THE HAGUE JUDGMENTS CONVENTION AND COMMONWEALTH MODEL LAW: A PRAGMATIC PERSPECTIVE

This book undertakes a systematic analysis, from a pragmatic perspective, of the 2019 Hague Judgments Convention, the 2017 Commonwealth Model Law on Recognition and Enforcement of Foreign Judgments, and the 2005 Hague Choice of Court Convention.

The book builds on the concept of pragmatism in private international law within the context of recognition and enforcement of judgments. It demonstrates the practical application of legal pragmatism by setting up a toolbox (pragmatic goals and methods) that will assist courts and policymakers in developing an effective and efficient judgments enforcement scheme at national, bilateral and multilateral levels.

Practitioners, national courts, policymakers, academics, students and litigants will benefit from the book's comparative approach using case law from the United Kingdom and other leading Commonwealth States, the United States, and the Court of Justice of the European Union. The book also presents interesting findings from empirical research on the refusal of recognition and enforcement in the UK and the Commonwealth statutory registration schemes respectively.

Volume 31 in the series Studies in Private International Law

Studies in Private International Law

Recent titles in the series

The Hague Judgments Convention and Commonwealth Model Law

A Pragmatic Perspective

Abubakri Yekini

·HART·

OXFORD · LONDON · NEW YORK · NEW DELHI · SYDNEY

HART PUBLISHING

Bloomsbury Publishing Plc

Kemp House, Chawley Park, Cumnor Hill, Oxford, OX2 9PH, UK

1385 Broadway, New York, NY 10018, USA

29 Earlsfort Terrace, Dublin 2, Ireland

HART PUBLISHING, the Hart/Stag logo, BLOOMSBURY and the Diana logo are
trademarks of Bloomsbury Publishing Plc

First published in Great Britain 2021

A catalogue record for this book is available from the British Library.

Library of Congress Cataloging-in-Publication data

Names: Yekini, Abubakri, author.

Title: The Hague Judgments Convention and Commonwealth Model Law :
a pragmatic perspective / Abubakri Yekini.

Description: Oxford, UK ; New York, NY : Hart, 2021. | Series: Studies in private international law ;
volume 31 | Based on author's thesis (doctoral - University of Aberdeen, 2020). |
Includes bibliographical references and index.

Identifiers: LCCN 2021011700 (print) | LCCN 2021011701 (ebook) | ISBN 9781509947072 (hardback) |
ISBN 9781509947119 (paperback) | ISBN 9781509947096 (pdf) | ISBN 9781509947089 (Epub)

Subjects: LCSH: Judgments, Foreign. | Convention on the Recognition and Enforcement of Foreign
Judgments in Civil or Commercial Matters (2019 July 2) | Hague Convention on Choice of Court
Agreements (2005 June 30) | Commonwealth (Organization). Office of Criminal and Civil Justice
Reform. Model Law on the Recognition and Enforcement of Foreign Judgments.

Classification: LCC K7680 .Y35 2021 (print) | LCC K7680 (ebook) | DDC 347/.077—dc23

LC record available at https://lccn.loc.gov/2021011700

LC ebook record available at https://lccn.loc.gov/2021011701

ISBN: HB: 978-1-50994-707-2
        ePDF: 978-1-50994-709-6
        ePub: 978-1-50994-708-9

Typeset by Compuscript Ltd, Shannon

www.bloomsbury.com

To find out more about our authors and books visit www.hartpublishing.co.uk.
Here you will find extracts, author information, details of forthcoming events
and the option to sign up for our newsletters.

This book is dedicated to the loving memory of my parents, Alhaj Yekini Gbadamosi and Mrs Morufat Yekini Giwa. May Allah make your graves a garden from the gardens of Jannah.

SERIES EDITOR'S PREFACE

This is the first book length work to analyse the Hague Judgments Convention 2019 and the Commonwealth Model Law on Judgments 2017. These are major new developments in the options made available to governments and legislatures to achieve the 'progressive unification of private international law' globally and in the incredibly diverse and exciting group of States that make up the Commonwealth. I am particularly excited by Abu's analysis of the Commonwealth Model Law. I am a Commonwealth Scholar (Dalhousie University, Halifax, Nova Scotia, Canada 1981–82) and am forever grateful for the opportunity it provided to me. I thoroughly enjoyed a wonderful time learning to write about private international law, two substantial term papers and a long LLM thesis on a natural forum based approach to jurisdiction. The feedback and guidance from Art Foote, Leon Trakman and Ron Macdonald really helped me to develop my critical skills in private international law building on the excellent foundation laid by the teaching and guidance of Elizabeth Crawford at the University of Glasgow. Throughout my career I have been encouraged by fruitful collaboration with excellent colleagues from different parts of the Commonwealth, notably David Goddard (New Zealand), Mary Keyes and Reid Mortensen (Australia), Mukarrum Ahmed (Pakistan and England) and Abubakri Yekini (Nigeria), the author of this book.

I had the privilege of being the main supervisor for Abu Yekini's PhD, at the University of Aberdeen, upon which this book is based. Abu worked hard to research the theory of pragmatism in private international law, delving back into its philosophical roots, as a foundation for this book. He makes a significant contribution to helping private international law scholars understand this theoretical approach to our subject.

I had the privilege and pleasure of representing the European Union as part of the Commission's team at the Hague Conference on Private International Law (HCCH) throughout all the negotiating stages of the Hague Judgments Convention 2019 in the 2010's under the very able chairing of David Goddard. I am delighted that the EU Commission on 4 May 2021 stated that: 'The Commission is planning to propose EU conclusion of the 2019 Hague Judgments Convention in the near future.' (see Communication from the Commission to the European Parliament and the Council: Assessment on the application of the United Kingdom of Great Britain and Northern Ireland to accede to the 2007 Lugano Convention COM(2021) 222 final at page 4). I hope the UK and many countries in the world will follow suit soon and ratify the Convention. Given that the Convention is based on minimum harmonisation, it is possible for Commonwealth States to select additional elements from the Commonwealth Model Law when implementing the Convention into national law (see P Beaumont, 'Some Reflections on the Way Ahead for UK Private International Law after Brexit' (2021) 17(1) *Journal of Private International Law* 1–17). They will find Abu's work very helpful when making decisions concerning the implementation of the Commonwealth Model Law.

Yekini carefully analyses the current predominant theories as to why foreign judgments are recognised and enforced (comity, reciprocity, legal obligation, and res judicata) before positing a theory based on pragmatism which promotes the goals of efficiency, fairness and justice. The key to this pragmatic theory of recognition and enforcement of judgments is trusting the wisdom of the treaty makers and model law designers to produce an efficient, fair and just system, and then to make that system operative in as many States as possible. There is in addition a role for judges to use a pragmatic approach to try to achieve uniform interpretation of the agreed Treaty and model law.

The book is a very useful guide to the current state of play in relation to the Commonwealth scheme for recognition and enforcement of judgments in civil or commercial matters which was created in the 1920's. It exposes how uneven the application of the scheme is between Commonwealth States and therefore how much could be gained by those States implementing the 2017 Commonwealth model law as part of implementing the Hague Judgments Convention 2019.

Another very practical feature of the book is the analysis of the findings of an empirical study conducted by the author on all reported judgments in the UK between February 1999 and February 2019 where the main defences against recognition and enforcement of civil and commercial judgments were discussed (natural justice and procedural fairness, fraud, and public policy).

At the global level, Abu Yekini wisely explains the development of the Hague Choice of Court Convention 2005 and the Hague Judgments Convention 2019 to show how they complement each other and should be seen as a package for the progressive unification of private international law in the field of recognition and enforcement of judgments on civil or commercial matters.

I wholeheartedly recommend this book to everyone interested in the recognition and enforcement of foreign judgments and to anyone interested in private international law theory.

Paul Beaumont
(University of Stirling)

PREFACE

This book develops the pragmatic theory of private international law set out by Kegel, Beaumont, and others in the context of the recognition and enforcement of foreign judgments. It identifies certain pragmatic goals and methods that can be used to develop an efficient judgments recognition framework at national, regional, and international levels. It further undertakes a systematic analysis of the Commonwealth Model Law 2017, the Hague Choice of Court Convention 2005, and the Hague Judgments Convention 2019 from this pragmatic perspective. This book concludes that those instruments skillfully address many of the practical problems facing cross-border litigants today. However, many Commonwealth States need to legislate to give effect to the model law for it to be significant in practice. No States have done so thus far. The 2005 Convention is in force for about 30 States and the Judgments Convention 2019 is not yet in force. They both have great potential to create a pragmatic solution to cross-border enforcement of judgments but the extent to which that potential will be realised depends on how many States become Contracting Parties to them.

ACKNOWLEDGEMENTS

Praise be to Allah by whose grace good deeds are completed.

I wish to express my profound appreciation to my supervisors, Professor Paul Beaumont and Dr Jonathan Fitchen, for their academic guidance and support throughout this PhD journey. I also benefitted immensely from all the members of the Centre for Private International Law (CPIL) and they deserve to be mentioned. To Dr Jayne Holliday, Dr Katarina Trimmings, Dr Justin Borg-Barthet, Dr Burcu Yüksel Ripley, Dr Onyoja Momoh, Hannah, and Ziyana, I say thank you all.

This PhD was largely funded by the Federal Government of Nigeria through Tertiary Education Trust Fund (TETFUND). My employer, Lagos State University, gave me study leave with pay for the four years I spent on the programme. I also got some funding from the CB Davidson Bequest when things were a bit tough. I must also acknowledge the Max Planck Institute Luxembourg for Procedural Law for offering me a visiting scholarship in 2019. The Institute funded my stay in Luxembourg. I benefitted from the rich library, excellent research fellows and supporting staff, the weekly Referentenrunde and the Lecture Series. Many thanks to all these institutions.

My stay in Aberdeen would have been miserable without my Aberdeen family. Many thanks to the Nigerian community in Aberdeen, Imam Ibrahim Alwawi and all members of the Aberdeen Muslim Community, Chaima, C137 friends, LRS members, and my ever-supportive landlord (Mr Mujeebul Islam). Timi Ojo, special thanks to you for helping with some proofreading.

To my sister Mrs Janet Adisa and other members of her family: Mr Julius Adisa, Tomi, Miriam and Joshua, May God bless you all for your support and encouragement always. To the Yekinis, I appreciate you all.

To my superwoman, Rukayat and my lovely kids, Mahabbatullah, Abdur-Rahman and Hibbatullah, thank you all for your love and prayers. The sacrifice is worth it and I am looking forward to reuniting with you all again.

CONTENTS

LIST OF ABBREVIATIONS

CML	Commonwealth Model Law
EU	The European Union
HCCA	Convention of 30 June 2005 on Choice of Court Agreements
Brussels Ia	Regulation (EU) No 1215/2012 of the European Parliament and of the Council of 12 December 2012 on jurisdiction and the recognition and enforcement of judgments in civil and commercial matters
CJEU	Court of Justice of the European Union
LFN	Laws of the Federation of Nigeria
HCPIL/ HCCH	Hague Conference on Private International Law

LIST OF CHARTS AND TABLES

Charts and Tables

TABLE OF CASES

EU

ECtHR

US

CANADA

AUSTRALIA

NEW ZEALAND

FRANCE

SINGAPORE

NIGERIA

MALAYSIA

SOUTH AFRICA

CAYMAN ISLANDS

ECUADOR

JERSEY

IRELAND

CHINA

GERMANY

RUSSIA

TABLE OF STATUTES/CONVENTIONS

1

General Introduction

I. Background of Study

Before the first wave of globalisation, civil litigation was essentially territorially defined. For instance, English courts would normally not exercise jurisdiction over a non-resident defendant because of the inconvenience of attending proceedings from a long distance.[1] Also, they would not be disposed to granting orders that could not be enforced by arresting the defendant or seizing his assets within the jurisdiction of the court except where there was an assurance that the non-resident defendant would comply with the judgment or the judgment would be enforced abroad.[2]

Ever since the period of the Industrial Revolution, the world has witnessed a growing transformation of businesses and social engagements. The advancements in telecommunication technologies and efficient means of mass transportation have practically eroded State borders and distances between different parts of the world.[3] One of the effects of these developments was an increase in economic flows, migration and capital transfer from Europe to other parts of the world, leading to the development of other economies in Asia, Africa and South America.[4] Statistics show that all regions continue to experience economic growth as a result of global economic integration and a reduction in trade costs.[5] The impact has been even more pronounced in the last two decades which saw an unprecedented increase in the number of Small and Medium Enterprises (SMEs) across the globe, a thriving gig economy and new business solutions that are added to the markets daily through numerous digital platforms.

The impact of globalisation is not limited to the commercial sphere. Rather, it permeates all areas of human endeavour including civil/personal relations.[6] The modern family is becoming increasingly international due to

---

[1] Lawrence Collins, *Essays in International Litigation and the Conflict of Laws* (OUP 1996) 228.
[2] Ibid, 233.
[3] Paul Schiff Berman, 'The Globalization of Jurisdiction' (2002) 151 *University of Pennsylvania Law Review* 311, 326–27.
[4] Ibid.
[5] Michael Mussa, 'Factors Driving Global Economic Integration' (IMF 2000): <https://www.imf.org/en/News/Articles/2015/09/28/04/53/sp082500> accessed 27 May 2020.
[6] Olusoji Elias, 'Globalisation and Private International Law: Reviewing Contemporary Local Law' [2001] 36 *Amicus Curiae* 5, 6.

the interconnectedness of today's societies, the booming international marriage brokering business, and the availability of several social networking platforms.[7] Apart from personal relationships, there is also an increasing internationalisation of tortious conduct such as online defamation via social media platforms, cross-border intellectual property theft, environmental degradation by foreign multinational corporations amongst others.[8]

The increase in cross-border trade, service and other interpersonal relationships have inevitably led to a corresponding increase in cross-border commercial and non-commercial conflicts. Unlike in the era before the Industrial Revolution, territorialism no longer exclusively defines civil litigation. The field of modern international civil procedure is complex and diverse owing to the absence of internationally harmonised civil procedure rules governing jurisdiction and judgments. Cross-border litigants are thus required to be very strategic in their choice of venue for litigation because that choice has implications for both the substantive outcome of the litigation and whether the successful party will be able to reap the benefits of his judgment.

As Professors Nadia de Araujo and Marcelo De Nardi rightly note, litigants may not always need to enforce foreign judgments. This situation may arise where the debtor complies with the judgment or where the creditor obtained a judgment in the jurisdiction where the debtor has enough assets to satisfy the judgment or where the case has no foreign element.[9] However, this is not always the case. In the modern era, it is much easier for a smart defendant to judgment-proof himself by cascading his assets to States that do not have personal jurisdiction over him or subject-matter jurisdiction over the impending dispute. To cite a few examples, in *Marex Financial Ltd v Sevilleja*,[10] a director asset-stripped his company by transferring a substantial part of the company's funds abroad to his personal account, leaving the company with minimal assets for enforcement proceedings. In a similar vein, *ICICI Bank UK Plc v Diminico NV*[11] illustrates how a company with a turnover of US$300m left only €2,600 in Belgium where it was sued. Fortunately, the judgment creditor was able to pursue some of the judgment debtor's assets in England.

For cross-border disputes, the probability is high that a judgment creditor may need to apply to the court of another State to enforce his judgment, since such disputes always have foreign elements. Thus, a cross-border litigant, especially a

---

[7] See Nicole Constable, 'International Marriage Brokers, Cross-Border Marriages and the US Anti-Trafficking Campaign' (2012) 38 *Journal of Ethnic and Migration Studies* 1137; Oksana Yakushko and Indhushree Rajan, 'Global Love for Sale: Divergence and Convergence of Human Trafficking with "Mail Order Brides" and International Arranged Marriage Phenomena' (2017) 40 *Women and Therapy* 190.

[8] Symeon C Symeonides, 'Choice of Law in Cross-Border Torts: Why Plaintiffs Win, and Should' (2009) 61 *Hastings Law Journal* 337, 339–40.

[9] Nadia de Araujo and Marcelo De Nardi, 'Consumer Protection Under the HCCH 2019 Judgments Convention' (2020) 67 *Netherlands International Law Review* 67, 68.

[10] *Marex Financial Ltd v Sevilleja* [2017] EWHC 918 (Comm).

[11] *ICICI Bank UK Plc v Diminico NV* [2014] EWHC 3124 (Comm).

judgment creditor, needs to consider the legal regimes of both the State where he intends to sue (S1) and other State(s) (S2) where he might need to enforce the outcome of the proceedings of S1.

While transactions are increasingly international, the legal regimes governing these transactions are largely national. The divergent national laws and policies create an unhealthy business environment for cross-border litigants because of the prevalent uncertainties concerning procedural laws and eventually the enforceability of foreign judgments. Besides, the role of the courts, the functions of law, the standards of justice, and States' interests differ. This has a great impact on the global circulation of foreign judgments. The civil law legal systems[12] generally recognise foreign judgments and allow them to be enforced after undergoing a special examination called 'an *exequatur*'. An *exequatur* proceeding enables a court addressed to examine the foreign judgment to ensure, among other things, that the foreign court had jurisdiction over the matter, the judgment debtor was given a fair trial, the enforcement is not objectionable to the forum's public policy, and also to consider whether its own judgments (the judgments of the court addressed) enjoy favourable treatment in the State of origin. The civil law tradition was exported from Europe to countries in the Middle East via Egypt,[13] the majority of the Latin American States[14] and Francophone countries in Africa.[15] It should be noted, however, that the details of foreign judgments laws and practices developed differently amongst the States.

Unlike the heterogeneous practices in the civil law jurisdictions, the judgments recognition rules of common law as developed in England were applied, uniformly to a large extent, in the Commonwealth. No recognition was accorded to foreign judgments *simpliciter*, as foreign courts were not part of the English courts of record.[16] However, common law courts often recognise the rights created by a foreign judgment through the doctrine of legal obligation. In other jurisdictions such as Canada, comity plays a key role in their judgments enforcement practice. Under civil and common law systems, certain hurdles usually present themselves when judgment creditors attempt to enforce foreign judgments.[17]

---

[12] There are differences in various legal systems within the civil law family even though they all have their roots in the Roman-Canon law. Some of the differences have been captured in many scholarly works. See Peter Schlosser, 'Jurisdiction and International Judicial and Administrative Co-Operation', *Recueil des Cours* (Martinus Nijhoff 2001) 39–42; Rudolf Graupner, 'Some Recent Aspects of the Recognition and Enforcement of Foreign Judgments in Western Europe' (1963) 12 *International and Comparative Law Quarterly* 367; Samuel P Baumgartner, 'How Well Do US Judgments Fare in Europe?' (2007) 40 *George Washington International Law Review* 173.

[13] Karim El Chazli, 'Recognition and Enforcement of Foreign Decisions in Egypt' (2013) XV *Yearbook of Private International Law* 387, 389–90. Egypt was a model for many of the Arab States.

[14] Carl Baudenbacher, 'Judicial Globalization: New Development or Old Wine in New Bottles?' (2003) 38 *Texas International Law Journal* 505, 506.

[15] Jeswald W Salacuse, *An Introduction to Law in French-Speaking Africa*, vol 1 (Michie Company 1969) 8.

[16] *Walker v Witter* (1778) 1 Doug KB 1, 5; 99 Eng Rep 1, 4.

[17] For the civil law systems, the challenges include international jurisdiction and proving reciprocity. On the extreme side, some Nordic countries do not recognise foreign judgments. A judgment creditor

The divergent national responses have not provided the required legal certainty and predictability for cross-border litigants. These challenges were noted as far back as the late nineteenth century by Mancini and Asser who were very concerned with the state of confusion arising from the divergent rules of various States, especially, their European neighbours. From their days at the *Institut de Droit International* (IDI), they had conceived the idea of forming a special body of lawyers to promote the progressive development and unification of private international law rules.[18] In 1869, Asser, in his writing in *Revue de Droit International et de Législation Compare* advocated for an international solution to the problems of recognition and enforcement of foreign judgments.[19] This, among other reasons, ignited his passion for the establishment of the Hague Conference on Private International Law (Hague Conference) for the progressive development of private international law in 1893.

In the last six decades, many States have realised the need for deeper legal and judicial cooperation as the most suitable way to resolve the numerous practical problems surrounding foreign judgments recognition and enforcement. It is considered that litigants need a simple and effective global legal framework through which they can make an informed decision concerning their commercial and non-commercial activities. Before the recent achievements from the Hague Conference, Several States concluded bilateral and regional judgments enforcement frameworks. In Latin America, examples of such regional legal frameworks on foreign judgments include the Inter-American Convention on General Rules of Private International Law,[20] the Inter-American Convention on Extraterritorial Validity of Judgments and Arbitral Awards[21] and the Inter-American Convention on Jurisdiction in the International Sphere for the Extraterritorial Validity of Foreign Judgments.[22] The EU also has several Regulations concerning foreign judgments and they have direct application in all Member States. Notable among them are Regulation (EU) No 1215/2012 of the European Parliament and of the Council of 12 December 2012 on jurisdiction and the recognition and enforcement of judgments in civil and commercial matters (Brussels Ia), Council Regulation (EC) No 2201/2003 of 27 November 2003 concerning jurisdiction and the recognition

---

must institute a fresh action. On the part of the common law, a very restricted attitude to international jurisdiction is maintained until today. Judgments can hardly be enforced against non-resident debtors. Fraud is also widely used as a defence to review foreign judgments altogether. See Tanya J Monestier, 'Foreign Judgments at Common Law: Rethinking the Enforcement Rules' (2005) 28 *The Dalhousie Law Journal* 163.

[18] Arthur Eyffinger, *Dreaming the Ideal, Living the Attainable: T.M.C. Asser [1838–1913] Founder of The Hague Tradition* (TMC Asser Press 2011) 27–28.

[19] Ibid, 18.

[20] The treaty was concluded in 1979, signed by 18 States and ratified by 10 States. Text is available at <http://www.oas.org/juridico/english/sigs/b-45.html>.

[21] The treaty was concluded in 1979, signed by 18 States and ratified by 10 States. Text is available at <https://www.oas.org/juridico/english/treaties/b-41.html>.

[22] The treaty was concluded in 1984, signed by 18 States and ratified by 2 States. Text is available at <https://www.oas.org/juridico/english/sigs/b-50.html>.

and enforcement of judgments in matrimonial matters and the matters of parental responsibility (Brussels IIa); Enforcement Order Regulation, European Account Preservation Order Regulation, European Small Claims Procedure Regulation, and European Payment Order Regulation.[23] Apart from the regional frameworks, there are several bilateral frameworks and court-to-court agreements across the globe.

At the global level, the Hague Conference has been working assiduously to deliver global conventions on jurisdiction and judgments. The first judgments convention was concluded in 1971 but that convention did not enjoy wide ratification amongst Member States of the Conference. Further work on judgments has produced a Convention of 30 June 2005 on Choice of Court Agreements (HCCA) and a broader brand-new Convention of 2 July 2019 on the Recognition and Enforcement of Foreign Judgments in Civil or Commercial Matters. Other relevant specialised conventions that affect foreign judgments' enforcement include the Convention of 23 November 2007 on the International Recovery of Child Support and Other Forms of Family Maintenance; the Convention of 19 October 1996 on Jurisdiction, Applicable Law, Recognition, Enforcement and Co-operation in Respect of Parental Responsibility and Measures for the Protection; and the Convention of 29 May 1993 on Protection of Children and Cooperation in Respect of Intercountry Adoption.[24]

II. Research Problem

The issues that are now associated with the recognition and enforcement of foreign judgments emerged from territorialism in eighteenth-century Europe as newly formed States began to guard their respective territories and sovereignty jealously against foreign sovereign acts. Judges were considered as sovereigns' agents and judicial decisions invariably became acts of State with no direct effects beyond the territory of the State of origin. This development posed a threat to the burgeoning cross-border trade and commerce in Europe and beyond.

The globalisation of businesses and socio-cultural interactions requires an international order, more than was needed in the nineteenth century. One can well imagine the chaotic situation that would ensue if there were no international frameworks regulating aviation, postal services, immigration, international trade and so on.

The absence of an effective global legal regime for jurisdiction and judgments continues to have a negative impact on global trade and access to justice. The first significant problem is that it leads to an increase in transaction costs, which

---

[23] The texts of all these instruments are available at <https://e-justice.europa.eu/content_european_judicial_atlas_in_civil_matters-321--maximize-en.do>.

[24] All the Hague conventions are available at <https://www.hcch.net/en/instruments/conventions>.

eventually limits the growth of trade worldwide.[25] An investor who is unsure of a prompt settlement of disputes and collection of the judgment sums arising from transactional disputes will factor those uncertainties into the cost of goods and services. It does not make any business sense for an investor to spend the profits he has made from a commercial transaction on endless litigation. Hence, a smart investor would assume that further litigation for recovering judgment sums in the absence of a global framework guaranteeing judgments' enforcement is of high probability.

Second, the absence of a global solution to judgments' recognition and enforcement encourages forum shopping and multiplicity of suits. A plaintiff will surely take advantage of the slightest connection his case has with a pro-plaintiff jurisdiction and file his suit there, even if that State is not the appropriate forum. A defendant will also deploy all strategies to block any attempt to haul him to a distant forum with which he is not familiar. Eventually, both parties may end up prosecuting two or more cases on the same cause of action. In some cases, this practice brings courts from different jurisdictions into conflict with each other, as witnessed in the Laker Airways antitrust litigation for instance.[26]

Third, where there is no harmonisation of judgments rules, foreign judgments are subjected to the diverse national laws and practices which are laden with different obstacles for both judgment creditors and debtors respectively.[27] For instance, in the Commonwealth, international jurisdiction grounds are restricted to 'presence' and 'submission'. This makes it difficult to enforce a judgment against a defendant who was not sued in his State of residence because all that such defendant needs to do to become judgment-proof is to stay away from foreign proceedings.[28] This is not appropriate in an interconnected world where parties can conclude transactions from any part of the world.

Fourth, unlike in the civil law tradition where judgments recognition rules are systemically codified, the civil procedures of many common law legal systems lack this means of systematisation and those systems are potentially subject to various court decisions that the doctrine of precedent endows with continuing relevance. The role of case law in common law legal systems may mean that well-settled rules may be suddenly overturned. The Canadian Supreme Court decision in *Beals v Saldanha*[29] quickly comes to mind. Even when that is not the case, there is no certainty that a case will be decided according to precedent, as lawyers and judges

---

[25] Richard Fentiman, *International Commercial Litigation* (OUP 2015) 6–7.
[26] Collins (n 1) 107–16.
[27] David Goddard, 'The Judgments Convention – The Current State of Play' (2019) 29 *Duke Journal of Comparative & International Law* 473.
[28] *Adams v Cape Industries Plc* [1990] Ch 433.
[29] *Beals v Saldanha* [2003] 3 SCR 416. In this case, the Canadian Supreme Court, for the first time, extended real and substantial connection, as a jurisdictional test for assessing a foreign court's jurisdiction, to international cases. Thus, a US judgment was allowed to be enforced against a debtor who had relied on the traditional common law jurisdiction grounds.

may manipulate the facts to arrive at another result. This contributes to legal uncertainty and unpredictability of results.

As the title suggests, this book aims to critically analyse the Hague Judgments Convention[30] and the Commonwealth Model Law[31] (CML), which are the latest multilateral responses that seek to address the practical challenges that international litigants often face when seeking to enforce judgments abroad. While a great deal of work exists on the previous Hague attempts, no significant work has been carried out on the 2019 Judgments Convention because it is a brand-new Convention. The CML has also not received much attention from academia. The analysis here is carried out from a pragmatic perspective. This entails the development of a pragmatic model for judgments recognition and enforcement and the application of this model as a tool for analysing the relevant Commonwealth and Hague instruments.

III. Research Questions

The Commonwealth Secretariat and the Hague Conference recently concluded a model law and convention respectively to address the inadequacies arising from the lack of a harmonised judgments enforcement scheme. The Hague Judgments Convention provides a floor and not a ceiling for recognition, thereby allowing for the continuous development of national and regional judgments frameworks. While assessing the international framework, the state of national schemes – with emphasis on the Commonwealth – and the role of the courts must be considered, since the ultimate success of the Hague Judgments Convention depends on the level of support and ratifications it enjoys from States. This book approaches these issues from a pragmatic point of view. This entails unravelling the theoretical foundations for judgments recognition schemes, a consideration of the suitability of the theoretical foundations in the light of the practical challenges international litigants face when enforcing judgments abroad, the desired approach for a pragmatic judgments framework and whether the new Commonwealth and Hague solutions are fit for purpose.

The above points prompt the following research questions which this book seeks to explore:

a.   What are the practical challenges that litigants face when they seek recognition and enforcement of judgments abroad?

---

[30] Convention of 2 July 2019 on the Recognition and Enforcement of Foreign Judgments in Civil or Commercial Matters. The text of the convention is available at: <https://www.hcch.net/en/instruments/conventions/full-text/?cid=137>.
[31] Model Law on the Recognition and Enforcement of Foreign Judgments. The text is available at <https://thecommonwealth.org/sites/default/files/key_reform_pdfs/D16227_1_GPD_ROL_Model_Law_Rec_Enf_Foreign_Judgements.pdf>.

b.   Why does a court addressed need to enforce foreign judgments?
c.   How effective and efficient are national laws and policies on foreign judgments?
d.   How does pragmatism apply to recognition and enforcement of foreign judgments?
e.   How pragmatic are the Commonwealth and Hague judgments frameworks?
f.   To what extent can both institutions and their frameworks support the agenda for a global liberalisation of judgments recognition and enforcement.

IV. Methodology

This book aims at unravelling the attitude of States towards foreign judgments, the challenges litigants face when seeking to enforce foreign judgments abroad and the effectiveness of recent multilateral frameworks that have been developed to address these challenges. In furtherance of these objectives, this book adopts a combination of doctrinal, comparative and empirical methodologies. A doctrinal research method is used to critically examine the underlying concepts and policies of judgments recognition schemes. It also enables the author to succinctly lay out the new multilateral frameworks that were recently adopted by the Commonwealth and the Hague Conference. The primary materials consulted for this book include judgments statutes from various Commonwealth States, the 2017 Commonwealth Model Law on Foreign Judgments, the 2005 Hague Convention on Choice of Court Agreements[32] (HCCA), the 2019 Hague Judgments Convention and relevant case law from Commonwealth States, the United States, the European Court of Justice and a few other courts around the world. Various secondary materials such as authoritative textbooks, articles in respected journals, explanatory reports, yearbooks, commissioned reports and law dictionaries were also engaged where necessary. These materials were mainly sourced from the University of Aberdeen Law School Library, the Commonwealth Secretariat Library in London, and the Max Plank Institute of Procedural Law Library in Luxembourg. Relevant electronic databases such as LexisNexis, Westlaw, and HeinOnline were also used. The University inter-library loan scheme was used to access books and other materials that are not available at the University of Aberdeen Library while Google Books was also helpful in some cases.

One of the objectives of this book is to examine the new frameworks to see the extent to which they solve practical problems. Comparative methodology was used to pursue this objective. This entails an examination of the divergent solutions offered by different legal systems and comparing those solutions with the ones offered by the new frameworks. This enables the author to form an

---

[32] The Hague Convention of 30 June 2005 on Choice of Court Agreements. The text is available at <https://www.hcch.net/en/instruments/conventions/full-text/?cid=98>.

informed opinion on whether the new frameworks are good, better, or worse than the extant frameworks and the costs and benefits of adopting the new models. This approach also helps in determining to what extent the Hague Convention aligns with or deviates from the fundamental policies of major legal systems since that is a key factor that will determine the success or failure of the Convention. The comparative inquiry is majorly based on cases and legislation from the leading Commonwealth States, the United States, and the EU. To find out how the laws work in practice, and whether the texts of both instruments address those practical challenges, some empirical research was carried out using English decisions as case studies.

Certain limitations were encountered during this research. While the judicial authorities in many Commonwealth States are accessible, that is not the case for others due to the level of development of law reporting in those jurisdictions. Efforts were made to ensure that cases from both developed and developing States were sourced to balance the outcome of the research. In any event, the position in many of the developing Member States represents the traditional common law and as such, the inability to obtain case law from all the States does not have any material effect on the research. Similarly, in the wider context of the Hague Judgments Project, only cases and materials that are available in the English language were accessed because of language barriers. The author, however, sufficiently engaged several English materials on judgments recognition laws of France, China, and Germany amongst others.

V. Significance of the Study

The law and practice of judgments recognition and enforcement in the Commonwealth have stagnated over the years. Most works that have addressed the subject matter are largely descriptive. Only a few commentators seem to engage with the theoretical infrastructure upon which the common law of foreign judgments is built. The much talked about pragmatism of the common law seems not to have much effect on the law of foreign judgments. The English courts, which guide the larger Commonwealth courts, have relaxed since the codification of the common law rules[33] and, possibly, since the UK's membership of the EU. Thus, the subject matter is under-theorised, stalled, and the laws are outdated. Beyond the Commonwealth, judgments' recognition laws face the same fate. Perhaps the EU is the only bloc where foreign judgments laws have received significant attention and reform.

The significance of this book is that it advances the pragmatic theory of private international law beyond the current frontiers. Specifically, it seeks to

---

[33] This refers to the Administration of Justice Act 1920 and the Foreign Judgments (Reciprocal Enforcement) Act 1933.

reconceptualise the theoretical framework for foreign judgments recognition and enforcement by integrating pragmatism into the discourse. This integration is expected to offer a better approach through which policymakers can retool judgments frameworks to become more responsive to the demands of the end-users of the law. It identifies certain pragmatic goals and methods that can best deliver an efficient judgments framework at national, regional, and international levels.

The book demonstrates the practical application of legal pragmatism by using the suggested pragmatic goals and methods to analyse the Commonwealth Model Law and the Hague Judgments Convention. Besides, the book will be the first major comprehensive work on these two instruments. It critically analyses the two instruments using case law from leading courts in the Commonwealth, the CJEU and the US courts, respectively. Litigants, lawyers, national courts, and policymakers will benefit from this analysis, particularly, the comparative approach, which identifies the convergences between national systems and the global framework. This analysis will strengthen uniform interpretation, certainty, and predictability of the rules. The identified gaps are highlighted to flag up areas to be improved upon by policymakers and to prepare litigants for the possible consequences of their choices.

VI. Literature Review

Private international law is often divided into three branches: jurisdiction, choice of law and enforcement of foreign judgments. Of the three branches, choice of law is arguably the most engaged by legal scholars. Outside the EU, only a little success has been achieved in the progressive development of judgments enforcement laws. Perhaps policymakers are simply content with the state of the law even when it no longer addresses many contemporary challenges faced by international litigants. This is not to say that there have been no scholarly engagements concerning foreign judgments. The Hague Conference listed over 250 contributions to the Hague Judgments Project. Other than these works, which are largely targeted at the previously failed exercises of the Hague Conference, most other works are largely historical or a restatement of the law from different national perspectives. The works that have been considered for this book are predominantly literature written in the English language.

Pavel Kalensky's work is, perhaps, one of the most comprehensive accounts of the historical development of private international law well before the statutist period.[34] That author set out the theoretical foundations for private international law. Although his analyses focus more on choice of law, there are many valuable points in the book that can be applied to recognition and enforcement of foreign

---

[34] Pavel Kalensky, *Trends of Private International Law* (Springer Netherlands 1971).

judgments. For instance, his chapter on universalism in the modern doctrine of private international law briefly discusses realism (which he equates with pragmatism) in private international law.[35] This idea essentially inspires this research and provides a platform from which it is launched. Professor Symeonides also discusses unilateral and multilateral approaches to solving private international law problems. Unlike Kalensky, Symeonides's work focuses on the application and impact of these ideas on the US choice of law revolution.[36] One major work, which specifically treats pragmatism as a theory of private international law is *Anton's Private International Law* edited by Professors Beaumont and McEleavy.[37] Unlike other Anglo-American texts, *Anton's Private International Law* is unequivocal in listing pragmatism as a theory of private international law. The best that can be seen in other works, such as *Cheshire, North & Fawcett*,[38] where theories and methods are given attention at all, is a general discussion on the American conflicts revolution or economic analysis of law. This may not be unconnected with the skepticism some scholars feel as to whether pragmatism can be described as a theory, since its basis is an aversion to theory.[39] Nevertheless, Professors Beaumont and McEleavy give a brief description of the pragmatic theory and how it has been the predominant approach being used by the European Group for Private International Law (EGPIL) and the Hague Conference. Pragmatism, as presented in their work, appears not to be sufficiently theorised, at least concerning foreign judgments. Beaumont, however, further demonstrates pragmatism in some of his recent works.[40]

Anselmo Reyes' edited work *Recognition and Enforcement of Judgments in Civil and Commercial Matters*[41] is the latest book on foreign judgments. The work compares the judgments recognition laws and practices of 15 Asian States, with the intent to discover a normative and rudimentary judgments enforcement system for the Asian bloc. One important feature of the book is the practical approach the editor adopts in analysing the various regimes, setting out in practical terms how receptive they are to foreign judgments and how they can be further developed to attract foreign investments to the region. The book further highlights the

---

[35] Ibid, 96–99.

[36] Symeon C Symeonides, *The American Choice-of-Law Revolution: Past, Present and Future* (M Nijhoff 2006) 357–75.

[37] Paul Beaumont and Peter McEleavy, *Anton's Private International Law* (3rd edn, W Green/ Thomson Reuters 2011) paras 2.87–2.99.

[38] Paul Torremans and others (eds), *Cheshire, North & Fawcett: Private International Law* (15th edn, OUP 2017) 21–75.

[39] Lara Walker, *Maintenance and Child Support in Private International Law* (Hart Publishing Ltd 2015) 6–7.

[40] For instance, see Paul Beaumont and Mihail Danov, 'Introduction: Research Aims and Methodology' in Paul Beaumont, Mihail Danov, Katarina Trimmings and Burcu Yuksel (eds), *Cross-Border Litigation in Europe* (Hart Publishing 2017) 1, 10–14; Lara Walker and Paul Beaumont, 'Empirical Study on the Early Operation of the EU Maintenance Regulation' in Paul Beaumont and others (eds), *The Recovery of Maintenance in the EU and Worldwide* (Hart Publishing 2014) 337–38.

[41] Anselmo Reyes (ed), *Recognition and Enforcement of Judgments in Civil and Commercial Matters* (Hart Publishing 2019).

uncertainties that abound in legal systems with less developed judgments schemes. Be that as it may, the approach adopted in the book reflects an aspect of pragmatism: finding out how laws work in practice. The book does not venture much into how to design a pragmatic framework which can serve the Asian States as a bloc and beyond. The yardsticks adopted for the analysis are restricted to reciprocity and choice of court agreements.

A great deal of work has been done on various aspects of foreign judgments, including international jurisdiction, which is the core of any foreign judgments framework. The leading text on private international law in the Anglo-American legal systems, *Dicey, Morris & Collins on the Conflict of Laws*, has two chapters on foreign judgments. The authors cover a wide range of topics on foreign judgments but from common law and European law perspectives. The book is largely descriptive; analysing the laws as pronounced by the courts. This position also applies to other standard texts written by learned writers such as James Fawcett and Janeen M Carruthers,[42] Trevor Hartley,[43] Adrian Briggs and,[44] Gilles Cuniberti,[45] amongst others.

The absence of harmonised rules on jurisdiction and enforcement of foreign judgments across the globe has a significant impact on international trade. Richard Fentiman[46] highlights the significance of certainty and predictability of laws in international trade and commerce and how their absence may lead to an increase in the costs of international trade and services. He further argues that the absence of international rules which support the free movement of judgments will also lead to transaction and litigation risks. He explains transaction risk as a fear harboured by a potential investor that his reasonable expectation concerning choice of laws and other legal aspects of his contract may not be met. Litigation risk is also described as a fear which may arise from not being allowed to litigate in the preferred forum or to defend an action in a desirable forum, and of course, enforcement risk is a subset of litigation risk. All these risks constitute hindrances to the growth of international trade and services. Closely related to what Richard Fentiman argues, Giesela Rühl[47] considers the economic aspect of differences in legal systems and the effect they have on trade and commerce. She considers the 'border effect' on trade, using economics theories and statistics. She identifies that, although pure economic issues may be responsible for a decline in cross-border trade and commerce, they are not the sole determinant. Citing examples of US and Canada that seem to have a homogeneous culture and a liberalised trade

---

[42] Torremans and others (n 38).

[43] Trevor C Hartley, *International Commercial Litigation: Text, Cases, and Materials on Private International Law* (Cambridge University Press 2009).

[44] Adrian Briggs, *The Conflict of Laws* (Oxford University Press 2013).

[45] Gilles Cuniberti, *Conflict of Laws: A Comparative Approach: Text and Cases* (Edward Elgar Publishing 2017).

[46] Fentiman (n 25).

[47] Giesela Rühl, 'The Problem of International Transactions: Conflict of Laws Revisited' (2010) 6 *Journal of Private International Law* 59.

relationship, she opines that the cross-border transactional decline in recent years must have, therefore, resulted not from economic but rather from legal factors. The author suspects that plurality of laws and 'constitutional uncertainties' are probable causes. Fentiman and Rühl's works demonstrate the huge cost litigants bear for the existing legal diversity and lack of legal certainty on States' recognition policies.

The obvious solution to the huge cost lies in a multilateral effort, which should be aimed at harmonising the divergent rules. The Hague Conference steps in to bridge this gap. The question is: what needs to be done and how can it be successfully delivered? Many works have been written on the past activities of the Hague Conference in this regard. The first Hague Judgments Convention,[48] which was delivered in 1971, failed for reasons which have been noted in the Kessedjian Report.[49] Commentators are in unanimity that the United States revived the current Hague Judgments Project. Paul Beaumont,[50] Arthur Von Mehren[51] and other academics attribute the revival of the Hague Judgments Project to the request from the US delegation to the Hague Conference Special Commission on General Affairs in 1992 for the negotiation of a mixed convention on recognition and enforcement of foreign judgments. David Bennett[52] gives an insight into the background of the negotiations at the first phase of the judgments project. There seem to be divergent views on why the initial attempts failed. Yuliya Zeynalova[53] blames the US constitutional limitations, an unwritten policy of avoiding international procedural treaties, the private-public law dichotomy and some elements of unilateralism. William O'Brian Jr[54] and Patrick J Borchers[55] note the jurisdictional problems inherent in the US due process and minimum contact philosophies, amongst others. To Arthur Von Mehren,[56] it is majorly a conflict

---

[48] Convention of 1 February 1971 on the Recognition and Enforcement of Foreign Judgments in Civil and Commercial Matters. The text is available at <https://assets.hcch.net/docs/bacf7323-9337-48df-9b9a-ef33e62b43be.pdf>.

[49] HCCH, 'International Jurisdiction and Foreign Judgments in Civil and Commercial Matters: Report Drawn up by Catherine Kessedjian', *Preliminary Document No 7 of April 1997 for the attention of the Special Commission of June 1997 on the question of jurisdiction, and recognition and enforcement of foreign judgments in civil and commercial matters* (1997) 7–8.

[50] Paul Beaumont, 'Hague Choice of Court Agreements Convention 2005: Background, Negotiations, Analysis and Current Status' (2009) 5 *Journal of Private International Law* 125.

[51] Arthur T Von Mehren, 'Recognition and Enforcement of Foreign Judgments : A New Approach for the Hague Conference ?' (1994) 1993 *Law and Conemporary Problems* 271.

[52] David Bennett, 'The Hague Convention on Recognition and Enforcement of Foreign Judgments – A Failure of Characterisation' in Talia Einhorn and Kurt Siehr (ed), *Intercontinental Cooperation Through Private International Law: Essays in Memory of Peter E. Nygh* (TMC Asser Press 2004).

[53] Yuliya Zeynalova, 'The Law on Recognition and Enforcement of Foreign Judgments : Is It Broken and How Do We Fix It ?' (2013) 31 *Berkeley Journal of International Law* 150.

[54] William E O'Brian, 'The Hague Convention on Jurisdiction and Judgments: The Way Forward' (2003) 66 *The Modern Law Review* 491.

[55] Patrick J. Borchers, 'A Few Little Issues for the Hague Judgments Negotiations' (1998) 24 *Brooklyn Journal of International Law* 157.

[56] Arthur T Von Mehren, 'Drafting a Convention on International Jurisdiction and the Effects of Foreign Judgments Acceptable World-Wide: Can the Hague Conference Project Succeed?' (2001) 49 *The American Journal of Comparative Law* 191.

over the appropriate convention format as differently viewed, principally, by the US and EU delegations. Yoav Ostreicher[57] submits that the failure is due to the mistrust and suspicion prevalent among key actors of the negotiation and the use of a Brussels-style convention at the Hague.

Paul Beaumont[58] sheds some light on the public international law aspect of the activities at the Hague Conference. Worthy of note is his discussion on the adoption of treaties by consensus, its evolution in The Hague and the political intrigues involved. He posits that such a move can allay the fears of some developed countries, such as the US, of being voted out by the EU bloc. Also, it may take care of concerns from developing countries of being handed a treaty devoid of their input. He concludes that, although consensus is a better way of delivering a widely acceptable convention, a voting option should also be available in exceptional cases to check States that may want to use consensus to frustrate a deal. In another work, Paul Beaumont and Lara Walker[59] prophesise the birth of the 2019 Judgments Convention. They analyse the Brussels I Recast and Hague Choice of Court Agreement with a view to suggesting pitfalls that the Hague Conference should avoid to realise the second fruit of the Judgments Project. While the prophecy of Beaumont and Walker came to pass with the adoption of the 2019 Judgments Convention, some of their recommendations, unfortunately, did not make it. The 2019 Judgments Convention has so far received only a few comments.[60] The Convention is radically different from the 1999 draft and as such needs a fresh assessment.

John David McClean is a major writer on private international law issues in the Commonwealth States. In his lecture at the Hague Academy of International Law,[61] he assessed the contributions of the Commonwealth States to the works of the Hague Conference. He noted the legal diversity in the Commonwealth, particularly the divergences in the conflicts of law generally. He identified Canada and Australia as Member States that have departed in some respects

---

[57] Yoav Oestreicher, 'The Rise and Fall of the "Mixed" and "Double" Convention Models Regarding Recognition and Enforcement of Foreign Judgments' (2007) 6 *Washington University Global Studies Law Review* 339.

[58] Paul R Beaumont, 'Reflections on the Relevance of Public International Law to Private International Law Treaty Making', *Collected Courses of The Hague Academy of International Law – Recueil des cours* (M Nijhoff 2010).

[59] Paul Beaumont and Lara Walker, 'Recognition and Enforcement of Judgments in Civil and Commercial Matters in the Brussels I Recast and Some Lessons from It and the Recent Hague Conventions for the Hague Judgments Project' (2015) 11 *Journal of Private International Law* 31.

[60] Lydia Lundstedt, 'The Newly Adopted Hague Judgments Convention: A Missed Opportunity for Intellectual Property' (2019) 50 *IIC – International Review of Intellectual Property and Competition Law* 933; David P Stewart, 'The Hague Conference Adopts a New Convention on the Recognition and Enforcement of Foreign Judgments in Civil or Commercial Matters' (2019) 113 *The American Journal of International Law* 772; Maria Blanca Noodt Taquela and Verónica Ruiz Abou-Nigm, 'The Draft Judgments Convention and Its Relationship with Other International Instruments' (2018) 19 *Yearbook of Private International Law* 449.

[61] John David McClean, 'The Contribution of the Hague Conference to the Development of Private International Law in Common Law Countries', *Collected Courses of The Hague Academy of International Law – Recueil des cours* (Nijhoff 1992).

from the traditional common law rules. One can add Singapore to the list, taking cognisance of the reforms it recently implemented.[62] Being a long-time expert representative of the Commonwealth at the Hague Conference, he, together with Professor KW Patchett, did considerable work on the pathetic status of foreign judgments law in the Commonwealth.[63] They presented a historical account of the common law and statutory schemes applicable in most of the common law jurisdictions. Their report traced the current statutory schemes to the Crown Debts Act of 1801, Judgments Extension Act, 1868, and the Administration of Justice Act, 1920, which was eventually transported to the various colonies. The report depicted that while a very few Commonwealth States, like the United Kingdom, Canada and Australia, have developed their laws to meet modern-day challenges, most of the Commonwealth States are still glued to the colonial legacy without any improvement. In fact, the legislation in some countries still bears pre-independence terms like 'colony'. Since the '80s, no work has been done to update intra-Commonwealth practices until Richard Oppong did a limited comparative review in 2015.[64] Oppong's work cuts across about 10 common law jurisdictions and five Roman-Dutch legal systems in Commonwealth Africa. The conclusion from his work confirms what other writers have said, that the Commonwealth schemes are no longer in tune with modern-day realities.

Tanya J Monestier[65] discusses the common law enforcement regime and how it is no longer effective for modern-day sophisticated transnational litigation. Her work examines the developments in the common law of Canada following the Canadian Supreme Court decisions in *Morguard*[66] and *Beals*[67] respectively. These decisions reveal that Canadian courts have moved away from the common law's bifocal lens of addressing international competence of courts (residence and submission). She commends the Canadian courts for a bold step in returning to the theory of comity while highlighting the injustice that may arise from a unilateral liberalisation of the enforcement regime. While Monestier is right to a large extent in her assessment of the moves by the Canadian Supreme Court to liberalise foreign judgments recognition, the approach created more problems than it attempted to solve, as it became difficult to set clear rules for what constitutes a substantial connection. Indeed, in another work, Monestier refers to this uncertainty as 'a mess'.[68] This strengthens the case for a pragmatic approach in dealing with judgments recognition problems.

---

[62] See the Reciprocal Enforcement of Foreign Judgments (Amendment) Act 2019 which came into effect on 3 October 2019. The Act departs from the common law and extant statutory schemes especially in the area of non-money judgments.

[63] JD McClean and Keith William Patchett, *The Recognition and Enforcement of Judgments and Orders and the Service of Process within the Commonwealth* (Commonwealth Secretariat 1977).

[64] Richard Frimpong Oppong, *Private International Law in Commonwealth Africa* (Cambridge University Press 2013).

[65] Monestier, 'Foreign Judgments at Common Law: Rethinking the Enforcement Rules' (n 17).

[66] *Morguard Investments Ltd v De Savoye* [1990] 3 SCR 1077.

[67] *Beals v Saldanha* (n 29).

[68] Tanya J Monestier, 'A "Real and Substantial" Mess: The Law of Jurisdiction in Canada' (2013) 36 *Fordham International Law Journal* 396.

By and large, the body of literature reveals the nature and extent of the diversity of laws and practices of judgments recognition and enforcement. It further unravels the delicate nature of the subject matter, especially when attempts are made to harmonise the divergent laws and States' interests and policies at a multilateral platform such as the Hague Conference. These works have contributed to the historical background and the theoretical frameworks for understanding both the legal and political intrigues of foreign judgments. While some of the works are very restricted in scope, focusing largely on the United States, United Kingdom, Canada and the EU, others dwell on the past activities of the Commonwealth Secretariat and the Hague Conference. One obvious gap that is easily observed from the existing literature is that there are only a few works that seek to engage or reassess the theoretical foundations for foreign judgments recognition. Similarly, the new multilateral frameworks which were recently concluded require a thorough examination. This book seeks to address these gaps by advancing the pragmatic theory of private international law and proposing a useful toolkit that may assist courts and policymakers in moulding an effective judgments enforcement scheme. It will further analyse the Commonwealth and Hague schemes from this pragmatic perspective.

VII. Conceptual Clarification

Some terms and concepts which may not be familiar to non-private international lawyers and cross-border litigants are used in this book. These terms and concepts are briefly explained in this section.

A. Foreign Judgments

Courts are primarily established by States to settle grievances between disputing parties. A court, as an unbiased arbiter, dispassionately listens to the case presented by the parties and gives a decision determining their respective rights and liabilities.[69] Courts' decisions are generally referred to as judgments and they may come in different forms. One of the broad classifications is *in personam* or *in rem* judgments. A judgment is *in personam* when it is rendered against the parties to a suit, and it binds only those parties against whom it is rendered. It is *in rem* when it decides the legal status of a person, an object or property. In this case, the judgment is said to be binding against the world.[70]

---

[69] Alan Uzelac (ed), *Goals of Civil Justice and Civil Procedure in Contemporary Judicial Systems* (Springer International Publishing 2014) 3.
[70] Tiong Min Yeo, 'Recognition and Enforcement of Foreign Judgments in Singapore' in Andrea Bonomi and Gian Paolo Romano (eds), *Yearbook of Private International Law. Vol XV* (Sellier European Law Publishers 2014) 452.

A court of law is established under the law of a State, and it is regarded as an agent or trustee of that State.[71] Its powers are limited to the territorial jurisdiction of the State. As such, its judgment does not have an extra-territorial effect of its own force.[72]

In private international law, the word 'foreign' means more than it ordinarily connotes.[73] Any action that has a connection with another distinct legal district is foreign even if both legal districts fall under the same political entity. For instance, in a federation such as the United States, the judgment of a Texas court is a foreign judgment in New York just as is a judgment from England. However, by constitutional arrangements,[74] judgments from sister-states or provinces are treated differently from judgments from foreign countries. In this chapter and the rest of the book, foreign judgments under consideration are judgments from foreign countries. Thus, a foreign judgment is defined as

> the final decision, decree or sentence of a judicial body or tribunal regularly established and exercising the jurisdiction conferred upon it by the law of the country or province of its creation, which determines the respective rights and claims of the parties to a suit therein litigated.[75]

This definition is apt as the nature, status and designation of courts differ from State to State. Thus, judgments from Dubai International Finance Centre (DIFC) Courts are regarded as foreign judgments even if they are not styled 'High Courts' as is widely used in other jurisdictions.

B. Recognition and Enforcement of Judgments

Recognition and enforcement of judgments are often used together but they mean different things and have different effects. Recognition is the preclusive effect that a court addressed grants to a foreign judgment. This implies that the court respects the decision of a foreign court and considers it to be final for the issues

---

[71] Paul B Stephan, 'Courts on Courts : Contracting for Engagement and Indifference in International Judicial Encounters' (2014) 100 *Virginia Law Review* 17, 20; Adrian Briggs, 'Recognition of Foreign Judgments: A Matter of Obligation (2013) 129 *Law Quarterly Review* 87.
[72] Lord Collins of Mapesbury and others (eds), *Dicey, Morris and Collins on the Conflict of Laws* (15th edn, Sweet & Maxwell Ltd 2012) 664; Briggs, *The Conflict of Laws* (n 44) 140.
[73] Torremans and others (n 38) 8.
[74] States do have some constitutional or statutory arrangements where full faith and credit apply to inter-state or provincial judgments. Examples of such arrangements are seen in Nigeria, the United States of America and others. See s 1, Article IV of the Constitution of the United States of America; s 104 Sheriffs and Civil Processes Act, LFN 2004 (Nigeria); ss 18 and 19 of Civil Jurisdiction and Judgments Act 1982 (UK). In other States like Canada where there is no explicit constitutional or statutory framework, it is implied by the doctrine of comity. See *Morguard Investments Ltd v De Savoye* (n 66).
[75] JG Castel, 'Recognition and Enforcement of Foreign Judgments in Personam and in Rem in the Common Law Provinces of Canada' (1971) 17 *McGill Law Journal* 11, 12.

or claims decided therein.[76] The parties are, therefore, barred from re-opening any of the issues or claims already decided by a previous judgment. On the other hand, enforcement entails the use of the machinery of the receiving State to give effect to a foreign judgment.[77] It involves taking an extra step to sanction and ensure compliance with the judgment. A judgment creditor may simply ask a court addressed to recognise a foreign judgment without seeking its enforcement. This may be the case where the aim is to prevent a claimant in a new suit from asserting his claims. However, enforcement necessarily entails recognition, as a court will only enforce a foreign judgment which it recognises.

C. Direct and Indirect Jurisdiction

Jurisdiction is the power of a court to adjudicate a dispute submitted to it and to issue decisions that bind the parties. This power to decide cases is often derived from the constitution, statutes and in some cases, from case law. This general understanding of jurisdiction is technically referred to as direct jurisdiction. It is also called judicial or adjudicatory jurisdiction. Thus, where a dispute is submitted to a court for adjudication, the court determines whether it has jurisdiction under its laws to entertain that dispute. Where jurisdiction is established, the court hears the matter and issues a judgment at the end of the proceedings.

On the other hand, a judgment creditor may need to enforce the judgment in another jurisdiction. The court where enforcement is sought – the court addressed – needs to determine whether the foreign court had jurisdiction over the subject matter or parties. This second jurisdictional inquiry is referred to as indirect jurisdiction.[78] It is indirect because the court addressed has no control over how the foreign court should exercise jurisdiction. Therefore, the court addressed will only enforce the judgment if, under its laws, the foreign court had jurisdiction. That jurisdiction is referred to as indirect jurisdiction or international jurisdiction or jurisdiction in the international sense.

D. State of Origin/State Addressed/Court Addressed

In this book, State of Origin refers to the State whose court delivered the relevant foreign judgment. The court of that State is also referred to as the court of origin or the rendering court. On the other hand, the State where recognition or

---

[76] Briggs, *The Conflict of Laws* (n 44) 140.

[77] Cedric C Chao and Christine S Neuhoff, 'Enforcement and Recognition of Foreign Judgments in United States Courts : A Practical Perspective' (2002) 29 *Pepperdine Law Review* 147.

[78] For a detailed analysis on the meaning and distinctions between direct and indirect jurisdiction, see Arthur T von Mehren and Donald T Trautman, 'Recognition of Foreign Adjudications: A Survey and a Suggested Approach' (1968) 81 *Harvard Law Review* 1601.

enforcement of a judgment is sought is the State addressed and the court where recognition or enforcement is sought is referred to as the court addressed.

VIII. Structure of the Book

This book is divided into three parts. Part I explores the theoretical foundations of foreign judgments recognition and enforcement, analysing the reasons and justifications offered by various legal traditions for enforcing judgments rendered abroad. The concept of pragmatism, as developed in philosophy and as applied in law, is also discussed in some detail. Thereafter, it considers the pragmatic theory of private international law and how it applies to foreign judgments. Part II is devoted to the CML and it is used as a practical example of how pragmatism can be applied by policymakers at the national level and international level between States with a shared legal culture. The Model Law is analysed against the backdrop of the pragmatic goals that have been suggested in Part I. Part III probes into the history of the Hague judgments project. It examines first, second and third attempts at arriving at a global judgments convention, especially between 1992 and 2019. The pragmatism in the making of the HCCA and the 2019 Judgments Convention is considered and the texts of both conventions are examined against the backdrop of the pragmatic goals suggested in Part I. The book concludes by considering the likelihood of ratification of the Judgments Convention by States and how the Commonwealth can work together with the Hague Conference to deliver a successful global judgments framework.

PART I

Theoretical Frameworks for Judgments Recognition and Enforcement

2

Recognition and Enforcement of Foreign Judgments: Theoretical Background

I. Introduction

Foreign judgments, generally, do not have extra-territorial effects. A litigant who is desirous of enforcing a foreign judgment needs the permission of the receiving State before such judgment can be given any effect. Whether the receiving State will grant such a request depends on several factors. These factors differ from one State to another. In many cases, the judgment creditor is faced with the stark reality that the judgment he obtained abroad is denied recognition, having spent huge resources and time. Nevertheless, why do courts need to enforce foreign judgments? The understanding of the underlying reasons will help us to appreciate the subject of inquiry. Broadly speaking, four theories have been offered to justify the enforcement of foreign judgments. These are comity, reciprocity, legal obligation, and *res judicata*. This chapter seeks to assess these theoretical bases, their practical application in various jurisdictions and their shortcomings. The chapter will then briefly discuss the emerging pragmatic approach to judgments recognition and enforcement, and how desirable or otherwise such an approach is.

An analysis of the theoretical framework will set the ground for the discourse in subsequent chapters and will serve as an eye-opener to help us form an understanding of the tricks and treats in judgments recognition and enforcement practices, why it took so long for States to come up with globally harmonised rules, the concerns and compromises, and, above all, the significance of the 2019 Judgments Convention and the CML.

II. Theoretical Bases for Enforcement of Foreign Judgments

A. Comity

(i) Meaning

The seventeenth century was a watershed in the annals of the development of private international law because of the gradual disintegration of the Holy Roman

Empire and the emergence of the city-states and eventually the post-Westphalian sovereign States. One of the immediate consequences was the demarcation and tying of populations to clearly defined territories.[79] Each State had absolute control over every person within its territory and the conduct of its internal and external affairs. It brought the idea of the universality of Roman law to an end, as each sovereign would now decide which law operated within its territory and the effects of foreign conduct on its soil. As Schultz and Mitchenson observe, the need to guard against the pre-Westphalian experiences required that invincible fences needed to be constructed along territorial borders in other to ensure good-neighbourliness.[80] These invincible fences did not, however, affect the growth of transboundary commerce. Similarly, people continued to crisscross from one territory to the other for education, leisure, and matrimonial purposes. These activities challenged the intelligentsia of that time, as there was the need to come up with a better way of addressing the evolving issues of territoriality and cross-border activities.

The Dutch jurists, such as Christian Rodenburg, Paul Voet, John Voet and Ulrich Huber (who was a leading figure),[81] were the leading theorists that responded to this challenge.[82] Huber published his seminal work *De Conflictu Legum* in 1689. The work was meant to address issues of conflict of laws arising from the relationship between laws of the emerging sovereigns in continental Europe.[83] Drawing from the works of Hugo Grotius, Huber advocated the principles of territorial sovereignty.[84] He was the doctrinal originator of the principle of territoriality[85] and the expression 'conflict of laws'.[86] By this doctrine, all laws are

---

[79] OECD, *Free Movement of Workers and Labour Market Adjustment: Recent Experiences from OECD Countries and the European Union* (OECD Publishing 2012) 279.

[80] Thomas Schultz and Jason Mitchenson, 'Navigating Sovereignty and Transnational Commercial Law: The Use of Comity by Australian Courts' (2016) 12 *Journal of Private International Law* 344, 347.

[81] Alex Mills, 'The Private History of International Law' (2006) 55 *International and Comparative Law Quarterly* 1, 25.

[82] The Dutch provinces grew into prominence as a major hub for maritime business due to their expanding economy, urbanisation, migration from the countryside and the dynamic labour market. See Joop De Jong, 'The Dutch Golden Age and Globalization: History and Heritage, Legacies and Contestations' (2011) 27 *Macalester International* 46, 50–51. The cosmopolitan nature of the cities and the diversity of the people possibly gave it the impetus to develop private international law. It should be added that other prominent writers like Bertrand D'Argentré of Brittany (France) also shared similar ideas. For a summary of their postulations and the point of divergence, see Ernest G Lorenzen, 'Huber's De Conflictu Legum' (1919) 13 *Illinois Law Review* 375, 375–78.

[83] William S Dodge, 'International Comity in American Law' (2015) 115 *Columbia Law Review* 2071, 2085; Donald E Childress III, 'Comity As Conflict: Resituating International Comity As Conflict of Laws' (2010) 44 *UC Davis Law Review* 11, 17.

[84] Mills (n 81) 25; Alan Golomb, 'Recognition of Foreign Money Judgments: A Goal-Oriented Approach' (1969) 43 *St John's Law Review* 604, 613.

[85] This is in relation to private international law. Although, some scholarly works before him like those of the statutists, and the Voets used elements of territoriality in formulating their theory, they are, however, not as succinctly articulated as that of Huber.

[86] H Patrick Glenn, *The Cosmopolitan State* (OUP 2013) 159.

territorial, and they have no extraterritorial application. His first two principles supported this notion. According to the influential scholar:

- The laws of each State have force within the limits of that government and bind all subjects to it, but not beyond.

- All persons within the limits of a government, whether they live there permanently or temporarily, are deemed to be subjects thereof.[87]

Huber's position is well understood, drawing from the circumstances of the newly independent Dutch Republic. The fledgling State needed to be protected from all forms of external control, and as such, any legal theorising must be able to justify the need for the State to have firm control over its territory and prevention of external incursions. However, if his doctrine were to be enforced to the letter, it would not only hamper the development of trade and commerce which the Dutch provinces were pursuing, but would also disrupt international sociopolitical relationships.[88]

Huber added a third principle thus:

- Sovereigns will so act by way of comity that rights acquired within the limits of a government retain their force everywhere so far as they do not cause prejudice to the powers or rights of such government [ie the receiving State] or of their subjects.[89]

Huber's third principle ushered in comity as a mechanism for addressing cross-border issues. The third rule admits foreign laws and other sovereign acts for convenience and the need to facilitate international commerce. It is also necessary for harmonious relations among sovereigns.

Huber's idea of comity was the first comprehensive principle to be used in analysing every aspect of private international law: jurisdiction, choice of law and enforcement of foreign judgments.[90] As it relates to foreign judgments, the decisions of foreign courts are regarded as a sovereign act, which only have the force of law within the territory of the State of origin. However, other States ought to receive, recognise and enforce such judgments in their respective territories provided they do not prejudice the sovereign interest of the receiving State. According to Huber, if foreign judgments would not have an effect outside their State of origin, it would cause great inconvenience and hamper the development of cross-border trade and commerce.

---

[87] Translation provided by Symeon C Symeonides, *Private International Law: Idealism, Pragmatism, Eclecticism: General Course on Private International Law* (M Nijhoff 2016) 42–43.

[88] Mills (n 81) 156.

[89] Symeonides (n 87) 43.

[90] Adrian Briggs, 'The Principle of Comity in Private International Law', *Hague Academy of International Law: Recueil des cours* vol 354 (Martinus Nijhoff 2011) 82.

Legal experts have understood Huber's proposition of comity differently. Huber, as a Grotian, might have intended that comity – as a general principle of international law – required recognition of judgments thereby having some obligatory character.[91] However, notable commentators after him were divided on whether comity requires foreign laws and rights to be recognised or it is a mere courtesy which can be withheld at will. One school understood it as presented above – mandatory[92] – while others submitted that it is a rule of domestic law, which is often extended out of mere courtesy.[93] It is not a surprise that Justice Gray in *Hilton v Guyot* placed it in between obligation and courtesy.[94] It has also been characterised by other commentators as a rule of reciprocity, and courtesy,[95] moral obligation, expediency, diplomacy, diplomatic immunity and so on.[96]

(ii) Practice

From the seventeenth century to date, comity has been regarded as a plausible answer to why a court should enforce a foreign judgment or apply foreign law. It gives both a theoretical and legal justification for the recognition of foreign judgments as dictated by convenience and the facilitation of trade and commerce. Comity – even if understood differently – has allowed commerce to flourish for ages, as investors are confident that the rights created in one jurisdiction will be respected and honoured in other jurisdictions.[97] It encourages harmonious relationships among States by giving recognition to foreign sovereign acts and deference to foreign sovereigns where their interests would be affected. In other words, it is 'essential to the establishment and maintenance of a stable international community'.[98] It also brings some form of orderliness to cross-border resolution of disputes.[99] Contrary to the reports of its 'demise', the reality is that the doctrine of comity is very much alive in many jurisdictions, especially in the United States

---

[91] Thomas Schultz and Niccolo Ridi, 'Comity and International Courts and Tribunals' (2017) 50 *Cornell International Law Journal* 576, 583; Mills (n 81) 26.

[92] Some commentators argue that it is part and parcel of public international law. See Rudolf Bernhardt, *Encyclopaedia of Public International Law* (Elsevier Science Publishers 1984) 41.

[93] Harold G Maier, 'Extraterritorial Jurisdiction at a Crossroads: An Intersection between Public and Private International Law' (1982) 76 *American Journal of International Law* 280, 281 (noting that 'the extension of comity to another nation is viewed as a unilateral decision of the forum, not as an act required by a rule of the public international system').

[94] *Hilton v Guyot* (1895) 113 US 159, 164.

[95] Gil Seinfeld, 'Reflections on Comity in the Law of American Federalism' (2015) 90 *Notre Dame Law Review* 1309, 1312.

[96] Zheng Sophia Tang, Yongping Xiao and Zhengxin Huo, *Conflict of Laws in the People's Republic of China* (Edward Elgar Publishing 2016) 142; Joel R Paul, 'The Transformation of International Comity' (2008) 71 *Law and Contemporary Problems* 19, 19–20.

[97] Justice James Allsop, 'Comity and Commerce' [2015] *Federal Judicial Scholarship* 27, para 25.

[98] Ho Li, 'Policies Underlying the Enforcement of Foreign Commercial Judgments' (1997) 46 *International and Comparative Law Quarterly* 443, 451.

[99] John Kuhn Bleimaier, 'The Doctrine of Comity in Private International Law' (1978) 24 *Catholic Lawyer* 327.

and some common law jurisdictions.[100] Although continental lawyers popularised it, it seems to be more prominently used in the common law jurisdictions than in continental Europe.[101]

The foundation for comity in its modern usage was laid in the seminal decision of the United States Supreme Court in *Hilton*[102] and it is the basis for enforcement of foreign judgments in many of the US states.[103] Hilton recognises the fact that foreign judgments should be recognised to do justice between parties and to foster friendly intercourse among nations. Apart from setting out *why* a foreign judgment should be enforced, it further answered the question of *which* judgments should be so enforced. In the standard set by the court, foreign judgments should be presumptively enforceable when a foreign court had properly exercised jurisdiction and observed due process.[104] *Hilton* has had a great influence on several courts in the Commonwealth.[105] For instance, when a Ugandan court was faced with a request to enforce a US judgment in *Christopher Sales v Attorney General*[106] in the absence of any treaty or bilateral arrangement, the court extensively relied on *Hilton* and found a solution in the doctrine of comity to enforce the said judgment.

In 2003, the Canadian Supreme Court adopted the doctrine of comity in *Beals v Saldanha*[107] to recognise a US foreign judgment under circumstances earlier preserved only for its own inter-provincial judgments. The Court noted that international comity is essential to 'facilitate the free flow of wealth, skills, and people

---

[100] For its relevance especially in jurisdictional restraint, see Lawrence Collins, 'Comity in Modern Private International Law' in J Fawcett (ed), *Reform and Development of Private International Law: Essays in Honour of Sir Peter North* (Oxford University Press 2002) 95 (noting that 'Comity may be a discredited concept in the eyes of the text-writers, but it thrives in the judicial decisions'). In *Adams v Cape Industries Plc* (ch 1, fn 28), the English Court of Appeal admitted the reality that comity plays some role in judgments' enforcement in the common law even though the widely accepted theory remains that of legal obligation. This view was also emphasised by Lord Collins in *Agbaje v Agbaje* [2010] UKSC 13.

[101] This is due to the primacy of the civil codes and limited discretionary powers of the courts in continental Europe. Generally, the courts apply foreign laws or enforce foreign judgments not out of respect but in accordance with the dictates of the codes. See Joel R Paul, 'Comity in International Law' (1991) 32 *Harvard International Law Journal* 1, 30–35 (discussing comity in the civil law countries). However, the concept of mutual recognition of judgments as practised in the EU under the Brussels regime can be said to be a resurrection of comity even though that is not expressly stated in the instruments.

[102] *Hilton v Guyot* (n 94).

[103] *Hilton* ushered in a liberal judgments enforcement regime by allowing all foreign judgments to be enforceable under the common law. Some states apply the common law as expounded in *Hilton* to foreign judgments, others apply the 1962 Uniform Foreign Money-Judgments Recognition Act or the 2005 Uniform Foreign-Country Money Judgments Recognition Act. See Ronald A Brand, 'Federal Judicial Center International Litigation Guide: Recognition and Enforcement of Foreign Judgments' (2013) 74 *University of Pittsburgh Law Review* 491.

[104] Chao and Neuhoff (ch 1, fn 77) 149.

[105] Lawrence Collins (n 100) 95 (noting that he came across no less than 30 such decisions in the British Commonwealth and more than 100 in the United States in the last 20 years).

[106] *Christopher Sales v Attorney General* [2013] UGHCCD 15 (High Court of Uganda at Kampala (Civil Division).

[107] *Beals v Saldanha* (ch 1, fn 29).

across State lines in a fair and orderly manner'.[108] The Court was swayed by *Hilton* and its own earlier decision in *Morguard*[109] and concluded that Canadian courts would recognise a foreign judgment if the foreign court had a real and substantial connection with the dispute. Recently, courts in the Cayman Islands, Guernsey, Australia, and Canada have also adopted comity to enforce foreign non-money judgments in a somewhat radical departure from the common law.[110]

Comity has also found its way into the jurisprudence of the Russian Federation. The legal consciousness of the Russian courts has been built around the protection of the sovereignty of the State and the propensity to defend the State's legal system from foreign interference.[111] For this reason, foreign judgments are hardly ever enforced in the absence of a treaty. However, in recent times, this perception seems to be changing in favour of a more internationalist approach. The Russian courts have enforced a few foreign judgments based on international comity. The Supreme Arbitrazh Court in *Rentpool BV*[112] ruled that a Dutch judgment could not be denied recognition because it originated from a competent court with valid legal norms. Similar considerations also influenced the recognition of an English judgment in *Boegli-Gravures SA*.[113]

While unrestricted usage of comity may lead to indiscriminate admittance of foreign judgments, its inbuilt discretionary device has been used to safeguard the rights of judgment debtors. Where it is just and convenient, a forum court will not provide its stamp of approval on a foreign judgment that has been inappropriately procured.[114] In this respect, comity preserves the integrity and sovereignty of the forum and more importantly, the need to do justice in deserving cases. Thus, to protect the fundamental policies of a receiving State by withholding recognition of foreign judgments is said to be compatible with comity. It has been used particularly in cases where foreign judgments were procured by fraud or where the independence of the foreign tribunal is strongly compromised.[115]

---

[108] Para 170.

[109] *Morguard Investment Ltd v De Savoye* (ch 1, fn 66).

[110] For discussions on some of these cases, see Graeme Halkerston, 'Enforcement of Foreign Non-Money Judgments at Common Law in Offshore Jurisdictions: Back to Basics?' (2015) 21 *Trusts & Trustees* 969; Jonathan Harris, 'Jurisdiction and Judgments in International Trusts Litigation – Surveying the Landscape' (2011) 17 *Trusts & Trustees* 236; Sara Collins, 'The Last Frontier: Enforcing Foreign Judgments against Offshore Trusts after Pattni v Ali' (2009) 15 *Trusts & Trustees* 18.

[111] Mikhail Antonov, 'Foreign Court Decisions, Arbitral Awards and Sovereignty in Russia' (2013) 38 *Review of Central and European Law* 317, 323.

[112] *Rentpool BV v OOO Podyemnye Tekhnologii*, Case No VAS-13688/09 (7 December 2009), cited in Antonov (n 111), 337–38. It does appear that the Russian courts require reciprocity as a precondition for the application of comity.

[113] *Boegli-Gravures SA v OOO Darsail-ASP and Andrei Pyzhov*, Sup Com Ct, 26 July 2012, Case No A40-119397/11-63-950. The summary of the case is discussed in ALRUD Law Firm, 'Enforcement of Foreign Court Judgments in Russia: A Wind of Change' (6 June 2017) <http://www.alrud.com/upload/iblock/dc5/Newsletter_recognition and enforcement.pdf> accessed 29 November 2017.

[114] Virginia A Fitt, 'The Tragedy of Comity: Questioning the American Treatment of Inadequate Foreign Courts' (2010) 50 *Virginia Journal of International Law* 1022, 1028.

[115] *Chevron Corp v Donziger*, 833 F.3d 74, 126 (2d Cir. 2016).

(iii) Criticism

Several Anglo-American commentators have criticised comity.[116] Huber's analysis only provides an answer to why a foreign judgment should be enforced, but not how and when. This lacuna forms one of the bases of criticising the doctrine. While commentators such as Story agree that foreign judgments are enforced only at the discretion of the receiving State, Dicey opposes this view and attacked comity from this perspective. In Dicey's view, comity is a very elastic concept and wrongly used to show that foreign law – or judgments – are honoured as a 'matter of caprice or option'.[117] He submits that rights acquired (under foreign judgments) ought to be enforced as a matter of justice and not at the discretion of the court.

Enforcing foreign judgments on the grounds of mere courtesy means a court can cherry-pick which foreign judgments to respect and when to respect them. It may be subject to abuse, as courts can easily create exceptions through the back door and re-examine the merits of foreign judgments at will.[118] This reduces the governance values[119] associated with comity, as an unfettered discretion to allow defences brings about waste of judicial resources in many cases. Also, it may create instability in the law, thereby leading to uncertainties. This criticism is linked to the lack of coherent principles guiding the exercise of comity because its contents and frontiers are left to judges to figure out. Hence, when a court should extend or withhold comity to foreign judgments and what factors the court should consider are questions which the doctrine fails to answer. While *Hilton* gives some guidelines, they are not uniformly applied in all jurisdictions.

The authors of *Cheshire and North* deride comity because it attempts to ascribe executive functions to the courts.[120] This criticism, perhaps, arises from their conception of comity as reciprocity. As Professor Briggs argues, comity is not reciprocity. It is simply an act of respecting the territorial sovereignty of other States in issues that fall within their competence.[121] Where private parties request courts

---

[116] FA Mann, *Foreign Affairs in English Courts* (Oxford University Press 1986) chapter 7; Torremans and others (ch 1, fn 38) 4.

[117] Albert Venn Dicey, *A Digest of the Law of England with Reference to the Conflict of Laws* (2nd edn, Stevenson & sons Ltd 1908) 10. The editors of the 15th edition, *Dicey, Morris and Collins on the Conflict of Laws*, however, admit that comity is now playing an increasing role in conflict of laws question. See Lord Collins of Mapesbury and others (ch 1, fn 72) 6–9.

[118] Courtland H Peterson, 'Res Judicata and Foreign Country Judgments' (1963) 24 *Ohio State Law Journal* 291, 308.

[119] Comity (judicial comity) has some governance values because it seeks to facilitate order and restraint in cross-boundary judicial activities. These values in turn ensure efficiency, judicial economy, and stability in the international order. See Christopher A Whytock, 'Enforcement of Foreign Judgments: Governance, Rights, and the Market for Dispute Resolution Services' in Hans-W Micklitz and Andrea Wechsler (eds), *The Transformation of Enforcement: European Economic Law in a Global Perspective* (Hart Publishing 2016) 50.

[120] Torremans and others (ch 1, fn 38) 4.

[121] Adrian Briggs (n 90) 82.

to enforce foreign judgments, the court is looking at private rights and the propri-etariness or otherwise of the basis of that right, ie the foreign judgment. If the judgment appears to be in order and the foreign court has properly exercised juris-diction, the forum court, ought to respect the integrity of the foreign court and its judgment. Hence, judicial comity has arisen as a separate form of comity distinct from others like legislative or executive comity, and may operate uniquely without executive interference.[122]

Despite the criticisms, comity represents a cornerstone of modern private international law, particularly in the area of recognition and enforcement of foreign judgments.[123] It supports the principle of efficiency by allowing a court which is more connected to a dispute to deal with it, while its decision is respected in other jurisdictions.[124] It is capable of stimulating cooperation among courts through mutual respect for foreign judicial proceedings and judgments.[125] It is very useful, particularly in today's cosmopolitan world where trade and commerce continue to defy territorial borders. The experience in *Hilton's* case alone proves that untold hardship will be met by judgment creditors who seek to realise the fruit of their labour against smart defendants who can become judgment-proof by merely changing location or moving assets.[126] Hence, comity has been able, largely, to curtail the frustration, inconvenience, injustice, and waste of scarce judicial resources that would have ensued if a strict territorial approach were maintained against foreign judgments. In all, it is opined that comity is a valuable theory not only because of its liberal outlook but also its support for efficiency and judicial economy.

B. Reciprocity

(i) Meaning

Reciprocity, like comity, is hard to define due to its broad and general usage. Its usage in the context of the external relations among sovereign States is what is intended in this chapter. In this regard, reciprocity means 'the relationship between two states, each of which gives the other, and its inhabitants, similar privileges'.[127]

---

[122] Michael D Ramsey, 'Comity' (1998) 1 *Iowa Law Review* 893 (discussing the three concepts as being grouped under 'international comity').

[123] This view is opposed by some of the leading English commentators. See Lawrence Collins (ch 1, fn 74) 91–92. However, in this similar work, Lord Collins agrees that comity remains very relevant as it is often cited in judicial decisions on enforcement of foreign judgments.

[124] Timothy Endicott, 'Comity among Authorities' (2015) 68 *Current Legal Problems* 1, 8–9.

[125] Schultz and Ridi (n 91) 13.

[126] In *Hilton* (n 94), while the French action was going through the appellate process, Guyot dissipated his assets in France in order to become judgment-proof there as it was obvious that the French judg-ment would be enforced against those assets.

[127] LB Curzon, *Dictionary of Law* (6th edn, Pearson Education Ltd 2002) 355.

Reciprocity was a feature of international relations even before the emergence of the modern State.[128] Before the development of modern international law, it was used to address the mutual concerns of sovereigns, induce cooperation and redress unfriendly conduct. For instance, the treaty of 1174 on the extradition of fugitive felons, signed between King Henry II of England and William, King of Scotland, was based on reciprocity.[129] Similarly, the French Code Michaud of 1629, which denied recognition and enforcement of foreign judgments against French nationals, was reciprocated with similar treatment for French judgments by some other sovereigns.[130] As rightly put by Parisi and Ghei, reciprocal treatment as a strategy 'permits cooperation in a state of nature, when no authority for enforcement of agreements exists'.[131]

Unlike the Hobbesian state of nature, modern international law regulates the relationships between States by creating certain norms and obligations. These norms are largely consensual. They arise from treaties or widely shared values.[132] The fulfilment of norms is necessary for the maintenance of international order and peaceful co-existence among States. Beyond agreed norms, a State is not obliged to act in any particular way. Unfortunately, international law lacks any effective supranational body to regulate and enforce compliance with obligations owed by States *inter se*.[133] No global court exists with mandatory jurisdiction to adjudicate on the breach of international norms and with the capacity to enforce compliance against the wish of a defaulting State.[134] A State is therefore at liberty to employ the usual remedial actions in retaliation for any violation of either legal or non-legal norms. It is also often used as a psychological attempt to compel State(s) to act in the desired way.

Foreign judgments are acts of sovereigns expressed through judicial pronouncements. No State is under any obligation to recognise and enforce them within its territory. However, commerce and other cross-border socio-political

---

[128] William G Southard, 'The Reciprocity Rule and Enforcement of Foreign Judgments' (1977) 16 *Columbia Journal of Transnational Law* 327.

[129] Arthur Lenhoff, 'Reciprocity in Function: A Problem of Conflict of Laws, Constitutional Law, and International Law' (1953) 15 *University of Pittsburgh Law Review* 44, 45.

[130] Ralf Michaels, 'Recognition and Enforcement of Foreign Judgments' in Rudiger Wolfrum (ed), *Max Planck Encyclopedia of Public International Law* (Oxford University Press 2009) 673.

[131] Francesco Paris and Nita Ghei, 'The Role of Reciprocity in International Law' (2003) 36 *Cornell International Law Journal* 93, 94.

[132] Eric A Posner and Alan O Sykes, 'Efficient Breach of International Law: Optimal Remedies, Legalized Noncompliance, and Related Issues' (2011) 110 *Michigan Law Review* 243, 252.

[133] Anu Bradford and Omri Ben-Shahar, 'Efficient Enforcement in International Law' (2012) 12 *Chicago Journal of International Law* 375, 381–82.

[134] The International Court of Justice, which can be referred to as the world court, can only assume jurisdiction with the consent of States. Where a State submits to the jurisdiction of the Court and a judgment is awarded, there is no effective international framework for the enforcement of such judgments, even though States do voluntarily comply in most cases. See Aloysius P Llamzon, 'Jurisdiction and Compliance in Recent Decisions of the International Court of Justice' (2007) 18 *European Journal of International Law* 815; Ian Brownlie, *Principles of Public International Law* (7th edn, Oxford University Press 2008) 710.

circumstances bring States and their subjects into closer interactions with one another. So, why, how, and when should State A enforce judgments from State B? The theory of reciprocity simply explains that State A should enforce judgments from State B if State B would enforce judgments from State A in return. This is a broad response. However, many other explanations support the above proposition.

One explanation is the emphasis on the equality of States and the defence of sovereignty. Reciprocity is used by States to strengthen their sovereignty, independence, and equality.[135] Of course, it undermines the principle of equality of States if a State accepts unfavourable treatment from another State without any consequence. As partners on the global platform, States are required to establish relationships that are based on mutual respect. This respect includes showing positive reception of one another's acts. This is the notion that informed the inclusion of reciprocity as a condition for the extension of comity in *Hilton*. A second explanation, which is closely related to the above, is the concept of nationalism and protectionism which held sway in the nineteenth century. Arthur Lenhof records that reciprocity was used by several European States to stop unfavourable and hostile treatment of their nationals in foreign territories.[136]

Again, in a world of divergent judgments enforcement practices, reciprocity is seen as a possible mechanism that can be used to induce cooperation from States to achieve a more liberalised regime. As various writers have explained this from an economic perspective, a State will be willing to cooperate and return reciprocal gestures where certain payoffs will be derived from such cooperation.[137] It is often believed that States act in self-interest and, as a 'rational entity', a State will reciprocate good gestures and vice versa. The policy behind reciprocity is, therefore, aimed at committing foreign States to respecting and recognising foreign judgments for the mutual benefit of all States and their subjects. A State which has an interest in seeing its judgments enforced abroad ought to enforce other States' judgments in return. This will eventually establish mutual cooperation amongst States and wider, if not global, circulation of judgments. Thus, reciprocity could serve as a source of global judicial efficiency and interdependence. It can also evoke a 'spirit of mutuality', which is necessary for the establishment of a transnational legal order.[138]

---

[135] Béligh Elbalti, 'Reciprocity and the Recognition and Enforcement of Foreign Judgments: A Lot of Bark but Not Much Bite' (2017) 13 *Journal of Private International Law* 184, 215; Samuel P Baumgartner, 'Understanding the Obstacles to the Recognition and Enforcement of U.S. Judgments Abroad' (2013) 44 *New York University Journal of International Law and Politics* 965.

[136] A Lenhoff, 'Reciprocity and the Law of Foreign Judgments: A Historical-Critical Analysis' (1955) 16 *Louisiana Law Review* 466, 479.

[137] The game theory has been used by various writers as an economic analysis of judgments' recognition practice. See Michael J Whincop, 'The Recognition Scene: Game Theoretical Issues in the Recognition of Foreign Judgments' (1999) 23 *Melbourne University Law Review* 416.

[138] Steven Chong, 'Cross-Border Dispute Resolution: Innovations From Singapore', *2nd China-ASEAN Justice Forum* (8 June 2017).

(ii) Application

Reciprocity is widely used both in civil and common law jurisdictions, though it is practised in different forms. The Commonwealth States have a statutory registration scheme that is only available to reciprocating States, usually within the Commonwealth.[139] Otherwise, other foreign judgments are only enforceable by legal action. Some of its members have extended the same privilege to non-Commonwealth States through various bilateral negotiations and treaties. Likewise, reciprocity has been customarily used in many States in Europe, Asia, Latin America, and the Middle East and as such only judgments from reciprocating States – as imposed by the relevant Code, case law or treaty – are usually enforced.[140]

Reciprocity has been successfully used to secure favourable treatment of foreign judgments by some States. Coyle[141] and Elbalti[142] did some empirical work in this respect. Their finding of partial effectiveness of reciprocal policy can be supported with more examples from the past and recent occurrences. The English Lord Chancellor's submission to the House of Lords on the reason for introducing a 1933 bill for direct registration of foreign judgments in England is very instructive. The Lord Chancellor informed the House that:

> The Bill owes its origin to a substantial grievance suffered by litigants in this country, mainly business men, when they recover judgment against a defendant whose assets are in a foreign country, and that grievance is this: they find it very difficult to enforce their judgment in the country where the assets are ... In some countries a foreign judgment is enforced quite readily if it comes from the Court of a country which itself grants similar facilities; in other words, if there is reciprocity. But when we are asked here whether we in England grant similar facilities, though our answer could be 'Substantially, yes', yet we are obliged to answer 'Technically, no'.... In practice hundreds of foreign judgments are enforced in England every year by a summary procedure without a fresh trial on the merits of the case, but very few of our judgments are enforced by foreign Courts and then often after trying the case all over again, the Court not being satisfied on the point of reciprocity.[143]

The English courts' doctrine of obligation which required creditors to file a new action on the judgment was considered to mean that English courts did not regard foreign judgments as final; hence the difficulty in enforcing English judgments in other States. The countermeasure of some civil law States necessitated the introduction of an alternative enforcement regime – statutory registration – by the

---

[139] McClean and Patchett (ch 1, fn 63). However, the 2017 model law, which is yet to be implemented by any State has removed the reciprocity requirement.
[140] Elbalti (n 135).
[141] John F Coyle, 'Rethinking Judgements Reciprocity' (2014) 92 *North Carolina Law Review* 1109.
[142] Elbalti (n 135).
[143] House of Lords, Foreign Judgments (Reciprocal Enforcement) Bill. (Hansard, 14 February 1933) 1933 vol 86, cols 671, 672.

United Kingdom.[144] Eventually, it led to the extension of the registration scheme to judgments from countries such as Belgium,[145] the Netherlands[146] and Norway[147] even before the accession of the United Kingdom to the EEC Brussels Convention. The Commonwealth States have also discarded reciprocity from the 2017 model law. However, there is no empirical study yet to determine if this move is due to the difficulties of enforcing their judgments abroad.

China is one of the few States that hardly enforce foreign judgments.[148] In 2016, China's Nanjing Intermediate People's Court in *Kolmar Group AG v Jiangsu Textile Industry (Group)*[149] gave a green light suggestive of possible enforcement of foreign judgments in China if evidence exists that Chinese courts' judgments have been previously enforced in the State in question.[150] In this case, the Court recognised a Singaporean judgment because a Chinese court's judgment had been earlier enforced in 2014 by Singapore in *Giant Light Metal Technology (Kunshan) Co Ltd v Aksa Far East Pte Ltd.*[151] The Court also realised that there was a need for a change in order to facilitate the China-led 'belt and road' global infrastructure development initiative. In walking the talk, China has proposed to relax its reciprocity requirement by adopting presumptive reciprocity in its Nanning Declaration of June 2017.[152]

In Russia, the Supreme Arbitrazh Court enforced an English judgment after considering the pro-enforcement stance of the English courts, the 1992 economic cooperation agreement signed between the two States and the 1997 Agreement on Partnership and Cooperation between the Russian Federation

---

[144] This position is also shared by Stevens who notes that the United Kingdom was induced to come up with a procedure like exequatur as result of the negative reactions from the neighbouring civil law countries. See Susan L Stevens, 'Commanding International Judicial Respect: Reciprocity and the Recognition and Enforcement of Foreign Judgments' (2002) 26 *Hastings International & Comparative Law Review* 115, 123.

[145] The Reciprocal Enforcement of Foreign Judgments (Belgium) Order in Council, 1936 (SR & O 1936, No 1169).

[146] The Reciprocal Enforcement of Foreign Judgments (The Netherlands) Order 1969.

[147] The Reciprocal Enforcement of Foreign Judgments (Norway) Order 1962.

[148] Jason Hsu, 'Judgment Unenforceability in China' (2013) 19 *Fordham Journal of Corporate & Financial Law* 201, 219. It is interesting to note that from an empirical research carried out by Tsang, it is discovered that the Chinese legal system was so restrictive that even in cases where enforcement action was brought before the Chinese courts under bilateral treaties, the Chinese courts usually reject enforcement on other extraneous grounds outside such treaties. See King Fung Tsang, 'Chinese Bilateral Judgment Enforcement Treaties' (2017) 40 *Loyola LA International & Comparative Law Review* 1, 32.

[149] The English summary of the case is reported at Stanford Law School, 'Kolmar Group AG, A Case of an Application for the Recognition and Enforcement of a Civil Judgment of the High Court of Singapore', *China Guiding Cases Project*, B & R Typical Case 13, 15 May 2017 at: <https://cgc.law. stanford.edu/wp-content/uploads/sites/2/2017/08/CGCP-BR-English-Typical-Case-13.pdf> accessed 12 December 2017.

[150] This is the case for commercial foreign judgments from States without any bilateral treaty. However, evidence exists of the recognition and enforcement of a few foreign judgments from certain States with a bilateral treaty. See Tsang (n 148) 39.

[151] *Giant Light Metal Technology (Kunshan) Co Ltd v Aksa Far East Pte Ltd* [2014] SGHC 16.

[152] Zheng Sophia Tang, '"The Belt and Road" and Cross-Border Judicial Cooperation' (2019) 49 *Hong Kong Law Journal* 121, 148.

and the EU.[153] The Russian courts have similarly enforced judgments from the Netherlands, Germany and more recently Japan.[154] This appears to be a change of attitude from the erstwhile restrictive regime. A few States have also abolished or downplayed reciprocity in their national laws. These States include Venezuela, Lithuania, Bulgaria, Macedonia, Poland, Montenegro, Italy, Switzerland, and Spain.[155]

(iii) Criticism

Despite the partial success of reciprocity, it remains a key hindrance to foreign judgments enforcement in many States. The recent developments in States like China and Russia, though suggestive of possible favourable reception of foreign judgments, may not help judgment creditors if any two States maintain the same reciprocity approach and neither is ready to provide a precedent first. For instance, *Kolmar* was successful because the judgment was from a common law jurisdiction which 'enforces' foreign judgments without necessarily investigating whether its own judgments are enforced abroad.[156] The common law unilateral gesture sets a precedent from which other States can draw inferences, thereby establishing a favourable reciprocal treatment by default. The situation would not have been the same if the Singaporean court maintained a strict reciprocal regime that required precedents of prior enforcement of its own judgments. Thus, a situation of *circulus inextricabilis* could be created.[157] The essence of reciprocity, ie inducement to cooperate, would have been defeated altogether. This is the current situation in Sino-Japanese judgments practice.[158] The Russian courts attempted to break such a circle in German-Russian relations by recognising a German bankruptcy judgment because German law did not have any provision that could potentially deny recognition to Russian judgments. However, a subsequent Russian judgment was not enforced in Germany despite the Russian precedent.[159]

[153] Anna Grishchenkova, 'Recognition and Enforcement of Foreign Judgments in Russia: Recent Trends' (2013) 15 *Yearbook of Private International Law* 439, 441.

[154] ALRUD Law Firm (n 113).

[155] Elbalti (n 135) 187–88; Tanja Domej, 'Recognition and Enforcement of Judgments (Civil Law)' in Jürgen Basedow and others (eds), *Encyclopedia of Private International Law* (Edward Elgar 2017) 1476.

[156] The common law judges see foreign judgments strictly as enforcement of private rights and, as such, this has nothing to do with the public law/foreign relations issues of whether a foreign State enforces the forum's judgments.

[157] Luke J Umstetter, 'Enforcing Foreign Judgments: In Search of a Treaty to Locate Assets Abroad' (2007) 3 *South Carolina Journal of International Law and Business* 85, 88; Anna Grishchenkova, 'Recognition and Enforcement of Foreign Judgments in Russia: Recent Trends' (2013) 15 *Yearbook of Private International Law* 439, 442.

[158] Wenliang Zhang, 'Recognition and Enforcement of Foreign Judgments in China: A Call for Special Attention to Both the Due Service Requirement and the Principle of Reciprocity' (2013) 12 *Chinese Journal of International Law* 143, 153–54; Elbalti (n 135) 213.

[159] A Schreiber, 'Granting of Reciprocity within the German-Russian Recognition Practice' (2017) 4 *Praxis des Internationalen Privat- und Verfahrensrechts (IPRax)* 368.

The result may be that future German judgments will most probably not be enforced by Russian courts.

Reciprocity may require formal and informal negotiations between willing States. It is not in all cases that a unilateral recognition step by a court addressed will yield a reciprocal return from other targeted States. It often takes time and in some cases, it is rejected, as evidenced in the German-Russian judgments practice.[160] Also, a call for bilateral negotiations may only come from States that have political and commercial interests to protect.[161] This makes it a complex matter, as time and resources, together with political will on the part of willing States, are required for this to be done. Due to various adverse political and economic impacts that foreign judgments may have on a receiving State, some States may not be willing to open their doors to certain judgments because of pressures from interest groups[162] or because the State's corporations engage in private cross-border commercial activities.[163] All these factors constitute a hindrance to cooperation.

Another major shortcoming in reciprocity practice of States is the difficulty of *proving* reciprocity. Many States have reciprocity legislation, which conflicts with actual judicial practice. It becomes a difficult task to satisfy foreign courts as to the real status of the law of the State of origin.[164] Also, the requirement of reciprocity differs from State to State. Some States require similarity in laws,[165] some require a treaty,[166] and others require actual precedent of prior enforcement of the

---

[160] Beckers gives a summary of a German court's ruling, which seems to support the assertion that a court addressed needs to initiate a move with the hope that the rendering court would return the gesture. According to him, the German court, while recognising an award from China for the first time, noted that 'for the principle of mutual recognition to apply, one country must always take the first step and that the legislature did not want to exclude this possibility with Section 328(1)(5) of the German Code of Civil Procedure. Rather, it was to be expected that the Chinese courts would in fact reciprocate and begin to recognize German court decisions'. See Philipp Beckers, 'German Court Takes First Step on Road to Mutual Recognition with China' (*International Law Office Newsletter*, 2007) <http://www.internationallawoffice.com/Newsletters/Arbitration-ADR/Germany/Ashurst/German-Court-Takes-First-Step-on-Road-to-Mutual-Recognition-with-China> accessed 23 September 2017. The same was reported of a Korean Court enforcing a Chinese judgment, hoping that it may pave the way for China's enforcement of Korean judgments. See Elbalti (n 135) 191.

[161] Andrew Henshaw, 'Reciprocity after Brexit' (2017) 2 *Journal of International Banking and Financial Law* 69.

[162] For instance, the US-UK attempt to negotiate a bilateral judgments treaty was marred partly because of pressures from UK interest groups like the manufacturers and insurance groups. See Paul R Beaumont, 'A United Kingdom Perspective On the Proposed Hague Judgments Convention' (1998) 24 *Brooklyn Journal of International Law* 75, 78.

[163] A good example is China. See Hsu (n 148) 219.

[164] In Nigeria for instance, despite the existence of reciprocity legislation which has not been extended to any State, its courts have admitted judgments from the United States, Liberia and Niger for direct registration, and the same conclusion therefore goes for judgments from other countries. See Abubakri Yekini, 'Foreign Judgments in Nigerian Courts in the Last Decade: A Dawn of Liberalization' (2017) 2 *Nederlands Internationaal Privaatrecht* 205. It is doubtful whether the liberal regime will satisfy courts in countries such as China, Japan, Russia, Tunisia, and Germany in the absence of evidence that their judgments have been registered.

[165] Sung Hoon Lee, 'Foreign Judgment Recognition and Enforcement System of Korea' (2006) 6 *Journal of Korean Law* 111, 134–35.

[166] Examples include Russia and the Nordic countries. However, the courts in many of these States find a way round the statutory prohibition on admitting foreign judgments in some instances. See Béligh

receiving State's judgments in the State of origin.[167] In some cases, the evidence available to the court may be mere conjecture, as seen in *Banque Libanaise Pour le Commerce v Khreich*[168] where a US court rejected an Abu Dhabi judgment because the expert said his firm was 'unaware of any Abu Dhabi courts enforcing United States' judgments'.[169]

Proving reciprocity comes at a cost. It requires extensive study of the jurisprudence and judicial practice of foreign States. It involves the hiring of experts in foreign law. Information about some foreign legal systems is very hard to secure due to lack of a serious law reporting system[170] or in cases such as Iran where courts' judgments are not published.[171] All these factors make it hard to get reliable information in some instances and generally the cost is always on the high side. Whether the cost is borne by the court or passed to the litigants, it is a needless waste of resources.[172]

Lastly, reciprocity seeks to pursue purely political and foreign affairs objectives at the expense of the justice of the case and the interests of a creditor who is a private party seeking the enforcement of his hard-earned rights. For a court addressed to go on a foray of examining what the rendering court does with its judgments does not assist the cause of a judgment creditor in any way. Hence, it unduly penalises a private litigant for an error of commission or omission by another.[173] In some cases, the applicant's country of nationality is a friendly State or he is a national of the receiving State, but he is denied access to justice or a 'means of executing justice'[174] simply because he is holding a judgment from a non-reciprocating State.[175] If reciprocity is assessed from the perspective of

Elbalti, 'Spontaneous Harmonization and the Liberalization of the Recognition and Enforcement of Foreign Judgments' (2014) 26 *Japanese Yearbook of Private International Law* 264, 266–68.

[167] For instance, China. See Elbalti (n 135) 202–5.

[168] *Banque Libanaise Pour le Commerce v Khreich* (1990) 915 F.2d 1000.

[169] See Vishali Singal, 'Preserving Power Without Sacrificing Justice' (2007) 59 *Hastings Law Journal* 943, 945. Meanwhile, Abu Dhabi law gives judges discretional powers to enforce foreign judgments.

[170] Tang, Xiao and Huo (n 96) 104 (noting that China's reciprocity practice will be hard to prove because there is no formal and systemic case-reporting system).

[171] This point was noted in paragraph 19 of Mr Justice Eady's judgment in *Kahangi and others v Nourizadeh* [2009] EWHC 2451 (QB) where the court was assessing expert opinion on the reciprocity practice of Iranian courts.

[172] Anke Meier, Steffen Burrer and Anna Fufurina (Noerr law firm), 'Hamburg Higher Regional Court: (Still) No Recognition and Enforcement of Russian Court Judgments in Germany Due to Reciprocity Not Being Warranted' (*Newsletter*, 2016) <https://www.noerr.com/en/newsroom/News/no-recognition-and-enforcement-of-russian-court-judgments-in-germany.aspx> accessed 15 July 2017 (narrates how the German court commissioned a detailed expert opinion on Russia reciprocity practice).

[173] Arthur T von Mehren and Donald T Trautman (ch 1, n 78) 1661.

[174] As used by Lady Justice Gloster in *Bestfort Developments LLP and Others v Ras Al Khaimah Investment Authority and Others* [2016] EWCA Civ 1099, para 75, quoting Mance LJ in *Nasser v United Bank of Kuwait* [2002] 1 WLR 1868.

[175] Pedro Alberto De Miguel Asensio, 'Recognition and Enforcement of Judgments in Intellectual Property Litigation: The CLIP Principles' in J Basedow, T Kono and A Metzger (eds), *Intellectual Property in the Global Arena – Jurisdiction, Applicable Law, and the Recognition of Judgments in Europe, Japan and the US* (Mohr Siebeck 2010) 246.

the desired objectives of an ideal judgments recognition practice, one tends to conclude that its demerits are enormous, even though it does achieve its purpose in some cases. This criticism, may, however, be qualified for multilateral judgments frameworks such as the Hague Choice of Court and Judgments Conventions where reciprocity has been used as an inducement for States to join clear frameworks that have been established by the Conventions.

C. Legal Obligation

(i) Meaning and Application

The eighteenth and nineteenth centuries witnessed the birth of legal positivism, which shook the foundation of natural law and all the legal theories founded on it.[176] The erstwhile fertile doctrine of comity was not spared.[177] The leading positivists of the era, such as Bentham and Story, distinguished between the realms of international and domestic transactions. According to Bentham, international law strictly speaking is merely a collection of rules that govern the transactions among sovereign States. All relationships arising from private transactions were excised from the purview of 'international law'.[178] Hence, private disputes could not be resolved by the law of nations or other universalist theories. Rather, they must be deferred to the domestic laws of each sovereign State.

Justice Story, in his Commentaries, classified the law governing these private cross-border transactions as private international law.[179] The positivists' influence probably led to the re-examination of the role of comity in resolving private international law disputes. Private international law disputes then began to be seen as purely domestic legal problems that could only be resolved by the internal law, in this case, English law. The response of the common law judges was to treat foreign judgments as creating obligations which a judgment debtor is obliged to fulfil.[180] This theoretical basis was well articulated in *Russell v Smyth*.[181] The case involved an action to recover costs awarded against a defendant who had

---

[176] Samuel P Baumgartner, *The Proposed Hague Convention on Jurisdiction and Foreign Judgments: Trans-Atlantic Law Making for Transnational Litigation* (Mohr Siebeck 2003) 24–25.

[177] Schultz and Ridi (n 91) 13.

[178] Jeremy Bentham, *The Collected Works of Jeremy Bentham: An Introduction to the Principles of Morals and Legislation* (JH Burns and HLA Hart eds, Oxford University Press 1996) quoted by Mark Weston Janis, *America and the Law of Nations 1776–1939* (Oxford University Press 2010) 14.

[179] Friedrich K Juenger, 'The Lex Mercatoria and Private International Law' (2000) 60 *Louisiana Law Review* 1133, 1143.

[180] The doctrine did not originate from any intellectual theorising. Historically, the English private international law developed largely from common law with little influence from legal theorists. See CGJ Morse, 'Making English Private International Law' in JJ Fawcett (ed), *Reform and Development of Private International Law: Essays in Honour of Sir Peter North* (Oxford University Press 2002) 276–77.

[181] *Russell v Smyth* (1842) 9 M & W 810. Although, some earlier reports, such as *Sadler v Robins* (1808) 1 Camp 253, were decided on a similar idea. The common law has always treated foreign decrees as evidence of debt and allowed an action in assumpsit to recover any sums due thereunder.

absconded following litigation in Scotland. The court justified why the action would be allowed even if it were unprecedented because 'the decree of the Court of Session creates a duty in the party to pay a debt' and an action to recover that debt was maintainable. The court held that:

> The action may be sustained on the ground of morality and justice. The maxim of the English law is to amplify its remedies, and, without usurping jurisdiction, to apply its rules to the advancement of substantial justice. Foreign judgments are enforced in these Courts, because the parties liable are bound in duty to satisfy them.[182]

Having laid the foundation in *Russell*, other English cases such as *Schibsby v Westenholz*[183] and *Williams v Jones*[184] simply adopted the ratio. It has continued to be the prevalent doctrine in England and Wales and most of the Commonwealth States to date.[185]

The doctrine of obligation is similar to the vested rights theory, which was postulated by Dicey and Beale.[186] The fulcrum of both theories is that legal rights are territorial and are enforceable in other jurisdictions. The focus of legal obligation, however, is the obligation to fulfil the right. It proceeded on the assumption that a defendant who submitted to the jurisdiction of a foreign sovereign is bound to comply with the obligations imposed by that sovereign. This position was confirmed by the statement of the English Court of Appeal in *Adams v Cape Industries*[187] that by 'making himself present he contracts into a network of obligations created by the local law and the local courts'. The foreign judgment is characterised as an implied contract, and, like other contracts created in a foreign land, it can be enforced everywhere. Thus, the common law allows a judgment creditor to sue his debtor in an action on the debt. This is the commonest mode of enforcing rights acquired under foreign judgments in almost all the common law jurisdictions.

The characterisation of a foreign judgment as debt is an ingenious one on the part of the English judges. It ably adapts some of the benefits of comity – extra-territorial recognition of rights – and avoids its major deficiency ie, courtesy. It dispenses with reciprocity altogether because judgment creditors are entitled

---

[182] Ibid, 819. It is interesting to note that a judgment from Scotland is a 'foreign' judgment in England and Wales even though it is a judgment in the same State because Scotland and England and Wales are two different legal systems.

[183] *Schibsby v Westenholz* (1870) LR 6 QB 155.

[184] *Williams v Jones* [1845] Eng R 394; 13 M & W 628.

[185] Despite various attempts to discredit the doctrine, the English courts have continued to affirm that it is the only bases for recognition and enforcement of foreign judgments. See *Adams v Cape Industries Plc* (ch 1, fn 28).

[186] Professor Jean-Gabriel Castel holds a different view. He opined that the doctrine has nothing to do with vested rights. Admittedly, the right which the judgment creditor seeks to enforce is not a foreign right; however, they share similarity in territoriality policy. See Castel, 'Recognition and Enforcement of Foreign Judgments in Personam and in Rem in the Common Law Provinces of Canada' (ch 1, fn 75). It is submitted that what the English court does is to convert the foreign acquired right into a local one for purposes of enforcement.

[187] [1991] 1 All ER 929, 1038–41.

to realise the fruit of their judgments *ex debito justitiae*. This aligns with the reasonable expectation of parties and promotes legal certainty and stability. The English courts combine the doctrine of legal obligation with other theories like *res judicata* to facilitate automatic recognition of foreign judgments, thereby achieving efficiency and judicial economy as well. Hence, in an action on a judgment debt, the principle of *res judicata* is applied to foreclose the reopening of the issues that has already been adjudicated upon in the foreign court.[188]

The doctrine of legal obligation supposedly answers the why, how and which foreign judgments should be enforced. In sum, the common law courts enforce foreign judgments because of the need to do justice between the parties, and to meet their reasonable expectations. On how such judgments should be enforced, the common law enforces all validly acquired rights in debt except where the enforcement will violate the public policy of the forum. Unlike comity, the court does not enforce rights by way of mere courtesy, but rather is obliged to do so. Lastly, not all judgments are enforceable. The English Court of Appeal in *Joint Stock Company (Aeroflot-Russian Airlines) v Berezovsky & Others*[189] summarised the conditions for recognition of foreign judgments as follows: the judgment must be final and conclusive; it must have been issued by a court that has international jurisdiction over the debtor; and the debtor must have no defence to the recognition.

(ii) Criticism

Although the doctrine of legal obligation has some practical utility, it is not free from criticism. It has been criticised as begging the question,[190] starting from a false premise by assuming that a foreign judgment creates a legal obligation, and failing to state why the forum court should ever enforce such an obligation in the first place.[191] The restrictive scope of the doctrine excludes many classes of judgments such as non-money judgments and preservative orders, which are essential for modern-day cross-border commercial litigation. Also, by not treating a foreign judgment as a judgment, so to speak, it allows room for unnecessary attacks by way of defence against the supposed debt. Its application may, therefore, lead to a waste of time and resources for the courts and litigants.

In the same vein, the doctrine of legal obligation seems to stand logic on its head when it posits that a cause of action does not merge with a foreign judgment. There is no sound justification why the rights created under a foreign judgment should be abandoned in pursuit of a fresh claim in the forum.[192] By giving a

---

[188] *Carl Zeiss Stiftung v Rayner & Keeler Ltd (No 2)* [1967] 1 AC 853.

[189] *Joint Stock Company (Aeroflot-Russian Airlines) v Berezovsky & Others* [2014] EWCA Civ 20.

[190] Michaels (n 130) 673.

[191] Willis L Reese, 'The Status in this Country of Judgments Rendered Abroad' (1950) 50 *Columbia Law Review* 783, 784.

[192] See Lord Wilberforce's view in *Carl Zeiss Stiftung* (n 188) 966.

claimant the right either to sue upon a foreign judgment or to commence a fresh cause of action, a claimant who lost the foreign action or didn't get maximum relief may abandon the foreign judgment and begin a new claim with the view of improving his lot.[193] This can work against legal certainty, efficiency, judicial economy and the essence of the underlying policy.

It is worth noting that the CML has discountenanced this doctrinal basis. Section 8 of the law expressly abolishes the common law action on a judgment debt. It remains to be seen when and how the model law will take effect in the Commonwealth Member States.

D. Res Judicata

(i) Meaning and Application

Res judicata pro veritate accipitur is a Latin maxim that means 'a matter adjudged is taken as truth'.[194] It has been suggested that the principle of *res judicata* was developed by Roman law.[195] What is well-known is that it features in almost every legal tradition in one form or the other.[196] The principle of *res judicata* stands on a tripod. First, public policy demands that there should be an end to litigation. Second, no man ought to be vexed twice over the same cause of action. Third, a judicial decision rendered by a competent court ought to be accepted as correct. The doctrine presupposes that once a litigant has had his day in court and presented his issues before an impartial judge and a decision has been rendered, that decision is final and disposes of the issues dealt with in that case. A party is estopped from reopening the case subsequently in a new proceeding. Applying this to foreign judgments, a judgment rendered abroad may be equated to a judgment of the forum court. The court addressed respects the foreign judgment, treats it as final and allows its own machinery to be deployed to give effect to it.

One of the policies underlying *res judicata* is one of legal certainty. Lady Justice Arden stresses this point in *Joint Stock Company (Aeroflot-Russian Airlines)* thus: 'legal certainty means the element of security that results from legal decisions becoming final and legal rules coming into force. Legal certainty is important because it smooths the way for social and commercial interaction'.[197] This suggests that parties should fairly expect that a judgment issued concerning their dispute has resolved the controversy one way or the other, the status

---

[193] Briggs, *The Conflict of Laws* (ch 1, fn 44) 140.
[194] Kevin M Clermont, 'Res Judicata as Requisite for Justice' (2016) 68 *Rutgers University Law Review* 1067, 1069.
[195] Ibid, 1071–72.
[196] Peter R Barnett, *Res Judicata, Estoppel, and Foreign Judgments: The Preclusive Effects of Foreign Judgments in Private International Law* (Oxford University Press 2001) para 1.12.
[197] [2014] EWCA Civ 20, at para 22.

of the rights of the parties is determined once and for all, and socio-economic commitments will proceed as usual.

Apart from the legal certainty that is derivable from the application of *res judicata*, the principle can also create judicial economy and efficiency in the conduct of litigation. It saves a litigant from vexatious suits from his adversary. It prevents unnecessary waste of litigants' resources and time in having to re-litigate the same issues a second time. This is the same for the courts. The policy enhances judicial economy and allows the court to allocate public resources only to deserving cases.[198] It aids certainty and predictability of results, as inconsistent judgments arise if litigants are given the option of re-opening an already decided issue. This is more likely to occur in international litigation because of differences in the substantive and procedural laws.

(ii) Criticism

Although the underlying policy of *res judicata* is a good one, its application presents some problems. There is a need to balance efficiency and justice when *res judicata* is applied to foreign judgments. While it is the desired goal to have an efficient justice system, one must not lose touch with the reality that some foreign courts are underdeveloped, and many others are influenced by their governments and highly connected litigants and counsel. A practical example is the Lago Agrio judgment scandal[199] and the Russian Court of Appeal judgment in *Yukos Capital*.[200] A blind application of the *res judicata* doctrine may well mean that many tainted foreign judgments will be recognised and possibly enforced because the foreign court has decided the matter between the parties and there must be an end to litigation. *Res judicata* may need to be supported by some other theories to protect the rights of judgment debtors in deserving cases.

One may also query the rationale behind forcing a litigant to litigate all his available claims, whether foreseeable or otherwise, arising from a cause of action. A plaintiff may have a genuine cause to seek procedural advantage in bringing part of a claim in one jurisdiction and not the other. Apart from the question of inconvenience to litigants, Lord Reid also raised valid concerns that can be encountered when applying *res judicata* to foreign judgments.[201] While the court agreed that it is desirable to apply the doctrine to foreign judgments, the differences in the

---

[198] Reese (n 191).

[199] In this case, it was alleged that the claimant's counsel wrote all or much of the US$19billion judgment awarded against Chevron by an Ecuadorian court in 2011. *Aguinda v Chevron Corp*, No 002-2003 (Superior Ct of Nueva Loja, 14 February 2011) (Ecuador). For the background of the case, see Manuel A Gómez, 'The Global Chase: Seeking the Recognition and Enforcement of the Lago Agrio Judgment Outside of Ecuador' (2013) 1 *Stanford Journal of Complex Litigation* 429.

[200] *Yukos Capital SARL v OJSC Oil Company Rosneft* [2014] EWHC 2188 (Comm). Here, it was alleged that the Russian Court of Appeal, which annulled an arbitral award obtained by Yukos, was biased and influenced by the Russian government.

[201] *Carl Zeiss Stiftung v Rayner & Keeler (No 2)* (n 188), 918.

procedural laws of the foreign and receiving States concerning what constitutes finality may pose practical challenges.

E. Pragmatism

(i) Meaning

Pragmatism began to feature in private international law thinking in the second half of the nineteenth century[202] but became prominent in the early part of the twentieth century.[203] At its inception, it was devoted to the choice of law and jurisdictional questions but it is gradually evolving in recognition and enforcement of foreign judgments.[204] Pragmatists view law as 'a body of practical tools for serving specific substantive goals'.[205] Laws should be empirically investigated to see whether they are serving the ends of justice. A pragmatic theory emphasises what the law ought to be as against what it is. As Walker puts it, it is about finding 'real solutions to deal with a specific legal problem'.[206]

Pragmatism opposes formalism, dogmatism, and other mechanical application of law and its principles to factual situations.[207] As Rabel wrote, conflict of laws just like other theories ought 'to serve reasonable purposes'.[208] Laws should be interpreted in such a way as to solve practical problems, and remedies should be advanced in a way that enhances the cause of justice and efficiency in the administration of justice.

Pragmatists are more interested in the best solution to a given problem. For instance, Ernst Rabel argued that no single conflicts rule can solve the myriad of complex problems presented before the courts. He noted that the nature of cross-border disputes requires carefully designed rules that are tailored towards the needs of cross-border litigants.[209] This point has also been emphasised by Symeonides,

---

[202] Gerhard Kegel, 'Fundamental Approaches' in Kurt Lipstein (ed), *International Encyclopedia of Comparative Law: Private international law* (JCB Mohr 1986) 13. Beaumont and McEleavy traced it to the works of Ernst Rabel. See Paul Beaumont and Peter McEleavy (ch 1, fn 37) 51.

[203] For its development in the US, see Symeon C Symeonides (ch 1, fn 36) and in the civil law countries, Paul Beaumont and Peter McEleavy (ch 1, fn 37) 51–54; Max Rheinstein, 'Comparative Law and Conflict of Laws in Germany' (1935) 2 *University of Chicago Law Review* 232, 232–69.

[204] Many of the works on pragmatism in conflict of laws are largely devoted to the choice of law rules. Some of these works include; Michael J Whincop, Mary Keyes and Richard A. Posner, *Policy and Pragmatism in the Conflict of Laws* (1st edn, Routledge 2017); Symeon C Symeonides (n 87); Erin O'Hara (ed), *Economics of Conflict of Laws* (Edward Elgar 2007).

[205] Robert S Summers, 'Pragmatic Instrumentalism in Twentieth Century American Legal Thought-A Synthesis and Critique of Our Dominant General Theory about Law and Its Use' (1980) 60 *Cornell Law Review* 861, 863.

[206] Lara Walker (ch 1, fn 39) 6.

[207] Richard A Posner, 'What Has Pragmatism to Offer Law?' (1990) 63 *Southern California Law Review* 1653, 1663; Ernst Rabel, 'Interim Account on Comparative Conflicts Law' (1948) 46 *Michigan Law Review* 625, 632.

[208] Rabel (n 207).

[209] See Rabel (n 207) 638.

who argues that modern conflict problems require a toolbox approach where useful ideas can be combined to deliver a workable system.[210]

Based on the foregoing, pragmatism in judgments recognition and enforcement practice dictates that policymakers should deploy the most effective mechanism that ensures that cross-border litigants have access to simple, clear and predictable frameworks that can guide them to make informed decisions concerning their transactions, and one that also promotes the enforcement of contractual rights. In this regard, some scholars opine that one of those pragmatic mechanisms through which the enforcement of those rights can be secured is international judicial cooperation. Noodt Taquela boldly asserts that foreign judgments and international judicial cooperation are two sides of a coin.[211] Peter Schlosser also notes that even before the popularisation of the doctrine of international comity by Huber and others, courts in Europe largely enforced foreign judgments based on mutual cooperation and the need to avoid unnecessary inconvenience.[212]

International judicial cooperation dispenses with unnecessary theoretical abstractions and methodological purism that were once the preoccupation of private international law scholars. Before the emergence of active judicial cooperation via multilateral platforms and treaties, records indicate that courts often engaged in passive judicial cooperation through transboundary mutual judicial assistance.[213] Today, both legislators and courts are increasingly focusing on mutual trust, legal and judicial cooperation in the field of private international law to meet the practical needs of cross-border litigants.

(ii) Application

Professors Beaumont and McEleavy once suggested that a pragmatic approach to solving conflict of laws problems ultimately would lead to innovative solutions, and one cannot but agree with them.[214] Many States have moved beyond theoretical barriers by looking in the direction of international legal and judicial cooperation to solve practical legal problems. Arguably pragmatism has been the force driving the development of EU private International law and, particularly judgments recognition. The EU seeks constant developments of its instruments by looking at concrete problems that confront litigants, carrying out comparative studies of the working of the instruments in EU Member States and updating the judgments enforcement frameworks accordingly. This is what

---

[210] Symeon C Symeonides, 'Private International Law: Idealism, Pragmatism, Eclecticism General Course on Private International Law' (n 87) 350.

[211] Maria Blanca Noodt Taquela, 'Applying the Most Favourable Treaty or Domestic Rules to Facilitate Private International Law Co-Operation', *Hague Academy of International Law: Recueil Des Cours* vol 377 (Brill Nijhoff 2015) 166.

[212] Schlosser (ch 1, fn 12) 33–34.

[213] Ibid, 31–34.

[214] Beaumont and McEleavy (ch 1, fn 37) 52.

led to the passage of the Brussels Ia, European Enforcement Order Regulation (Recast Brussels Regulation) amongst others.[215]

Outside the EU, Latin America has equally achieved significant progress in the recognition and enforcement of foreign judgments through international judicial cooperation. Some of the conventions that are in force in that region include the Inter-American Convention on Extraterritorial Validity of Foreign Judgments and Arbitral Awards 1979, and the Protocol on Judicial Cooperation and Assistance in Civil, Commercial, Labour and Administrative Matters 1992. The same can be said of the Middle East countries. In 1983, the Council of Arab Ministers of Justice concluded the Riyadh Arab Agreement for Judicial Cooperation.[216] The Convention entered into force on 30 October 1985. The Convention has been ratified by 16 States.

At a broader level, similar experiences have been recorded in the Commonwealth and Hague Conference platforms. For a century now, the Commonwealth has operationalised a simple registration scheme for intra-Commonwealth judgments. The English Administration of Justice Act 1920 (AJA) was replicated in virtually all the Commonwealth States to facilitate the enforcement of judgments between the United Kingdom and other Commonwealth Member States and amongst Member States *inter se.* The Hague Conference comprises members from every region of the world and has been responsible for the progressive development of private international law at the global level. Pragmatism has been the approach used at the Hague Conference by its Member States in negotiating and preparing its conventions, including the HCCA and the 2019 Judgments Convention.[217]

One must add the emerging court-to-court agreements on the enforcement of judgments. These arrangements are being put in place by courts in the absence of relevant treaties in force between their respective States. Such agreements have been signed by the Supreme Court of Singapore with Abu Dhabi Global Market Court;[218] and by Dubai International Financial Centre Courts (DIFC) with various courts in Malaysia, Hong Kong, Zambia, China, Australia, United States and Kenya.[219] Others include the Nanning Statement signed between Singapore and Peoples Republic of China[220] and a memorandum of

---

[215] Monique Hazelhorst, *Free Movement of Civil Judgments in the European Union and the Right to a Fair Trial* (TMC Asser Press 2017) 3–6.

[216] See <https://jusmundi.com/en/document/pdf/treaty/ar-riyadh-arab-agreement-for-judicial-cooperation-1983-riyadh-convention-1983-wednesday-6th-april-1983> (accessed 10 october 2020).

[217] Beaumont and McEleavy (ch 1, fn 37) 51.

[218] Singapore International Commercial Court, 'Guidance Notes on Enforcement Signed with Courts in Abu Dhabi, UAE, and Victoria, Australia' (*SICC News*, 2017) <http://www.sicc.gov.sg/documents/docs/SICC_News_Issue_5.pdf> accessed 22 November 2017.

[219] See 'Protocols and Memoranda' <https://www.difccourts.ae/courts-programmes/protocols-and-memorandums-of-understanding/ >.

[220] See Memorandum of Guidance between the Supreme People's Court of the People's Republic of China and the Supreme Court of Singapore on Recognition and Enforcement of Money Judgments in Commercial Cases (31 August 2018). The text is available at <https://www.supremecourt.gov.sg/docs/default-source/default-document-library/spc-mog-english-version---signed.pdf>.

guidance on enforcement of judgments between DIFC Courts and the English Commercial Court.[221]

(iii) Criticism

Pragmatism has been criticised as a concept without any theoretical basis. It is said to have no consistent legal doctrine and thus favours the whims of judges or policymakers. While pragmatists urge that legal principles should be applied to achieve the best outcomes, there is no standard guidance on evaluating such outcomes.[222] It is therefore said to be a threat to legal certainty and predictability, which are the markers of the rule of law. In fairness to the critics, the practical application of pragmatism as described above seems to support their position. For instance, while various court-to-court agreements are helpful, they will eventually create a complex regime, as there will be countless agreements with different scopes and contents.

Pragmatism is not as unprincipled as it has been projected, however. It shares features of other theoretical foundations in both content and analysis. Its significant difference lies in its flexibility of choosing options that best address the issues at hand. Hence, comity, *res judicata*, legal obligation and judicial cooperation are all elements of pragmatism, with useful principles that can guide courts and policymakers in designing appropriate legal frameworks. Be that as it may, there is a need to further theorise pragmatism in judgments recognition and enforcement so that it does not become a 'just-do-it' approach, as claimed by its critics. Such a task will seek to identify the pragmatic goals that policymakers and judges may pursue and the methods that can be used to deliver on those goals. This will ensure that pragmatism is engaged and applied in a principled manner to deliver the desired legal certainty and predictability.

III. Conclusion

The chapter has set out the theoretical background and policies underlying recognition and enforcement of foreign judgments. It provides key information that informs the attitudes and views of courts about foreign judgments. The underlying policies clarify the diversity in judgments enforcement practices from different jurisdictions. Also, it lays the groundwork for a better appreciation of the discourse in subsequent chapters of the book.

---

[221] Memorandum of Guidance as to Enforcement between the DIFC Courts and the Commercial Court, Queen's Bench Division, England and Wales 2013. The text is available at <https://www.judiciary.uk/wp-content/uploads/JCO/Documents/Guidance/uk-uae-protocol-with-logos.pdf>.
[222] Douglas Lind, 'The Mismeasurement of Legal Pragmatism' (2012) 4 *Washington University Jurisprudence Review* 213, 237.

The chapter identifies the basic challenges that State sovereignty and territoriality foist on private citizens who transact across borders. Territorial borders do not make it impossible for citizens from various States to do business, maintain family life, or carry out actions that may harm others in other States. The borders are more porous today than they were in the nineteenth century, with the advent of the internet and advancement in telecommunication technologies and means of transportation. These advancements have practically eroded State borders. The current challenges are how judgments obtained in one State should be recognised and enforced in other States; how to ensure global judicial economy and the growth of international trade and commerce.

The response of earlier jurists to these challenges was to use comity to file the rough edges of States' borders in order not to cause hindrances to the growth of international trade. This theory proved effective to a large extent as it has since formed the basis for recognition and enforcement of foreign judgments in many jurisdictions. Its discretionary character is the major shortcoming observed in its application. Other policy considerations like reciprocity, legal obligation, and *res judicata* also have some utility, as presented earlier in this chapter. However, the major challenge is how courts have held on to these theoretical bases rigidly despite their shortcomings.

The chapter finds that the formalistic approach of courts to one doctrinal basis or another – without considering whether it meets the end of justice, business efficacy, efficiency, parties' reasonable expectations, legal certainty and judicial economy – has led to the need for a reconsideration of these theoretical frameworks. As Professor Atiyah noted in the 39th Hamlyn Lecture Series, law is a practical subject and so should be the response to it.[223] Solutions to practical legal problems should not be hindered by blind adherence to legal theories. It must be acknowledged that the world is fast-moving and so the law must respond to catch up with it. These theoretical foundations might fit the environment, circumstances, and the reality of previous centuries but certainly not the modern era. Adhering to these policies without adaptation to fit current realities has led to the denial of justice, less efficiency in judicial administration and increased litigation costs, and has hindered the growth of international trade and commerce.

It is suggested that a pragmatic approach is desirable. Apart from the fact that it is a modern approach to addressing private international law issues, it is most suited for the question of recognition and enforcement of foreign judgments because of the cluster of interests involved in this branch of private international law. Only a pragmatic approach can address the deep divergences of States' practices and interests, and the complicated issues of modern cross-border litigation. The next chapter will explore pragmatism in detail and will seek to identify the pragmatic goals for judgments recognition and enforcement, and the methods that can be used to deliver these goals.

---

[223] PS Atiyah, *Pragmatism and Theory in English Law* (Stevens & Sons 1987) 4.

3

A Pragmatic Model for Recognition and Enforcement of Foreign Judgments

I. Introduction

Professor Gerhard Kegel once wrote that the creative solutions being proposed by leading academic writers for private international law problems in the United States were developed principally for the law of obligations.[224] This seems to also represent the position in Europe and elsewhere. The statement is as correct today as it was four decades ago when it was made. Enforcement of foreign judgments has not received much attention, unlike jurisdiction and choice of law. This is not to say that there is a dearth of literature on foreign judgments. A great deal of scholarly work has been produced up to the present day. However, the innovative solutions being developed over the years have largely been directed at other aspects of private international law, especially the choice of applicable law. For instance, the American conflicts revolution and the law and economics discussions have had very little impact on the recognition and enforcement of foreign judgments. Thus, discussions on foreign judgments have generally followed the line of traditional private international law doctrines. Only a few academic works connect these new approaches to foreign judgments.[225]

Traditional private international law doctrines have helped in resolving conflict problems from time immemorial. The challenge, however, is how effective these doctrines can be at solving the practical problems posed by changes in time and circumstances. While these doctrines might have been suitable at the time they were formulated, can the same be said for today? Let us take, for instance, the concept of territoriality, which forms the theoretical foundation for international

---

[224] Gerhard Kegel, 'Paternal Home and Dream Home: Traditional Conflict of Laws and the American Reformers' (1979) 27 *The American Journal of Comparative Law* 615.

[225] Few authors have specifically treated foreign judgments from pragmatic and economic perspectives. They include: Whincop, Mary Keyes and Richard A Posner (ch 2, fn 178); Ronald A Brand, 'Transaction Planning Using Rules on Jurisdiction and the Recognition and Enforcement of Judgments' (2014) 62 *Netherlands International Law Review* 485; Ronald A Brand, 'Recognition of Foreign Judgments as a Trade Law Issue: The Economics of Private International Law' in JS Bhandari et al (eds), *Economic Dimensions in International Law* (Cambridge University Press 1997); Golomb (ch 2, fn 84); Monestier, 'Foreign Judgments at Common Law: Rethinking the Enforcement Rules' (ch 1, fn 17); Beaumont and Walker (ch 1, fn 59).

jurisdiction under the common law.[226] In the nineteenth century and afterwards, the English courts rarely exercised jurisdiction over non-resident defendants, partly because of the practical difficulties that might be experienced by defendants in attending English proceedings from abroad. By extension, the English court would not recognise foreign judgments rendered against non-resident defendants who did not submit to the jurisdiction of the foreign court.[227] Admittedly, such assumptions might be acceptable in an era where moving from one part of the world to another was a significant undertaking, but not today when the world is said to be a global village. Do principles moulded on the theories of territoriality and power suffice as exclusive bases for exercising jurisdiction (or enforcing foreign judgments) when almost all the variables have changed?

The menu of problems popping up in the courts gives an overview of the challenges that cross-border litigants encounter and the need for some creative solutions. An assessment of reported cases from different jurisdictions reveals that in an era of free movement of persons, globalisation of assets, complex corporate structures, and easier movement of assets across borders, judgment debtors can easily render all the efforts of the judgment creditors worthless.[228] In *Marex Financial Ltd v Sevilleja*,[229] a company's director asset-strips his company by transferring a substantial part of the company's funds abroad to his personal account, leaving the company with minimal assets for enforcement proceedings. In *ICICI Bank UK Plc v Diminico NV*,[230] the issue before the English court was whether the court could grant a worldwide freezing order and disclosure against the defendant in respect of working capital provided through a facility agreement for some contracts in Belgium. The claim against the defendant was US$25 million. The defendant's published accounts showed that its turnover was about US$300 million. Yet, it maintained only €2,600 as a credit balance in its Belgian account. Neither the defendant nor the contract was connected to England. Although the claimant partially succeeded in getting reliefs against assets based in England, this would have been entirely impossible if the traditional common law rules had been applied. While pre-judgment preservation orders are available in almost all jurisdictions, their effectiveness over non-resident defendants or assets located abroad remains a challenge.[231]

---

[226] *Sirdar Gurdyal Singh v Rajah of Faridkote* [1894] AC 670, 683–84 (PC).

[227] *Emanuel v Symon* [1908] 1 KB 302; *Rousillon v Rousillon* (1880) 14 Ch D 351.

[228] Hayk Kupelyants, 'Recognition and Enforcement of Foreign Judgments in the Absence of the Debtor and His Assets within the Jurisdiction: Reversing the Burden of Proof' (2018) 14 *Journal of Private International Law* 455, 455–56.

[229] *Marex Financial Ltd v Sevilleja* [2017] EWHC 918 (Comm).

[230] *ICICI Bank UK Plc v Diminico NV* [2014] EWHC 3124 (Comm).

[231] Campbell McLachlan, 'The Continuing Controversy over Provisional Measures in International Disputes' (2005) 7 *International Law Forum* 5, 11–13 (noting that such measures are unenforceable under the common law, and the foreign court in whose jurisdiction the defendant has assets will not grant a preservative order if it has no strong connection with the subject-matter of the order).

One indisputable fact is that many of the circumstances which brought about the extant theoretical foundations and the judgments recognition frameworks in most legal systems have changed today. Global markets and burgeoning international trade, with free movement of capital, goods, services and persons across national borders, have challenged the concerns of sovereignty and territoriality. Most judiciaries today are advanced, including those of the third world countries. As such, it would be untenable to categorise any legal system as barbaric or uncivilised or to characterise their judgments as substandard by default.[232] In fact, judicial cosmopolitanism and judicial cooperation are inevitable in addressing complex cross-border issues of today.[233] What these changing circumstances portray is that the legal thoughts and solutions of the past centuries may not be sufficient for the twenty-first century. After all, a Latin maxim says *cessante rationale legis, cessat ipsa lex* ('when the reason for a law ceases, the law itself ceases').

This aim of this chapter is to develop a pragmatic model or approach as a viable alternative to the extant divergent national approaches to judgments' recognition and enforcement. Contrary to the individualistic – and in some cases parochial – national approaches, the chapter proposes that a pragmatic judgments framework should essentially be founded on legal certainty and predictability, mutual trust, conflicts justice and multilateralism. In deserving cases, it would also consider some elements of unilateralism and material justice (eg overriding forum policy and States' interests). This suggests that the major task for the legislators is to arrive at acceptable connections (jurisdictional filters)[234] between a foreign court and the underlying dispute or parties. In this regard, judges would only need to screen foreign judgments to ensure that they comply with the checklist (jurisdictional filters) and other safeguards that are drawn up by the legislators. A foreign judgment that complies with the checklist should be generally respected and enforced elsewhere, save for limited grounds that can be invoked as safety valves.

In developing a pragmatic judgments framework, this chapter proposes that the legislators or treaty-makers, as the case may be, should adopt a pluralist theory, which is driven by pluralist goals and methods. Three principal goals are suggested: efficiency, fairness, and justice. These substantive goals are not to be construed by unnecessary abstractions and absolute principles. Rather, their analysis is to be guided by practical experience, and comparative and empirical methodologies. The pragmatic model which is developed by this chapter shall then be used to analyse the CML and the Hague Conventions in subsequent chapters.

---

[232] Paul B Stephan, 'Foreign Court Judgments and the United States Legal System' in Paul B Stephan (ed), *Foreign Court Judgments and the United States Legal System* (Brill 2014) 87.

[233] Judicial cooperation in the enforcement of judgments was emphasised in the March 2015 'Vision and Action Plan on the Belt and Road Initiative' and the Nanning Statement of June 2017. See Zheng Sophia Tang (ch 2, fn 152) 148.

[234] Jurisdictional filters are the jurisdictional grounds upon which a foreign court (rendering court) can validly exercise jurisdiction. It is also referred to as international jurisdiction or indirect jurisdiction.

II. Pragmatism as a Philosophical Thought

Pragmatism is a concept that is commonly used in different fields of knowledge. As such, it means different things to different people. To be pragmatic may imply: being practical; common sense; being down to earth; eclecticism; reasonableness, amongst other connotations. It does not come as a surprise that both as a philosophical and legal term, there has been no unanimity amongst scholars on its content and frontiers. To demonstrate this, Charles S Peirce, one of the founders of pragmatism, even suggested that the idea he was theorising was pragmaticism, distinguishing it from pragmatism as coined by William James.[235] Susan Haack gives a catalogue of how it has been described among legal scholars: an aversion to theory; freedom from theory-guilt; looking at problems concretely, without illusions; rejection of an overarching set of immutable principles; synthesis of contextualism and instrumentalism; anti-foundationalism; and anti-formalism, amongst others.[236] As the British pragmatist FSC Schiller says, there are as many pragmatisms as there are pragmatists.[237] Thus, it will be a futile exercise attempting to define pragmatism. Nevertheless, a general understanding of pragmatism, as a rejection of universal a priori principles as the foundation of knowledge and truth, shall be used in this book.

Pragmatism has its roots in philosophy. It is often referred to as philosophical pragmatism in this context.[238] It began from the informal discussions at the Metaphysical Club founded by Charles S Peirce (1839–1914) of which William James (1842–1910), John Dewey (1859–1952) and Oliver Wendell Holmes Jr (1841–1935) were members.[239] This movement began in the mid-nineteenth century in the United States at a time when the intellectual space was effectively dominated by Continental rationalism and British empiricism.[240] The rationalists took abstractions, a priori principles and indubitable beliefs as the foundation of knowledge and truth. They were typically religious, dogmatic, and optimistic.[241] On the other hand, the British empiricists stood in sharp contrast to the rationalists. They reject all forms of absolutism. To them, real knowledge is only derivable from bare data obtained from facts and experimentation.[242] They were characteristically

---

[235] Raimo Siltala, *Law, Truth, and Reason* (Springer Netherlands 2011) 98.

[236] Susan Haack, 'On Legal Pragmatism: Where Does "The Path of the Law" Lead Us?' (2005) 50 *The American Journal of Jurisprudence* 71, 72.

[237] Robert Almeder, 'A Definition of Pragmatism' (1986) 3 *History of Philosophy Quarterly* 79.

[238] Susan Haack, 'The Pluralistic Universe of Law: Towards a Neo-Classical Legal Pragmatism' (2008) 21 *Ratio Juris* 453, 456; D Luban, 'What's Pragmatic About Legal Pragmatism?' (1996) 18 *Cardozo Law Review* 43, 46.

[239] Siltala (n 235) 97; Thomas C Grey, 'Holmes and Legal Pragmatism' (1989) 41 *Stanford Law Review* 787, 864.

[240] Brian Z Tamanaha, *Realistic Socio-Legal Theory: Pragmatism and a Social Theory of Law* (Clarendon Press 1997) 26.

[241] Ibid, 27.

[242] Grey (n 239) 799.

sceptical and irreligious.[243] The pragmatists sought to find a balance between these two extremes of absolutism and scepticism.

The major preoccupation of the leading pragmatists at that time was the determinant of knowledge, the theory of meaning and the nature of truth. While they differed in their approach and methodology, they agreed that such phenomena ought not to be determined by a priori beliefs and other overarching principles derived from deductive syllogism. Their backgrounds in different fields of knowledge and their peculiar socio-political experiences[244] might have contributed to their divergent approaches. From their discussions at the Club, they reasoned that the nature of propositions could only be determined in relation to the practical effects they produce. A proposition will be true because it has been tested and produced the desired result. Knowledge can be attained, and truth can be ascertained through an investigative process. While Peirce argued for a strict objective and scientific investigative process, others, like James, a psychologist, argued that not all claims could be verified through the scientific method. He posited that beyond the field of scientific inquiry, issues concerning religious, moral and other ethical questions could as well be verified by other subjective factors such as experience, opinions, and beliefs.[245] Largely, their expositions ushered in a new way of thinking about critical issues that affect human existence. They broke away from the prevalent doctrine of rationalism as a basis of philosophical thought and set the cornerstone for the foundation of a new path to critical thinking, not just in philosophy but also in other fields of knowledge, including law.

III. Pragmatism as a Legal Theory

Like their counterparts in philosophy, many legal theorists in the Enlightenment era and afterwards shared the view that law is autonomous, logically ordered and rationally determinate.[246] A legal rule is correct and valid if it reasonably and logically follows from established propositions. The function of a judge in the administration of justice is to discover and apply the law to the established facts. Reason plays a vital role in decision-making, as it provides an objective means of analysing the legitimacy and validity of decisions.[247] The correctness of decisions lies in their adherence to logical order from certain a priori principles established

---

[243] Ibid.

[244] Charles Peirce was a mathematician, William James was a psychologist, Dewey was an educationalist, and Holmes trained as a lawyer. The American Civil War had a great impact on their views about ideas. The ideological fanaticism and violence resulting from the War shaped their thoughts. Holmes in particular fought as an Army Captain and had first-hand experience of the havoc of the War. See Louis Menand, *The Metaphysical Club* (Flamingo 2002) 3–4.

[245] Grey (n 239) 791; Siltala (n 235) 98–99.

[246] Paul N Cox, 'An Interpretation and (Partial) Defense of Legal Formalism' (2003) 36 *Indiana Law Review* 57, 59–60; Daniel Z Epstein, 'Rationality, Legitimacy, & the Law' (2014) 7 *Washington University Jurisprudence Review* 1, 7.

[247] Ibid, 7.

by law. The judicial decision-making process, therefore, ought to be a deductive system. This generally describes legal formalism and rationalism, which were the hallmark of judicial reasoning in the nineteenth century.[248]

In the civil law tradition, legal formalism is inevitable due to the influence of analytical positivism. Judicial reasoning begins and ends with the civil codes. Answers to legal questions are to be located in the codes and there is generally no recourse to non-legal materials or other moral considerations.[249] Cases are often decided by a mechanical application of the rules existing in the codes. The codes are all-embracing and contain self-sufficient premises. The facts of a case present the minor premise and there should be no difficulty in drawing conclusions. Judges neither have discretion nor can they rationalise based on set values and prejudices.[250] This is commonly referred to as 'judicial syllogism' in Continental literature. It explains why judgments in the civil law tradition are usually not as elaborate as their common law counterparts.[251] It is not for the judge to discuss the workability of the rules, what effects they produce or questions touching on social policy.[252]

On the other hand, the common law is essentially judge-made. Common law judges are not so restrained as their colleagues in the civil law system. Nevertheless, they share some elements of formalism as well. The doctrine of stare decisis requires that judicial decisions should flow from the body of established principles and precedents.[253] While judges in the civil law tradition proceed from the general premises provided in the codes, common law judges often rationalise from general principles that have been settled by precedents. From there, lower-level rules are derived which are syllogistically applied to the factual case in issue. Over time, the common law systematically became formalised under the influence of Continental traditions. As Lon Fuller notes, the pragmatism of the common law 'was debauched' and it 'became abstract and conceptual'.[254] While this represents the formalistic aspect of judicial reasoning in the common law, the inherent powers of the judges to tinker with the process in deserving cases to meet the ends of justice, brings the common law method a little closer to pragmatism.

---

[248] Epstein (n 246) 3; Steven M Quevedo, 'Formalist and Instrumentalist Legal Reasoning and Legal Theory' (1985) 73 *California Law Review* 119, 121.

[249] Scott Shapiro, *Legality* (Harvard University Press 2011) 246. Shapiro notes that some positivists, like Hart, however, reject formalist judicial reasoning. For a comparative analysis of legal and judicial reasoning in civil and common law traditions, see: George Mousourakis, *Comparative Law and Legal Traditions: Historical and Contemporary Perspectives* (Springer 2019); Ugo Mattei and Luca G Pes, 'Civil Law and Common Law: Toward Convergence?' in Gregory A Caldeira, R Daniel Kelemen and Keith E Whittington (eds), *The Oxford Handbook of Law and Politics* (OUP 2008); Konrad Zweigert and Hein Kötz, *Introduction to Comparative Law* (3rd edn, OUP 1998) 256–75; Lyndel V Prott, 'Judicial Reasoning in the Common Law and Code Law Systems' (1978) 64 *Archives for Philosophy of Law and Social Philosophy* 417.

[250] Roberto G MacLean, 'Judicial Discretion in the Civil Law' (1982) 43 *Louisiana Law Review* 45, 45–46.

[251] Eva Steiner, *French Law : A Comparative Approach* (2nd edn, OUP 2018) 112–13.

[252] Charles H Koch, 'The Advantages of the Civil Law Judicial Design as the Model for Emerging Legal Systems' (2004) 11 *Indiana Journal of Global Legal Studies* 139, 151.

[253] *Willers v Joyce* [2016] UKSC 44.

[254] LL Fuller, 'American Legal Realism' (1934) 82 *University of Pennsylvania Law Review* 428, 438.

The situation in the classroom is not entirely different from what is obtainable in the courtroom. From Continental Europe to England and the United States of America, legal education is dogmatic. It is more about critical analysis of the system and structure of the law, basic concepts and their distinctions, syllogistic application of those abstract concepts to facts, and adherence to forms and procedures.[255] From their first year in the law school, law students are introduced to syllogistic legal reasoning, how to identify issues, relating them to statements of law and drawing conclusions.[256] There is little or no room for the use of non-legal tools in legal analysis.

Formalism in its extreme form is rarely practised today, not even in the civil law tradition. There is no doubt that logic and reason are necessary tools for both legal theorising and judicial decision-making. The central question is what degree of relevance should be accorded to them? Should judges be confined exclusively to the rationality of their decisions or could they find legitimacy in other non-legal norms? Should judges simply discover and declare the law? Should they take note of the consequences and effects of their decisions? These are the questions which pre-occupied legal discourse towards the twilight of the nineteenth century.

Legal pragmatism shares a somewhat similar historical background with philosophical pragmatism.[257] Justice Wendell Holmes Jr – a member of the Metaphysical Club and contemporary of Peirce, James and Dewey – was amongst the early legal theorists to introduce elements of pragmatism to law.[258] Holmes' views about law were in tandem with the discussions at the Metaphysical Club. In *The Common Law*, Holmes declared that:

> The life of the law has not been logic: it has been experience. The felt necessities of the time, the prevalent moral and political theories, intuitions of public policy, avowed or unconscious, even the prejudices which judges share with their fellow men, have had a good deal more to do than the syllogism in determining the rules by which men should be governed. The law embodies the story of a nation's development through many centuries, and it cannot be dealt with as if it contained only the axioms and corollaries of a book of mathematics.[259]

---

[255] Hasso Hofmann, 'From Jhering to Radbruch: On the Logic of Traditional Legal Concepts to the Social Theories of Law to the Renewal of Legal Idealism' in Damiano Canale and Others (eds), *A Treatise of Legal Philosophy and General Jurisprudence: Vol 9: A History of the Philosophy of Law in the Civil Law World, 1600–1900* (Springer 2009) 301; Martijn Willem Hesselink, *The New European Private Law : Essays on the Future of Private Law in Europe* (Kluwer Law International 2002) 18; MH Hoeflich, 'Law & Geometry: Legal Science from Leibniz to Langdell' (1986) 30 *The American Journal of Legal History* 95, 108.

[256] Michael BW Sinclair, 'What Is the "R" in IRAC' (2003) 46 *New York Law School Law Review* 457.

[257] For instance see Richard A Posner, *How Judges Think* (Harvard University Press 2008) 232. Posner indeed suggested that the common law judges before Holmes were influenced by pragmatism in the development of the common law. It should be noted that several legal writers in Continental Europe, such as Jhering, Erhlich and others, shared similar thoughts to Holmes. However, their impact was not strong enough to cause a systemic change in legal theory and judicial reasoning like that of the United States. See Hesselink (n 255) 26.

[258] Thomas C Grey, *Formalism and Pragmatism in American Law* (Brill 2014); Richard A Posner, 'Legal Pragmatism' (2004) 35 *Metaphilosophy* 147.

[259] Oliver Wendell Holmes, *The Common Law* (William S Hein & Company 1881) 1.

Holmes analysed the developments of the common law – in the areas of liability, contract, tort and others – and its progressive development in form and substance in meeting the needs of the time, even though such development may be stultified or hindered by precedent. His views were also shared by some of his contemporaries such as Roscoe Pound who argued that law 'must be judged by the results it achieves, not by the niceties of its internal structure'.[260] Pound maintained that the inherent value of the law is to be measured by the result it produces and not by blind adherence to rules.

The underlying assumption that informs Holmes' position is that law must continue to grow organically, and the growth should be influenced by factors both within and outside the law. History, economics, sociology, and experience are other relevant factors that should shape law and the judicial decision-making process. He also demonstrated this in his dissenting judgment in *Lochner v New York*,[261] where he declared that 'general propositions do not decide concrete cases'. He opposed the lead judgment, which interpreted the state of New York's Bakeshop Act from an economic perspective without considering the practical problems that Congress was trying to address by the statute.[262] His approach essentially favoured anti-foundationalism and instrumentalism. However, Holmes did not call himself a pragmatist, even though many legal commentators have described him as such.[263]

Since the turn of the twentieth century, legal theorising and judicial reasoning have been much influenced in both the United States and elsewhere by pragmatism. There has been a growing resentment toward formalism, and this is evident from the legal scholarship emerging since then.[264] Legal pragmatists prioritise the functionality of laws. They seek to constantly appraise the workability of laws and their progressive development in addressing specific challenges of the time. They reject a one-size-fits-all approach to law where legal problems are addressed mainly through the prism of absolute principles and logical neatness.

IV. Legal Pragmatism Today

From Holmes to Pound, the seed of legal pragmatism has been firmly sown, and the idea is well known in the literature. The advent of globalisation, the triumph of

---

[260] Roscoe Pound, 'Mechanical Jurisprudence' (1908) 8 *Columbia Law Review* 605, 605.

[261] *Lochner v New York* 198 US 45, 76 (1905).

[262] The Act forbade workers from working above 10 hours a day or 60 hours a week in total. The Supreme Court ruled that the statute infringed on freedom of contract. Holmes's major argument was that the Court ought to consider the social policy and other public health issues that necessitated Congress to pass the Act.

[263] F Kellogg, 'American Pragmatism and European Social Theory: Holmes, Durkheim, Scheler, and the Sociology of Legal Knowledge.' (2012) IV *European Journal of Pragmatism & American Philosophy* 107, 108; Haack (n 236) 454.

[264] Various movements which opposed formalistic judicial decision-making emerged in the United States and elsewhere. These include legal realism, Critical Legal Studies, law and economics, amongst others. See Hesselink (n 255) 24.

laissez-faire capitalism, and the emergence of the law and economics movement gave the impetus for the resurgence of the modern legal pragmatist movement. Richard Posner is regarded as a leading proponent of modern legal pragmatism.[265] He has written extensively on the subject, gave it some theoretical underpinnings and strongly defended it, perhaps, more than anyone else.

Posner shares similar views with earlier pragmatists. His work on pragmatic adjudication, which he describes as 'judgments in facts and consequences rather than in conceptualisms and generalities',[266] is more relevant to this research work. His view on pragmatic adjudication is no different from what many earlier commentators have argued. Luban contends that if pragmatism had not meant more than eclecticism and a result-oriented approach to judicial decision-making, it would not have been different from the views of many legal thinkers today, because that is the prevailing practice in the judicial process.[267] No wonder Thomas Grey agrees that legal pragmatism is essentially banal.[268] However, legal pragmatism is becoming more theorised and acquiring a distinct character beyond the views held in the past.

Judge Posner's theory of pragmatic adjudication is anchored on what he calls 'everyday pragmatism'. By this, he argues that pragmatism is nothing more than a common-sense approach to solving problems.[269] A pragmatic judge is one that makes the 'most reasonable decision ... all things considered'.[270] This implies that judges should consider all the peculiar facts of the case; the ends of justice; the social policy behind laws; the utility of the different solutions at hand; business and commercial efficacy; common sense; and reasonableness, in arriving at the best decision. The judge's inherent and discretionary powers should be effectively utilised in selecting the best result. In other words, a judge must dig down to the root of the issue at hand and deal with it without regard to any theoretical, conceptual, or absolute principles which might stand as obstacles in his way. Also, a pragmatic judge should not be fettered by unnecessary adherence to precedent if such would produce inefficient results.[271]

An anti-theoretical and common-sense judicial approach, or what some have called 'brass-tacks pragmatism',[272] has been criticised by several scholars. Dworkin contends that a case-specific, forward-looking approach would create infidelity within the law. The unguided use of discretion and a fixation on the facts of the case, the ends of justice and social policy would lead to unbridled judicial activism, arbitrariness in the use of judicial powers, and a break away from adherence to

---

[265] Michael N Sullivan and Daniel J Solove, 'Can Pragmatism Be Radical? Richard Posner and Legal Pragmatism' (2003) 113 *Yale Law Journal* 687, 688.
[266] Richard Posner, 'Legal Pragmatism' (2004) 35 *Metaphilosophy* 147, 150.
[267] Luban (n 238) 45.
[268] Grey (n 258) 132.
[269] Richard A Posner, *Law, Pragmatism, and Democracy* (Harvard University Press 2005) 52.
[270] Ibid, 64.
[271] Ibid, 60.
[272] John CP Goldberg, 'Pragmatism and Private Law' (2012) 125 *Harvard Law Review* 1640.

precedents.[273] Consequently, this would cause manipulation of precedents, uncertainty and unpredictability of laws. Professor Atiyah also expresses similar fear about pragmatic adjudication and notes that it may lead to 'ad hockery'.[274]

This criticism raises legitimate concerns. While other legal pragmatists simply preferred that pragmatism should remain anti-theoretical, Posner offers further arguments as a response. He reconstructs his idea of pragmatic adjudication, clothing it with some normative ideals of economic efficiency. As a rider to everyday pragmatism, efficiency is a widely held value, and pragmatic judges are expected to produce efficient results bearing in mind the present and future needs of the society.[275] These results can be determined, inter alia, by judicial empiricism.[276] Posner admits that pragmatism is not hostile to all forms of theory but 'it is friendlier to some forms of theory than legal formalism is, namely, theories that guide empirical inquiry, such as economics'.[277]

From the foregoing, the preponderance of modern pragmatists believe that judicial reasoning cannot be completely devoid of some theoretical assumptions and principled reasoning. This can address the question of unrestrained use of judicial preferences and discretions. As Posner argues, judges must observe principles and consider the 'systemic consequences' of their decisions.[278] For instance, concepts such as the reasonable expectations of parties, legal certainty and predictability – because of their inherent values – are relevant factors that judges must bear in mind when carrying out judicial functions. It is only in deserving cases, when confronted with unique challenges that the body of precedents ought to be adjusted to accommodate new realities.[279] In the same vein, a pragmatic judge must be flexible enough in his choice of theories. The ultimate goal is to make a choice that produces useful results. Such evaluations should be carried out through a pragmatic inquiry that considers both historical and current experiences.[280]

V. Legal Pragmatism in Private International Law

Pragmatism stands as a useful tool to private international law compared to other areas of law because of the multi-layer complexities involved in conflicts questions.

---

[273] Ronald Dworkin, *Law's Empire* (Belknap Press 1986) 148–50; Michael Sullivan, 'Pragmatism and Precedent: A Response to Dworkin' (1990) 26 *Transactions of the Charles S. Peirce Society* 225.

[274] Atiyah (ch 2, fn 223) 129.

[275] Richard A Posner, 'Pragmatic Adjudication' (1996) 18 *Cardozo Law Review* 1, 5; Richard A Posner, 'Legal Pragmatism Defended' (2004) 71 *University of Chicago Law Review* 683, 685.

[276] Posner, *Law, Pragmatism, and Democracy* (n 269) 60; Posner, 'Pragmatic Adjudication' (n 275) 11–12.

[277] Posner, 'Legal Pragmatism' (n 266) 152.

[278] Ibid, 154.

[279] Ibid, 150–151.

[280] Sullivan and Solove (n 265) 716.

Legal scholarship and judicial reasoning in private international law before the era of legal pragmatism were, largely, based on a theoretical and abstract analysis of concepts and rules without much regard for results. The emergence of pragmatism challenged legal commentators to evolve alternative thoughts, which advanced result-selectivism and justice as opposed to formalistic legal solutions. The choice of law revolution, which took place in the United States, is a manifestation of pragmatic thought. Following the codification of the vested rights theory as the foundation for the choice of law rule in the First Restatement, numerous writers challenged the 'ordainment' by coming up with solutions that focused on results and the unique nature of transnational disputes.[281] Thus, Juenger advocated a 'best law' approach, which should be specifically crafted for international cases.[282] Luther M McDougal, Arthur T von Mehren and Donald T Trautman also favoured this result-oriented approach. According to McDougal, 'the best rule of law is one that best promotes net aggregate long-term common interests.'[283] To this category one may add other commentators such as Cavers, who criticised the mechanical nature of the traditional methodology and compared it with a slot machine, programmed to select laws robotically without regard to the controversies in issue.[284] He argued that judges ought to examine and understand the case at hand and the rules applicable, and then select the rule that seeks to do better justice for the case. Professor David Cavers' approach requires judges to 'scrutinize the event or transaction', 'compare carefully the proffered rule of law and the result which its application might work', and 'appraise these results in the light of those facts' from the standpoint of 'justice between the litigating individuals or of those broader considerations of social policy', before arriving at the proper law.[285] The approaches that were advanced, from Cavers to Juenger, could therefore be described as pragmatic.

From the Continental perspective, Savigny blazed the trail with his universalist approach to private international law problems. However, his theory was fixated on the localisation of legal relations and the identification of the State whose law governed a given transaction.[286] This solution favoured conflicts justice as against substantive justice. In contrast, some scholars who came after him, such as the German jurist Rudolph von Jhering, had argued for a paradigm shift from the

---

[281] For a summary of the result-selective approach, see Symeon C Symeonides, 'Result-Selectivism in Conflicts Law' (2009) 46 *Williamette Law Review* 1.

[282] Friedrich K Juenger, *Choice of Law and Multistate Justice* (Martinus Nijhoff Publishers 1993) 197.

[283] Luther L McDougal III, 'Toward Application of the Best Rule of Law in Choice of Law Cases' (1983) 35 *Mercer Law Review* 483, 484.

[284] Symeon Symeonides, *American Private International Law* (Kluwer Law International 2008) 94.

[285] David Cavers, 'A Critique of the Choice-of-Law Problem' (1933) 47 *Harvard Law Review* 173, 192. Professor Cavers later developed this thought by coming up with what he called 'principles of preference'. This is a set of principles that can serve as a premise from which courts can derive the best solution to a given problem, see David Cavers, *The Choice-of-Law Process* (University of Michigan Press 1965).

[286] Jürgen Basedow, 'Methods of Private International Law' in Jürgen Basedow and others (eds), *Encyclopedia of Private International Law* (Edward Elgar Publishing 2017) 1404.

jurisprudence of conceptions to a jurisprudence of results.[287] Jhering's writings perhaps watered the ground for the development of comparative law, which was one of the earliest methodologies used by private international lawyers to import pragmatism into Continental jurisprudence.[288] The paradigm shift from mechanical jurisprudence was vigorously pursued by Franz Kahn, Ernst Rabel and others. Professor Rabel, a leading comparative law scholar of the twentieth century, wrote that legal theorists and judges should focus on comparative law to juxtapose the solutions offered by different legal systems for similar factual situations and to decide which of those solutions better addressed the problem at hand.[289] Rabel practicalised this approach in his *A Draft of an International Law of Sales*. After examining the nature of international sales contracts, and the different, unsatisfactory and complicated rules of common law – as applied in the United States and England – and civil law, he opted for a draft which squarely focused on business common sense and commercial realities. This mix-and-match approach is said to 'draw its fundamental elements not from any legally moulded concepts but directly from the facts appearing during the execution of sales. Its fundamental notions are not legalistic but "natural". They are based on typical facts'.[290]

Rabel's works on private international law generally followed an anti-theoretical approach. He prescribed a functional comparative method through which judges and legislators can avoid the unproductive results usually seen in cross-border cases due to adherence to abstract concepts of national laws.[291] The Hague Conference and the European Group for Private International Law also follow this approach.[292]

VI. A Pragmatic Approach to Recognition and Enforcement of Foreign Judgments

The challenges posed by private international law issues are unique and characteristically different from those of national laws that deal with issues arising within the confines of the territory of a State. Globalisation has continued to defy State borders. Cross-border business and social transactions continue to expand, as

---

[287] Morris Raphael Cohen and Felix S Cohen, *Readings in Jurisprudence and Legal Philosophy* (Beard Books 2002) 425.

[288] Konrad Zweigert and Kurt Siehr, 'Jhering's Influence on the Development of Comparative Legal Method' (1971) 19 *The American Journal of Comparative Law* 215, 222.

[289] David J Gerber, 'Sculpting the Agenda of Comparative Law: Ernst Rabel and the Facade of Language' in Annelise Riles (ed), *Rethinking the Masters of Comparative Law* (Hart Publishing 2001).

[290] Ernst Rabel, 'A Draft of an International Law of Sales' (1935) 5 *The University of Chicago Law Review* 543, 549.

[291] Ralf Michaels, 'Comparative Law and Private International Law' in Jürgen Basedow and others (eds), *Encyclopedia of Private International Law* (Edward Elgar Publishing 2017) 418.

[292] See for instance HCCH, Catherine Kessedjian Report: International Jurisdiction and Foreign Judgments in Civil and Commercial Matters, Preliminary Document No 7 of April 1997; EGPIL, 'Summary of Working Sessions: Twentieth meeting Copenhagen, September 17 to 19, 2010' <https://www.gedip-egpil.eu/reunionstravail/gedip-reunions-20-fr.htm> accessed 12 January 2019.

do the modes of delivering them. Today, we have e-commerce, e-money, virtual companies, social media, and other platforms, which provide access to people from every part of the world without much hindrance and interference. Burgeoning global trade and innovative business solutions have transformed the menu of issues that the courts have to deal with today. The courts have struggled to fashion acceptable jurisdictional grounds to exert over non-resident, transient, and evasive defendants. With the globalisation of corporations, markets, and assets, insolvency proceedings with significant cross-border implications[293] are on the increase. So is the threat of dissipation of assets and the need for worldwide preservation orders amongst other measures.

The main objective of a pragmatic judgments framework is to have an efficient mechanism that facilitates a global exchange of judgments with minimal inconvenience to cross-border litigants. The myriad of knotty issues arising from the enforcement of foreign judgments touch on divergent national policies, values, and interests. The challenges are global and, as such, they require a well-designed global framework to be negotiated on a multilateral platform where those knotty issues can be thoroughly addressed. Besides the global solution, pragmatic ideals can also be beneficial to national legislators who may be considering reforming national judgments frameworks.

While Posner's idea of everyday pragmatism (judicial development), or America's result-selectivism (best law approach) might work for other branches of private international law, it is doubtful whether they will produce a good result for judgment recognition and enforcement. The focus of a pragmatic judgments framework should be legal certainty and predictability, conflicts justice and not material justice, multilateralism and not unilateralism. The emphasis, therefore, is on the formulation of clear and predictable jurisdictional connections between a foreign court and the underlying dispute or parties, with an assurance that judgments from courts which are substantially connected to a dispute are enforceable in other jurisdictions. The task for a court addressed is to screen a foreign judgment to ensure that the foreign court had an acceptable basis of jurisdiction. The court addressed should be discouraged as much as possible from interfering with the merits of a case except where such judgment violates some fundamental policy of the forum. Even for this limited role, the treaty-makers must ensure that the grounds for denial are intended to be interpreted narrowly to reduce the risk of judges applying them inappropriately.

The framework described above aggregates different theoretical and methodological issues of private international law. Thus, while focusing on conflicts justice and multilateralism, it also factors in material justice and unilateralism (States' interests, public policy, and overriding mandatory norms) as may be exceptionally required in deserving cases.

---

[293] See *Rubin v Eurofinance SA* [2012] UKSC 46, paras 11–14. Also, in the empirical research reported in section VI.B below, insolvency cases form a large percentage of the cases categorised as 'commercial'.

A. Competing Values and the Inherent Tensions

The preceding paragraph highlights the central tenets of our idea of a pragmatic judgments recognition and enforcement framework. What is apparent in this proposed model is the inherent tension between some of the suggested substantive values. This tension runs through the analysis of the rest of the chapters of this book. On the one hand, there is a perceived tension between legal certainty (and predictability) and flexibility, which are both required to deliver a pragmatic judgments framework that meets the needs of the time. There is also the tension between conflicts justice and material justice, and how to strike a balance between these two substantive values. Yet, it can also be noticed that there is further tension between the need to prioritise private parties' interests and the accommodation of States' or societal interests. Besides, one also needs to justify why national interests should give way for a global interest in the harmonisation of judgments rules.

Our position is that the question is beyond conflicts justice vs material justice or unilateralism vs multilateralism. There is hardly any private international law system today that is wholly and exclusively built on any of these values. A pragmatic judgments framework will integrate these values, focusing on the utility of each of them, since the ultimate goal is to solve practical legal problems. The task of resolving the tensions is an onerous one. It is best suited for the legislators or treaty-makers who can devote time and energy to consider the utilities therein and to what extent each of these values should be adopted and for which purpose.

In balancing the tensions, legislators and treaty-makers should target specific substantive goals upon which the framework shall be built. It is suggested that a global judgments framework, and national frameworks by extension, ought to prioritise efficiency, fairness, and justice. The methods of achieving these goals are practical experience, comparativism and empiricism. Efficiency, fairness and justice are normative goals that address the specific problems arising from enforcement of foreign judgments, and the methods that have been chosen are meant to ensure that the legislators and policymakers can discover the practical problems and come up with solutions that best suit those identified problems. The broader goals of efficiency, fairness and justice can assist law-makers in striking a balance amongst the competing values of legal certainty and predictability, conflicts justice, material justice and state interests.

B. Efficiency

The issue at stake in an application for the enforcement of foreign judgments is quite different from those in other areas of private international law such as jurisdiction and choice of law. Unlike those others, there is usually no competition between different national laws or national courts. It solely involves the status and effect of foreign judgments, evidencing rights already determined by a foreign court. An enforcement application is principally a private law issue, although sometimes State immunity or national public policy may be an issue. A private law approach, which focuses on the interests of individual parties and the maximisation of their welfare, should therefore be adopted.

Empiricism is a key aspect of pragmatism, as it gives a clear picture of what the real issues are. The assumption is that most cases on foreign judgments relate to the protection and distribution of private assets, the allocation of resources and coordination of State powers. Thus, legislators must focus on efficiency when designing judgments recognition frameworks. This assumption is confirmed by an empirical study of UK decisions on foreign judgments for the past two decades. The data obtained shows that most of the reported cases on recognition and enforcement of foreign judgments concern commercial transactions. From 203 reported cases that came up before the UK courts between January 1998 and December 2018, 56 per cent were commercial disputes, ranging across construction contracts, carriage of goods by sea, unfair competition, insolvency and general commercial contracts.[294] This confirms that the foundation of most cases is transactional. These cases involved the questions of whether a foreign court should be assisted by a court addressed in the collection and distribution of assets, whether a foreign court had an acceptable basis of jurisdiction, and so on. It is arguable; therefore, that one of the underlying policies to be considered by legislators and treaty-makers is the efficiency of the judgments enforcement rules, the support for private business actors, the maximisation of their overall welfare and efficient coordination and utilisation of judicial resources.

Table 1 Reported cases on recognition and enforcement of foreign judgments in the UK: 1998–2018

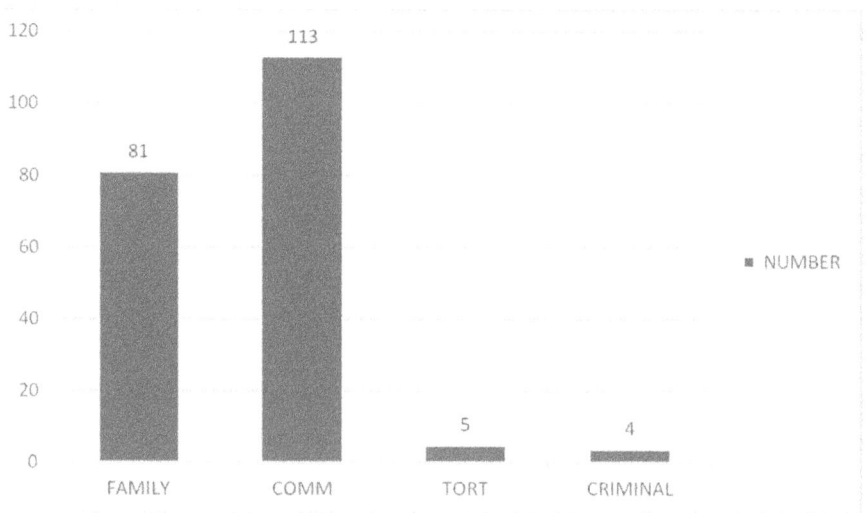

---

[294] These cases were obtained from Lexis and Westlaw UK databases. While there is a possibility that a few cases within the years reviewed might have been omitted, such cases, if any, would not have any significant effect on the general outlook of the result.

(i) Party Autonomy/Protection of Legitimate Expectations

For transnational trade and commerce to flourish, States ought to prioritise private interests, the security of their transactions and the protection of their property rights.[295] These factors have been identified as necessary ingredients for the global exchange of goods and services.[296] To achieve this, in designing rules for judgments enforcement, legislators should seek an enforcement regime that helps parties to meet their legitimate reasonable expectations. Parties who conclude commercial transactions in a jurisdiction may be deemed to have made voluntary and informed litigation choices.[297] As rational actors, they have sought to benefit from their transactions and the legal system which they have expressly or impliedly chosen. It is only reasonable that the law should help them to fulfil their contractual obligations. Non-enforcement of contracts and the benefits arising therefrom have a social cost. It can influence parties' behaviour towards the sanctity of contracts.[298]

Foreign judgments establish private rights and obligations. In cases where there is an underlying contract wherein parties have chosen the foreign court that rendered the judgment in question, or the judgment debtor, in the course of the proceedings, had chosen or acquiesced in the choice of the foreign court, a court addressed should treat that foreign judgment as an extension of the underlying contract between the parties.[299] As Gascon J notes in *Chevron Corp v Yaiguaje*, 'the only purpose of the action is to allow a pre-existing obligation to be fulfilled'.[300] The court addressed should therefore graciously permit its machinery to be deployed to give effect to the foreign judgment in furtherance of the contract between the parties. It seems more pragmatic for a foreign judgment to crystallise the rights obtained under the underlying contract – which is then imported – than treating it as creating a new obligation (contract) which requires a fresh action to be enforced.[301]

The common law and, more recently, several civil law jurisdictions favourably enforce foreign judgments under the circumstances related above, even though their underlying assumptions are couched in different terms. Barring any

---

[295] Wenliang Zhang, 'Sino-Foreign Recognition and Enforcement of Judgments: A Promising "Follow-Suit" Model?' (2017) 16 *Chinese Journal of International Law* 515, 516.

[296] Giuliana Palumbo and others, 'Judicial Performance and Its Determinants: A Cross-Country Perspective', *OECD Economic Policy Papers No 05* (June 2013).

[297] Kevin E Davis and Helen Hershkoff, 'Contracting for Procedure' (2011) 53 *William & Mary Law Review* 507.

[298] Michael Whincop, 'Three Positive Theories of International Jurisdiction' (2000) 24 *Melbourne University Law Review* 379, 381.

[299] In the same vein, a court may rightly refuse to enforce a judgment that was issued in contravention of a choice of forum clause. See Adrian Briggs, 'Distinctive Aspects of the Conflict of Laws in Common Law System: Autonomy and Agreement in the Conflict of Laws' (2005) 57 *The Doshisha Law Review* 21, 33.

[300] *Chevron Corp v Yaiguaje*, 2015 SCC 42 at para 42.

[301] In one breath, the common law action on judgments could be described as a pragmatic solution in the nineteenth century when many States did not ordinarily recognise foreign judgments. However, its pragmatic outlook seems no longer impressive considering the cost and procedural hurdles that judgment creditors may face in such actions.

fundamental defect, foreign judgments are hardly ever impeachable where a judgment debtor chose the foreign court. Recently, in *Vizcaya Partners Ltd v Picard*,[302] the Privy Council went further to rule that submission can be presumed from the conduct of the judgment debtor or the surrounding circumstances. Courts ought to entertain objections only on a narrow ground of fairness, such as cases where a foreign court does not have a strong connection with the case, or where there are other fundamental defects which may vitiate the judgment just like the underlying contract.

This approach was adopted under the HCCA and the 2019 Hague Judgments Convention.[303] The practical value from this approach is that it aids certainty and predictability of laws. There is anecdotal evidence that litigants prefer arbitration clauses to choice of court clauses because of the ease of enforceability of the former.[304] With these two conventions, a more effective enforcement regime is now available for judgment creditors. In this connection, it is not only pragmatic to enforce judgments from agreed courts, but also to deny recognition to judgments obtained in breach of a choice of court agreement.[305]

It is part of pragmatism that parties' legitimate expectations should be protected. Parties who transacted in a particular State ought to be deemed to have ordinarily subjected themselves to the courts of that State in respect of any dispute arising from such transactions, having taken advantage of its legal and economic conditions. This used to be part of the common law until it was rejected in *Emanuel v Symon*.[306] In the *Bank of Australasia v Nias*,[307] it was held that there might be an implied contract for parties who transacted in a jurisdiction to be bound by the procedure of the courts of that State. Mr Justice Blackburn was prepared to arrive at the same conclusion in *Schibsby v Westenholz*.[308] However, this is no longer the case at common law. As many enforcement actions have shown, it is very difficult

---

[302] *Vizcaya Partners Ltd v Picard* [2016] UKPC 5.
[303] <https://www.hcch.net/en/instruments/conventions/status-table/?cid=98>. The 2005 Convention is in force for 30 States and 1 Regional Economic Integration Organisation (the EU).
[304] Louise Ellen Teitz, 'The Hague Choice of Court Convention : Validating Party Autonomy and Providing an Alternative to Arbitration' (2005) 53 *The American Journal of Comparative Law* 543, 548.
[305] See for instance, s 7(4)(b) of the Australian Foreign Judgments Act 1991 (No 112 of 1991); s 32 of UK Civil Jurisdiction and Judgments Act 1982. Recently, the English courts granted worldwide anti-enforcement injunctions against judgments obtained in breach of choice of court agreements. See *Ust-Kamenogorsk Hydropower Plant JSC v AES Ust-Kamenogorsk Hydropower Plant LLP* [2013] UKSC 35; *Bank St Petersburg v Arkhangelsky* [2014] EWCA Civ 593; *Ecobank Transnational Inc v Tanoh* [2015] EWHC 1874 (Comm). See also Art 7(1)(d) of the 2019 Hague Judgments Convention.
[306] *Emanuel v Symon* [1908] 1 KB 302 (CA) 306–7. The case outlines the common law rules on international jurisdiction. In this case, the English court rejected contracting in a State as a jurisdictional ground for international jurisdiction. This represents the traditional common law rule to date except in Canada. Many scholars have criticised this position. For instance, Briggs describes it as odd. See Adrian Briggs, 'Crossing the River by Feeling the Stones: Rethinking the Law on Foreign Judgments' (2004) 8 *Singapore Year Book of International Law* 1, 11.
[307] *Bank of Australasia v Nias* (1851) 16 QB 717.
[308] *Schibsby v Westenholz* (1870–71) 6 QB 155. See also *Copin v Adamson* (1875) 1 Ex D 17 where the court reasoned that a man who contracted to obtain shares in a French company should be deemed to have contracted to submit to the jurisdiction and procedure of the French courts.

to enforce foreign judgments against non-resident defendants because of the restrictive scope of the concept of international jurisdiction.

Litigants should not be at liberty to disregard a court which has a very strong link to the underlying contract especially in this era where people criss-cross borders with ease for business activities. Having benefitted from a State's economy, both parties should presumably 'take the rough with the smooth'[309] and be amenable to the processes of that State's court. Defining acceptable links with foreign courts for every transaction remains a Herculean task,[310] possibly because it has been pursued by judges, who are not best suited for the task.[311] It is suggested that such a task can best be undertaken by legislators through extensive negotiations at a multilateral level. From that platform, they can define some acceptable connections which will reflect the reasonable legitimate expectations of parties.

(ii) Judicial Economy

Having noted the need to respect party autonomy, the security of transactions and property rights, a pragmatic judgments enforcement regime also needs to protect States' needs and ambitions.[312] Many States are battling with dwindling revenue resources and an ailing economy. This economic downturn affects budgetary allocation to the judiciary and the eventual performance of the courts. Judicial economy is, therefore, a global concern. The courts are faced with extremely busy dockets without a corresponding expansion of court structures, equipment, and personnel. In enacting policy frameworks for foreign judgments, it is only logical that the legislators should think of judicial economy by discouraging the re-examination of the merits of a case. This ensures that scarce judicial resources are not further wasted on matters that are already decided. It also helps the litigants in preserving as much cost as possible.

To this end, the doctrine of *res judicata* and mutual trust are essential tools that can support judicial economy. A legal framework that requires a judgment creditor to file a fresh action on a foreign judgment fails the pragmatic test. The new action helps neither the court's docket nor the pocket of the litigants. In terms of cost, the

---

[309] In *Adams v Cape Industries Plc* (ch1, fn 28) at 519, Scott J used this phrase to justify why someone who is present within a State's territory would be regarded as amenable to the processes of the State's court. Doing business in a State should be more justifiable as litigants took voluntary and rational steps to obtain some benefits (and burdens) by transacting in that State.

[310] Ardavan Arzandeh, 'The English Court's Service-Out Jurisdiction in International Tortious Disputes' (2017) 133 *Law Quarterly Review* 144 (discussing the confusion arising from English courts' interpretation of the 'jurisdictional gateway' for international torts); Jean-Gabriel Castel, 'The Uncertainty Factor in Canadian Private International Law' (2007) 52 *McGill Law Journal* 555 (discussing the uncertainty and undesirability of the Canadian test); Tanya Monestier, '(Still) A "Real and Substantial" Mess: The Law of Jurisdiction in Canada' (2013) 36 *Fordham International Law Journal* 396.

[311] Mary Keyes, *Jurisdiction in International Litigation* (Federation Press 2005) at 3 notes that the jurisdictional principles, as developed by judges in Australia, are incoherent, inconsistent and lacking clear objectives.

[312] John CP Goldberg (n 272) 642.

judgment creditor and debtor will finance the litigation in the second jurisdiction for the second time. For fresh actions, the litigants will face rising litigation costs, which may go as high as £10,000 for filing fees in jurisdictions like England.[313] This is exclusive of lawyers' fees[314] and other sundry costs that are attached to litigation. This is a needless waste of resources, which invariably leads to a higher cost of doing business. There are also procedural issues that judgment creditors may face in serving claims outside the jurisdiction of the court addressed[315] or in establishing direct jurisdiction over the non-resident judgment debtor – who may not have assets within the jurisdiction. This has always been a litigious point, as seen in several cases including *Chevron Corp v Yaiguaje, Yukos Capital SARL v OAO Tomskneft VNK*,[316] *Demirel v Tasarruf Mevduati Sigorta Fonu*,[317] *Abu Dhabi Commercial Bank PJSC v Saad Trading, Contracting and Financial Services Co*,[318] *Ahmad Hamad Al Gosaibi & Bros Co v Standard Chartered Bank*.[319]

The cost of adjudication is a factor which the legislators should consider when designing a judgments framework. A pragmatic example is the Brussels Ia regime, which is built on mutual trust. It establishes a hassle-free foreign judgments registration scheme by removing intermediate measures that may lead to an unnecessary waste of judicial and litigants' time and resources.[320] A speedy process is also available in some of the states in the US,[321] in many European States for non-EU judgments,[322] and under the new

---

[313] The filing fee is capped at £10,000 for claims above £200,000. See HM Courts and Tribunals Service, 'Civil and Family Court Fees From 6 April 2015' (2015) <http://hmctsformfinder.justice.gov.uk/courtfinder/forms/ex050-eng.pdf> accessed 30 August 2018.

[314] Rising lawyers' fees has been a topical issue in recent times. Unlike the German system where fees are fixed and determinable, such is not the case in most common law jurisdictions. It has been reported, for instance, that lawyers' fees have risen to an hourly rate of around £1000 in top English firms. See Martin O'Neill, 'Top London Lawyers Charge £1,000 an Hour, Study Finds', *Financial Times* (2 May 2016) <https://www.ft.com/content/29151078-ca73-11e5-a8ef-ea66e967dd44> accessed 23 August 2018. This has necessitated a call for the introduction of a fixed fee regime in England as rising costs negatively impacts access to justice. See Lord Justice Jackson, 'Speech by Lord Justice Jackson: Fixed Costs – The Time Has Come', *IPA Annual lecture* (2016): https://www.judiciary.uk/wp-content/uploads/2016/01/fixedcostslecture-1.pdf.

[315] *Abela v Baadarani* [2013] UKSC 44 is a recent UK Supreme Court decision, which showcases the problems that litigants may face in serving claims on uncooperative foreign defendants. In this case, the respondent obviously frustrated every attempt to serve the court processes on him in Lebanon by refusing to disclose his address.

[316] *Yukos Capital SARL v OAO Tomskneft VNK* [2014] IEHC 115.

[317] *Demirel v Tasarruf Mevduati Sigorta Fonu* [2007] EWCA Civ 799.

[318] *Abu Dhabi Commercial Bank PJSC v Saad Trading, Contracting and Financial Services Co*, 86 N.Y.S.2d 454 (App. Div. 2014).

[319] *Ahmad Hamad Al Gosaibi & Bros Co v Standard Chartered Bank*, 98 A.3d 998 (D.C. 2014).

[320] Beaumont and Walker (ch 1, fn 59) 32–33.

[321] Brand notes that a few US states have extended the 1964 Act, which provides for a simple registration process for local judgments, to include foreign judgments. Ronald A Brand, 'Federal Judicial Center International Litigation Guide: Recognition and Enforcement of Foreign Judgments' (2014) 74 *University of Pittsburgh Law Review* 491, 499.

[322] Foreign judgments are enforceable in most European States by an application for the recognition of the judgment (*exequatur* proceeding). Unlike the common law jurisdictions where that is a fresh action, the *exequatur* proceedings are not necessarily so. The judge is merely requested to confirm whether the foreign judgment passes the prescribed conditions for recognition. The procedure differs

CML.[323] An enforcement regime with an underlying policy of judicial economy will enhance efficiency and solve many practical problems faced by litigants.

C. Justice and Fairness

Traditionally, justice and fairness to the parties have been the underlying assumptions for recognition of foreign judgments under the common law.[324] This has enabled the courts to set broad standards and open-ended principles to address various questions surrounding foreign judgments. As mentioned elsewhere in this chapter, justice and fairness must be redefined and their underlying policy should now be the subject of multilateral negotiations rather than judicial development.

Justice in judgments recognition policy requires that the judgment creditor should reap the fruit of his labour and the judgment debtor should be protected against an improperly procured judgment. Since the merits of the case have been determined and it is generally agreed that the standards of justice of foreign legal systems are equally as good as that of the State addressed, foreign judgments should then be tolerated and recognised even if a somewhat different result would have obtained if the matter had been litigated in the State addressed.[325] The question of justice here is very narrow and is restricted to fairness in the exercise of jurisdiction, the integrity of the foreign proceedings and not the justness of the substantive decision. Thus, justice in this sense entails conflicts justice and material justice, and both are relevant in setting up a pragmatic judgments framework.

Conflicts justice requires that negotiators should search for appropriate connections that a court addressed can simply verify to determine the propriety of a foreign judgment. The framework should be designed in such a way that judgments which conform with the checklist are treated with mutual respect, and therefore enforceable without much ado. This aligns with the primary goal of private international law: the coordination and allocation of governance authority among nations.[326] Justice, fairness, and reasonableness have some role to play in

---

in detail from one State to another. Recently, some States have enacted a more efficient *exequatur* procedure, which forbids the court from reviewing the merits of the case, abolished reciprocity and allows for limited defences from the debtor. See for instance, Art 119 of the Bulgarian Code of Private International Law 2005, available at <http://www.ifrc.org/Docs/idrl/868EN.pdf>. For similar development in Hungary, see Katalin Raffai, 'The New Hungarian Private International Law Act – a Wind of Change' (2017) 6 *Acta Universitatis Sapientiae: Legal Studies* 119, 133.

[323] Commonwealth Secretariat, 'Improving the Recognition of Foreign Judgments: Model Law on the Recognition and Enforcement of Foreign Judgments Commonwealth Secretariat' (2018) 43 *Commonwealth Law Bulletin* 545.

[324] Andrew Dickinson, 'Keeping up Appearances: The Development of Adjudicatory Jurisdiction in the English Courts' (2017) 86 *British Yearbook of International Law* 6, 67.

[325] This is a semblance of what Alex Mills refers to as 'justice pluralism'. See Alex Mills, 'Variable Geometry, Peer Governance, and the Public International Perspective on Private International Law' in Horatia Muir Watt and Diego P Fernández Arroyo (eds), *Private International Law and Global Governance* (OUP 2014) 247.

[326] Christopher A Whytock, 'Conflict of Laws, Global Governance, and Transnational Legal Order' (2016) 1 *UC Irvine Journal of International, Transnational, and Comparative Law* 117, 121.

setting up acceptable jurisdictional standards. Ideally, the primary consideration for determining jurisdictional connections should be proximity, foreseeability, and effectiveness. In some cases, these primary considerations may give way for justice and fairness to the defendant. Many States might want to protect a certain class of defendants by giving them access to home courts or restricting where these defendants can be sued on grounds of justice and fairness. Examples are consumers and employees. Also, the underlying issues of some foreign judgments are not transactional, as Table 1 shows. These may include judgments whose causes of action relate to torts, some quasi-criminal claims, family law and others. Thus, it is for legislators to consider the divergent policy objectives and agree on what is just and fair for 'special defendants'.

There is also a meritorious argument for material justice considerations in judgments recognition frameworks. A court addressed should normally not be interested in the justness of the substantive outcome of a case. A review of the merits of foreign judgments should be prohibited except where the foreign judgment violates some fundamental due process. Therefore, the other task for the legislators or treaty-makers is to define the limited grounds upon which a foreign judgment may be denied. This should take care of possible mandatory forum policies and other grounds that can be invoked in a second jurisdiction as safety valves to check any improperly procured judgment. It is just and fair to both the creditor and the debtor that a judgment which emanates from a court that is substantially connected to the dispute/parties and which has been properly procured should be enforceable, as the interests of both parties have been adequately considered.

The legislators must be cautious in prescribing grounds for denial of recognition. They must be well tightened to ensure that they do not become an avenue through which judges can review foreign judgments as that will create uncertainty and unpredictability

D. Comparativism

In the nineteenth century and early part of the twentieth century, private international law was essentially a branch of domestic law. With increasing cross-border transactions and the burgeoning global market, it became imperative that unilateral (or national) approaches could not offer effective solutions to the emerging problems.[327] Since the formation of the Hague Conference on Private International Law and the EU single market, private international law has taken on a new dimension. The conclusion of several bilateral and multilateral treaties on private international law subjects means that it would be incorrect to continue to view it as a matter of domestic concern.[328] Current and future legislative frameworks for

---

[327] Michaels (n 291) 423.

[328] Lord Mance, 'The Future of Private International Law' (2005) 1 *Journal of Private International Law* 185, 186, 188–89; Giesela Rühl, 'Private International Law, Foundations' in Jürgen Basedow and others (eds), *Encyclopedia of Private International Law* (Edward Elgar Publishing 2017) 1382–93.

judgments must consider the transnational character of the problems to be solved. In this context, the solution to be offered must have some bearing on transnational legal theory.[329] This is where Ernst Rabel's functional comparative law methodology can be a useful toolkit in dealing with the problems of judgments recognition.

Comparative law investigation expands the horizons of legislators and treaty-makers. It exposes them to the structure, style, and quality of foreign legal systems and the diversity of available solutions on a given problem.[330] It gives them first-hand information about developments in the laws and practices of other jurisdictions, the problems posed by similar laws, the difficulties encountered in the application of such laws and the various outcomes obtainable elsewhere. All these will enable them to measure the practicality and usefulness of one solution as against another.

Comparativism will be useful in building a system of law through which divergences in different jurisdictions can be harmonised. It strengthens global integrity and fairness of the law as similar issues will probably be treated in a fairly similar way.[331] As Lord Reed notes, this is a practical value which should drive the legislators (and perhaps courts) to adopt solutions that will work in harmony with those developed by the legislators and courts in other countries.[332] Eventually, comparativism contributes to legal certainty and predictability. This translates to economic efficiency because fairly uniform legal regimes will lead to reduced transaction costs.[333]

Comparative jurisprudence is a significant methodology that can serve as a bridge to traverse the seemingly irreconcilable concepts and conceptions prevalent in different jurisdictions, because it is anti-theoretical.[334] It can be used to wriggle out of the impasses that are usually encountered when negotiating model laws or conventions on jurisdiction and judgments. A practical example is reflected in the negotiations of the Judgments Convention. The Conference failed to arrive at an acceptable draft at its second attempt largely because of the EU-US divergences in juridical concepts and legal traditions.[335] However, the drafters were able to make significant progress by a mix-and-match approach, in arriving at an agreed

---

[329] Horatia Muir Watt, 'Globalization and Private International Law' in Jürgen Basedow and others (eds), *Encyclopedia of Private International Law* (Edward Elgar Publishing 2017) 849–50.

[330] Thomas Kadner Graziano, 'Is It Legitimate and Beneficial for Judges to Compare ?' in Mads Andenas and Duncan Fairgrieve (eds), *Courts and Comparative Law* (Oxford University Press 2015) 44; Zweigert and Siehr (n 288) 219.

[331] Graziano (n 330) 38–39.

[332] Lord Reed, 'Comparative Law in the Supreme Court of the United Kingdom' (Centre for Private Law, University of Edinburgh, 2017) <https://www.supremecourt.uk/docs/speech-171013.pdf> accessed 22 August 2018.

[333] Ibid (noting that jurisdictions sharing a common approach tend to be more attractive to each other as destinations for investment).

[334] Ralf Michaels, 'The Functional Method of Comparative Law' in Mathias Reimann and Reinhard Zimmermann (ed), *The Oxford Handbook of Comparative Law* (OUP 2006) 376.

[335] Ronald A Brand, 'Community Competence for Matters of Judicial Cooperation at the Hague Conference on Private International Law: A View from the United States' (2002) 21 *Journal of Law and Commerce* 191,197.

draft which was eventually adopted by the Diplomatic Conference in 2019. Ralf Michaels mentions that such theoretical divide was witnessed in the negotiations of the Hague Conventions on Evidence and Service. However, the Conference was able to wriggle out of the problem by relying on extensive comparative research on the issues.[336] The 2005 Hague Choice of Court Agreements Convention can be added to the list. This approach takes and blends ideas from the divergent legal traditions.

It is worth mentioning that this methodology plays some roles in the drafting process of the new CML as well. The Secretariat synchronises the developments in different Commonwealth countries and the works of the Hague Conference.[337] This brings the works of the Commonwealth closer to the Hague Conference and generally the emerging trends across the globe. Thus, it can be predicted that in the future, foreign judgments laws and practices will converge more. Subsequent chapters will be devoted to examining how this approach was used to arrive at the relevant texts of the HCCA, 2017 CML and the 2019 Judgments Convention.

While the main task is for the legislators to provide policy directions, there is a minor role for judges within the framework set out by the legislators and treaty-makers. First, judges also need a comparative methodology to achieve a harmonious interpretation of the model law or convention. Second, there may also be a need for some judicial intervention in addressing some gaps that might become apparent in the application of laws. A comparative approach is therefore inescapable. Judges must necessarily reach out to their counterpart in other jurisdictions. This will stimulate judicial cooperation across the globe and, through that medium, many emerging hurdles in the enforcement of foreign judgments can be cleared. Currently, this has delivered several bilateral court-to-court agreements on foreign judgments enforcement,[338] favourable treatment of foreign judicial requests, and recently an increasing number of States signing up to the court-to-court communications and co-operation in cross-border insolvency cases,[339] an initiative which was floated by the Chief Justice of Singapore.

Several other examples abound to justify why comparative inquiry can aid the interpretative functions of judges. In *Jiangsu Overseas Group Co Ltd v Reitman*,[340] the Israeli Supreme Court adopted a liberal interpretation of the reciprocity requirement of its law when it granted recognition to a Chinese judgment despite the absence of a treaty between the two States. The Court particularly emphasised the need to deepen mutual cooperation between Israeli and foreign judicial systems. It had earlier approved the recognition of a Russian judgment,[341] having

---

[336] Michaels (n 291) 419.

[337] Commonwealth Secretariat, 'Improving the Recognition of Foreign Judgments: Model Law on the Recognition and Enforcement of Foreign Judgments' (n 323) 546.

[338] For instance, see Singapore International Commercial Court (ch 2, fn 218).

[339] Steven Chong (ch 2, fn 138) 7–9.

[340] Cited in Zhang (n 295) 524.

[341] *Gazprom Transgaz Ochta Ltd v Double K Oil Products 1996 Ltd*, DCC 30752-05-11, Tel Aviv District Court, cited in Elbalti (ch 2, fn 135) 195.

considered the developments in Russian case law. Comparative analysis played a crucial role in moving the Court to interpret reciprocity to mean a reasonable potential of enforcement by a foreign court. In *Züblin International GmbH v Wuxi Woke General Engineering Rubber Co Ltd*,[342] a German court embarked on a similar exercise and also adopted a liberal interpretation of reciprocity. Having considered the deadlock that might ensue if it followed a strict approach adopted by Chinese courts, the Court considered that it would be worthwhile to 'blink first', hoping that the Chinese courts would reciprocate the gesture in the future. The German and Israeli courts' comparative assessments assisted them in concluding that their judgments would be favourably treated in China and Russia respectively if they provided a precedent, thereby, breaking what could have potentially been an endless cycle of non-recognition. In a similar development, the Chief Justices of China and Singapore jointly signed the Nanning Declaration in June 2018, urging members of the China-ASEAN Justice Forum to adopt presumptive reciprocity for foreign judgments recognition and enforcement.[343]

The Canadian real and substantial connection test, which revolutionised Canadian judgments enforcement law, was influenced by the House of Lords decision in *Indyka v Indyka*[344] and the Court also noted similar developments in the United States and Europe.[345] Also, the UK Supreme Court has considered these developments in *Rubin v Eurofinance SA*,[346] but preferred that such a big jump be better taken by Parliament than the courts. The point being made is that comparative law helps the treaty-makers as much as it can help the judges in their limited role of interpreting the legislative policy behind judgments model laws and conventions. It will ensure that a harmonious global regime is achieved, particularly in these circumstances where there is no supranational court to oversee the development of the judgments model law and convention.

E. Empiricism

The hallmark of pragmatism is empiricism. A law properly so-called in a world driven by global economy is one that works. To know whether a law works in the real sense is to know how the law operates in practice and whether it is achieving the desired results. The legislators are generally responsible for law reforms. Several commentators have rightly argued that they are in a better position to do

---

[342] *German Züblin International Co Ltd v Wuxi Walker General Engineering Rubber Co Ltd*, Judgment of the Court of Appeal of Berlin 18 May 2006, Document Number 20 SCH 13/04, cited by Zhang (n 295) 523.
[343] Zheng Sophia Tang (n 152) 148.
[344] *Indyka v Indyka* [1966] 3 All ER 583. See also Vaughan Black, 'Enforcement of Foreign Non-Money Judgments: Pro Swing v. Elta' (2005) 81 *Canadian Business Law Journal* 81.
[345] H Patrick Glenn, 'Foreign Judgments, the Common Law and the Constitution: *De Savoye* v. *Morguard Investments Ltd*' (1992) 37 *McGill Law Journal* 537, 540.
[346] *Rubin and another v Eurofinance SA and others* [2012] All ER (D) 258.

so because they possess the wealth, skill, and diversity to discuss policies and other contemporary problems facing the application of laws. They are part of the society and might also have first-hand experience of some of these problems. They can constitute specialised groups to study the workability and suitability of the laws and deploy necessary funding to achieve the task. However, it is also a known fact that, often, they are more interested in heat-of-the-moment reactions than serious issues of evidenced-led law reform.[347]

As Lord Collins rightly observes in *Rubin*,[348] painstaking reforms are better carried out by the legislative bodies. This will enable the laws to be subjected to a thorough investigatory process which ensures that the stakeholders are carried along, empirical data are collected on the workings of the law and at the end, an objective truth about the practicalities of the laws is discovered. A classic example is the Heidelberg Report that was carried out on the efficacy of the Brussels I Regulation. In conducting that research, the views of judges, lawyers, notaries, bailiffs, relevant groups, economic operators, and individual citizens who are affected one way or the other by the Regulation were sought. The empirical work confirmed the assumption that the Brussels I Regulation was generally working fine,[349] and some areas that needed improvement were discovered. This formed the basis for the Brussels Ia. Today, the EU could be said to have the most effective judgments enforcement scheme owing to its empirical approach to law reforms. This approach is desirable for all judgments model laws and conventions.

VII. Conclusion

The value of legal rules lies in their ability to solve the everyday practical problems for which such rules were created in the first place. Rules must be reviewed periodically to respond to challenges of the time, since human society and the idiosyncrasies of its inhabitants are never static. To ensure a functional system, rules must organically grow to align with the society and the activities of its end users. Logically, a non-alignment of these variables will lead to a dysfunctional system.

In the years before globalisation, certain assumptions were presumed to be right and suitable for the needs of that time. Judicial reasoning was influenced by

---

[347] Christopher Forsyth, 'The Eclipse of Private International Law Principle? The Judicial Process, Interpretation and the Dominance of Legislation in the Modern Era' (2005) 1 *Journal of Private International Law* 93, 96. Some English authors are, however, opposed to legislative law reforms. For instance, Lord Wilberforce and Dr FA Mann thought that it would paralyse legal developments. See CGJ Morse, 'Making English Private International Law' in JJ Fawcett (ed), *Reform and Development of Private International Law: Essays in Honour of Sir Peter North* (Oxford University Press 2002) 286.

[348] [2012] All ER (D) 258. The Irish Supreme Court in *Re Flightlease (Ireland) Ltd (in Voluntary Liquidation)* [2012] IESC 12 shared a similar sentiment while noting that adopting the Canadian 'real and substantial connection' test would amount to judicial legislation.

[349] B Hess, T Pfeiffer and P Schlosser, 'Report on the Application of Regulation Brussels I in the Member States' (CF Müller 2007) 8.

the dominant political and intellectual ideologies. This was a period when nationalism and protectionism held sway. Certain legal systems were just evolving, and it was not unreasonable to be circumspect about their judgments. Generally, most national legal systems were not open to foreign ideas and influences. However, the reality on the ground has changed. Many of these concerns have been relegated to the background, if not totally vanished. Cosmopolitanism, the ease of doing business, and the movement of people and assets seamlessly across borders all demand that the legal theories built on the old assumptions be reconsidered.

The dominant legal theories on recognition and enforcement of foreign judgments – comity, obligation, reciprocity, *res judicata* – all have some practical benefits. One way or the other, they have contributed to the liberalisation of foreign judgments over the years, albeit, to different degrees. The major deficiency in the use of these theories is their application to legal problems without examining the results they produce. This blind application has stultified the liberalisation of judgments enforcement globally, resulted in hindrances to the growth of commerce and exchange of wealth, and produced injustice in some cases.

This deficiency calls for a new approach. The chapter suggests pragmatism as a better approach and goes further to examine how it can apply to foreign judgments. Since pragmatism, like other legal concepts, is susceptible to different meanings, it is imperative to clearly set out its content and context, particularly how it is best suited for recognition and enforcement of judgments. The chapter builds on existing works that have considered pragmatism as a theory of private international law. Beyond current frontiers, it identifies what aspect of pragmatism is suited for foreign judgments, offers some normative arguments, and sets out the substantive goals of a pragmatic judgments framework. It further identifies comparativism and empiricism as useful methodologies to pursue these goals.

The chapter argues that the tasks are better performed by legislators or treaty-makers following an extensive negotiation at a multilateral level. Legislative solutions provide a clear path for the courts to follow. The limited role for national judges is to ensure a harmonious interpretation and application of the law. The overall objective of the framework is to achieve conflicts justice, legal certainty and predictability of results. Since the existence of a foreign judgment presupposes that the underlying dispute between the parties had been determined by a foreign court, the legislators should be more interested in defining the propriety of the connection between a foreign court and a dispute, and the limited grounds upon which a court addressed may deny recognition.

Having set out what pragmatism in judgments recognition and enforcement entails, the substantive goals to be pursued and the method of delivering the framework, the subsequent chapters shall be devoted to examining the CML and the Hague Judgments Conventions from the perspective of the pragmatic model that has been developed in this chapter.

PART II

Commonwealth Model Law on the Recognition and Enforcement of Foreign Judgments

4

Foreign Judgments Enforcement in the Commonwealth

I. Introduction

The intra-Commonwealth judgments enforcement schemes have largely remained untouched in the vast majority of the Member States for nearly a century.[350] The schemes, which are largely a codification of the traditional common law, are one of the enduring legacies of the former British Empire. Some Commonwealth Member States, such as Singapore,[351] Belize[352] and Botswana,[353] which revised their judgments laws in recent times did not depart from the old regime in any significant way. The theoretical foundations of the schemes, which are based on the doctrines of obligation and reciprocity, have been widely criticised by academic writers and law reformers. The Commonwealth Secretariat undertook the task of reforming the CML as far back as the 1970s. Professor JD McClean did extensive work in this regard for the Secretariat.[354] However, the efforts yielded no positive result. A new impetus was received in 2005 when the Law Ministers charged the Secretariat with resuming work on a model law.[355] The painstaking efforts of the Secretariat led to the conclusion and adoption of the Model Law on the Recognition and Enforcement of Foreign Judgments (CML) by the Law Ministers in Nassau, The Bahamas in 2017.[356]

---

[350] The intra-Commonwealth judgments' enforcement schemes are modelled on the UK's Administration of Justice Act 1920 and Foreign Judgments (Recognition and Enforcement) Act 1933. The equivalents of these statutes apply to date in most Member States of the Commonwealth without any changes.

[351] Reciprocal Enforcement of Foreign Judgments Act (chapter 265) 2001 Revised Edition (Singapore) as amended in 2019. The amended Act retained reciprocity and the restrictive concept of international jurisdiction. Unlike the earlier revised version of the 2001 Act, non-money judgments are now enforceable by virtue of the 2019 amendment.

[352] Reciprocal Enforcement of Judgments Act (Revised Edition) 2000.

[353] Judgments (International Enforcement) Act 1981.

[354] McClean and Patchett (ch 1, fn 63).

[355] Commonwealth Secretariat, *2005 Meeting of Commonwealth Law Ministers and Senior Officials, Accra, Ghana, 17-20 October 2005* (The Commonwealth Secretariat 2006).

[356] See the introductory text to the CML, available at: <https://thecommonwealth.org/sites/default/files/key_reform_pdfs/D16227_1_GPD_ROL_Model_Law_Rec_Enf_Foreign_Judgements.pdf> accessed 20 December 2019.

This chapter examines the model law from the perspective of the pragmatic theory of judgments recognition and enforcement espoused in Chapter three. It assesses the Commonwealth as an institution, its unique nature and why the Secretariat settled for a model law and not other forms of harmonisation such as a convention. The chapter also considers the relationship and key differences between the extant laws and the CML and the key aspects of the CML such as international jurisdiction, grounds for denial of recognition, the abolition of reciprocity, and the recognition of non-money judgments amongst others. This chapter finds that the extant statutory frameworks available in the Commonwealth present many obstacles that hinder the recognition and enforcement of foreign judgments in the Commonwealth, and are also obsolete. It concludes that the extant frameworks are long overdue for reform.

II. The Commonwealth

A. Formation

The Commonwealth is a unique association. It started as 'the British Commonwealth of Nations' which was formed after a series of Imperial Conferences held between 1887 and 1926.[357] Its formation was not accidental. It could rather be described as a child of necessity. One of the lessons that Great Britain learnt from the American Revolution was the need to retain colonies' loyalty by granting them as much liberty as possible in the management of their internal affairs. It did not come as a surprise that one of the key recommendations of Lord Durham's Report on the Affairs of British North America, following the uprising in Lower and Upper Canada between 1837 and 1838 was the establishment of a 'responsible government' for the colonies.[358] Although a very controversial report, its recommendation on responsible government was upheld by the British Parliament. Self-governance or 'government by consent of the governed' became a cardinal policy of the British colonial government.

From 1839, Britain began the process of granting self-rule to her colonies. Ontario and other Canadian provinces became a British dominion. Australian and South African colonies followed suit. As more dominions were created, it was thought that there was a need to keep the imperial unity, the ties and friendship already existing among these dominions *inter se* and between them and the British Empire.[359] The British government constituted the self-governing dominions into federating units. Thus, the Dominion of Canada, the Commonwealth of Australia, the Dominion of New Zealand, the Union of South Africa, the Irish Free State, and

---

[357] Thomas M Leonard (ed), *Encyclopedia of the Developing World* (Routledge 2006) 373.
[358] Andrew Walker, *The Commonwealth: A New Look* (Pergamon Press 1978) 6; Leonard (n 357) 373.
[359] Leonard (n 357) 373–373.

Newfoundland unofficially became the States of the British Commonwealth.[360] In these circumstances, the British Commonwealth of Nations began with the British-descended dominions and was essentially Anglo-centric.[361] The status of the dominions and their relationship with the British Empire were, however, formalised under the Balfour Declaration of 1926 and the Statute of Westminster of 11 December 1931.[362] The status and relationship were defined thus:

> They are autonomous communities within the British Empire, equal in status, in no way subordinate to one another in any aspect of their domestic or external affairs, though united by a common allegiance to the Crown, and freely associated as members of the British Commonwealth of Nations.

The next three decades after the Statute of Westminster changed the character of the British Commonwealth of Nations. The Empire continued to shrink as more colonies began to demand self-rule or outright independence. This led to the independence of many States in Asia, Africa, and the Caribbean. With the entry of India, Pakistan, Nigeria, Ghana, Jamaica, Malaysia, Cameroon and so on, as newly independent sovereign States, the association lost its Anglo-centric status.[363] It could no longer be genuinely described as 'British' in the light of the admission of these new members.

Having transformed from the British Commonwealth of Nations to the Commonwealth in the early 1960s, it became necessary to further redefine the nature of the association and what role(s) it should play with the spatially and culturally diverse members. One of the first set of issues that confronted the Commonwealth was the definition of some of the phrases used in the Balfour Declaration such as 'common allegiance' and 'freely associated'. This is against the backdrop of the fact that the erstwhile British Commonwealth of Nations was more or less a platform, which was used to further the interests of the British Empire.[364] For instance, one of the policies of the pre-war British Commonwealth was that a declaration of war by Britain meant that all other Commonwealth members were automatically at war.[365] It became difficult to juxtapose how Commonwealth States could have an 'allegiance to the Crown' and yet, the institution be described as a 'free association'. What became of the new Commonwealth was that members were

---

[360] Walker, *The Commonwealth: A New Look* (n 358) 7.

[361] As rightly noted by Professor Wheare, a good number of the Dominions' population were not British. There were French populations in Canada, and majority non-British Europeans in the Union of South Africa. See Kenneth C Wheare, 'Is the British Commonwealth Withering Away?' (1950) 44 *The American Political Science Review* 545, 545–46.

[362] Statute of Westminster 1931 (c 4). The Statute granted legislative autonomy to the Dominions with a caveat that the British Parliament would not legislate for the Dominions except with their consent.

[363] Alan Watt, *The Evolution of Australian Foreign Policy: 1938–1965* (Cambridge University Press 1968) 269; William Dale, 'Is the Commonwealth an International Organisation?' (1982) 31 *International and Comparative Law Quarterly* 451; Walker, *The Commonwealth: A New Look* (n 358) 9–10.

[364] Krishnan Srinivasan, 'Nobody's Commonwealth? The Commonwealth in Britain's Post-Imperial Adjustment' (2006) 44 *Commonwealth & Comparative Politics* 257, 260.

[365] Donal K Coffey, 'The Right to Shoot Himself': Secession in the British Commonwealth of Nations' (2018) 39 *Journal of Legal History* 117, 125.

free to join and exit the association; to exclusively determine their foreign policies including the declaration of wars; and to recognise the 'King' as a symbol and head of the Commonwealth.[366] In this regard, Burma, Aden (Yemen) and Sudan opted not to join the Commonwealth after gaining independence.[367] Also, the Maldives[368] recently left the association voluntarily and returned in February 2020.

B. The Modern Commonwealth

Before the establishment of the Commonwealth Secretariat in 1965,[369] the association had no charter with any set objectives to be pursued. Some prominent members such as the United Kingdom, Canada and South Africa have consistently opposed suggestions aimed at formalising the association.[370] At some point, it was thought that a formal structure would cause frictions and, eventually, ill feelings amongst members of the Commonwealth and that this would undermine the ties and friendship they already enjoyed as a family. The Australian government had always felt otherwise and continued to push for the establishment of a structure, which could serve as a platform for consultation and cooperation amongst the Commonwealth States. The significance of the Australian request was underscored by Gordon Greenwood, who opined that 'without full and frank consultation, which does not necessarily imply a binding collective decision, the Commonwealth as an organization has little, if any meaning'.[371] The absence of such a formal structure and policy directive for the Commonwealth led to huge embarrassment and discontent amongst its members over the unilateral decision of the United Kingdom to invade the Suez Canal.

The post-Suez developments led to the establishment of the Commonwealth Secretariat in 1965. The formalisation of the association took it beyond just a family club to what could be regarded as a proper inter-governmental organisation. It was modelled, along the lines of the suggestion made by Gordon Greenwood in 1957, as a platform for consultation and cooperation where non-binding decisions are taken by consensus and communicated through a communiqué. Since the Secretariat came on board, the association has been transformed into an institution which pursues certain shared values and objectives for the Commonwealth as a whole.

---

[366] Zelman Cowen, 'The Contemporary Commonwealth: A General View' (1959) 13 *International Organization* 204, 205–6.

[367] William David McIntyre, *A Guide to the Contemporary Commonwealth* (Palgrave 2001) 22.

[368] See Commonwealth Secretariat, 'Maldives Becomes 54th Member of Commonwealth Family' <https://thecommonwealth.org/media/news/maldives-becomes-54th-member-commonwealth-family> accessed 31 May 2020.

[369] The Secretariat was established in 1965 following an agreed memorandum adopted at the 1965 Commonwealth Prime Ministers' Meeting. It was to serve as a coordinating platform for cooperation amongst members without any executive functions. See Peter Slinn, 'The Commonwealth and the Law' in James Mayall (ed), *The Contemporary Commonwealth: An Assessment 1965–2009* (Routledge 2010) 28.

[370] McIntyre (n 367) 21; Walker, *The Commonwealth: A New Look* (n 358) 13.

[371] Gordon Greenwood, 'Australia's Triangular Foreign Policy' (1957) 35 *Foreign Affairs* 689, 699.

Today, the Commonwealth is a voluntary association of 54 sovereign States from every continent of the world, with Rwanda being its latest member. It continues to pride itself on being an association with great diversity and global reach. This also confirms the paradigm shift from the old Commonwealth, which was regarded as a vehicle of former British colonies. The Commonwealth remains a unique and important association with a population of about 2.4 billion people.[372] It is also the world's oldest political association of sovereign States.[373] It has two G7 and three OECD members and some high-ranking developing countries such as Nigeria, Malaysia and South Africa amongst others.[374]

A strategic focus for the association was laid out in 1971 at the Singapore Heads of Government Meeting. The meeting came up with the 1971 Declaration of Commonwealth Principles.[375] These principles stipulated the goals and objectives of the Commonwealth and its consensual working method. They have been reaffirmed in various subsequent declarations and communiqués. They were also reproduced in the Charter of the Commonwealth signed by Queen Elizabeth, the Head of the Commonwealth in 2013.[376] The new Commonwealth, as envisioned, is to be an association of friendship, consultation and cooperation that shall strive to achieve democracy, peace and the pursuit of economic development amongst its Member States.

The Commonwealth has shown more interest in trade and development since the turn of this millennium. This may not be unconnected with the advent of globalisation, and the potential therein for attracting foreign direct investment (FDI) and stimulating growth and development, especially for the developing and least developed States which constitute most of the Commonwealth. The association has come to realise that the prosperity of its Member States lies in pushing the intra-Commonwealth trade frontiers forward. This point is consistently stressed in the communiqués issued from the various Ministerial meetings.[377] The 'Commonwealth advantage'[378] is the new catchphrase in recent Commonwealth Trade Reviews. Some

---

[372] Commonwealth Secretariat, *Commonwealth Trade Review 2018: Strengthening the Commonwealth Advantage* (The Commonwealth Secretariat 2018) 41.

[373] House of Commons Foreign Affairs Committee, *The Role and Future of the Commonwealth: Fourth Report of Session 2012–13* (The Stationery Office Limited 2012) 13.

[374] Amitav Banerji, 'The Commonwealth of Nations: A Force for Democracy in the 21st Century?' (2009) 97 *The Round Table* 813, 814.

[375] Commonwealth Secretariat, 'Singapore Declaration of Commonwealth Principles 1971' <http://thecommonwealth.org/sites/default/files/history-items/documents/Singapore Declaration.pdf> accessed 26 February 2019.

[376] Commonwealth Secretariat, 'Charter of the Commonwealth' (2013) <https://thecommonwealth.org/about-us/charter>.

[377] Commonwealth Secretariat, 'Declaration on the Commonwealth Connectivity Agenda for Trade and Investment' (2018): <https://www.chogm2018.org.uk/sites/default/files/DeclarationontheCommonwealthConnectivityAgendaforTradeandInvestment%20pdf.pdf>.

[378] The Commonwealth advantage represents the shared history of its members, the common language and familiar legal and administrative mechanisms and procedures. Secretariat, *Commonwealth Trade Review 2018: Strengthening the Commonwealth Advantage* (n 372) 65; House of Commons Foreign Affairs Committee (n 373) Ev 31.

Commonwealth States are amongst the fastest growing economies and thus, major destinations for investment.[379] The Commonwealth's contribution to global production has increased. Intra-Commonwealth trade continues to show a positive outlook. There are concerted efforts to further explore the 'Commonwealth advantage' in boosting intra-Commonwealth trade because of the ongoing political and economic uncertainty that may be brought by *Brexit* and the suggestion of an imminent global trade war between the leading economies of the world.

Private international law has a role to play in facilitating intra-Commonwealth trade, investment and exchange of goods and services. There is a plethora of scholarly literature that seeks to explain the relationship between efficient legal institutions and frameworks, and growth in cross-border trade.[380] Businesspersons tend to patronise jurisdictions that support businesses and those that guarantee efficient enforcement schemes. They are interested in a wide range of issues, like to what extent they can freely determine the jurisdiction to litigate and the law that applies to their contract; whether the legal system has good preservative measures in support of actions; whether there would be any hurdles in enforcing judgments, amongst others. More gains are likely to be derived where several jurisdictions have largely harmonised legal regimes, because investors need not worry about the cost of modifying their investment plans to suit the law of every target State.[381] In these circumstances, the Commonwealth has made significant efforts in the harmonisation of some aspects of its private international law such as recognition and enforcement of foreign judgments. The 2017 model law is a modest project, which the Commonwealth is committed to implementing to deepen the Commonwealth advantage and foster trade and developments both within and outside the Commonwealth. The Commonwealth is expected to receive a boost in the progressive development of its private international law as the United Kingdom hopefully gives more priority to the Commonwealth post-*Brexit*.

III. Civil Justice and Cooperation in the Commonwealth

One of the aspects of the Commonwealth advantage is the familiar legal culture and administrative machinery amongst the vast majority of Member States.

---

[379] House of Commons Foreign Affairs Committee (n 373).

[380] OECD, 'Better Civil Justice Systems Can Boost Investment, Competition, Innovation and Growth' (2013): <http://www.oecd.org/economy/betterciviljusticesystemscanboostinvestmentcompetitioninnovation andgrowthoecdsays.htm> accessed 27 February 2019; World Bank Group, 'Enforcing Contracts' <http://www.doingbusiness.org/en/data/exploretopics/enforcing-contracts/why-matters> accessed 27 February 2019; Lorenzo Bini Smaghi, 'Legal System and Financial Markets', *Legal issues related to the financial markets* (26 October 2007): <https://www.ecb.europa.eu/press/key/date/2007/html/sp071026.en.html> accessed 27 February 2019.

[381] Secretariat, *Commonwealth Trade Review 2018: Strengthening the Commonwealth Advantage* (n 372) 64; House of Commons Foreign Affairs Committee (n 373) 67.

A cardinal policy of British colonial rule was the extension of the English common law, doctrines of equity and statutes of general application, to the colonies. To date, these laws still apply in several Member States subject to local variations from time to time. The Privy Council, sitting in London, remains the apex court for about 13 Commonwealth States and other British Overseas Territories.[382] The UK Supreme Court which is made up of largely the same judges as the Privy Council still enjoys the privilege of a 'head prefect' because most common law judiciaries are usually persuaded or influenced by its decisions.

The relationship between Commonwealth Member States and the UK was largely asymmetric. From trade to politics and beyond, everyone looked in its direction for guidance. It maintained a direct relationship with each member, often stronger than how members related to one another. Before the creation of the Commonwealth Secretariat and the opening of the Commonwealth to all sovereign States, there seemed to be not much formal discussion about intra-Commonwealth civil and judicial cooperation. The colonial government usually legislated for the colonies in some subject matters. The ultimate legal authority was vested in the Crown and such powers were exercised on its behalf by its assigns in the respective colonies.[383] The UK Parliament could make laws directly for the colonies or extend the application of some laws to them. Such was the case of the Administration of Justice Act 1920, which could be described as the first uniform law on judgments recognition and enforcement in the Commonwealth. This piece of legislation was reproduced in most colonies. It enabled a simpler framework for registration of foreign judgments between the United Kingdom and each colony on the one hand, and among willing dominions. Similar reasons necessitated the Foreign Judgments (Reciprocal Enforcement) Act 1933, though with a broader objective of facilitating trade relationships with the neighbouring European States.[384] The same Act was replicated in most of the colonies and often continues to apply.[385]

The need for a conscious and symmetric legal cooperation within the Commonwealth began after the independence of former British colonies. For obvious reasons, each State needed to grow according to its needs and circumstances. As independent sovereigns, they were no longer bound by legal developments in the UK. It must be added that many of the new members have diverse legal backgrounds distinct from the common law. The legal system in some Asian countries such as India, Brunei, Maldives, Pakistan, Bangladesh, and Sri Lanka are to a greater or lesser extent influenced by Islamic, Buddhist and Hindu laws. Those in the South African region such as South Africa, Botswana and Zimbabwe are of Roman-Dutch origin. Cameroon, Malta, and Seychelles display more features of

---

[382] House of Commons Library, 'The Privy Council' (*Briefing Paper: Number CBP7460*, 8 February 2016).
[383] BO Nwabueze, *A Constitutional History of Nigeria* (C Hurst 1982) 32–35.
[384] House of Lords, Foreign Judgments (Reciprocal Enforcement) Bill 1933 (Hansard 14 February 1933).
[385] See Table 2 below.

civil law or at best are a combination of civil and common law traditions.[386] In the same vein, some of the members have nothing in common or any shared agenda other than being former British colonies. The majority of the Commonwealth States are small States[387] with less sophisticated legal infrastructures compared to what obtains in jurisdictions like the United Kingdom, Canada, and Australia. The constitutional structure of the Member States differs as well. Some have constitutional or absolute monarchies[388] while others are republics. The Commonwealth Law Ministers noted these diverse national peculiarities while commending the Secretariat on the new model law.[389] In the absence of any concerted efforts to address this legal diversity, the only reasonable conclusion is that it would be difficult to have any harmonised legal regime on important matters that affect international trade and development within the Commonwealth.

Since 1966, the Secretariat, through its legal section, has provided a platform for Commonwealth Member States to discuss legal developments within the Commonwealth and ways to deliver effective legal regimes that would support cross-border trade and commerce. Some work was done in the late' 70s on intra-Commonwealth arrangements in the fields of service of process, recognition of grants of administration, the enforcement of maintenance orders and money judgements.[390] Little success was achieved, perhaps due to the absence of political will on the part of the Secretariat and Member States. With the signing of the Commonwealth Charter, there was a perceived impetus on the part of the Secretariat and Member States to push for serious law reforms.

In 2017, the Office of Civil and Criminal Justice Reform (OCCJR) was established to facilitate these reforms. Its major responsibility is to 'make available good legislative practice from across the Commonwealth through model laws, standards, templates, legal insight and legal networks.'[391] Harmonisation through model laws is a step in the right direction for the Commonwealth States. Some degree of

---

[386] See Jacques Du Plessis, 'Comparative Law and the Study of Mixed Legal Systems' in Mathias Reimann and Reinhard Zimmermann (eds), *The Oxford Handbook of Comparative Law* (1st edn, OUP 2006) 483–87; Vernon Valentine Palmer (ed), *Mixed Jurisdictions Worldwide: The Third Legal Family* (2nd edn, Cambridge University Press 2012) 25–26.

[387] 31 of the 54 Member States are small States with a population of 1.5 million people or less. See Commonwealth Secretariat, 'Small States and the Commonwealth: Strengthening Resilience for Sustainable Development' (2014).

[388] The United Kingdom, Brunei, Lesotho, Malaysia, Eswatini (Swaziland) and Tonga.

[389] Commonwealth Secretariat, 'Meeting of Commonwealth Law Ministers and Senior Officials: Outcome Statement' (16-19 October 2017, Nassau, The Bahamas).

[390] Commonwealth Secretariat, *Recognition and Enforcement of Judgments and Orders and the Service of Process within the Commonwealth: A Report of a Working Meeting Held at Apia, Western Samoa, 18–23 April 1979* (Commonwealth Secretariat 1979); Commonwealth Secretariat, 'Recognition and Enforcement of Judgments and Orders and the Service of Process within the Commonwealth – Multiple Damages Judgments: LMM(80)24' in *1980 Meeting of Commonwealth Law Ministers: Barbados, 28 April–2 May 1980: Memoranda* (Commonwealth Secretariat 1980).

[391] Commonwealth Secretariat, 'Praise for Commonwealth's New "Momentous" Justice Reform Office' (*News*, 2017) <https://thecommonwealth.org/media/news/praise-commonwealths-new-momentous-justice-reform-office>.

certainty arising from similarities in the laws of Member States, a common and efficient intra-Commonwealth enforcement mechanism will encourage cross-border trade and commerce within and beyond the Commonwealth bloc.[392] Further evidence can be adduced from the latest Commonwealth Strategic Plan where the Secretariat asserts that a common legal system, amongst other benefits, costs Member States 19 per cent less compared to trade deals with other countries' pairings.[393] Also, model laws allow States to integrate internationally-shared commitments into local legislation while accommodating domestic concerns where necessary. It is easier to negotiate model laws compared with conventions because of the flexibilities they offer.

In furtherance of the above-mentioned objective, the Secretariat has reviewed several outdated laws, including that of foreign judgments recognition and enforcement, in order to keep pace with developments in the world. Nevertheless, one cannot deny the fact that in the absence of a strong political will and effective coordination from the Commonwealth Secretariat, the model law may just remain a model law without implementation by Member States. Apart from Canada, Singapore, South Africa, New Zealand, Australia, and the United Kingdom,[394] which have active law reform agencies, other Member States rarely take an interest in the progressive development of private international law.[395]

IV. The 1920 and 1933 Statutory Schemes

A. From Common Law to Administration of Justice Act 1920 (AJA)

The traditional common law of judgments recognition and enforcement could be said to be pragmatic to some extent. At a time when many legal systems were hostile to foreign judgments, common law judges had formulated rules which were predicated on justice, fairness, and efficiency. They were able to achieve

---

[392] HM Government, 'Review of the Balance of Competences between the United Kingdom and the European Union Civil Judicial Cooperation' (2014), 55: <https://assets.publishing.service.gov.uk/government/uploads/system/uploads/attachment_data/file/279228/civil-judicial-cooperation-report-review-of-balance-of-competences.pdf> accessed 3 November 2018.

[393] Commonwealth Secretariat, *Commonwealth Secretariat Strategic Plan: 2017/18–2020/21* (Commonwealth Secretariat 2017) 2.

[394] Some of these law reform agencies have recently carried out some work on judgments recognition and enforcement. See eg Singapore Academy of Law, 'Report of the Law Reform Committee on Enforcement of Foreign Judgments' (July 2005); South African Law Reform Commission, 'Report: Consolidated Legislation Pertaining to International Judicial Co-operation in Civil Matters' (December 2006).

[395] For instance, the Nigerian legislators and the Justice Minister have been nonchalant towards the country's convoluted statutory registration scheme despite several Supreme Court decisions on the subject matter. See generally Abubakri Yekini, 'Foreign Judgments in Nigerian Courts in the Last Decade: A Dawn of Liberalization' (2017) 2 *Nederlands Internationaal Privaatrecht* 205.

this through the doctrines of international comity and *res judicata*. In the early part of the nineteenth century, the doctrine of obligation replaced international comity. The basic rule, until now, has been that all money judgments are enforceable provided the foreign court had international jurisdiction and natural justice and due process were observed. Although this is a seemingly straightforward legal framework, it has its weaknesses.

Judicial transnationalism and the inter-governmental 'cooperative dimension' to judgments enforcement have their pedigree in English law.[396] As far back as 1801, the UK Parliament passed the Crown Debts Act for the 'speedy and effectual' enforcement of debts due to the Crown as adjudged by the English and Irish courts through a simple registration procedure. By 1868, the Judgment Extension Act legislated for a similar framework to cover judgments from the superior courts in other parts of the United Kingdom.[397] The first attempt to devise a more pragmatic judgments enforcement law in the Commonwealth was made in 1920 when the United Kingdom passed the Administration of Justice Act 1920 (AJA). The Act was extended to the colonies and other British Overseas Territories. Cross-border cooperation in judgments enforcement has always been motivated by the need to facilitate smooth transnational trade. The AJA came to be as a result of several complaints from colonial trading companies who could not collect judgments against debtors because the latter usually ran away to foreign lands thereby becoming judgment-proof.[398] It was considered that the registration system, which already existed in the United Kingdom, should be extended to the colonies. Thus, Part II (reciprocal enforcement of foreign judgments) of the AJA was replicated throughout the British colonies to facilitate enforcement of judgments between the United Kingdom and the colonies.

B. From AJA to Foreign Judgments (Reciprocal Enforcement) Act 1933

The process leading to the AJA was similar to that which led to the enactment of the Foreign Judgments (Reciprocal Enforcement) Act 1933. This is another piece of legislation that is widely adopted throughout the Commonwealth. The pragmatism of the AJA brought about an efficient judgments enforcement regime among the reciprocating States. The success story is captured in the Lord Chancellor's remark while moving for the adoption of the Bill thus: '[t]here has now been an experience of the working of these reciprocal arrangements over a period of more than ten years – it is believed with universal satisfaction'.[399] The case was made

---

[396] Olusoji Elias, *Judicial Remedies in the Conflict of Laws* (Hart Publishing 2001) 54.

[397] Trevor C Hartley, *International Commercial Litigation: Text, Cases, and Materials on Private International Law* (Cambridge University Press 2009) 361.

[398] Richard Frimpong Oppong, 'Recognition and Enforcement of Foreign Judgments in Ghana: A Second Look at a Colonial Inheritance' (2005) 31 *Commonwealth Law Bulletin* 19, 20.

[399] House of Lords, Foreign Judgments (Reciprocal Enforcement) Bill 1933 (Hansard 14 February 1933).

for a similarly simple and faster judgments enforcement procedure between the United Kingdom and other key trading partners outside the Commonwealth.

The two Acts are similar but not the same. An examination of their key differences is not necessary here because they have been addressed by several writers;[400] more so, a new model law, which will hopefully replace these Acts in the Commonwealth, has been concluded. Be that as it may, they represent earlier successful pragmatic attempts at producing a judgments enforcement scheme that promotes justice and efficiency.

C. Current Status of the Reciprocal Regime in the Commonwealth

Having noted the pragmatism of the 1920 and 1933 Acts, it must be added that the efficiency of the schemes has been weakened by other factors. The first problem is that these laws stayed in force too long before they were considered for review in some Member States and in the Commonwealth as a whole. The obvious result is that the laws are not addressing modern challenges. One of the inadequacies in the schemes is the reference to judgments from a 'superior court'. Many countries no longer pay any serious attention to this historical classification. For the sake of efficiency, the monetary jurisdiction of lower courts has been increased so that the high courts can deal with more substantial and complex matters. With the extant laws in most jurisdictions, judgments from magistrates' courts or other lower courts nevertheless cannot be enforced by registration even among reciprocating States. For instance, in *Su'a v Imex Company Ltd*,[401] a Samoan court set aside the registration of a judgment from a district court of New Zealand because it was regarded as an inferior court. This is notwithstanding that the applicant took the said judgment back to New Zealand to have it endorsed and re-issued with a certificate of judgment signed by a Deputy Registrar of the High Court of New Zealand.

The absence of any collective review has led to wider divergences in the foreign judgments laws and practices in the Commonwealth. This leads to greater uncertainty and unpredictability of the judgments recognition and enforcement, with attendant costs for litigants. In States such as Vanuatu and Nauru, a registration scheme is not available to any foreign judgment including those from the Commonwealth.[402] Australia and Kenya have enacted modern legislation with some changes from the 1920/1933 statutes, while Canada is developing broad autonomous private international law rules on recognition and enforcement.

---

[400] Adewale A Olawoyin, 'Enforcement of Foreign Judgments in Nigeria: Statutory Dualism and Disharmony of Laws' (2014) 10 *Journal of Private International Law* 129; Richard Frimpong Oppong (ch 1, fn 64).

[401] *Su'a v Imex Company Ltd* [2004] WSSC 6.

[402] For Vanuatu, see *Naylor v Kilham* [1999] VUSC 11 (SC); *In Re the Foreign Judgment (Reciprocal Enforcement) Ordinance* [1997] VUSC 2. Nauru has a Foreign Judgments (Reciprocal Enforcement) Act 1973 but the Act has not been extended to any country.

The dualist/multiple regimes prevalent in many Member States have also contributed to the problems in judgments enforcement laws in the Commonwealth.

The reciprocity regime has produced a negative result in the Commonwealth. It is unthinkable that despite the much talked about 'Commonwealth factor' or 'Commonwealth advantage' judgments from many Member States are not registrable in other parts of the Commonwealth. Apart from the United Kingdom, New Zealand, Grenada and Uganda, which have extended the reciprocal statutes to most or all of the Commonwealth countries, reciprocity practice for other States suggests that it only follows colonial and, in some cases, close geographical connections.[403] It is surprising to see that some States with substantial trading interests do not have any reciprocal arrangement in place for judgment registration. For instance, in Nigeria's Q4 2018 Foreign Trade in Goods Report, India, South Africa and Canada were leading export destinations for Nigeria.[404] Yet, none of its judgments statutes has been extended to these countries.

Table 2 List of Commonwealth States, the extant judgments legislation, and reciprocating States

S/N	State	Statute(s)	Commonwealth State extended to[405]
1	Antigua & Barbuda	The Reciprocal Enforcement of Judgments Act 1922	United Kingdom, Grenada, St. Vincent, Guyana, Trinidad, Antigua, St Kitts & Nevis, St Lucia, Jamaica, The Bahamas, Nigeria, Australia (New South Wales)
2	Australia	Foreign Judgments Act 1991 The Trans-Tasman Proceedings Act 2010	United Kingdom, Western Samoa, Tuvalu, Tonga, Solomon Islands, Sri Lanka, Singapore, Seychelles, St Vincent & the Grenadines, St Kitts & Nevis, Papua New Guinea, Malawi, Grenada, Fiji, Dominica, The Bahamas, New Zealand, Canada (Provinces of Manitoba, British Columbia, and Alberta)

(continued)

---

[403] See Table 1 in Chapter 3 above.

[404] National Bureau of Statistics, 'Foreign Trade in Goods Statistics (Q4 2018)', <https://www.nigerianstat.gov.ng/download/900> (accessed 11 March 2019).

[405] The list was compiled from both primary and secondary sources. Most Member States' statutes and statutory instruments are accessible online. Few others were gathered or confirmed from recent scholarly works from academic writers and practitioners. These secondary sources include: Thomas H Reynolds, *Foreign Law Guide* (Brill 2000); Richard Frimpong Oppong (ch 1, fn 64); Mandi Rossouw, *The Harmonisation of Rules on the Recognition and Enforcement of Foreign Judgments in the Southern African Customs Union* (Pretoria University Law Press 2016); Lawrence W Newman (ed), *Enforcement of Money Judgments* (Juris Publishing LLC 2000); Thomson Reuters Practical Law (online).

Table 2 *(continued)*

S/N	State	Statute(s)	Commonwealth State extended to
3	Bangladesh	Code of Civil Procedure, 1908	United Kingdom, Pakistan, Fiji, Singapore, New Zealand, Western Samoa, Australia (Australian Capital Territory and Northern Territory of Australia)
4	Barbados	Foreign and Commonwealth Judgments (Reciprocal Enforcement) Act 1922	United Kingdom, Grenada, St Vincent, Guyana, Trinidad, Antigua, St Kitts & Nevis, St Lucia, Jamaica, The Bahamas, Nigeria, Australia (New South Wales)
5	Botswana	Judgments (International Enforcement) Act 1981	United Kingdom (Maintenance Orders Only) Lesotho, Swaziland Zambia, Zimbabwe, South Africa, Malawi, Uganda, India, Pakistan, Australia, New Zealand, Kenya
6	Brunei	Reciprocal Enforcement of Foreign Judgments Act 1996	Malaysia, Singapore
7	Belize	Reciprocal Enforcement of Judgments Act 1922	United Kingdom, The Bahamas, Barbados Antigua & Barbuda, St Kitts & Nevis, Jamaica, Nigeria, Australia
8	Cameroon	Law No 2007/001 of 19 April 2007	None[406]
9	Canada	Various Acts domesticating the UK-Canada judgments treaty	United Kingdom[407]

(continued)

---

[406] *Exequatur* applies under this law. This is a proceeding which enables a court addressed to determine if a foreign judgment is enforceable. It is a common practice in civil law jurisdictions. Reciprocity is one of the factors that is often considered in an *exequatur* proceeding. *Exequatur* proceedings also apply in Rwanda and Mozambique.

[407] Each Canadian province has a reciprocal enforcement statute for inter-provincial judgments and judgments from the United Kingdom. Few provinces extend their statutes to Australia. However, Saskatchewan and Quebec do not require reciprocity.

Table 2 *(continued)*

S/N	State	Statute(s)	Commonwealth State extended to
10	Cyprus	The Reciprocal Execution of certain Judgments of the Commonwealth Countries Law, 130(I) of 2000. The Decisions of Foreign Courts (Recognition, Registration and Enforcement) Act of 2000 (Law No 121(1)/2000) Civil Procedure (Reciprocal Enforcement of Judgments) Law 1921	United Kingdom, Grenada, Australia (New South Wales)
11	Dominica	Commonwealth Judgments (Reciprocal Enforcement) Act 1922 Foreign Judgments (Reciprocal Enforcement) Act, Chapter 4:72, 1959	United Kingdom, Bahamas, Barbados, Belize, Grenada, Guyana, Jamaica, St Lucia, St Vincent & Grenadines, Trinidad & Tobago, Nigeria, India, Canada, Australia, Singapore
12	Fiji	Foreign Judgments (Reciprocal Enforcement) Act (1935)	United Kingdom, India, Tonga, Papua New Guinea, Australia
13	Ghana	The Courts Act 1993 (Act 459)	United Kingdom
14	Grenada	Foreign Judgments (Reciprocal Enforcement) Act 1958	United Kingdom, Antigua & Barbuda, Kiribati, Sierra Leone, Australia, Lesotho, Singapore, The Bahamas, Malawi, Solomon Islands, Bangladesh, Malaysia, Sri Lanka, Barbados, Maldives, Swaziland, Belize, Malta, Tanzania, Botswana, Mauritius, Tonga, Brunei, Namibia, Trinidad & Tobago, Canada, Nauru, Tuvalu, Cyprus, New Zealand, Uganda, Dominica, Nigeria, The Gambia, Pakistan, Vanuatu, Ghana, Papua New Guinea, Western Samoa, Guyana, St Kitts & Nevis, Zambia, India, St Lucia, Jamaica, St Vincent & The Grenadines, Kenya, Seychelles

(continued)

Table 2 *(continued)*

S/N	State	Statute(s)	Commonwealth State extended to
15	Guyana	Judgments Extension Act, Cap 27, 1953 Foreign Judgments (Reciprocal Enforcement) Act 1961	United Kingdom, Trinidad & Tobago, Grenada, St Lucia, Barbados, Antigua & Barbuda, St Kitts & Nevis, Belize, Jamaica, St Vincent, The Bahamas, Australia (New South Wales), Nigeria
16	India	Code of Civil Procedure, 1908	Bangladesh, Malaysia; Fiji, New Zealand; Western Samoa; Papua New Guinea; Singapore; Trinidad & Tobago; United Kingdom, Australia (Victoria), Canada (Ontario)
17	Jamaica	The Judgments and Awards (Reciprocal Enforcement) Act of 1923 The Judgments (Foreign) (Reciprocal Enforcement) Act of 1936	United Kingdom[408]
18	Kenya	Foreign Judgments (Reciprocal Enforcement) Act (2012)	United Kingdom, Australia, Malawi, Seychelles, Tanzania, Uganda, Zambia, Rwanda
19	Kiribati	Foreign Judgments (Reciprocal Enforcement) Ordinance (1965)	United Kingdom, Papua New Guinea
20	Lesotho	Reciprocal Enforcement of Judgments Proclamation No 2 of 1922	United Kingdom, Swaziland, Zambia, Tanzania, Malawi, Kenya, Uganda, New Zealand, Australia
21	Malawi	British and Colonial Judgments Act 1922 Service of Process and Execution of Judgments Act 1956	United Kingdom, Kenya, Uganda, Tanzania, Zambia

(continued)

---

[408] Other countries to which the Judgments and Awards (Reciprocal Enforcement) Act of 1923 was extended are not accessible.

Table 2 *(continued)*

S/N	State	Statute(s)	Commonwealth State extended to
22	Malaysia	Reciprocal Enforcement of Judgments Act 1958	United Kingdom, Singapore, New Zealand, Sri Lanka, India, Brunei Darussalam
23	Malta	The British Judgments (Reciprocal Enforcement) Act 1924	United Kingdom, Australia (New South Wales, Western Australia and Victoria)
24	Mauritius	The Foreign Judgments (Reciprocal Enforcement) Act 1961 The Reciprocal Enforcement of Judgments Act 1923	United Kingdom[409]
25	Mozambique	Code of Civil Procedure 1966	None
26	Namibia	Enforcement of Foreign Civil Judgments Act No 28 of 1994	South Africa
27	Nauru	Foreign Judgments (Reciprocal Enforcement) Act 1973	None
28	New Zealand	Trans-Tasman Proceedings Act 2010. Reciprocal Enforcement of Judgments Act 1934	Antigua & Barbuda, Australia, Bahamas, Bangladesh, Barbados, Belize, Botswana, Canada, Cameroon, Cyprus, Dominica, Fiji, Gambia, Ghana, Grenada, Guyana, India, Jamaica, Kenya, Kiribati, Lesotho, Malawi, Malaysia, Malta, Mauritius, Nauru, Nigeria, Pakistan, Papua New Guinea, Seychelles, Sierra Leone, Singapore, Solomon Islands, Sri Lanka, St Lucia, St Vincent & the Grenadines, Swaziland, Tanzania, Tonga, Trinidad & Tobago, Tuvalu, Uganda, United Kingdom, Vanuatu, Western Samoa, Zambia

(continued)

---

[409] Others are inaccessible.

Table 2 *(continued)*

S/N	State	Statute(s)	Commonwealth State extended to
29	Nigeria	The Reciprocal Enforcement of Foreign Judgments Ordinance, 1922 The Foreign Judgment (Reciprocal Enforcement) Act, 1961	United Kingdom, Ghana, Sierra Leone, The Gambia, Barbados, Guyana, Grenada, Jamaica, Antigua and Barbuda, St Kitts & Nevis, St Lucia, St Vincent, Trinidad & Tobago, Canada (Newfoundland), Australia (New South Wales and Victoria)
30	Pakistan	Civil Procedure Code,1 1908	United Kingdom, Bangladesh, Fiji, Singapore, Australia (the Australian Capital Territory, the Northern Territory of Australia), New Zealand, Western Samoa
31	Papua New Guinea	Reciprocal Enforcement of Judgments Act 1976	Australia, Bahamas, Fiji, Grenada, India, Kenya, Malaysia, Canada (Manitoba), New Zealand, Niue, Pakistan, Sierra Leone, Singapore, St Lucia, Tonga, Trinidad & Tobago, United Kingdom, Western Samoa
32	Rwanda	Code of Civil Procedure 2012	None
33	Western Samoa	Reciprocal Enforcement of Judgments Act 1970	New Zealand, Australia (Western Australia)
34	Seychelles	Foreign Judgments (Reciprocal Enforcement) Act 1961 Reciprocal enforcement of British Judgments Act 1922	United Kingdom, Kenya, Australia, and all countries which recognise the Queen of England as the Head
35	Sierra Leone	Foreign Judgments (Reciprocal Enforcement) Act 1935	United Kingdom, Nigeria and the Gambia
36	Singapore	Reciprocal Enforcement of Commonwealth Judgments Act, 1985 Reciprocal Enforcement of Foreign Judgments (Amendment) Act 2019	United Kingdom, Malaysia, Brunei Darussalam, Pakistan, Sri Lanka, India (except the state of Jammu & Kashmir), Australia, New Zealand, Papua New Guinea

(continued)

Table 2 *(continued)*

S/N	State	Statute(s)	Commonwealth State extended to
37	Solomon Islands	Foreign Judgments (Reciprocal Enforcement) Act 1988	Papua New Guinea, Australia.[410]
38	South Africa	Enforcement of Foreign Civil Judgments Act 32 of 1988	Namibia
39	Sri Lanka	Enforcement of Foreign Judgments Ordinance No. 4 of 1937 Reciprocal Enforcement of Judgments Ordinance No 41 of 1921	United Kingdom, Mauritius, Australia, Tanzania, Uganda, Malaysia New Zealand, Western Samoa
40	St Christopher & Nevis	Foreign Judgments (Reciprocal Enforcement) Act 8 of 1969 Reciprocal Enforcement of Judgments Act 1922	United Kingdom, The Bahamas, Barbados, Belize, Bermuda, Trinidad & Tobago, Guyana, St Lucia, St Vincent, Grenada, Jamaica, Nigeria, Australia (New South Wales)
41	St Lucia	Enforcement of Foreign Judgments Act 1991	Unavailable
42	St Vincent & the Grenadines	The Foreign Judgments (Reciprocal Enforcement) Act, 1958 The Commonwealth Countries Judgments Enforcement Act, 1988	United Kingdom, Singapore, The Bahamas, Barbados, Belize, Grenada, Guyana, Jamaica, St Lucia, St Vincent, Trinidad & Tobago, Nigeria, India, Canada, Australia, Singapore
43	Swaziland (Kingdom of e-Swatini)	Reciprocal Enforcement of Judgments Act No 4 of 1922	United Kingdom, Lesotho, Botswana, Zambia, Zanzibar, Malawi, Kenya, New Zealand, Tanzania, Uganda, Australia (Western Australia, New South Wales, Victoria, Territory of North Australia, and the Territory of Southern Australia)
44	Tanzania	Reciprocal Enforcement of Foreign Judgment Act No 8 [Re 2002] Judgments Extension Act Cap 7 [Re 2002]	United Kingdom, Lesotho, Botswana, Sri Lanka, Mauritius, Australia (New South Wales), Zambia, Seychelles, Swaziland, Kenya, Uganda, Malawi

(continued)

[410] The statute was extended to 'Courts of Commonwealth'. Unfortunately, this is not clear, as 'Courts of Commonwealth' was not defined.

Table 2 *(continued)*

S/N	State	Statute(s)	Commonwealth State extended to
45	The Bahamas	Reciprocal Enforcement of Judgments Act, 1924	United Kingdom, Barbados, Jamaica, Antigua & Barbuda, St Kitts & Nevis, St Lucia, Trinidad & Tobago, British Guyana, British Honduras (Belize) and Australia
46	The Gambia	Reciprocal Enforcement of Judgments Act 1922 Foreign Judgments Reciprocal Enforcement Act 1936	United Kingdom, Nigeria
47	Tonga	Reciprocal Enforcement of Judgments Act 1967	New Zealand, Papua New Guinea, United Kingdom, Australia
48	Trinidad & Tobago	Judgments Extension Act 1921	United Kingdom, Guyana, Grenada, St Vincent, Barbados, St Lucia, Leeward Islands (Antigua & Barbuda, St Kitts & Nevis) The Bahamas, Jamaica, States of Australia, Papua New Guinea, Nigeria, India
49	Tuvalu	Foreign Judgments (Reciprocal Enforcement) Act 1965	Papua New Guinea, Australia
50	Uganda	Judgments Extension Act, 1908 Reciprocal Enforcement of Judgments Act, 1922 Foreign Judgments (Reciprocal Enforcement) Act.	All Commonwealth countries
51	United Kingdom	Administration of Justice Act 1920 The Foreign Judgments (Reciprocal Enforcement) Act 1933.	Antigua and Barbuda, Australia, Barbados, Bahamas, Belize, Botswana, Canada, Cyprus, Dominica, Fiji, The Gambia, Ghana, Grenada, Guyana, India, Jamaica, Kenya, Kiribati, Lesotho, Malawi, Malaysia, Malta, Mauritius, New Zealand, Nigeria, Pakistan, Papua New Guinea, Seychelles, Sierra Leone, Singapore, Solomon Islands, Sri Lanka, St Christopher & Nevis, St. Helena, St Lucia, St Vincent & the Grenadines, Swaziland, Tanzania, Tonga, Trinidad & Tobago, Tuvalu, Uganda, Zambia.

(continued)

Table 2 *(continued)*

S/N	State	Statute(s)	Commonwealth State extended to
52	Vanuatu	None[411]	None
53	Zambia	The Foreign Judgments (Reciprocal Enforcement Act 1937 The Service of Process and Execution of Judgments Act 1957	Tuvalu, Kiribati, Solomon Islands, Malawi

V. Conclusion

The development of common law, which is the foundation of the legal systems of most Commonwealth States, has stagnated for a while. From the choice of jurisdiction to applicable law and recognition and enforcement of judgments, the rules are antiquated and 'have passed their use-by date', as Professor Adrian Briggs puts it.[412] They are no longer suitable for the modern era.

The codification of judgments enforcement rules in the Commonwealth may be responsible for its stagnation. This is further aided by the judicial policy of deference to the legislators in the area of law reforms and development. Deference to legislators has its merits, considering the Canadian experience of judicial experimentation which has led to uncertainties in the jurisdictional law for instance. The main drawback is that law-makers do not often take an interest in the development of private international law. This is glaring from Table 2, which depicts that the vast majority of the Commonwealth States still apply the 1920 AJA or Foreign Judgments (Reciprocal Enforcement) Act 1933.

What is more worrisome is that despite the similarities in language, law and administration of justice (ie the 'Commonwealth advantage'), the statutory enforcement schemes are not widely extended to foreign countries either within or outside the Commonwealth. It is, therefore, a welcome development that the Member States have resolved to reform the Commonwealth model laws on judgments recognition and enforcement, after about a century of operationalising the current models.

---

[411] Foreign judgments can only be enforced by action, see Part 13, Civil Procedure Rules 2002 and *Naylor v Kilham* [1999] VUSC 11 (SC).

[412] Briggs, 'Crossing the River by Feeling the Stones: Rethinking the Law on Foreign Judgments' (ch 3, fn 306) 2.

5

Commonwealth Model Law

I. Introduction

The Commonwealth Law Ministers at their 2017 triennial meeting in Nassau, The Bahamas, considered and adopted the 2017 Model Law on the Recognition and Enforcement of Foreign Judgments (CML). The work is the product of an exercise that has been ongoing for about three decades.[413] The final impetus came in 2005 when the Law Ministers and Attorneys-General of Member States tasked the Secretariat to review the extant intra-Commonwealth legal frameworks on recognition and enforcement of money judgments, which the meeting regarded as long overdue.[414] The introductory text captures the rationale for the new model law as follows:

> While international trade and commercial activity have rapidly evolved as a result of globalisation, mechanisms to resolve international commercial disputes have not been developed at the same speed or with similar enthusiasm. Legal arrangements that are currently in place, in the Commonwealth and elsewhere, fail to meet the expectation that judgments will be enforced in foreign jurisdictions[415]

The first element of pragmatism in the making of the model law is the identification of the problems at hand and the resolve to come up with solutions that will be targeted at addressing these problems. This foretells that the work will be remarkably different from the extant laws. In other words, from the onset, the Secretariat had formed a clear policy objective that was centred on solving practical problems associated with the enforcement of foreign judgments. This mind-set shaped the procedure and the overall outcome of the exercise.

The Secretariat was, to a great extent, methodical in its approach. Unlike the 1920 and 1933 Acts that were colonial legacies, the 2017 model law was a product of some comparative and empirical work. The Secretariat also maintained a close connection with the Hague Conference and its Judgments Project with a view to incorporating global developments into the model law. The developments in Commonwealth Member States were also given attention. The Secretariat

---

[413] See McClean and Patchett (ch 1, fn 63).
[414] Commonwealth Secretariat, *2005 Meeting of Commonwealth Law Ministers and Senior Officials* (The Commonwealth Secretariat, 2006) xiii.
[415] Commonwealth Secretariat, 'Model Law on the Recognition and Enforcement of Foreign Judgments' (The Commonwealth Secretariat, 2018).

was careful enough not to design a legal framework that appeared appropriate for the working group alone. The Law Ministers of the Commonwealth were engaged as major stakeholders. For instance, in the Meeting of Senior Officials of Commonwealth Law Ministries of October 2007, the complexities of the issues surrounding foreign judgments were discussed. Pursuant to the discussions, questionnaires concerning the key areas of the proposed law were delivered to Law Ministers for their views.[416] Some of the issues covered by the questionnaire include the nature and types of judgment to be enforceable; jurisdictional filters concerning contract, tort, and trust cases; grounds upon which enforcement of foreign judgments should not be allowed; and the efficiency of the methods of enforcement, amongst others. The reports were discussed at the Law Ministers' Meetings of 2008 in Edinburgh[417] and of 2014 in Gaborone.[418] This chapter examines in some detail the key provisions of the CML. It finds that the policy objectives of the CML emphasise efficiency, *res judicata* and to some extent, legal certainty. Some shortcomings arising from the simplistic, restrictive, and in some cases, overly broad approach generally adopted by the drafters concerning the jurisdictional filters are also highlighted in this chapter.

II. Preliminaries

A. Reciprocity and its Abandonment

The CML delivers a simple legislative framework, which prioritises the rights of the private litigants over political considerations. It abandons reciprocity and extricates altogether the complex problems surrounding a typical reciprocal framework. The title of the model law is described as 'the Foreign Judgments Act'. In the explanatory text, the drafters reasoned that this title 'gives the simplest possible formulation' and that a 'reference to "Reciprocal Enforcement", found in many current acts, is no longer appropriate'.[419]

Neither the explanatory text nor the report on the responses from Commonwealth Member States to the questionnaires gives any further clues on why reciprocity is no longer appropriate. However, some justifications can be offered. There is no gainsaying that the removal of reciprocity as a condition for recognition and enforcement will enhance the free circulation of judgments in the Commonwealth, particularly in these circumstances where Member States

---

[416] Commonwealth Secretariat, 'Commonwealth Practice in the Recognition of Foreign Judgments' (2009) 35 *Commonwealth Law Bulletin* 345, 345–46.

[417] Commonwealth Secretariat, 'Meeting of Commonwealth Law Ministers, Edinburgh, 7–10 July 2008: Communiqué' (2009) 35 *Commonwealth Law Bulletin* 85, 89.

[418] Commonwealth Secretariat, 'Meeting of Commonwealth Law Ministers and Senior Officials' (5–8 May 2014, Gaborone, Botswana).

[419] See explanatory text on clause 1.

are pursuing a common legal and economic agenda.[420] It promotes justice and equal treatment of judgment creditors whose property rights should be enforceable not based on the State of origin of such rights. A simplified legal framework can lead to greater certainty for litigants, their lawyers and the courts.[421] A litigant need not worry about whether his judgment will be enforced in other parts of the Commonwealth. The tasks for the lawyers and judges are much more simplified because they are relieved of the confusion which attends a convoluted regime where several statutes apply to judgments from different States.

More importantly, Table 1 shows that reciprocity barely adds any value to the free movement of judgments in the Commonwealth. Rather, it has hindered judgments' circulation as only a few States have widely extended the registration scheme in nearly a century. Also, there are growing numbers of States that have discontinued its usage across the globe. Therefore, apart from the practical benefits outlined above, it is in line with the modern trend. This can stimulate the Commonwealth members to join the Hague judgments project, since they are poised to open their legal systems to foreign judgments from within and beyond the Commonwealth. Such a move will accelerate global liberalisation of judgments enforcement considering the collective size of the Commonwealth States.

B. Foreign Court

The model law (section 2(1)) defines a court of the State of origin to be:

(a) a court of civil jurisdiction; or
(b) a court of criminal jurisdiction in respect only of a civil claim it is competent to entertain under the law of that state for damages or restitution based on an act giving rise to criminal proceedings;

One of the obstacles presented by the Administration of Justice Act 1920[422] and Foreign Judgments (Reciprocal Enforcement) Act 1933[423] is that they apply only to judgments from 'superior courts'. The rationale for the choice of superior courts might not be unconnected with the distinction between the jurisdictional powers and status of the superior and inferior courts in England. This distinction is historical as Her Majesty's judges (of the superior courts) were regarded as 'the fount of the common law'[424] with unlimited powers compared to circuit and district judges who were appointed for specific roles and under specific statutes.[425] Other than

---

[420] Secretariat, *Commonwealth Trade Review 2018: Strengthening the Commonwealth Advantage* (ch 4, fn 372) xx–xxv.

[421] Thalia Kruger, 'The Quest for Legal Certainty in International Civil Cases', *Recueil Des Cours* vol 380 (Martinus Nijhoff 2016) 405.

[422] Section 9.

[423] Section 1.

[424] Richard Harrison, 'Why Have Two Types of Civil Court?' (1999) 149 *New Law Journal* 65, 66.

[425] Gary Slapper and David Kelly, *The English Legal System* (Cavendish Publishing Ltd 2004) 331.

this historical distinction, judgments of both courts have the same effect on the parties.

In modern times, there is less emphasis on the status and importance of the courts. At best, many systems now focus on efficiency in the allocation of jurisdictional powers. In the last few decades, many judiciaries have been reformed. Apart from some inherent powers of high courts as courts of general jurisdiction, magistrate, district, or circuit courts now enjoy almost the same powers as high courts in civil proceedings. Their monetary jurisdiction has been increased and this makes them the appropriate venue for small and medium claims. For instance, in Nigeria, the Lagos State Magistrate Courts' jurisdiction has been increased to claims not exceeding N10,000,000 (US$28,000);[426] South Africa increased its District Magistrate Courts' jurisdiction to R200,000 (US$15,000) in 2014;[427] Australia increased District and Magistrate Courts' jurisdiction to AUS$750,000 and AUS$150,000 respectively in 2010;[428] Kenya increased its Magistrates Courts' jurisdiction to 20,000,000 shillings (US$195,000) in 2015[429] amongst others. Lifting the embargo on inferior courts will admit many judgments which would have otherwise been unenforceable under the current schemes. It takes care of cases such as *ABSA Bank Limited v Moorosi Ezekiel Latela*,[430] and *Su'a v Imex Company Ltd*,[431] where foreign judgments could not be registered because they were issued by magistrate and district courts respectively.

Another point worthy of note is the broad approach adopted by the Secretariat in describing foreign courts. A foreign court whose judgment is enforceable is any 'court of civil jurisdiction'. This broad classification clears up the uncertainties that may arise from the varied designation of courts around the world. Emphasising the nature of the proceeding and not the appellation would admit judgments from Islamic civil courts, for instance, which are prevalent in several Commonwealth States such as Brunei, Nigeria, Malaysia, and Pakistan. It also takes care of uncertainties that may arise from judgments from other quasi-civil courts and/or tribunals. This is one of the issues raised recently in *State Bank of India v Mallya*.[432] In this case, the State Bank of India sought to enforce in England, a judgment to the value of £385.9 million of the Bangalore Debt Recovery Tribunal against Dr Mallya. Some of the conditions imposed by the English 1958 Order-in-Council, which extended the application of the 1933 reciprocal statute to India, are that the foreign court should be a superior court whose civil jurisdiction has no pecuniary limit and the judgment must bear a seal stating that the jurisdiction of the court has no pecuniary limit. The judgment debtor contended that the judgment from

---

[426] See s 28, Magistrates' Court Law of Lagos State 2009.
[427] Government Notice No 216 of 27 March 2014: <http://www.justice.gov.za/legislation/notices/2014/2014-03-27-gg37477_gon216.pdf>.
[428] The Civil and Criminal Jurisdiction Reform and Modernisation Amendment Act 2010.
[429] Section 7, The Magistrates' Courts Act, 2015.
[430] *ABSA Bank Limited v Moorosi Ezekiel Latela* [2004] LSHC 47 (High Court of Lesotho).
[431] *Tuigamala Su'a v Imex Company Ltd* [2004] WSSC 6 (Supreme Court of Samoa).
[432] *State Bank of India & Others v Mallya & Others* [2018] EWHC 1084 (Comm).

the Tribunal did not qualify for registration because it was neither from a superior court nor did the court's enabling law prescribe any procedure for sealing (ie stating that its jurisdiction has no pecuniary limit). This, amongst other issues raised by the judgment debtor, necessitated the calling of expert witnesses – two former Indian judges – to testify on the nature of the Debt Recovery Tribunal, its enabling law and procedure. The English court rejected all the objections of the judgment debtor by adopting a purposive interpretation of the Order-in-Council, noting the policy objective of the reciprocal regime and the fact that it would be against the principle of comity to resolve the questions by an 'unduly narrow or technical approach'.[433]

This broader approach had earlier been adopted in *Habib Bank Ltd v Ahmed*.[434] In this case, the judgment debtor sought to set aside the registration of a Pakistani judgment because the foreign court (the High Court of Sindh) had sat as a banking tribunal which was not a court recognised under section 4(1)(a)(i) of the Foreign Judgments (Reciprocal Enforcement) Act 1933. The English court discountenanced the objection and held that the nature of the proceeding was what mattered, not the capacity in which the court acted. The utility of broadly defining a court of the State of origin is that the kind of uncertainties and hassles observed in *State Bank of India* and *Habib Bank Ltd* would be reduced, if not eradicated.

Nevertheless, one shortcoming is observed in this broad definition. The explanatory text states that arbitral tribunals are excluded from the scope of the model law. It also notes that it was argued that other courts such as religious courts should be excluded. The Secretariat was of the considered view that these issues were satisfactorily addressed in the definition of a foreign court, particularly, by stating 'a court of civil jurisdiction'. This view seems to be misplaced as the contrary is ordinarily suggested. As mentioned elsewhere, several Commonwealth Member States have religious courts exercising civil jurisdiction. In Nigeria for instance, shariah courts (also referred to as Area courts in some Nigerian states) exercise civil jurisdiction with no monetary limitation. Therefore, the application of the model law in some Commonwealth Member States may create some uncertainties if the explanatory text were to be given any weight. A better approach is to explicitly mention the category of courts/tribunals that are excluded from the scope of the law.

C. Types of Judgment

Section 2(1) defines a 'foreign judgment' as:

> a final decision (however described, and including a judgment, order, decree, decision, writ of execution or determination of costs by an officer of a court) made by a court of a foreign state deemed to have had jurisdiction on any of the grounds set out in section 5, and which is a money-judgment or a non-monetary judgment;

---

[433] Ibid, para 64.
[434] *Habib Bank Ltd v Ahmed* [2001] EWCA Civ 1270.

The model law departs from the traditional common law doctrine of obligation by recognising both money and non-money judgments. This is a welcome development, as the exclusion of non-money judgments has been consistently criticised by academic writers. The recognition of non-money judgments brings the Commonwealth system closer to what obtains in other parts of the world. The model law defines the scope of enforceable non-money judgments. It provides that:

> 'non-monetary judgment' means a foreign judgment:
> (a) ordering specific performance of a contractual obligation;
> (b) ordering the transfer of a specified item or specified items of movable property; or
> (c) prohibiting the judgment debtor from acting in a specified way;

The explanatory report is, however, silent on the rationale for enumerating these three classes of judgment.

Much scholarly work has been done on the efficacy of enforcement of non-money judgments.[435] Some law reform agencies in the Commonwealth have argued in support of such orders as well.[436] Concerns have also been raised about the practicalities of their enforcement, particularly as observed from the Canadian Supreme Court decision in *Pro Swing Inc v Elta Golf Inc*.[437] However, there seems to be a consensus that it is unrealistic to deny enforcement of all non-money judgments altogether. Notable among non-money judgments are anti-suit injunctions, *Mareva* injunctions, *Anton Piller* orders, specific performance orders, restitution orders, disclosure orders and orders connected to insolvency proceedings.

Paragraphs (a) and (b) of the above definition cover cases of specific performance and restitution orders. The Privy Council had earlier moved to recognise these kinds of orders by way of judicial pragmatism. In *Pattni v Ali*, Lord Mance expressed the support for this view thus:

> [W]here a court in state A makes, as against persons who have submitted to its jurisdiction, an in personam judgment regarding contractual rights to either movables or intangible property (whether in the form of a simple chose in action or shares) situate in state B, the courts of state B can and should recognise the foreign court's in personam determination of such rights as binding and should itself be prepared to give such relief as may be appropriate to enforce such rights in state B. The extent to which this is possible might be limited by the law of state B, as the situs or in the case of shares as the place of incorporation of the relevant company (in this case, as both)[438]

Other Commonwealth courts from the Cayman Islands and Jersey did uphold the enforcement of restitution and specific performance orders under the common

---

[435] Stephen GA Pitel, 'Enforcement of Foreign Non-Monetary Judgments in Canada (and Beyond)' (2007) 3 *Journal of Private International Law* 241; Richard Frimpong Oppong, 'Enforcing Foreign Non-Money Judgments: An Examination of Some Recent Developments in Canada and Beyond' (2006) 39 *University of British Columbia Law Review* 257; Vaughan Black, 'Enforcement of Foreign Non-Money Judgments: *Pro Swing v. Elta*' (2005) 42 *Canadian Business Law Journal* 81.

[436] Singapore Academy of Law (ch 4, fn 394) 27; South African Law Reform Commission (ch 4, fn 394) 37.

[437] *Pro Swing Inc v Elta Golf Inc* [2006] 2 SCR 612, 2006 SCC 52.

[438] *Pattni v Ali and Another* [2006] UKPC 51, para 27, [2007] 2 All ER (Comm) 427 at 441.

law in *Miller v Gianne*,[439] *Bandone Sdn Bhd v Sol Properties Incorporated*[440] and *Brunei Investment Agency v Fidelis Nominees Ltd*.[441] The model law has provided the required change in this regard. Paragraph (c) could technically be described as an injunction. Literally, this may cover asset-freezing orders (*Mareva* injunctions), anti-suit injunctions and *Anton Piller* orders generally. The limitation of paragraph (c) is that it binds only the judgment debtor in person. Thus, freezing orders and disclosure orders which may require some third parties to act may not be enforceable.

The restriction of non-money judgments to final judgments and their particularisation will limit their utility. Sadly, pre-judgment orders and other interim reliefs which are often useful in transnational litigation are not covered under this law. While it is conceded that the enforcement of pre-judgment and other interim relief needs a cautious approach,[442] excluding them totally defies practicality as it fails to appreciate their inherent practical benefits. The points being made are not theoretical. It seems the drafters did not take cognisance of the developments in some Commonwealth jurisdictions such as England, Canada and Australia. There are cases which demonstrate that there is a need for a review of extant judgments frameworks in the Commonwealth to support a simple procedure for enforcement of non-money judgments and orders, particularly worldwide asset-freezing orders and ancillary disclosure orders for instance. The practical importance of these orders cannot be overemphasised due to the complexity of modern transactions, the nature of transnational litigation and the seamless movement of assets across borders.[443] That reality was established three decades ago in *Babanaft International Co SA v Bassatne and Another*,[444] where the English courts approved the grant of worldwide post-judgment freezing orders, and in deserving cases, pre-trial worldwide injunctions.[445] It is now well established in the Commonwealth.[446]

---

[439] *Miller v Gianne* [2007] CILR 18.

[440] *Bandone Sdn Bhd v Sol Properties Incorporated* [2008] CILR 301.

[441] *Investment Agency v Fidelis Nominees Ltd* [2008] JRC 152. These three cases were cited and discussed in Halkerston (ch 2, fn 84); Harris (ch 2, fn 110).

[442] This is because the jurisdictional requirements to grant such orders and the extent of their reach are yet to fully converge in the Commonwealth. See Trevor C Hartley, *International Commercial Litigation: Text, Cases, and Materials on Private International Law* (Cambridge University Press 2009) 428. In addition, their enforcement may implicate the right to privacy and the privilege against self-incrimination. For instance, Art 7 of the Hague Convention on Choice of Court Agreements leaves out issues concerning the grant, refusal or termination, recognition or enforcement of interim measures. See Trevor Hartley and Masato Dogauchi, 'Explanatory Report: Convention of 30 June 2005 on Choice of Court Agreements' (2005). See also *Crédit Suisse Fides Trust SA v Cuoghi* [1998] QB 818 (discussing disclosure orders and the privilege against self-incrimination).

[443] Pepin Aslett, 'Cross-Border Asset Protection: An Offshore Perspective' (2003) 10 *Journal of Financial Crime* 229; Verónica Ruiz Abou-Nigm, 'Ancillary Jurisdiction for Interim Measures of Protection in Support of Cross-Border Litigation' (2005) 10 *Uniform Law Review*.

[444] *Babanaft International Co SA v Bassatne and Another* [1989] 1 All ER 433. See also *Republic of Haiti v Duvalier* [1990] 1 QB 202, *Derby and Co Ltd v Weldon (No 1)* [1990] Ch 48, and *Derby and Co Ltd v Weldon (Nos 3 and 4)* [1990] Ch 65.

[445] *Babanaft*, [1989] 1 All ER 433, Kerr LJ, 441, 447.

[446] See Lawrence Collins, 'The Territorial Reach of Mareva Injunctions' (1989) 105 *Law Quarterly Review* 262 (for developments and case law in other leading Commonwealth jurisdictions such as Australia and Canada).

Disclosure orders often follow worldwide freezing orders. By their nature, they can potentially affect third parties (for instance, banks) who may have some connections with the assets of the judgment debtor.[447] If it is common practice to grant such orders, it makes sense that the legislators should make provision for their reception in other jurisdictions.

In *Davis v Turning Properties Pty Ltd*,[448] an Australian court for the first time granted a *Mareva* order in support of the Bahaman court's *Mareva* order over the assets of the defendant in Australia. In *Cyprus Popular Bank Public Co Ltd v Vgenopoulos & Others*,[449] the English court registered a freezing order from Cyprus[450] (based on EU law) but denied a similar order from Nigeria in *Standard Chartered Bank v Zungeru Power Ltd*,[451] because a freezing order and the ancillary disclosure order are not supported by the Administration of Justice Act 1920. In *Federal Republic of Nigeria v Dariye and another*,[452] an English court refused to transfer a suit to Nigeria, which was the natural forum because the applicant's counsel successfully convinced the court that the applicant would not be able to enforce Nigerian disclosure orders against English banks that were holding the defendant's funds. Thus, despite having over 20 witnesses residing in Nigeria, the matter proceeded in England simply because there was no scheme for the enforcement of such orders. Having noted these practical problems, the model law ought to make provisions that effectively tackle them.

Enforcement of pre-judgment preservative orders could help judgment creditors tie down a debtor's foreign assets in the event a possible transfer to jurisdictions where enforcement may be impracticable or frustrated. It helps judgment creditors to scale jurisdictional obstacles that may lie ahead if the orders were to be requested from foreign courts where the assets are located or transferred to. It does make sense that a litigant procures the order in the court that is more connected with the dispute and then uses it to track the judgment debtor's assets anywhere in the world.[453] This is more appealing, since such orders are now routinely granted and their conditions have been largely standardised, at least, among the leading Commonwealth States.[454] The drafters would have added more value to the model

---

[447] Fentiman (ch 1, fn 25) 570–74; Lawrence Collins, 'The Territorial Reach of Mareva Injunctions' (n 442) 269, 281; Campbell McLachlan, 'The Jurisdictional Limits of Disclosure Orders in Transnational Fraud Litigation' (1998) 47 *International & Comparative Law Quarterly* 3, 7.

[448] *Davis v Turning Properties Pty Ltd* (2005) 222 ALR 676 at 682.

[449] *Cyprus Popular Bank Public Co Ltd v Vgenopoulos & Others* [2016] EWHC 1695 (QB).

[450] Both countries are members of the Commonwealth and of the EU. The registration in question is governed by EU law.

[451] *Standard Chartered Bank v Zungeru Power Ltd* [2014] EWHC 4714 (QB).

[452] *Federal Republic of Nigeria v Dariye and another* [2007] EWHC 708 (Ch).

[453] Jeremy Andrews and Charles Allin, 'Developments in Freezing Foreign Assets' (2015) 2 *Journal of International Banking and Financial Law* 111.

[454] See Lord Millett in *Crédit Suisse Fides Trust SA v Cuoghi* [1998] QB 818, 824 where he notes that 'such orders are nowadays routinely made in cases of international fraud and the conditions necessary in order to preserve international comity and prevent conflicts of jurisdiction have become standardised'.

law by stating that final judgments include final and interlocutory decisions. A good template is the Australian and Singaporean texts that define judgments to include a final or interlocutory judgment or order given or made in a civil proceeding.[455]

It should be added that 'foreign judgment' refers to only a judgment issued by a court of origin which has jurisdiction over the merits of the case and which meets any of the jurisdictional filters. The English Court of Appeal has ruled in *Strategic Technologies Pte Ltd v Procurement Bureau of the Republic of China Ministry of National Defence*[456] that judgment obtained in one Commonwealth State to enforce a money judgment obtained in another would not qualify for registration under the statutory schemes in the UK as a third such State. This caveat will be more relevant if any Member State decides to introduce reciprocity in the implementation of the model.

III. Excluded Matters

Certain types of judgments are excluded from the scope of the model law by section 4(1). They are:

(a)   relating to the status and legal capacity of a natural person
(b)   relating to a family law matter, including a matter relating to maintenance obligations, matrimonial property and other rights or obligations arising out of marriage or similar relationships
(c)   arising out of bankruptcy, insolvency, composition or analogous proceedings
(d)   for the recovery of taxes
(e)   for the recovery of monetary fines or penalties
(f)   that recognize the judgment of another foreign state
(g)   made in proceedings commenced before the coming into force of this Act.

The exclusion of certain types of judgment from the scope of the law is understandable because of their peculiar nature. For family law related judgments, for instance, Commonwealth Member States have diverse legal views on the foundations of matrimony, and the rights and responsibilities arising therefrom. Those issues are rooted in public policy. It may require painstaking efforts to agree on some key provisions if an agreement is ever possible. It is also observed that the use of 'similar relationships' shows that the model law takes cognisance of other forms of 'marriages' such as civil partnership, registered cohabitation and recognised cohabitations.[457]

The exclusion of fines, penalties and taxes is also not surprising as it has long been established that a forum court will not act as a debt collector for a foreign

---

[455] Section 3(1) Foreign Judgments Act 1991 (Australia); s 2 Reciprocal Enforcement of Foreign Judgments Act (chapter 265) 2001 Revised Edition, as amended in 2019 (Singapore).
[456] *Strategic Technologies Pte Ltd v Procurement Bureau of the Republic of China Ministry of National Defence* [2020] EWCA Civ 1604.
[457] See explanatory note.

sovereign. The view was reinforced by the English court in *Government of India v Taylor*.[458] In *United States v Harden*,[459] the Canadian Supreme Court confirmed the application of the rule in Canada when it upheld the lower court's decision not to recognise a US$640,000 US income tax judgment against Harden who had moved, together with all her assets, from the US to Canada after the said US judgment was entered against her. Arguably, such judgments do not fall within the scope of private international law because the judgments are often in favour of States themselves when exercising sovereign powers.[460] Nevertheless, interested States may enter bilateral relationships for the enforcement of tax judgments. A few examples exist. In Australia, judgments in respect of income tax from New Zealand and Papua New Guinea are enforceable by registration.[461] The UK has also signed some treaties and implemented some EU Directives which seek to facilitate the collection of taxes for other EU Member States.[462]

For insolvency judgments, the nature of the proceedings requires courts to cooperate with one another to ensure efficient distribution of assets that are scattered in different jurisdictions. Enforcement of insolvency orders was a big issue in *Rubin v Eurofinance SA*,[463] where the Supreme Court had the opportunity to extensively consider the nature of such judgments and their importance. The Court was prepared to enforce insolvency judgments provided Parliament would do the needful by setting out in legislation what would be the acceptable jurisdictional connection(s) between the Court and the debtor/subject matter.

Rubin shows that there are practical problems which the Commonwealth needs to address to enhance the efficiency of the intra-Commonwealth judgments scheme. The Secretariat missed this opportunity. The courts should be willing to assist foreign courts as much as practicable. At the international level, the Evidence and Service Conventions are examples of such assistance even in areas that implicate State sovereignty.[464] The Secretariat would have added more value to the model law by engaging Law Ministers on the desirability or otherwise of addressing the recommendations of *Rubin*. Alternatively, the model law could be silent rather than expressly excluding it. This may well mean that some Commonwealth Member States, who have neither modernised their insolvency law[465] nor adopted

---

[458] *Government of India v Taylor* [1955] 1 All ER 292. See also *Pocket Kings Ltd v Safenames Ltd and another* [2010] Ch 438 on the prohibition of enforcing foreign penal laws.

[459] *United States v Harden* [1963] SCR 366.

[460] This does not include cases where sovereign powers are exercised on behalf on private citizens. In *United States Securities & Exchange Commission v Manterfield* [2009] EWCA Civ 27, the Court of Appeal recognised a US judgment because the SEC's action in the US was for the disgorgement of misappropriated funds and such were to be returned to the injured investors.

[461] Foreign Judgments Act 1991 (Cth) s 7(3)(a).

[462] Campbell McLachlan, *Foreign Relations Law* (Cambridge University Press 2014) 456.

[463] *Rubin v Eurofinance SA* [2012] UKSC 46.

[464] Convention of 18 March 1970 on the Taking of Evidence Abroad in Civil or Commercial Matters, entered into force on 7 October 1972, with 62 contracting parties as at March 2019; Convention of 15 November 1965 on the Service Abroad of Judicial and Extrajudicial Documents in Civil or Commercial Matters, entered into force on 10 February 1969, with 74 contracting parties as at March 2019.

[465] By implementing the UNCITRAL Model Law on Cross-Border Insolvency (1997).

the 2018 UNCITRAL Model Law on Insolvency Judgments,[466] may be willing to enforce such judgments under the CML, especially since recognition is no longer limited to money judgments.[467] A practical example of this suggestion is the Ugandan case of *Re: Application by Michael Ndichu Mburu (Receiver/Manager of Mandeeq Africa Ltd (In Receivership)*,[468] where an 'insolvency-related judgment' was registered under the extant Commonwealth statutory scheme. In this case, the applicant got an order from a Kenyan High Court authorising him to attach all the assets of Maandeeq Africa Ltd (In Receivership), which were charged under a debenture. The directors of the company transferred most of the assets to Uganda after the said order was made. The Kenyan judgment was registered under the Reciprocal Enforcement of Judgments Act, 1961 without much ado.[469] This may help litigants to enforce some less controversial insolvency judgments pending relevant Member States' adoption of the modern insolvency model laws. It is hoped that the Commonwealth States would take cognisance of this emerging trend in the future judgments works.

Foreign judgments against sovereign States or their agencies are not excluded from the scope of the model law. This is, however, without prejudice to the rights and privileges they enjoy under international law. Again, it is well settled that execution cannot be levied against State-owned assets except where such assets are specially utilised or earmarked for commercial purposes, the burden of proving which rests on the judgment creditor. This has always been a problem for judgment creditors who have sought to enforce judgments against sovereign States, as seen in the recent UK decisions such as *NML Capital Ltd v Republic of Argentina*,[470] *SerVaas Incorporated v Rafidain Bank*[471] and *LR Avionics Technologies Limited v Federal Republic of Nigeria*.[472] The model law is similar to the 2019 Judgments Convention on this point. The exclusion is analysed further in Chapter seven below.

Section 3 of the CML allows for the severance of parts of a foreign judgment, which are enforceable from those that are not. Severance is a good attempt at saving judgments that would have otherwise been rejected altogether. For instance, a judgment may contain heads of damages (eg punitive damages) which offend a forum's public policy. Rather than reject the whole judgment, a court addressed

---

[466] UNCITRAL Model Law on Recognition and Enforcement of Insolvency-Related Judgments 2018.

[467] The only shortcoming in this suggestion is the uncertainty that may arise from the absence of clear jurisdictional connections for insolvency cases.

[468] *Re: Application by Michael Ndichu Mburu (Receiver/Manager of Mandeeq Africa Ltd (In Receivership)* Miscellaneous Cause 09 of 2008. Available at: https://ulii.org/ug/judgment/commercial-court/2008/70.

[469] It should be mentioned that the Ugandan court did not make any reference to the fact that the order was not a money judgment. It cannot be ascertained whether this is an omission or a conscious attempt to liberalise the judgment regime. The Ugandan government has extended the registration scheme to all Commonwealth countries through the Foreign Judgments (Reciprocal Enforcement) (General Application) Order No 35 of 2002. This might have influenced the decision of the court.

[470] *NML Capital Ltd v Republic of Argentina* [2011] UKSC 31.

[471] *SerVaas Incorporated v Rafidain Bank* [2012] UKSC 40.

[472] *LR Avionics Technologies Limited v Federal Republic of Nigeria* [2016] EWHC 1761 (Comm).

can now enforce the acceptable part of the judgment awarding general and special damages (compensatory damages) while rejecting the punitive damages. This is also useful for judgments which contain fines and penalties. A court addressed may enforce the compensatory part which is to the benefit of the judgment creditor, and reject the fines and penalties which would otherwise render the judgment unenforceable altogether. There are a few cases under the English common law where severance has been utilised as mentioned above. In *Raulin v Fischer*,[473] a victim's compensation in a criminal prosecution for negligence in France (*partie civile*) was adjudged to be severable and enforceable in England. This is a good development that takes care of *partie civile* since there are now sizeable civil law jurisdictions in the Commonwealth. Similarly, in the Singaporean case of *Alberto Justo Rodriguez Licea v Curacao Drydock Co Inc*,[474] the plaintiffs, who were victims of a forced labour scheme, obtained a default judgment in the US against the defendant for compensatory and punitive damages. They filed a common law action in Singapore to enforce the compensatory part of the US judgment. The defendant sought to set aside the Singaporean summary judgment claiming that the US judgment contained punitive damages. The Court held that the plaintiffs had severed the legitimate aspect from the objectionable aspect of the US judgment by proceeding only on the compensatory part.

This discretion already exists under the Australian statutory enforcement scheme.[475] It was also applied under Australian common law in *Schnabel v Lui*[476] where a US judgment was sought to be enforced by action. The judgment included both compensatory and punitive damages. The New South Wales Supreme Court allowed enforcement of the compensatory part and severed the punitive part because it formed part of American penal/public law. The approach adopted under the Canadian Uniform Enforcement of Foreign Judgments Act is to empower a court addressed to limit enforcement of punitive, multiple or excessive damages to comparable values under the forum law.[477] The model law has a similar provision under section 14. The benefit to be derived from the combination of severance (section 3) and limitation of damages (section 14) is that punitive damages which cannot be severed can still be enforced, albeit to the extent permitted by the forum law.

---

[473] *Raulin v Fischer* [1911] 2 KB 93. Severance was also applied recently by an English court in an enforcement proceeding involving a US judgment, part of which violated s 5 of the UK's Protection of Trading Interests Act 1980. The main compensatory part of the US judgment was enforced while the punitive damages awarded under the Racketeer Influenced and Corrupt Organizations Act 1970 (the RICO Act) were held to be unenforceable. See *Lewis v Eliades (No 2)* [2003] EWHC 368 (QB).

[474] *Alberto Justo Rodriguez Licea v Curacao Drydock Co Inc* [2015] 4 SLR 172.

[475] Foreign Judgments Act 1991, s 6(13).

[476] *Schnabel v Lui* [2002] NSWSC 15, discussed in Kent Anderson and Jim Davis, 'Annual Survey of Recent Developments in Australian Private International Law 2000–2003' (2005) 24 *Australian Year Book of International Law* 443.

[477] Section 6 of the model law.

IV. International Jurisdiction

The jurisdiction of the foreign court is one of the cornerstones of any judgments recognition scheme. Jurisdiction is often said to be the life-blood of any litigation and no matter how beautifully a trial is conducted, the proceedings and judgment rendered by a court which lacks jurisdiction amount to a nullity. Such judgments will not be recognised elsewhere. It is often the first item examined in an enforcement proceeding.

From time immemorial, jurisdiction has always been a contentious matter because it is often regarded as an exercise of sovereignty.[478] It becomes more problematic when it is exercised over persons and objects that are not within the territorial reach of the State of origin. To avoid any friction which may result in an attempt to regulate the direct jurisdiction of courts, it is said to be desirable to defer the issue of jurisdiction to the enforcement stage. Hence, whilst States may exercise jurisdiction as they deem fit, a court addressed would enforce only those judgments which are rendered on a jurisdictional basis that it regards as acceptable. As mentioned in Chapter three above, the courts are not well equipped to formulate acceptable jurisdictional filters, it is therefore appropriate that the Secretariat took up this task by allowing the Law Ministers to consider appropriate 'international jurisdictional' grounds for recognition and enforcement. Section 5 of the CML sets out these grounds.

The CML retains the traditional common law heads of jurisdiction and adds new grounds in the light of modern realities and some of the consensus reached in The Hague.[479] For ease of presentation and clarity, the usual classifications of jurisdiction as general and special (specific) shall be adopted here.

A. General Jurisdiction

(i) Residence (Natural Person)

Section 5(1)(d) reads:

> the judgment debtor, being an individual, was ordinarily resident in the state of origin;

Residence differs from one branch of law to the other. Residence for tax, immigration or matrimonial purposes may be different from the idea of residence contemplated for jurisdiction concerning civil and commercial judgments.[480] Residence is approved by common law as the strongest link between a defendant and a foreign court. The drafters did not give any reason why they adopted

---

[478] Alex Mills, 'Rethinking Jurisdiction in International Law' (2014) 84 *The British Yearbook of International Law* 187, 196–98.

[479] See the explanatory texts to the model law.

[480] Lord Collins of Mapesbury and others, *Dicey, Morris and Collins on the Conflict of Laws* (ch 1, fn 72) 193–96 (discussing the variations in the degree of permanence required for those subject matters).

'ordinary residence' as against 'habitual residence' which is found in the Hague Conventions.[481] What does it mean to be ordinarily resident in the State of origin? Does 'ordinarily' connote that there must be some degree of permanence or presence of the judgment debtor in the State of origin at the time of the commencement of the foreign proceedings. This distinction is necessary because an individual can be ordinarily resident in Nigeria but have another home in England, which he regularly or occasionally visits. If he ordered some goods in Nigeria from a seller in London, can the seller sue in England claiming that the buyer is resident in England? The explanatory text simply says, 'an individual must be "ordinarily resident" and not merely "resident". This explanation begs the question. The question remains what it means to be resident in a State whether 'ordinarily' or 'merely'.

Case law from several Commonwealth courts seems to suggest that having a physical address in the State of origin is enough to establish residence even if the judgment debtor was not present in that State at the time of the proceedings. The residence need not be a permanent home. It suffices that it is a residential address irrespective of the purpose of the stay. In the Nigerian case of *VAB Petroleum v Momah*,[482] the Supreme Court held that a UK address which the judgment debtor filed on incorporation documents (register of directors) sufficed to prove that he was resident in the United Kingdom.

In the Scottish case of *Zigal v Buchanan*,[483] the plaintiff sought to enforce a Hong Kong judgment against the defendant. Both parties had a business relationship in Hong Kong. The defendant rented an apartment in Hong Kong for that purpose. The plaintiff sued him in respect of the business association. On the claim form, he listed the addresses of the defendant in Hong Kong and Glasgow, but the service was allegedly effected on him in Hong Kong in July 2016. A default judgment for HK$774,430 and US$99,927 was entered against him. He claimed to have left Hong Kong in July 2015 when his visa expired and thus the foreign court did not have jurisdiction as he was not resident in the country as at the time of the commencement of the proceeding in January 2016. On the question of residence, the Scottish court held that he was resident in Hong Kong as he could not establish by credible evidence that he had left the apartment by showing any travel document evidencing that he left Hong Kong or any document showing the termination of the lease (the flat being a rented apartment). The court also rejected his attempt to establish that he was resident in Glasgow at the relevant time. The court noted that his UK lease commenced in December 2016 and the utility bills of earlier dates could not confirm that those utilities were used by the defendant or someone else. This case suggests that residence in the State of origin is a question

---

[481] For instance, see Art 5 of the 2018 draft of the Hague Judgments Convention.

[482] *VAB Petroleum v Mike Momah* (2013) LPELR–19770 (SC). An English court came to the same conclusion in *Key Homes Bradford Ltd & Others v Patel* [2014] EWHC B1 (Ch) while interpreting s 1140 of the Companies Act 2006, that a foreign director who has a UK residential address on the register of directors is deemed to be resident in the UK. This is, however, in respect of the service of an originating process.

[483] *Zigal v Buchanan* [2018] CSOH 94; [2019] CSIH 16.

of fact and the continued presence of the judgment debtor at a known address at the time of proceedings is relevant to establish residence.

A recent Australian case also throws up the question of residence of a judgment debtor. In *Suzhou Haishun Investment Management Co Ltd v Zhao & Others*,[484] the plaintiff applied to enforce three Chinese default judgments against the defendants. The interesting point in this case is that there is a 'hukou system' in China which requires all Chinese citizens to have a registered address, and it is not permitted for a Chinese person not to have a known hukou residence. The summons was advertised in the daily newspapers because it was not received at the defendant's hukou address. The Supreme Court of Victoria ruled that the defendant was resident in China at the time of the proceedings there and the service was valid under Chinese law. These cases portray that the question of ordinary residence of the debtor is not as straightforward as it may appear. The cases have treated it more as a question of law and fact. These cases demonstrate that the Commonwealth courts will likely treat 'ordinary residence' simply as 'residence' or 'mere residence'. The terminology used in the model law and the case law is somewhat different from the approach of the Hague Conventions as will be seen in Chapter seven below.

The common law concept of transient jurisdiction, which has been reaffirmed as an acceptable basis of international jurisdiction in several cases such as *Adams v Cape Industries plc*[485] (UK), *Richman v Ben-Tovim*[486] (SA), and *Beals v Saldanha*[487] (Canada) did not make the list. This is a welcome development because transient jurisdiction has been regarded as being exorbitant. This will ensure that judgments which are rendered by courts that are not substantially connected with the subject matter or defendant are not enforceable. This further drives the efficiency and fairness theories of jurisdiction, as it would be unfair and costly for a litigant to be ambushed for trial in any country that he sets his feet on. It will lay to rest the uncertainty as to whether presence without more is sufficient.[488]

In the same vein, citizenship will not qualify as a substantial connection under the model law, although this has never been recognised by most Commonwealth States except Australia. In *Independent Trustee Services Ltd v Morris*,[489] the UK pension regulator appointed the plaintiff, a professional trustee company, in connection with fraudulent mismanagement of £52 million of pension scheme assets by two former trustees. Morris, one of the defendants was found to be liable in breach of trust. He was ordered to pay £52 million on account. He was resident in Australia at the time of the proceedings. He was served in Australia but chose to ignore the English court. The Australian court enforced the English judgment

---

[484] *Suzhou Haishun Investment Management Co Ltd v Zhao & Others* [2019] VSC 110.
[485] [1990] Ch 433 (ch 1, fn 28).
[486] *Richman v Ben-Tovim* [2007] 2 All SA 234.
[487] *Beals v Saldanha* [2003] 3 SCR 416.
[488] For the controversy, see Briggs, 'Crossing the River by Feeling the Stones: Rethinking the Law on Foreign Judgments' (ch 3, fn 306) 3–4.
[489] *Independent Trustee Services Ltd v Morris* [2010] NSWSC 1218.

and held that the English court had a substantial connection with the dispute and the defendant because he was a UK citizen. This principle was also applied in two recent Australian cases: *Liu v Ma & Another*[490] and *Suzhou Haishun Investment Management Co Ltd v Zhao & Others*.[491] This judicial pragmatism[492] would have been unnecessary under the model law as the judgments can be enforced under other specific heads of jurisdiction.

(ii) Residence (Corporation)

Section 5(1)(e) reads:

> the judgment debtor, not being an individual, was incorporated in the state of origin, exercised its central management in that state or had its principal place of business located in that state;

This provision deals with general jurisdiction over corporations. It seeks to replace the extant rule, which restricts general jurisdiction to the State where a company has its principal place of business. Indeed, this is one area where the Hague Conference's influence on the Commonwealth is obvious. This head of jurisdiction identifies three connecting factors for a corporate defendant: its place of incorporation, its place of central management, and its principal place of business. The additions are borrowed from other international instruments such as the Hague Conventions where the statutory seat and place of central administration have long been recognised.[493] The explanatory text notes that 'the word "seat" familiar in civil law usage is not used, but actually has the same effect'. Therefore, the place of incorporation and central management are alternatives to statutory seat and the place of central administration respectively as often used in the Hague and other international instruments.

The expansion of the connecting factors for corporate defendants brings the Commonwealth law in tune with the reality of the day. The concept of 'principal place of business' has been interpreted narrowly in most Commonwealth Member States to mean the place of incorporation, even if the company practically does not do any business there.[494] In *PMG Motors v Firstrand Bank*,[495] the South African Court of Appeal held that a company is resident at the site of its registered office. The Court reasoned that it is a 'convenient fiction' because the company has

---

[490] *Liu v Ma & Another* [2017] VSC 810.

[491] *Suzhou Haishun Investment Management Co Ltd v Zhao & Others* [2019] VSC 110.

[492] For a critique of the *Morris* case, see Sirko Harder, 'Recent Judicial Aberrations in Australian Private Law' (2012) 19 *Australian International Law Journal* 161, 170–73.

[493] See Art 4, HCCA; Art 3, Judgments Convention.

[494] The principal place of business is also used in the EC Treaty and Brussels I Regulation, but it is not the same as the place of incorporation. The understanding of the concept in EU law is the same as the 'real seat' theory in German law. See *Young v Anglo American South Africa Ltd & Others* [2014] EWCA Civ 1130.

[495] *PMG Motors v Firstrand Bank* [2014] ZASCA 180. See also *Bisonboard Ltd v K Braun Woodworking Machinery (Pty) Ltd*, 1991 (1) SA 482.

established a physical presence there, records relating to its business dealings are there, most of its employees may be located there, and these factors may make litigation against the company convenient in that forum. It is observed that this rule is rooted in English company law and practice, from which most Commonwealth States derive their laws. Under the English Companies Act, registered companies can only be served processes at their registered address.[496] This is the address of the principal place of business supplied to Companies House at the time of incorporation. Theoretically, the registered address, which is often the address of the principal place of business, is the headquarters and the place of central management of the company. It follows that only the court of the State of incorporation can exercise general jurisdiction over companies.

While this may have been true in 1933 when the extant Act was enacted, the reality is that modern corporate structures have grown more sophisticated beyond that position. Company promoters are moved by several factors when making decisions on corporate formation and management. A company may be formed in a country for tax or other financial considerations while its real principal place of business is located elsewhere for other economic reasons.[497] The CJEU case law provides practical examples. *R (Daily Mail and General Trust plc) v HM Treasury and Commissioners of Inland Revenue*,[498] *Centros Ltd v Erhvervs-og Selskabsstyrelsen*,[499] and *Uberseering BV v Nordic Construction Baumanagement GmbH*,[500] amongst others, are cases where companies which are formed in State A seek to move their businesses to State B while retaining State A as the place of incorporation. In other words, the companies are deemed to be State A companies, but their central management or major businesses are in State B.

This draft improves on extant laws and takes cognisance of what principal place of business means theoretically and practically by retaining the States that have real and genuine connections with a company. State of incorporation does not need further explanation as it can easily be determined. The guidance from English case law is that the place of central management or principal place of business is a question of fact. This may be the 'real seat' where the company carries out its business activities, the place where entrepreneurial decisions are taken, or where those who carry out serious responsibilities in the company have their place of work.[501]

---

[496] Section 1139, Companies Act 2006 (UK).

[497] See *Alberta Inc v Katanga Mining Ltd & Others* [2008] EWHC 2679 (Comm) where a company was registered in Bermuda, resident in Canada for tax purposes, and had its central administration in London.

[498] Case 81/87 *R (Daily Mail and General Trust plc) v HM Treasury and Commissioners of Inland Revenue*.

[499] Case C-212/97 *Centros Ltd v Erhvervs-og Selskabsstyrelsen*.

[500] Case C-208/00 *Uberseering BV v Nordic Construction Baumanagement GmbH*.

[501] See *The 'Rewia'* [1991] 2 Lloyd's Rep 325; *Ministry of Defence of Iran v Faz Aviation* [2008] 1 All ER (Comm) 372; *Alberta Inc v Katanga Mining Ltd & Others* (n 497).

B. Special Jurisdiction

(i) Submission

Section 5(1)(a)–(c) reads:

(a)   the judgment debtor expressly agreed to submit to the jurisdiction of the court;
(b)   the judgment debtor submitted to the jurisdiction of the court by appearing voluntarily in the proceedings;
(c)   the judgment debtor was plaintiff in, or counterclaimant in, the proceedings;

The consent of the judgment debtor clothes the foreign court with the requisite authority to adjudicate a matter, whether he sued as a claimant (and counterclaimant) or is sued as a defendant. This is akin to the Latin maxim *volenti non fit injuria*. It is just and fair that a judgment debtor who chose a foreign court or voluntarily participated in its proceedings should not be heard to complain about the propriety of the foreign court's jurisdiction. In *Naraji v Shelbourne*,[502] the claimant filed a negligence suit in Indiana, United States, against some surgeons over a knee operation and medical aftercare carried out in the United States and England. When the Indiana suit was dismissed, he filed a second suit in England. The defendants relied on the Indiana judgment to bar the second, English proceeding. The English High Court rejected the claimant's argument that the Indiana court had no personal jurisdiction over him because he was neither resident nor present in that jurisdiction. The Court noted that 'a claimant who brings proceedings confers upon the court jurisdiction to determine those proceedings either for or against him'.[503]

The practical problem in the application of these heads of jurisdictions is the determination of what constitutes submission and appearance. A closer look at the drafting of paragraph (a) reveals that its application in practice may produce some uncertainties. It refers specifically to judgment debtors and without any reference to a contract. A question arises as to whether this refers to express choice of court agreement? Must such agreement be reached by both parties or does a unilateral promise from the judgment debtor suffice? This was the issue in *Adams v Cape Industries Plc* where the plaintiff sought to rely on a non-contractual 'agreement to submit'. Scott J in the High Court was of the view that:

> a unilateral statement of willingness to accept the jurisdiction of a foreign court does not, of itself, have any obvious binding effect. It ought, in my view, like any other non-contractual statement of future intention, to be capable of being withdrawn, at any rate, until acted on.[504]

The draft has only settled the ambiguities that may arise from cases like *Vizcaya Partners Limited v Picard and another*[505] where the Privy Council held that submission can be an implied term of a contract, taking account of the circumstances of

---

[502] *Naraji v Shelbourne* [2011] EWHC 3298 (QB).
[503] Ibid, para 135.
[504] *Adams* [1990] Ch 433, 463.
[505] *Vizcaya Partners Limited v Picard* [2016] UKPC 5.

the case.[506] The draft fails to take cognisance of the problem identified in *Adams* of whether a submission should be contractual or non-contractual.

At first blush, voluntary submission seems to be simple and straight forward. It is also trite that a conditional appearance, or what is otherwise known as appearance under protest, does not amount to submission. The courts, however, differ as to what conduct constitutes 'protest'. For instance, a letter written to a court by a judgment debtor denying liability or offering some explanations has been held to be a submission by some courts[507] and a protest by others.[508] Similarly, where a judgment debtor appeared in the foreign court in respect of claim A, does that submission extend to amendments to the claims? Does it extend to the joinder of other co-defendants who may counterclaim and thereby bring in other claims that are connected to A?[509] In *Giant Light Metal Technology (Kunshan) Co Ltd v Aksa Far East Pte Ltd*,[510] the defendant voluntarily submitted in Chinese proceedings but the parties discontinued the action for out-of-court settlement. When the defendant reneged on the settlement, the plaintiff refiled the suit, but the defendant did not appear in the second suit. The plaintiff sought to enforce the default judgment in Singapore. The defendant unsuccessfully challenged the enforcement proceedings on the basis that he had not submitted to the jurisdiction of the court in the second case. Can it be said that section 5(1)(b) of the model law covers this situation? It is suggested that where a suit is reinstated, an earlier submission should suffice because the second suit is a continuation of the first. The answer will be different where there is a substantial amendment to the main claim. A defendant should be allowed to decide whether he wishes to submit to the new claim(s) or not.

To address some of the ambiguities, the drafters proposed that where a defendant appeared for the following purposes, there is no submission (section 5(2)). These are:

(a) to contest the jurisdiction of the court;

(b) to ask the court to dismiss or stay the proceedings on the ground that the dispute in question should be submitted to arbitration or to the determination of the courts of another country;

(c) to protect, or obtain the release of, property seized or threatened with seizure in the proceedings;

---

[506] Lord Collins, giving the judgment of the Privy Council, at paras 59–60 said: 'there must have been an agreement to submit to the jurisdiction of the foreign court, and that agreement may arise through an implied term. Terms implied as a matter of fact depend on construction of the contract in the light of the circumstances.' See also Michael Driscoll QC, 'Common Law Recognition of Foreign Judgments by English and Commonwealth Courts: What Are You Implying?' (2016) 7 *Journal of International Banking and Financial Law* 396.

[507] *Re Overseas Food Importers & Distributors Ltd* (1981) 126 DLR (3d) 422 (decided that a judgment debtor's letter, sent through the German Consulate in Canada to a Bavarian court, explaining her inability to attend proceedings and reasons for the loss suffered by the judgment creditor was a submission).

[508] *De Santis v Russo* [2001] QCA 457 (decided that a letter sent by the judgment debtor to the Queensland court was partly an objection to the jurisdiction of the Italian court and an answer to the merits of the case).

[509] *Murthy v Sivajothi* [1999] 1 WLR 467.

[510] *Giant Light Metal Technology (Kunshan) Co Ltd v Aksa Far East Pte Ltd* [2014] SGHC 16.

These provisos are in *pari materia* with section 33(1) of the UK Civil Jurisdiction and Judgments Act 1982 (CJJA), a statute that was enacted to take care of cases where a defendant objected to the jurisdiction of the foreign court but participated in the proceedings for (b) and (c) purposes.[511] Admittedly, the three provisos give some guidance, but the list does not exhaustively address typical problems encountered in practice. The point was noted by Scott J in *Adams v Cape Industries Plc*[512] that some ambiguities remain in cases where a defendant not only contested the jurisdiction of the foreign court but also took some steps to prepare for trial.

This interesting point is the fulcrum of a recent decision of the Canadian Supreme Court in *Barer v Knight Brothers LLC.*[513] The case concerns the registration of a US (Utah) default judgment in Quebec, Canada. Barer was personally sued, alongside the companies he allegedly controlled, for breach of contract and fraudulent misrepresentation. Barer argued in his motion that the trial court did not have personal jurisdiction over him and that the claim for fraudulent misrepresentation against him was barred at law. The Utah court dismissed his motion and a default judgment was entered against all the defendants. The Canadian Supreme Court, in a plurality decision, held that Barer had submitted to the jurisdiction of the foreign court and the 'save your skin' approach would not assist him. The majority, seven judges, held that he had submitted by arguing a substantive point – that the claim was barred – in his motion in Utah. Brown J held that he did not submit but the court had jurisdiction on another ground: the claim on false misrepresentation was ancillary to the main claim. Côté J held that it was not proven that the Utah court had jurisdiction under the contract and the fact that Barer did raise a substantive point in the motion did not amount to submission. The extent to which a person can raise substantive arguments alongside jurisdictional objections and not be deemed to have submitted to the foreign court's jurisdiction for the purpose of recognising and enforcing the resulting judgment is the key issue in this case. This issue is not clearly determined by the terms of the model law and the explanatory text is silent on it. The majority judgment in *Barer*, written by Gascon J, says that a defendant submits to the jurisdiction of a foreign authority 'when the defendant presents substantive arguments which, if accepted, would resolve the dispute – or part of the dispute – on its merits'.[514] However, the dissenting judgment of Côté J takes into account the 'subjective intent'[515] of the person who is alleged to have submitted to the jurisdiction and adopts a much less rigid test than the majority:

> I would adopt a more flexible approach in determining whether a defendant has submitted to a foreign authority's jurisdiction. A defendant that wishes to contest the

---

[511] Under common law, a judgment debtor who challenged the jurisdiction of the foreign court and lost would be deemed to have submitted and be bound by the decision of the court. See *Henry v Geoprosco International Ltd* [1976] QB 726. The criticisms levied against this rule made Parliament reconsider it. The amendment was codified in s 33(1).

[512] [1990] Ch 433, 464.

[513] *Barer v Knight Brothers LLC*, 2019 SCC 13.

[514] Para 69.

[515] Para 212.

jurisdiction of a foreign authority should be able to argue why the authority lacks jurisdiction without risking being found to have submitted to that jurisdiction. Further, in jurisdictions where procedure requires that arguments on the merits be made simultaneously with objections based on jurisdiction, a defendant should not be prejudiced by raising substantive arguments at that stage.[516]

Barer confirms how vaguely defined concepts can become a nightmare in practice. Gascon J, writing for the majority, made a very important point that '[c]ourts must indeed protect the plaintiff's legitimate interest in knowing, at some point in the proceedings, whether or not the defendant has submitted to jurisdiction.'[517] This point is unassailable. However, like other concepts, this task is better addressed by the legislators and not judges. As much as the plaintiff has a legitimate interest, so also does the defendant. There is a need for a balance, through clear rules, to enable both parties to know when a jurisdictional contest subsists and when it is lost. Côté J, in his dissenting judgment, aptly states the precarious situation of judgment debtors thus:

> This would leave defendants in a 'catch-22' situation. If they attempt to challenge the jurisdiction of a foreign authority, they risk being found by a Quebec court to have submitted to that jurisdiction. If they do not, they will likely be faced with a foreign default judgment which could seriously limit their ability to conduct business (or any other activities) in the foreign jurisdiction. The practical implications are real and serious.[518]

It becomes dicier where the defendant is not represented by counsel, as seen in cases such as *De Santis v Russo*[519] and *Von Wyl v Engeler*.[520] It should be added that in some jurisdictions, the civil procedure laws require a party to answer to the merits of the case and raise whatever objection he has in the defence.[521] For a statutory registration framework where a receiving court is to be discouraged from reviewing foreign judgments, the jurisdictional rules should be as explicit and succinct as possible. It is suggested that a court addressed should be able to review the jurisdictional question where a debtor had raised an objection in the foreign proceedings within the time frame permitted by the rules of the foreign court. This is closer to the solution provided under the Hague Judgments Convention.

The last point on submission is that the CML maintains a similarly broad approach to counterclaims. A counterclaimant is treated as a plaintiff without any qualification. Where the judgment is awarded against him, he is deemed to have submitted because he presented the counterclaim before the court. It does not make any difference whether the counterclaim is wholly connected to the main claim or not. For this purpose, the counterclaim is treated as a self-standing suit.

---

[516] Para 213.
[517] Para 62.
[518] Para 216.
[519] [2001] QCA 457.
[520] *Von Wyl v Engeler* [1998] 3 NZLR 416.
[521] See for instance, Order 24 of the High Court of Lagos State (Civil Procedure) Rules 2019. A similar issue was observed in *Adam v Cape Industries Plc*, [1990] Ch 433, p 460.

Section 5(1)(c) does not, however, cover a counterclaimant who is a judgment creditor. In this situation, he must seek enforcement under section 5(1)(a) and (b) or other jurisdictional grounds.

(ii) Contract

Section 5(1)(g) reads:

> the proceedings related to a contractual obligation that was or should have been performed in the state of origin;

A special jurisdiction founded on contract performed in the State of origin is a new development that will be welcomed by litigants and legal practitioners as well. Obviously, it widens the net to accommodate the enforcement of more foreign judgments in the Commonwealth. The model law expands the heads of international jurisdiction beyond the frontiers of the traditional common law and extant statutory schemes. Under the extant statutory framework, litigants find it so easy to evade legal obligations and proceedings in jurisdictions that are otherwise substantially connected to an underlying contract. This makes it easier for them to judgment-proof their assets. There are judicial authorities in almost every Commonwealth jurisdiction where judgment debtors simply ignore validly commenced proceedings from a State where they transacted business. Such defendants do so without hesitation because they know judgments will not be enforced against non-resident defendants who did not participate in such proceedings. This will no longer be the case when the model law is adopted by Member States. It is a big step that addresses specific problems encountered within the Commonwealth jurisdictions.

Having underscored the importance of the inclusion of this head of jurisdiction, the adequacy of the text can then be considered. The drafters did not offer any explanation why they have restricted this head of jurisdiction to the place of performance and whether this is the best they could offer. The long-arm statutes, as applied in most Commonwealth States, recognise the place of performance and the place of formation as strong links on the basis of which courts can validly exercise direct jurisdiction in contract-related disputes.[522] The two links are strong, although the place of performance may be presumably stronger because the place of formation can be fortuitous in some cases. Also, the policy behind indirect jurisdiction is to ensure that the foreign court is substantially connected with the underlying dispute and that such court is reasonably foreseeable to the parties. It thus makes sense that this ground is restricted to the State where a contract is or ought to be performed since that State has potentially the strongest link to the contract.

---

[522] See for instance, Order 11 Rule 1(d), The Civil Procedure Rules 1998 (UK). Other Commonwealth States have similar rules.

For many contracts, the place of performance may not be difficult to determine either because that place is stipulated by the contract itself or it is fairly straightforward from the nature of the contract itself. Using the example offered in the 2016 UNIDROIT Principles,[523] if A contracts with B to build luxury flats in State C, the place of performance is State C where the construction is to take place. However, not all contracts are as straightforward as the given scenario. International contracts can be very complex, with different obligations to be performed in different places.[524] For instance, *JEB Recoveries LLP v Judah Eleazar Binstock*[525] involved an agency contract wherein Binstock appointed one Wilson to identify and acquire a publicly quoted company which would be interested in acquiring Binstock's business assets. In the course of perfecting Binstock's instructions, Wilson carried out several activities in England, Spain and France. The question, in this case, turned out to be whether Wilson could sue on the contract in England as the place of performance simply because he met some auditors in London and agreed to form an English liability partnership in furtherance of perfecting Mr Binstock's instructions. As the facts of *Rehder v Air Baltic Corp*[526] also confirm, an airline which is domiciled in State A may undertake to fly a customer from State B to States C and D. One can see that there are different categories of contract which a single rule – the place of performance – may not adequately cover.

Another problem with the text is that it fails to stipulate whether what is being considered here is a specific obligation, otherwise known as 'the obligation in question' or the characteristic obligation. This is a novel provision in all the Commonwealth judgments frameworks except for that of Canada where indirect jurisdiction is based on real and substantial connection. One wonders how the Commonwealth courts will interpret this text when the model law is adopted. English law may not reflect the understanding of the Commonwealth courts in this area because case law and the CJJA have been influenced by the EU Brussels Convention/Regulation. For instance, the CJJA domesticates the Brussels Convention, which confers jurisdiction 'in matters relating to a contract' on 'the courts for the place of performance of the obligation in question'. There are only a few cases from other Commonwealth States on this point and this makes it difficult to predict how the courts will interpret 'the place of performance' and whether they will go for the 'obligation in question' approach or 'the characteristic obligation' (ie the main obligation) approach.

In *Lilydale Cooperative Limited v Meyn Canada Inc*,[527] *Lilydale*, a company based in Alberta, contracted with *Meyn*, an Ontario company, for the design and

---

[523] International Institute for the Unification of Private Law, *UNIDROIT Principles of International Commercial Contracts 2016* (UNIDROIT 2016) 193.

[524] Paul Beaumont and Burcu Yüksel, 'Cross-Border Civil and Commercial Disputes Before the Court of Justice of the European Union' in Paul Beaumont and others (eds), *Cross-Border Litigation in Europe* (Hart Publishing 2017) 513–24; Jonathan Hill, 'Jurisdiction in Matters Relating to a Contract under the Brussels Convention' (1995) 44 *International & Comparative Law Quarterly* 591.

[525] *JEB Recoveries LLP v Judah Eleazar Binstock* [2016] EWCA Civ 1008.

[526] Case C-204/08 *Rehder v Air Baltic Corp*.

[527] *Lilydale Cooperative Limited v Meyn Canada Inc*, 2015 ONCA 281.

delivery of a 'fryer and oven system'. *Meyn* carried out the design, chose the components and arranged to obtain them in Ontario. The only work it did in Alberta was to deliver and install the system. Both parties commenced proceedings in Alberta and Ontario respectively for negligence and breach of contract. *Lilydale* applied for the Ontario action to be struck out for want of jurisdiction because the place of performance of the contract was Alberta and not Ontario. The Ontario Court of Appeal agreed with the lower court that this was not a contract of sale but one of 'design and sale'. As such, most of the aspects of the contract were performed in Ontario and not Alberta, and the lower court was right to choose which of the obligations should be overriding. The Court did not discuss characteristic obligation or obligation in question perhaps, because those concepts are not popular in the Commonwealth. This suggests that some Commonwealth courts may approve an international jurisdiction based on the performance of some or part of the obligations in the State of origin without necessarily considering whether it is the obligation in question or the characteristic obligation.

The approach of the English court is to consider the obligation in question. This obligation may be a single activity to be performed in one State or several obligations to be performed in different States, in which case, the court will consider the place for the provision of the main service(s). In *IHP Ltd v Fleming*,[528] it was held that England, the place of business of the seller, was the place of performance of an obligation to pay for the supply of chickens to the respondent in Scotland. In *Canyon Offshore Ltd v GDF Suez E&P Nederland BV*,[529] it was held that the place of performance of the obligation to pay for certain engineering works carried out on the Dutch continental shelf was England or Scotland, as stipulated on the invoice issued to the respondent. In *JEB Recoveries LLP v Judah Eleazar Binstock*, the Court of Appeal set out objective criteria to determine the place of performance where the overall obligation in question comprises several obligations that are performed in more than one State. The Court noted the need for proximity and foreseeability while deciding the place of performance in this instance. Thus, where several places have been agreed or no specific place was agreed, the place of performance would be that place where the principal obligation was carried out (assuming that can be determined), or where most of the obligations were carried out, or, if none of the above can be determined, the place where the party performing the obligation is domiciled.

For modern legislation, the drafters ought to take cognisance of the developments within and outside the Commonwealth. In the absence of a shared meaning or an autonomous definition which has evolved or been prescribed by the drafters, a more nuanced provision with some details to address some of the uncertainties that have been recorded elsewhere would have been appropriate.

---

[528] *IHP Ltd v Fleming* (QBD, 10 July 2009), [2009] 7 WLUK 279.
[529] *Canyon Offshore Ltd v GDF Suez E&P Nederland BV* [2015] ILPr 8, [2014] EWHC 3810 (Comm).

Assuming the drafters wanted to go for the strongest connection, ie, the 'place of performance' rule, a simple and broad rule may not address the practical problems as shown above and as further discussed in Chapter seven below. The rule will likely be subjected to different interpretations by different courts, thereby jeopardising legal certainty and predictability. While the goals of the drafters are praiseworthy, presenting the rules in such a way that will achieve their goal is equally important. Therefore, they could have been more explicit on the standards that can guide courts on how to determine the place of performance where the contract is silent on that point.

It is suggested that the courts should follow an approach that prioritises proximity and foreseeability. The place where an obligation in question is to be performed will meet these two criteria. Thus, where the cause of action concerns the delivery of goods, that should be the place where the goods are/ought to be delivered; for provision of service(s), the place where the service is/ought to be performed; for payments, the place where payment is/ought to be made; and for other obligations to be performed in different States, the place where the main obligation is/ought to be performed. In borderline cases where the obligations are weighed equally, then both or all the places are substantially connected and can be regarded as places of performance. This is similar to the English court's guidelines as stipulated in *JEB Recoveries LLP* and is therefore recommended for the Commonwealth courts.

(iii) Tort

Section 5(1)(h) reads:

> the proceedings related to tort or a non-contractual obligation and the wrongful act occurred in the state of origin;

Defining what is a real and substantial connection for torts has never been an easy task. Under their national laws, courts do exercise direct jurisdiction where a tort has any connection with the forum. However, this is not the case for indirect jurisdiction. Neither the common law nor the extant statutory schemes recognise any jurisdiction exercised based on the location of a wrongful act or where damage is suffered. To this extent, section 5(1)(h) is another positive step by the Commonwealth countries at modernising their judgments enforcement scheme.

The drafters appear to have attempted to avoid the controversies surrounding the divergent approaches of Commonwealth Member States to the appropriate forum for torts by limiting the plaintiff's choice to the place of the wrongful act. The explanatory text shows that the previous drafts also included the place where the damage was suffered. The discussants noted that there are some torts whose consequential damage is multi-jurisdictional, and this can make the tortfeasor liable to answer claims in different jurisdictions, some of which might not be foreseeable.

The argument has its merits. The place of the wrongful act provides more certainty and predictability since the State where the tort occurred is the natural forum and, arguably, may have the strongest link to the dispute.[530]

The Canadian Supreme Court seems to favour a broader approach to the question of jurisdiction in tort cases.[531] In *Spar Aerospace Ltd v American Mobile Satellite Corp*,[532] the Court was of the view that real and substantial connection had to be interpreted so as to consider the interests of both the plaintiff and the defendant. It reasoned that what matters is that the court should have *a* real and substantial connection, not *the most* real and *most* substantial connection. Thus, a court of the place where harm is suffered may validly assume jurisdiction. It would not matter whether this is an interprovincial or international case. This is part of the Canadian common law development and the application of its 'real and substantial connection' in the context of tort. The Court favoured a broader approach since the doctrine of *forum non conveniens* can always act as a 'counterweight' to an inappropriate exercise of direct jurisdiction.[533] In other words, a broader indirect jurisdictional ground which vests jurisdiction in the court of the State where a wrongful act occurs or where harm is suffered should not pose any serious challenge because *forum non conveniens* can be used by the respondent to redirect the action to its natural forum. Where such is the case, the result should normally be that judgments would come from the State where the tort occurred. The weakness in this argument is that *forum non conveniens* is discretionary, and it is not available in many jurisdictions outside the Commonwealth. Within the Commonwealth, there is no certainty that courts will stay proceedings in tort cases where damage – whether initial or secondary – was suffered within the jurisdiction. Indeed, if the practicalities of litigation were to be considered, a court would rather allow a plaintiff who was injured in an accident to sue at home because it would be inconvenient for him to litigate abroad.

Be that as it may, the place where a wrongful act occurred has its interpretative difficulties. The use of 'wrongful act' signifies that the drafters intended to provide a simple rule to determine the appropriate venue for tort claims. The emphasis is on the wrongful act and not the damage. This will be obvious for many torts, as the wrongful act which caused the damage can be easily identified. However, this may not be the case for other torts like negligent misstatements and product liability cases where the wrongful act(s) may consist of a series of actions which may be multi-jurisdictional as well.

---

[530] This may, however, not be the case always, as some torts can be fortuitous. Also, the State where damage occurred, at times, may have stronger connection to a tort. Fairness and justice may also require that the plaintiff sue in his home court. This is the rationale for the Canadian approach, which integrates damage as a causative factor. See *Poirier v Williston* (1981) 118 DLR (3d) 252, 1981 CanLII 3027 (ON CA); *Muscutt v Courcelles* (2002) 60 OR (3d) 20, 2002 CanLII 44957 (ON CA).

[531] This extends to other heads of jurisdiction such as contract.

[532] *Spar Aerospace Ltd v American Mobile Satellite Corp* [2002] 4 SCR 205.

[533] Paras 57–60.

There is also the problem of characterisation of what the wrongful act is. This explains why in the Canadian jurisprudence, any significant element, including damage suffered by the plaintiff, will be relevant. Thus, by the 'last event' theory, the damage completes the tort.[534] *Gulevich v Miller*[535] also holds that in determining the place where a tort was committed, 'it is necessary and sufficient that the last ingredient of the cause of action [damage], the event which completes the cause of action and brings it into being, has occurred within the jurisdiction'.

The Anglo-Australian approach to direct jurisdiction considers the place where the 'substance of the claim' – ie, the substance of the tort – occurred. This was laid down in *Distiller's Co (Biochemichals) Ltd v Thompson*[536] and *The 'Albaforth'*[537] line of authorities. It requires the court to look at the series of events and ask: 'Where in substance did this cause of action arise?'. The rationale offered by Robert Goff LJ in *The 'Albaforth'* is that 'if the substance of an alleged tort is committed within a certain jurisdiction, it is not easy to imagine what other facts could displace the conclusion that the courts of that jurisdiction are the natural forum'.[538]

As Yeo Tiong Min rightly notes, the Anglo-Australian approach offers a balance between certainty and flexibility,[539] at least theoretically. However, determining the substance of the tort claim also brings a problem of characterisation and other subjective factors. It is a question of which of the factors the court emphasises. This explains why some decisions are irreconcilable on this point. It is not surprising that in *VTB Capital plc v Nutritek International Corp and Others*,[540] the issue of the place of the tort was litigated up to the UK Supreme Court with different considerations emphasised by the trial court, the Court of Appeal and the Supreme Court.

For a judgments enforcement framework, clarity and certainty should be key objectives that lawmakers must strive to achieve to enable litigants to make informed choices of litigation venue. Given the ambiguities arising from the case law, it will be useful for lawmakers to identify certain factors which courts should assess or consider in determining the place of the wrongful act.[541] It makes the assessment of a foreign court's jurisdiction easier at the enforcement stage without the need to go into the merits of the case.

---

[534] Tiong Min Yeo, 'Jurisdiction Issues in International Tort Litigation: A Singapore View' (1994) 7 *Singapore Academy of Law Journal* 1, 5.

[535] *Gulevich v Miller*, 2015 ABCA 411, para 29.

[536] *Distiller's Co (Biochemichals) Ltd v Thompson* [1971] AC 458 (PC).

[537] *Cordoba Shipping Co Ltd v National State Bank, Elizabeth, New Jersey (The 'Albaforth')* [1984] 2 Lloyd's Rep 91.

[538] Ibid.

[539] Yeo (n 534) 12.

[540] *VTB Capital plc v Nutritek International Corp and Others* [2013] UKSC 5.

[541] A similar suggestion was made in *Muscutt v Courcelles* (n 530) concerning the assumption of jurisdiction over out-of-province torts.

(iv) Branch/Agency

Section 5(1)(f) reads:

> the judgment debtor, being a defendant in the court of the state of origin, had an office or place of business in that state and the proceedings were with respect to a transaction effected through or at that office or place;

This is another ground of novel indirect jurisdiction that is being introduced in the Commonwealth judgments scheme. Unlike section 5(1)(e), this head of jurisdiction applies to corporate and non-corporate defendants such as sole proprietorships, partnerships, and other unincorporated associations. It confers specific jurisdiction on the State of origin where the debtor has a place of business and in respect of transactions conducted through that office. There should be no serious difficulty in applying this paragraph to non-corporate defendants. However, for companies who do business in foreign countries through a branch, an agent or other establishments, there is a need for some examination.

This paragraph suggests that where 'a transaction' was conducted through an office or a place of business in the State of origin, the judgment from that court is enforceable. What does an office or a place of business mean? Does it include non-business premises? Does a single transaction in the State of origin suffice? Is the emphasis on the place, or the business, or both? These questions are prompted because the drafters did not indicate whether this head of jurisdiction means 'branch jurisdiction' or 'doing business' jurisdiction. Since the drafters are largely inspired by the developments in The Hague, it can be argued that they intended to follow the Brussels/Hague approach. Thus, 'office' and 'place of business' will be treated as branch, agency and other establishments.

'An office' means a permanent location associated with the judgment debtor.[542] In *Re Oriel Ltd*, the Court of Appeal noted that a company which transacts business in the public rooms of a hotel in London would have 'carried on business' in England, but it would be difficult to hold that hotel rooms are an established place of business. It seems that a 'place of business' as used in the model law would be interpreted to mean a business office. Thus, a foreign company which transacted business in a hotel room cannot be said to have transacted through an office or a place of business in that State of origin. The focus of this head of jurisdiction is on the established business location of the debtor and the transaction(s) effected through that location. Thus, international jurisdiction will not be validly exercised merely because the defendant does business in the State of origin via a website,[543] or in a hotel through some employees.[544]

One other key point that should be mentioned is that neither common law nor the 1933 Act provides for branch jurisdiction. As such, jurisdiction has been

---

[542] *Re Oriel Ltd* [1986] 1 WLR 180, 185.
[543] *HMB Holdings Limited v Attorney General of Antigua and Barbuda*, 2019 ONSC 1445.
[544] *Littauer Glove Corp v FW Millington (1920) Ltd* (1928) 44 TLR 746.

analysed based on 'residence' of foreign corporations through local branches or agents. These cases prescribe two criteria for international jurisdiction over foreign corporations: one, they must be resident (through a local agent/branch) at a fixed place; two, they must have carried on business over a period of time.[545] While the first condition is supported by the model law, the second condition will not apply because that condition is meant for 'doing business'. What is required under this new head of jurisdiction is that 'the proceedings were with respect to a transaction effected through or at that office or place'. Thus, a foreign judgment is enforceable even if it relates to the single transaction a company carried out in the State of origin, provided it was a transaction effected through its branch in that State.

The model law fails to address some ambiguities that surround the relationship between the parent company and the branch. Can the foreign principal be impleaded for transactions carried out by its branch in the State of origin? Will it make any difference if the branch has a separate legal personality? What if the branch does not have the authority to bind the principal? The Commonwealth courts will likely follow *Adams v Cape Industries Plc* on these issues.

(v) Real Property

Section 5(1)(i) reads:

> the proceedings related to a dispute concerning title to real property located in the state of origin;

The *lex situs* rule remains one of the settled private international law rules. Since title to land can only be dealt with in the manner required by the law of the *situs* and may require the rectification of a government register, it goes without saying that the court of the *situs* is in the best position to deal with such disputes. This is often referred to as the *Moçambique* rule.[546] Thus, a foreign judgment determining title to land in the receiving State would normally be unenforceable. In *Singh v Kaur Bal*[547] two brothers had a dispute over some properties in Malaysia. The plaintiff sued the defendant in the Supreme Court of Western Australia for transferring lands held on constructive trust to his wife and daughter with intent to defraud. The defendant unsuccessfully challenged the jurisdiction of the Australian court thereby leading to a default judgment against him. Thereafter, the defendant sued the plaintiff in Malaysia and got an injunction restraining the plaintiff from relying on the Australian judgment or acting upon it except through a Malaysian enforcement proceeding. It may be a fruitless exercise to sue for title to land in foreign courts. Similarly, in an earlier Canadian case of *Duke v Andler*,[548] a court

---

[545] See *Adams v Cape Industries Plc* [1990] Ch 433; *Vogel v R and A Kohnstamm Ltd* [1973] QB 133.
[546] *British South Africa Co v Companhia de Moçambique* [1893] AC 602 (HL).
[547] *Singh v Kaur Bal (No 3)* [2012] WASC 243, cited as *Singh v Singh* in Jack Wass, 'The Court's *In Personam* Jurisdiction in Cases Involving Foreign Land' (2014) 63 *International & Comparative Law Quarterly* 103.
[548] *Duke v Andler* [1932] SCR 734.

in California ordered the execution of a conveyance concerning land in British Columbia in favour of the judgment creditor following a refusal by the defendant to do the same. The Canadian Supreme Court held that the conveyance could not be binding in Canada even though the California court had validly exercised *in personam* jurisdiction over the parties and thereby had the power to order the defendant to convey the land.

The *situs* rule has remained unchanged even though individuals and corporations that claim interests in land are increasingly mobile.[549] While the rule remains well established in most jurisdictions, its utility in the modern age has been criticised by several writers.[550] This criticism may be sound, particularly, in cases where the parties voluntarily submitted to the jurisdiction of the foreign court and the court applied the *lex situs* so that the result would not have been different from what the court of the *situs* would arrive at. This view is gaining ground and has been applied by some courts in the Commonwealth. In *Monteiro v Monteiro*,[551] Madam Justice Burke held that a Portuguese order in a matrimonial proceeding affecting a property in British Columbia can be enforced in British Columbia under section 10(k) of the Court Jurisdiction and Proceedings Transfer Act.[552] The Supreme Court of British Columbia declined jurisdiction in favour of the pending proceeding in Portugal and also noted that Mrs Monteiro had pled British Columbia law in the Portuguese proceeding and there was no issue that the law would apply.

While it is settled that a court does not have jurisdiction in matters involving titles to foreign land, the areas of interest, as observed from case law in different Commonwealth jurisdictions, are whether a court of origin can exercise jurisdiction over equitable claims concerning foreign land, whether a court of origin can entertain contractual, trust or tort disputes concerning foreign land, and whether any *in personam* judgment (money or non-money) rendered in those proceedings can be enforced.[553] A good example is *Lightning v Lightning Electrical Contractors Ltd*[554] where Mr Lightning claimed to be a beneficiary under a resulting trust for land, which the defendant company bought in Scotland, but which Mr Lightning paid for. The defendant went into receivership. Scots law does not

---

[549] Wass (n 547) 104.

[550] Keyes (ch 3, fn 311) 75 (argues that the rule should be retained only where it will result in effecting corrections in registers); Stephen Lee, 'Title to Foreign Real Property in Transnational Money Claims' (1995) 32 *Columbia Journal of Transnational Law* 607 (describing the rule as a nineteenth-century academic construct).

[551] *Monteiro v Monteiro*, 2015 BCSC 1543 (CanLII).

[552] Court Jurisdiction and Proceedings Transfer Act (S.B.C. 2003).

[553] *Murakami Takako v Wiryadi Louise Maria* [2009] 1 SLR 508 (CA) (where an executor of the estate of a deceased sought to amend a claim in Singapore to include money in two Australian banks and other foreign immovables); *L Manimuthu v L Shanmuganathan* [2016] 5 SLR 719 (a claim involving a composite agreement by two brothers over their deceased father's immovable properties in Singapore and India).

[554] *Lightning v Lightning Electrical Contractors Ltd* [1998] NPC 71, (1998) 23(1) *Trust Law International* 35.

recognise equitable interests. Both parties were based in England. The English Court of Appeal held that the property or its proceeds of sale was held in trust for Mr Lightning.[555] Although an English court cannot adjudicate on a *title to land* located in Scotland, Mr Lightning should be able to enforce a judgment which ruled on a beneficial interest in the *proceeds of the sale* of the land. It is not clear whether this ground as drafted in section 5(1)(i) covers these types of proceedings which do not 'directly' determine title to land.

Other interesting issues are jurisdiction over movable property and the enforce-ability of judgments from those proceedings. Section 2(1) of the CML defines enforceable non-money judgments to include orders for 'the transfer of a speci-fied item or specified items of movable property'. However, acceptable connections over movable property are not included under section 5. Movable property can be the subject of a distinct claim for possessory rights, rights of security over the property or authority to dispose of the said property. Clearly, a contractual rule on the place of performance does not apply to these examples, as these are not contractual disputes. Unfortunately, these issues are not addressed as a result of the restrictive scope adopted under this head of jurisdiction.

(vi) Trust

Section 5(1)(j) reads:

> the proceedings related to the validity or administration of a trust established in the state of origin or to trust assets located in that state, and the trustee, settlor or benefi-ciary had his or her ordinary residence or its principal place of business in the state of origin; or the court of origin was a court of a country designated in the trust instrument as having jurisdiction for this purpose;

Trust is a creation of equity and it is a concept that is widely used in common law jurisdictions. Jurisdiction over equitable actions is generally *in personam*. This suggests that irrespective of where the subject matter of a trust is located, a court has jurisdiction to decide disputes concerning such trust provided the defend-ant is within its territorial reach. With the emerging developments in the area of trust establishment and administration, the field is becoming more sophisticated, with trust properties, trustees and beneficiaries scattered in different jurisdictions. Undoubtedly, it has developed beyond the frontiers of the traditional equitable principles. With the frequency of foreign elements in trust administration, inevita-bly, the rules of jurisdiction and enforcement of judgments concerning trust assets must be revisited. Such revision has been limited or non-existent until recent times. The inclusion of international jurisdiction for trust disputes in the model law should be applauded.

As mentioned above, *in personam* jurisdiction over trustees may result in judgments from courts that have little or no connection with the trust assets.

---

[555] For other cases of *in personam* action concerning foreign land, see Wass (n 547).

The jurisdictional ground provided under the model law is generally based on efficiency. By this, courts that have a substantial connection with a trust establishment would have their judgments recognised and enforced abroad. The drafters noted various options that were suggested during the negotiation of the Hague Judgments Convention. However, they settled for a simple 'serviceable rule' that can be easily implemented. In line with the promotion of party autonomy, any court designated in a trust instrument is sufficiently connected even if the trust assets or administrators are located elsewhere. When the judgment involved the validity or administration of the trust, the originating State where the trust was established has indirect jurisdiction, or when the judgment concerned trust assets located in that State the courts of that State have indirect jurisdiction, provided that in both either the settlor, trustee or beneficiary was ordinarily resident or had their principal place of business in the State of origin.

There are, however, a few points to be noted on this paragraph. A definition or description of what constitutes a trust should be offered, since the Commonwealth has some civil law members who may not have a comparable concept in their laws. Although trust is defined in the Hague Convention of 1 July 1985 on the Law Applicable to Trusts and on their Recognition, only Australia, the United Kingdom, Canada, Cyprus and Malta are Commonwealth members who are party to that Convention. Other members may have a different understanding of what a trust is, what is included and what is excluded.

(vii) Product/Service Liability

Section 5(1)(k) reads:

> the proceedings related to a dispute concerning goods made or services provided by the judgment debtor and the goods and services were acquired or used by the judgment creditor when the judgment creditor was ordinarily resident in the state of origin and were marketed through the normal channels of trade in the state of origin.

There is a difficulty in the categorisation of this head of jurisdiction because the ground as drafted is unique. No such ground exists under common law or the extant statutory schemes. It is also neither in the Hague Conventions nor the Brussels Ia Regulation. The drafters stated that 'it is essentially a consumer protection rule'. Perhaps it is a restrictive consumer protection rule, since it is not as broad and detailed as standard jurisdiction rules for consumer contracts as seen in Brussels Ia for instance. What is more appropriate is that this head of jurisdiction governs products and services liability. The explanatory text gave the reason as follows:

> Suppose that A spends some time working in the United States. He or she buys a product manufactured in, for example, Germany but marketed in the US. The product turns out to be defective and indeed dangerous; A is injured. Although the German manufacturing company is in no sense present in the relevant US jurisdiction and there is no contractual relationship between A and the company, most US states will claim jurisdiction on the ground that by targeting a US market, the company has exposed itself to the

risk of litigation there. Few Commonwealth courts would themselves take jurisdiction on such a ground, but there seems no good reason to deny A enforcement of any judgment obtained on that basis elsewhere.

The scenario puts it beyond doubt that the paragraph deals with products and services liability. In most cases, product liability claims fall under non-contractual obligations. Most of those scenarios can be covered by the jurisdictional ground for torts because the injuries often occur in the place where the products are used. The plaintiff should still be able to sue in his place of residence (assuming he bought the goods there) even where the event leading to the injury did not occur at his residence. This may cover defects arising from the design or manufacturing of the goods. Thus, if a manufacturer is sued in a jurisdiction where its goods are marketed which was also the ordinary residence of the victim at the time of the goods being used or acquired, the judgment obtained in such proceedings is enforceable. It is unclear how the paragraph applies to liability for services because the notion of acquiring and using services is quite novel, as is what is meant by marketing services. This kind of provision has some familiarity in the context of applicable law in product liability rather than services liability (eg the Hague Convention on Product Liability and the Rome II Regulation). The scenarios that may come under this paragraph are negligent/fraudulent misrepresentations arising from service contracts (eg professional advice, financial services, etc) or contracts that comprise goods and services (eg design). This paragraph, therefore, permits a buyer or user to sue foreign manufacturers/service providers at home, even in cases where there is no contractual relationship between them, and have judgment in his favour enforced elsewhere.

Another problem with this head of jurisdiction is that it is difficult to reconcile the explanatory note (consumer protection rule) with the text. The basis for providing an alternative forum for a consumer – his residence – is that he is often a weaker party who needs some form of protection against sellers who, presumably, have enough resources to defend actions abroad.[556] In jurisdictions where such rule is available, it protects business to consumer, and not business to business contracts.[557] However, what we have under this head does not protect consumers enough. Where a consumer changes his residence after purchasing some goods but before receiving them, he cannot benefit from this ground because the connection applies only when the place where the goods or services were acquired or used is the place where the person was ordinarily resident. On the other hand, the rule is arguably overbroad because corporate plaintiffs are protected by the rule.

---

[556] Joakim St Øren, 'International Jurisdiction Over Consumer Contracts in E-Europe' (2003) 52 *International and Comparative Law Quarterly* 665; Beatriz Añoveros Terradas, 'Restrictions on Jurisdiction Clauses in Consumer Contracts within the European Union' (2003) *Oxford University Comparative Law Forum* 1.

[557] See Article 17(1) of Brussels Ia. It is thought that corporate entities usually act in a business capacity even though there are a few borderline cases which may suggest otherwise.

It is a big win for them, as they can sue at home for product and service liability cases and have judgment in their favour enforced elsewhere.

V. Recognition, Enforcement and Defences

A pragmatic judgments enforcement framework ensures that disputes are litigated in jurisdictions that are substantially connected to the parties or disputes. The jurisdictional filters are succinctly laid out to help litigants make informed choices. Once a judgment emanates from a court with a substantial connection, all that is required by the court addressed is to verify the jurisdictional grounds and check whether the judgment does not violate the receiving State's fundamental policies. Section 6(1) and (2) of the CML stipulate that a foreign judgment which meets the jurisdictional requirements of section 5 should be recognised without much ado, and the merits of such judgments shall not be reviewed under any guise.

Denial grounds are safety valves against foreign judgments that might have been improperly procured or those that violate the fundamental values of the enforcing State. This is the essential function they perform in a judgments enforcement framework. While these grounds are indisputably essential, legislators and treaty-makers need to ensure that they are restricted to securing the right to a fair trial and reflecting the public policy of the receiving State. Where these grounds are excessively broad, they may reduce the efficiency of the judgments framework.

An empirical assessment of UK judgments delivered between February 1999 and February 2019 was carried out to see how these denial grounds (defences) were raised in practice and how they have been treated by the courts. The essence of this is to see whether there is justification or need for the grounds, whether they have been broadly or narrowly applied by the courts and whether the text of the model law can adequately take care of any perceived problem. The United Kingdom was selected because of its status in the Commonwealth and the persuasive effect of its decisions in all common law jurisdictions. The last two decades were chosen for two reasons. One is to get as many cases as possible to arrive at conclusions that can fairly represent the courts' practice. Second, the last two decades should fairly represent the contemporary views of the courts. The research was done by consulting two electronic databases: WestlawUK and LexisNexis. These two platforms offer access to not only the appellate decisions but also cases decided by the lower courts, which may not be captured in the law reports.[558] The relevant cases considered are those in which the defences were specifically raised

---

[558] About 866 cases were retrieved with the search phrase 'foreign judgment' for the period of enquiry. The search was further narrowed down to 'foreign judgment' AND 'public policy', 'foreign judgment' AND 'fraud', 'foreign judgment' AND 'natural justice'. 50 cases were retrieved for natural justice, 260 were retrieved for public policy and 246 were retrieved for fraud. Some cases were further excluded. These are non-UK judgments, and judgments concerning family, insolvency and criminal law matters.

to set aside recognition or enforcement of foreign judgments (and in a few cases arbitral awards which were connected with foreign judgments) and whose subject matter falls within the scope of this book. These defences are natural justice (19), fraud (21), public policy (41). The following sections will examine the grounds for denial under the model law.

A. Natural Justice and Procedural Fairness

A judgment that was delivered in a proceeding that violated 'the principles of procedural fairness and natural justice' shall not be entitled to recognition.[559] This provision is similar to but not identical with what is available in the extant laws. The current laws specify that a foreign judgment shall not be recognised if the judgment debtor was not duly served[560] or given enough time to prepare his defence.[561] This is more limited in scope compared to the broad provision of the model law. The drafters took cognisance of modern trends and expressions found in other judgments recognition treaties such as the Hague Judgments Convention.

There is no gainsaying that every litigant has a fundamental right to a fair hearing. This is a universal right, which is entrenched in almost all constitutional charters both within and outside the Commonwealth. The right to a fair hearing is broad. The details differ from one jurisdiction to another. Case law and extant statutory laws emphasise issues of service of the processes of the foreign court and adequacy of time to prepare the defence. This has come to be generally understood in the Commonwealth as natural justice.[562] However, it remains to be seen how the courts will consider 'procedural fairness' as newly introduced in the model law. Is procedural fairness an emphasis on the shared understanding of natural justice? Is it to be taken as a new form of defence which means that the court addressed may consider the totality of the fairness of the procedure of the foreign court? In the absence of any explanatory note on this, different Commonwealth Member States may interpret and apply 'procedural fairness' differently. This may lead to an undesirable result where litigants would simply invite a court addressed to review the procedure of foreign courts. This closely represents what transpired in *Adams v Cape Industries Plc*. In this case, a foreign judgment was attacked based on a procedural defect. The English Court of Appeal refused to enforce an award of the sum of US$75,000 as compensation to each plaintiff without an objective assessment of the extent of the defendant's obligation and upon proof by the plaintiff of the relevant facts. For the sake of legal certainty and predictability, whatever is sought

---

[559] Section 6(3)(c).
[560] Section 9(2)(c), 1920 Act.
[561] Section 4(1)(a)(iii), 1933 Act.
[562] Hill and Chong referred to them as traditional categories. See Jonathan Hill and Adeline Chong, *International Commercial Disputes: Commercial Conflict of Laws in English Courts* (Hart Publishing 2010) 427.

to be achieved by 'procedural fairness' may, as well, be achieved by 'natural justice' as understood under the extant laws.

Be that as it may, the proceedings of the foreign court are presumptively regular. The court addressed knows fully that national courts' procedures and substantive laws differ. Thus, the mere fact that a foreign court treated some procedural matters in a rather different way should not lead to denial.[563] The judgment debtor must show that he was not notified of the proceedings, did not have adequate time to prepare for trial or that he was denied other rights to a fair trial such as an impartial tribunal.[564] For efficiency, the debtor should also be required to attempt to seek redress in the State of origin provided he has time to do so.

From the empirical research, the result reaffirms that there is a need for the natural justice defence. In many of these enforcement proceedings, judgment debtors sought to overturn the registration of foreign judgments or asked that such judgments be denied recognition on the ground of natural justice. Natural justice was used in the broader sense to cover procedural irregularities, such as non-service of originating processes or the service but non-receipt of originating processes, and inadequacy of time to prepare for trial. It was also used as a ground for other fundamental rights such as partiality of judges,[565] incapacity to present a defence,[566] excessive delay of trial,[567] award of damages on points not addressed at trial,[568] and deficiency in the judicial reasoning of foreign courts,[569] amongst others.

Nineteen cases were identified and reviewed in total. The judgment debtors succeeded in seven cases (37 per cent) and failed in 12 cases (63 per cent).[570] The seven successful cases are *Malicorp Ltd v Egypt*,[571] *Maronier v Larmer*,[572] *Tavoulareas v Tsavliris & Others*,[573] *Reeve v Plummer*,[574] *Kanoria v Guinness*,[575] *Laserpoint Ltd v Prime Minister of Malta*[576] and *Masters v Leaver*.[577] *Laserpoint Ltd*

---

[563] *Pace Europe Ltd v Dunham* [2012] EWHC 852 (Ch); *Keller v Cowen (Foreign judgments)* [2000] 7 WLUK 121.

[564] See *Laserpoint Ltd v Prime Minister of Malta* [2016] EWHC 1820 (QB).

[565] *Smith v Huertas* [2015] EWHC 3745 (Comm).

[566] *Ajay Kanoria and Others v Tony Francis Guinness* [2006] EWCA Civ 222.

[567] *Smith v Huertas* [2015] EWHC 3745 (Comm); *Laserpoint Ltd v Prime Minister of Malta* (n 564).

[568] *Malicorp Ltd v Arab Republic of Egypt* [2015] EWHC 361 (Comm).

[569] *Superior Composite Structures LLC v Parrish* [2015] EWHC 3688 (QB).

[570] The cases where the defence failed are: *Pace Europe Ltd v Dunham* [2012] EWHC 852 (Ch); *Keller v Cowen (Foreign judgments)* [2000] 7 WLUK 121; *Midtown Acquisitions LP v Essar Global Fund Limited* [2018] EWHC 2545 (Comm); *Superior Composite Structures LLC v Parrish* [2015] EWHC 3688 (QB); *Smith v Huertas* [2015] EWHC 3745 (Comm); *Open Joint Stock Company Alfa-Bank v Georgy Trefilov* [2014] EWHC 1806 (Comm); *Commercial Innovation Bank Alfa Bank v Victor Kozeny* [2002] UKPC 66; *OJSC Bank of Moscow v Chernyakov* [2016] EWHC 2583 (Comm); *JSC VTB Bank v Skurikhin* [2014] EWHC 271 (Comm); *Ningbo Jiangdong Jiemao and Export Company Limited v Universal Garments International Limited* [2017] 11 WLUK 660; *Starlight International Inc v A.J Bruce and Others* [2002] EWHC 374; *TSN Kunststoffrecycling GmbH v Jurgens* [2002] EWCA Civ 11.

[571] [2015] EWHC 361 (Comm).

[572] *Maronier v Larmer* [2002] EWCA Civ 774.

[573] *Tavoulareas v Tsavliris & Others* [2006] EWCA Civ 1772.

[574] *Reeve v Plummer* [2014] EWHC 4695 (QB).

[575] [2006] EWCA Civ 222.

[576] [2016] EWHC 1820 (QB).

[577] *Masters v Leaver* [2000] ILPr 387.

is an exceptional case. The company was sued for fire damage that occurred in a conference it organised in Malta in 1987. The writ was served on the company's registered address in London. However, the address had been changed by then, but the change was not effected timeously by Companies House. Since the company was not represented, a copy of the writ was served on curators appointed for the company in Malta. The trial dragged on for a long time. In the process, the company's predecessor was dissolved around 2003. The trial was suspended and reinstated in 2007 but no further communication was served on the company. A default judgment was entered in 2007. The company challenged the enforcement of the judgment in England. The English court held that the appellant had been denied the right to a fair hearing because it was not contacted before judgment was given and the trial was excessively long. The circumstances in *Maronier* were similar to those of *Laserpoint Ltd*. In this case, a Dutch judgment was denied recognition because the suit was stayed for 12 years and reactivated without notice to Mr Larmer who had by then relocated to England. The Court of Appeal ruled that he was denied a right to a fair trial. In *Tavoulareas*, recognition was denied to a Greek judgment because Mr Tavoulareas only got to know of a parallel Greek proceeding in the witness statement that was served on him in an English proceeding. In *Reeve*, a Belgian judgment against Mr Reeve was set aside because he, together with other appellants had been served by substituted service. They only became aware of the suit after the judgment was obtained. The High Court allowed his application because he had taken steps to challenge the proceedings in Belgium.[578]

The other two cases are for the enforcement of arbitral awards. These cases are relevant because the result would not have been different if they were foreign judgments. They were decided under section 103(2)(c) of the England and Wales Arbitration Act 1996 which provides that enforcement may be set aside on the ground that the judgment debtor 'was not given proper notice of the appointment of the arbitrator or of the arbitration proceedings or was otherwise unable to present his case'. In *Malicorp Ltd*, the claimant entered into a concession agreement for the construction of an airport in Egypt. The contract was revoked by the Egyptian government and an arbitration proceeding was commenced. Malicorp Ltd claimed compensation for breach of contract. The arbitral tribunal ruled that the contract was void but went on to rely on Articles 120 and 121 of the Egyptian Civil Code and ordered damages in favour of Malicorp Ltd. The award was set aside by the Egyptian Court of Appeal. Malicorp Ltd, having unsuccessfully attempted to enforce the award in France, applied to the English court. The Egyptian government claimed that the proceedings leading to the award had violated natural justice because damages were awarded on a basis that was neither claimed nor argued by the parties. The English court agreed that the award was unenforceable because Egypt had been unable to present its case and that constituted a breach of

---

[578] It should be noted that Art 34(2) of Brussels Ia, which applies to this action, requires that a judgment debtor must take steps to challenge the judgment in the foreign court.

natural justice. In *Kanoria*, the respondent was served with a notice of arbitration concerning a contract his English company had entered into with the applicant. He notified the arbitrators that he would be away for 12 weeks for a course of radiotherapy for cancer. The arbitration proceeded in his absence. He opposed the enforcement of the award in England. The English court noted that he had not been given proper notice for 'a highly material part of the arbitration proceedings' and thus had been unable to present his case. In *Masters*, recognition was denied because a US court assessed and awarded damages in breach of the procedure set out by the same court.

The results show that the English judges are very pragmatic in the application of the natural justice defence. It is largely restricted to cases where the judgment debtors were able to specifically prove that they did not receive notice of the proceedings or where they received notice but were not allowed to be heard. The courts rejected this defence where it was raised to discredit foreign courts' procedures or to make a blanket attack on foreign judges, their judgments or foreign legal systems.[579] It was also denied where a debtor argued that he had not raised the question of fraud and bad faith in the foreign court because of extra-judicial risks,[580] and where a debtor was served at his address but claimed that the summons was not received,[581] amongst other reasons.

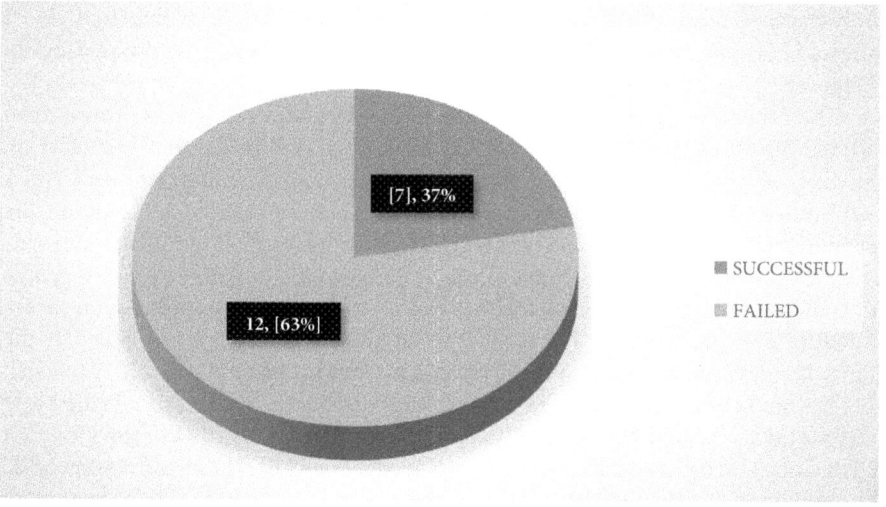

Natural Justice Defence

---

[579] Eg *Superior Composite Structures LLC v Parrish* (n 569); *Smith v Huertas* (n 565).
[580] *JSC VTB Bank v Skurikhin* (n 570).
[581] Eg *Open Joint Stock Company Alfa-Bank v Georgy Trefilov* (n 570); *Keller v Cowen (Foreign judgments)* (n 563); *OJSC Bank of Moscow v Chernyakov* (n 570).

B. Fraud

Section 6(3)(e) provides that a foreign judgment shall not be recognised if 'the judgment was obtained by fraud'. This text, as rightly noted by the Secretariat, is very much similar to the extant legislation in the Commonwealth. The Explanatory Report indicates that the Secretariat deliberated on the possible adoption of the text of the HCCA, which restricts the scope of the fraud defence to matters relating to procedure.[582] The utility of that approach is that it will limit the extent to which debtors can resort to the fraud defence as a decoy to invite a court addressed to review the merits of foreign judgments. That proposal was eventually dropped in favour of a broader text which is analogous to that of the 2019 Judgments Convention.

Fraud is a serious matter, and judgment debtors should be protected against fraudulently procured judgments. The tricky task is how to ensure that the enforcement process remains efficient so that crying 'fraud' does not become a magic wand through which foreign judgments become easily reviewable. The traditional common law rule in *Aboulof*,[583] which allows judgments to be reviewed on any allegation of fraud, can produce undesirable results, especially in many common law jurisdictions where judges have wide discretionary powers and can easily manipulate open-ended rules. In *Westacre Investments Inc v Jugoimport-SDRP Holding Company Ltd & Others*,[584] Lord Justice Waller in the Court of Appeal wondered why the fraud defence applies to domestic and foreign judgments differently. He reasoned that:

> It does seem anomalous that enforcement of a foreign judgment can be attacked without any requirement that the evidence must be evidence not available at the trial, and apparently without regard to the question whether the impact of that evidence would be likely to be decisive.

The Court further noted a few English cases such as *House of Spring Gardens v Waite*[585] and *Owens Bank Ltd v Etoile Commerciale SA*,[586] where *Aboulof* had been weakened or applied restrictively. Specifically, *Owens Bank Ltd* mooted the idea that there is a strong case for according foreign judgments the same finality accorded to domestic judgments: only fresh and cogent evidence could be allowed to set aside a final judgment.[587] Also, Lord Collins in the Privy Council in *AK Investment CJSC v Kyrgyz Mobil Tel Ltd*[588] noted that since the issue is governed by statute, a change is better effected by the legislature and not the judiciary.

---

[582] Commonwealth Secretariat, 'Model Law on the Recognition and Enforcement of Foreign Judgments' (n 415) 12–13.

[583] *Aboulof v Oppenheimer* (1882) 10 QBD 295.

[584] *Westacre Investments Inc v Jugoimport-SDRP Holding Company Ltd & Others* [2000] QB 288, [1999] EWCA Civ 1401.

[585] *House of Spring Gardens Ltd v Waite* [1991] 1 QB 241.

[586] *Owens Bank Ltd v Etoile Commerciale SA* [1995] 1 WLR 44.

[587] Paras 48–49.

[588] *AK Investment CJSC v Kyrgyz Mobil Tel Ltd* [2011] UKPC 7, [2012] 1 WLR 1804, para 112.

Other Commonwealth States such as Canada,[589] some parts of Australia[590] and Singapore,[591] only allow the fraud defence if such fraud could not have been reasonably discovered at the time of the foreign proceedings and it was material to the outcome of the dispute, thereby ascribing equal status to domestic and foreign judgments. This is pragmatic because it allows the foreign courts to deal with the issue, and parties can reasonably expect that their rights have been settled in those foreign proceedings. In Australia, the courts are divided. New South Wales[592] and Victoria[593] seem to favour the Canadian approach. Some authorities share that sympathy but prefer that the needed change should be made by Parliament.[594] Thus, the preferred approach is that any allegation of fraud, if it could be reasonably discoverable at the time of trial, should be raised and decided in the foreign proceedings. The judgment debtor should make use of any remedy available in the foreign legal system to litigate the fraud question, as seen in *House of Spring Gardens v Waite*. The foreign court's determination on the issue of fraud should not be reviewable save in extreme cases where the ruling was reached in bad faith. The Commonwealth Secretariat should have seized this opportunity to come up with a text that incorporates this restrictive approach that has been favoured by the courts of the Commonwealth Member States.

From the empirical research conducted on the fraud defence, the defence was raised to set aside recognition in 21 cases. It succeeded in six cases (29 per cent) and failed in 15 cases (71 per cent).[595] The six cases where the fraud defence was admitted for trial are *Korea National Insurance Co v Allianz Global Corporate & Specialty AG*,[596] *HJ Heinz Co Ltd v EFL Inc*,[597] *Habib Bank Ltd v Ahmed*,[598] and *Stati & Others v Kazakhstan*,[599] *AK Investment CJSC v Kyrgyz Mobil Tel Ltd*[600] and *Yukos Capital SARL v OJSC Rosneft Oil Company*.[601]

---

[589] *Beals v Saldanha* (n 487); *Union of India v Bumper Development Corp* [1995] 7 WWR 80 (Alberta QB).

[590] *Keele v Findley* (1990) 21 NSWLR 444; *Wentworth v Rogers (No 5)* (1986) 6 NSWLR 534.

[591] *Hong Pian Tee v Les Placements Germain Gauthier Inc* [2002] 2 Sing R 81 (Sing CA).

[592] *Keele v Findley* (1990) 21 NSWLR 444 and *Wentworth v Rogers (No 5)* (1986) 6 NSWLR 534.

[593] *Doe v Howard* [2015] VSC 75.

[594] *Yoon v Song* [2000] NSWSC 1147.

[595] The cases where the defence failed are: *Irish Response Ltd v Direct Beauty Products* [2011] EWHC 37 (QB); *Parkes v MacGregor* [2011] CSIH 69; *Clarke v Fennoscandia Ltd & Others* [2007] UKHL 56; *Mengiste v Endowment Fund for the Rehabilitation of Tigray* [2017] EWCA Civ 1326; *Midtown Acquisitions LP v Essar Global Fund Ltd* (n 570); *OJSC Bank of Moscow v Chernyakov* (n 570); *JSC VTB Bank v Skurikhin* (n 570); *Gelley v Shephard* [2013] EWCA Civ 1172; *Superior Composite Structures LLC v Parrish* [2015] EWHC 3688 (QB); *Smith v Huertas* [2015] EWHC 3745 (Comm); *Open Joint Stock Company Alfa-Bank v Georgy Trefilov* (n 570); *Arran Coghlan v Daniel Bailey, The National Crime Agency* [2014] EWHC 924 (QB); *Chantiers de L'Atlantique SA v Gaztransport & Technigaz SAS* [2011] EWHC 3383 (Comm); *Westacre Investments Inc v Jugoimport-SDPR Holding Co Ltd* (n 584); *Malicorp Ltd v Egypt* (n 568).

[596] *Korea National Insurance Co v Allianz Global Corporate & Specialty AG* [2008] EWCA Civ 1355.

[597] *HJ Heinz Co Ltd v EFL Inc* [2010] EWHC 1203 (Comm).

[598] *Habib Bank Ltd v Ahmed* [2001] EWCA Civ 1270.

[599] *Stati & Others v Kazakhstan* [2017] EWHC 1348 (Comm).

[600] [2011] UKPC 7.

[601] *Yukos Capital SARL v OJSC Rosneft Oil Company* [2012] EWCA Civ 855.

In *Korea National Insurance Co*, the Court of Appeal set aside the lower court's ruling that a fraud allegation was non-justiciable because it would embarrass diplomatic relations between North Korea and the United Kingdom. In this case, *Korea National Insurance Co* obtained a money judgment in North Korea against a reinsurance company which had refused to reimburse it for payments made over a helicopter crash. In enforcement proceedings in England, the reinsurance company alleged that the underlying claim was a scam as the incident never happened. It claimed that it was an attempt to raise money for North Korea or its leader. The Court of Appeal, therefore, ordered that the allegation should proceed to trial. Similarly, in *Ahmed*, the English Court of Appeal ordered a new trial on a fraud allegation. The Bank had obtained a judgment against the appellant in Karachi over some guarantee forms the appellant signed to secure some additional facilities for his company. The appellant signed blank forms with the understanding that the Bank's Executive Committee would approve the discussed terms and his brothers, who are co-owners, would also sign the forms. This was confirmed by the contemporaneous manuscript notes and figures noted by the Bank's official who negotiated the terms. There was no evidence that either of the two conditions was fulfilled. The Bank nevertheless filled the blank forms and backdated them with terms that would enable the Bank to wind up the company and sue Mr Ahmed. The Court of Appeal allowed the application to order a trial because the lower court had not given full reasons why it rejected Ahmed's allegation, despite the existence of documentary evidence supporting his claim.

In *Stati*, the applicants applied to enforce an arbitral award in England, but Kazakhstan opposed the application based on certain fraud that was discovered after the award. The State got some documents from discovery proceedings in the US which showed that the applicants had inflated the value of the liquefied petroleum gas plant (their investment) in a failed oil exploration contract. The arbitral award was based on the valuation submitted by the applicants. The English High Court ruled that there was a prima facie case to be tried and therefore sustained Kazakhstan's objection. The fraud case proceeded to trial. The applicants, however, subsequently applied to discontinue the enforcement proceedings. *HJ Heinz Co Ltd* also involved a motion for an injunction against the enforcement of a foreign arbitral award in England. A substantial part of the Hungarian arbitral award was based on the breach of some Distribution and Settlement Agreements which the defendant purportedly signed with a third party. HJ Heinz Co Ltd claimed before the arbitration panel and Hungarian courts that the distribution agreements were forged, and the signatories were never called to testify. Although the company was unsuccessful in the Hungarian courts, the English court was of the view that the defendant's application opposing the motion for an injunction should be dismissed, as there was a serious issue to be tried. In *Yukos Capital SARL*, one of the questions posed to the Court of Appeal was whether Rosneft was estopped from challenging, in England, a Dutch court's finding that a Russian court's decision setting aside an award was obtained by fraud, corruption and bias. The Court of Appeal held that English courts were not bound by the Dutch court's finding and the question would have to be tried because the public policies of the two countries may differ. In *AK Investment CJSC*, the Privy Council agreed that a fraud allegation could be raised against a Kyrgyzstan judgment which granted specific performance of a Transfer Agreement in favour of one of the appellants when the latter was not a party to the agreement. On the one hand, the Kyrgyz court ruled that the judgment creditor was a party to the agreement, and on the other hand, that it was not bound by the jurisdiction clause in favour of England because it had not signed it. The Privy Council wondered how the judgment creditor, which did not sign an agreement, was nevertheless a party to the agreement. It was therefore concluded that the judgment would have been improperly procured.

The result shows that for a judgment debtor to succeed, the fraud allegation must be specific, and cogent enough to significantly affect the outcome. This shows why the success rate is low. In all other cases it was used as a mere 'artificial construct', or a blanket allegation against foreign judges or arbitrators. General allegations that the foreign court is pro-government,[602] an appendage of the executive,[603] or biased[604] are routinely rejected.

The application of the fraud defence in setting aside arbitral awards was slightly different. This relates to whether the defence can be raised at any time or must be raised in the foreign proceedings. Other than this, the treatment of the substance of the defence was similar. Perhaps it would have been more efficient if the defence were limited to frauds that could not be reasonably discovered before the conclusion of the foreign proceedings. This would reduce the frequency of its usage.

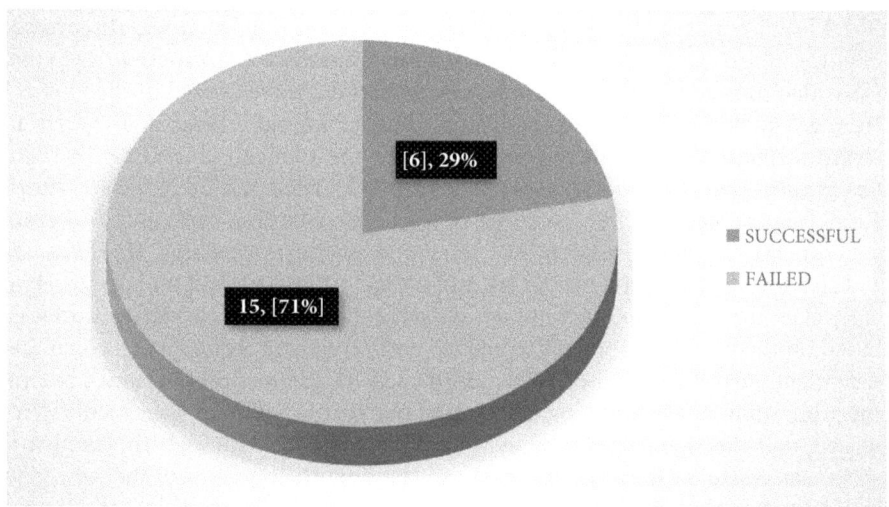

Fraud Defence

---

[602] *Malicorp Ltd v Egypt* (n 568).
[603] *Korea National Insurance Co v Allianz Global Corporate & Specialty AG* (n 596).
[604] *OJSC Bank of Moscow v Chernyakov* [2016] EWHC 2583 (Comm).

C. Public Policy

Section 6(3)(d) provides that a foreign judgment shall be denied recognition if it is 'manifestly contrary to public policy' of the court addressed. The public policy defence is well entrenched in every legal system. The drafting is largely similar to the provisions of the extant statutes. The notable difference is the addition of 'manifestly' in the model law. Also, it departs from the 1920 Act, which emphasises the underlying cause of action.[605]

Public policy is a useful safeguard that protects the rights of the judgment debtor and most importantly the fundamental values and sovereignty of the enforcing State. As Gross J rightly observed in *IPCO (Nigeria) Ltd v Nigerian National Petroleum Corporation*,[606] the defence is not intended to create an 'open-ended escape route' to attack foreign awards or judgments. It is only available where the effect of the enforcement of a foreign judgment will violate some fundamental value of the legal order of the forum.

Commonwealth Member States' courts have largely resisted attempts by judgment debtors to frustrate enforcement proceedings through the public policy defence. The standards imposed on foreign judgments are higher than their domestic counterparts. Enforcement action bears on the foreign judgment and not the original cause of action, and in most cases, the law of the court addressed whose policy is sought to be engaged by way of defence to enforcement may not be directed at foreign judgments or causes of action litigated abroad.[607] Thus, the word 'manifestly' suggests that some more fundamental, or possibly mandatory forum policy must be violated.

National substantive public policy cannot be regulated or harmonised. However, the courts do realise that it is not every foreign judgment that violates local statutes that will be contrary to public policy. Otherwise, the whole idea of comity and deference to foreign law, which is the bed-rock of conflicts jurisprudence will be destroyed.[608] In dealing with public policy defence, courts need to do some 'interest analysis'. While it is conceded that parliament does not usually express a specific policy or interest in statutes, the courts should nevertheless engage the public policy defence only where such policy is clearly expressed and intended to cover causes of action that arise within and outside the country. Otherwise, there should be a presumption against the extraterritorial application of statutes. This is a pragmatic approach to prevent foreign judgments from being reviewed in undeserving cases. A practical application is seen in the way various

---

[605] Section 9(2)(f) of the Administration of Justice Act 1920 (UK) provides that 'No judgment shall be ordered to be registered under this section if the judgment was in respect of a cause of action which for reasons of public policy or for some other similar reason could not have been entertained by the registering court'.

[606] *IPCO (Nigeria) Ltd v Nigerian National Petroleum Corporation* [2005] 2 Lloyd's Rep 326.

[607] *Westacre Investments Inc v Jugoimport-SPDR Holding Co Ltd and others* [2000] QB 288, 305.

[608] *Boardwalk Regency Corp v Maalouf* (1992) 88 DLR (4th) 612, 620.

Commonwealth countries such as Malaysia,[609] Singapore,[610] and Canada[611] have dealt with the question of enforcement of foreign judgments concerning gambling contracts.

The empirical survey on public policy defence confirms that the courts have been very pragmatic in its application. Usually, judgment debtors use it together with other defences like natural justice and fraud. In the period of review, it was used in a total of 41 cases. It was upheld in nine cases (22 per cent) and failed in 32 cases (78 per cent).[612] It is interesting to note that in the nine cases where it was successfully raised, the specific allegations therein are non-service of court proceedings – natural justice (four cases); a judgment violating a mandatory European Software Directive 91/250/EEC (one case); a judgment that was contrary to the UK's Protection of Trading Interests Act 1980 (one case); a judgment that was in breach of the principle of legal certainty as enshrined in the European Convention on Human Rights (one case); and judgments in breach of an English arbitration agreement and an anti-suit injunction (two cases).

Toulevarais, Maronier, Laserpoint Ltd and *Reeve* have been discussed under the natural justice defence. In these cases, natural justice, the breach of the right to a fair trial, and public policy, were taken together. Only in five cases was the public policy defence upheld independently of other grounds. In *Service Temps Inc v MacLeod*,[613] it was held that a US anti-trust judgment which also awarded treble damages was contrary to the broad intention of Parliament under section 5 of the Protection of Trading Interests Act 1980. The statute was aimed at discouraging extra-territorial enforcement of anti-trust judgments and measures. Even if the Act did not apply, Lord Hodge was of the view that the judgment would still be

---

[609] *The Aspinall Curzon Ltd v Khoo Teng Hock* [1991] 2 MLJ 484.
[610] *Liao Eng Kiat v Burswood Nominees Ltd* [2004] 4 SLR(R) 690.
[611] *Boardwalk Regency Corpn v Maalouf* (n 608) 612.
[612] The cases where the defence failed are: *Westacre Investments Inc v Jugoimport-Spdr Holding Co Ltd* (n 584); *Orams and another v Apostolides (British Residents' Society intervening)* [2010] 1 All ER (Comm) 992; *JSC VTB Bank v Skurikhin* (n 570); *Eastern European Engineering Ltd v Vijay Construction (Proprietary) Ltd* [2017] EWHC 797 (Comm); *Superior Composite Structures LLC v Parrish* (n 569); *Smith v Huertas* (n 565); *Midtown Acquisitions LP v Essar Global Fund Ltd* (n 570); *Bach v Davis* [2013] EWHC 4459 (QB); *Banco Nacional de Comercio Exterior SNC v Empresa de Telecomunicaciones de Cuba SA* [2007] All ER (D) 138; *Nomihold Securities Inc v Mobile Telesystems Finance SA* [2011] EWHC 2143 (Comm); *Gater Assets Ltd v Nak Naftogaz Ukrainiy* [2008] 1 All ER (Comm) 209; *Zigal v Buchanan* [2018] CSOH 94; *West Tankers Inc v Allianz SpA and another* [2012] EWCA Civ 27; *Reeve v Plummer* (n 574); *Walton v Shanley* [2012] CSOH 64; *Hamsah Investments Ltd v Liberia* [2009] 11 WLUK 644; *Baden-Wurttembergische Bank AG, Petitioner* [2009] CSOH 19; *Tenaga Nasional Berhad v Frazer-Nash Research Limited, Kamkorp Limited* [2018] EWHC 2970 (QB); *Marie Brizzard et Roger International SA v William Grant & Sons Ltd (No 2)* [2002] SLT 1365 (OH); *Agrokor DD, Re* [2017] EWHC 2791 (Ch); *OJSC Bank of Moscow v Chernyakov* (n 570); *Tanir v Tanir* [2015] EWHC 3363 (QB); *Spliethoff's Bevrachtingskantoor BV v Bank of China Ltd* [2015] EWHC 999 (Comm); *Malicorp Ltd v Egypt* (n 568); *Open Joint Stock Co Alfa-Bank v Trefilov* (n 570); *Desarrollo Immobiliario Y Negocios Industriales De Alta v Kader Holdings Co Ltd* [2014] EWHC 1460 (QB); *Citibank NA v Rafidian Bank* [2003] EWHC 1950 (QB); *Nikolay Viktorovich Maximov v Open Joint Stock Company 'Novolipetsky Metallurgichesky Kombinat'* [2017] EWHC 1911 (Comm); *DHL GBS (UK) Ltd v Fallimento Finmatica SpA* [2009] EWHC 291 (Comm).
[613] *Service Temps Inc v MacLeod* [2013] CSOH 162.

contrary to public policy at common law and under Article 1 of Protocol number 1 of the European Convention on Human Rights.[614] *SAS Institute Inc v World Programming Ltd*[615] involved a breach of a software licence and copyright agreement. Having failed to get any remedy against the defendant in an English court, *SAS Institute Inc* commenced another proceeding in the US and obtained damages for US$26 million against the defendant. The judgment was partly[616] rejected because it violated the Protection of Trading Interests Act 1980 and also because the terms of the licence violated the public policy objective of Directive 91/250/EEC on the legal protection of computer programmes. In *Merchant International Company Ltd v Natsionalna Aktsionerna Kompaniia Naftogaz*,[617] MIC obtained a judgment against Naftogaz in the Commercial Court of the City of Kiev (CCCK) and it was later confirmed by the Supreme Commercial Court of Ukraine (SCCU) in 2006. It filed an action to enforce the said judgment under common law. After MIC had obtained a judgment in England, Naftogaz applied to SCCU to review the 2006 decisions of SCCU and that of CCCK based on newly discovered facts. SCCU repealed those two decisions in 2011 and remitted the case for a new trial. Naftogaz then applied to the English court to set aside its decision, based on the 2011 decision of SCCU. The trial court and the Court of Appeal upheld the argument of MIC that the 2011 judgment was contrary to public policy and legal certainty as enshrined in Article 1 of Protocol number 1 and Article 6 of the European Convention on Human Rights. In *AK Investment CJSC v Kyrgyz Mobil Tel Ltd*,[618] the Privy Council held that the recognition of a Kyrgyzstan judgment would be contrary to public policy because it was obtained in breach of an English arbitration agreement and anti-suit injunction. A similar decision was reached in *Ust-Kamenogorsk Hydropower Plant JSC v AES Ust-Kamenogorsk Hydropower Plant LLP*,[619] where the English Court of Appeal declined to recognise a Kazakhstan judgment that ruled on a contract that was subject to an English arbitration clause.

Other attempts failed the higher threshold of public policy analysis in conflict of laws largely because the respondent could not support the claims with any credible or prima facie evidence. Some of the complaints include the inability to present a defence because of war;[620] judges alleged to be pro-government;[621]

---

[614] See para 43.
[615] *SAS Institute Inc v World Programming Ltd* [2018] EWHC 3452 (Comm). However, in *Lewis v Eliades (No 2)* [2003] EWCA (Civ) 1758, the Court of Appeal allowed the compensatory part of a US judgment to be enforced while the punitive part was denied under s 5 of the Protection of Trading Interests Act 1980. The case was not included in this empirical result because it was not specifically raised and discussed by the court.
[616] Enforcement was also denied because the judgment was inconsistent with the judgment delivered in the earlier English suit.
[617] *Merchant International Company Ltd v Natsionalna Aktsionerna Kompaniia Naftogaz* [2012] EWCA Civ 196.
[618] [2011] UKPC 7.
[619] *Ust-Kamenogorsk Hydropower Plant JSC v AES Ust-Kamenogorsk Hydropower Plant LLP* [2011] EWCA Civ 647.
[620] *Hamsah Investments Ltd v Liberia* (n 612).
[621] *Malicorp Ltd v Egypt* (n 568).

perjury and bribery, which were held to not to be decisive;[622] that the debtor's application for leave to appeal is pending before the foreign court,[623] or that he had an intention to appeal against the foreign judgment;[624] procedural unfairness which was not raised in the foreign proceedings;[625] fraudulent misrepresentation which could not be proved;[626] the inability of the judgment debtor to put up effective legal representation in the foreign proceedings because of sanctions against Iraq;[627] a judgment in breach of a jurisdiction agreement but the debtor submitted to the foreign court,[628] amongst others. Thus, the current draft of the model law can be said to be adequate given the established judicial practice.

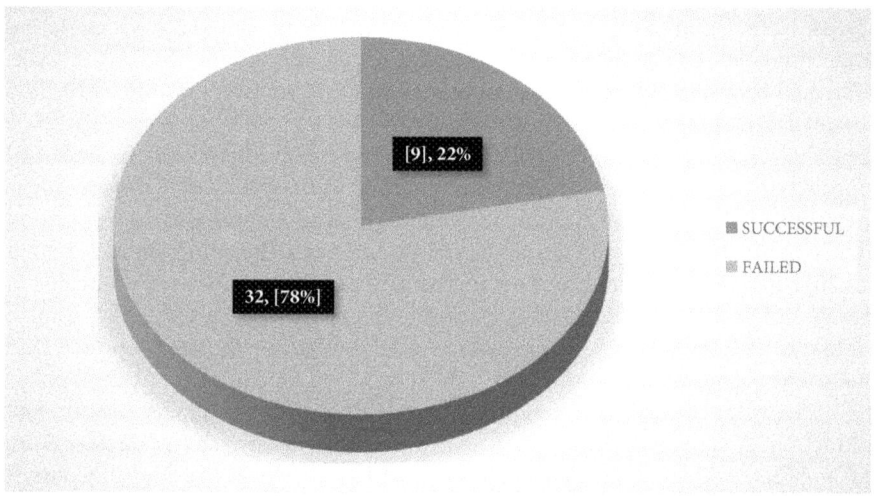

Public Policy Defence

D. Other Grounds

The model law provides for two additional grounds that can lead to the denial of recognition. It states that:

> (3) A foreign judgment is not to be recognised in [.......] if at the time the judgment is relied upon in proceedings in [.......],[629]

---

[622] *Westacre Investments Inc v Jugoimport-Spdr Holding Co. Ltd. and Others* (n 584).
[623] *Tenaga Nasional Berhad v Frazer-Nash Research Limited, Kamkorp Limited* (n 612).
[624] *Walton v Shanley* (n 612).
[625] *Smith v Huertas* (n 565).
[626] *Superior Composite Structures LLC v Parrish* (n 569).
[627] *Citibank NA v Rafidian Bank* (n 612). In this instance, the court noted that there were 'some (unsuccessful) efforts' to have the Dutch Judgment set aside and that was fatal by reason of Art 29 of the Brussels Convention. There was also evidence that the Bank had access to non-frozen funds via the Iraqi regime.
[628] *Spliethoff's Bevrachtingskantoor BV v Bank of China Ltd* (n 612).
[629] Section 6(3) CML.

(a) proceedings between the same parties and having the same subject matter were pending before a court of [.......], having been commenced before the proceedings that gave rise to the judgment were commenced;
(b) the judgment is inconsistent with a judgment made, either in [.......] or in another foreign state, provided that in the latter case the judgment meets the conditions for recognition in [.......];

According to section 6(3)(a), recognition is to be denied where a judgment arose from a proceeding commenced after an earlier proceeding between the same parties over the same subject before a court in the receiving State. This provision is novel in the Commonwealth and, unfortunately, there was no explanatory note on it. This is not a case of inconsistent judgment but one of commencement of proceedings elsewhere after the court addressed was already seised. It is difficult to find any rational justification for this ground. It is submitted that section 5 has extensively discussed acceptable jurisdictional bases. There is no need for it to feature as a distinct ground for denial of recognition. This ground does not require that the court addressed should have exclusive jurisdiction. All that a judgment debtor needs to do is to rush to a jurisdiction (possibly, its home court) to commence proceedings to forestall the enforcement of any foreign judgment in that jurisdiction, even though that jurisdiction may not be the 'natural forum' for that dispute. This ground may be abused by litigants. The legislators might need to have a rethink on it.

Section 6(3)(b) deals with inconsistent judgments. It combines Articles 7(1)(e) and (f) of the Hague Judgments Convention. The first shortcoming observed in the text is that it does not expressly specify that the competing judgments must relate to the same cause of action and parties. Secondly, there is no priority rule as between an inconsistent foreign judgment and a judgment of the court addressed and between two inconsistent foreign judgments. It may be presumed that the judgment of the court addressed trumps an inconsistent foreign judgment even if it was later in time because the foreign judgment ought to have been raised in the ongoing proceedings in the receiving State before judgment was rendered.[630] As between competing foreign judgments, the priority rule is desirable for legal certainty.

The gaps can be filled from well-established principles in case law. The English courts have dealt with a few cases on inconsistent judgments in recent times. In *SAS Institute Inc v World Programming Ltd*,[631] a US judgment was denied recognition because its finding contradicted an earlier English judgment between the same parties. This is the only case that emerged from the empirical research. The decision is consistent with *Vervaeke v Smith*,[632] an earlier case where conflicting foreign and English judgments were considered. In *Vervaeke*, a petitioner failed to get a decree of nullity for an English marriage in England but successfully got one

---

[630] For instance, see *Naraji v Shelbourne* [2011] EWHC 3298 (QB).
[631] *SAS Institute Inc* (n 615).
[632] *Vervaeke v Smith* [1983] 1 AC 145.

in Belgium thereafter. She then applied for the recognition of the Belgian judgment under the 1933 Foreign Judgments (Reciprocal Enforcement) Act. Recognition was refused because the judgment was inconsistent with an earlier judgment of the English court.

There are a few other cases that have considered competing foreign judgments. The approach of the English courts is to apply the doctrine of estoppel *per rem judicatam* to bar the second judgment.[633] By this doctrine, a valid judgment precludes a reconsideration of the cause of action and any issue of fact or law determined therein, provided the parties and the subject matter (cause of action and/or issue) are the same.[634] In essence, once a judgment is rendered in a suit, it effectively disposes of the issues(s), and any other subsequent judgment from elsewhere will not be recognised by the court addressed. The second condition is that the first judgment must be enforceable. This entails that the foreign court is properly seised, the judgment is final on the merits, and not perverse or contrary to the public policy of the court addressed.[635] These conditions are well captured in the Hague Judgments Convention. These two conditions can be illustrated with *Phillips v Avena*[636] and *Showlag v Mansour*.[637] *Phillips* was a dispute over the ownership of the shares of a company in Panama, between the personal representatives of a deceased and the defendant with whom the deceased had had a relationship. Avena sued Phillips in Alberta and Panama respectively. Her claim was dismissed in Alberta in April 2005 while the one in Panama was upheld in June 2005. Philips asked the English court to recognise the Alberta judgment to pre-empt any action that Avena might present before the English courts. The court agreed that the Alberta judgment was preferred, and the Panama judgment was not entitled to recognition because the Alberta court had jurisdiction, and the judgment was final, conclusive and first in time. Similarly, in *Showlag*, Mansour was employed by a Saudi businessman, Shaykh Abdul Ahmed Showlag, in connection with his business affairs in London. Shortly before his death, some deposits held in London banks by the deceased were transferred to Showlag SA, a company owned by Mansour, in Switzerland. The legal representatives of the deceased got to know about this transaction, and believing that the money was stolen, they instituted actions in England and Egypt amongst others. In December 1990, an English court found that the money was not a gift but had been obtained by fraud. In 1991, an Egyptian court concluded otherwise. The Privy Council was asked to determine which of the competing judgments was entitled to recognition in proceedings in Jersey. It was held that the English judgment, which was the earlier of the two competing foreign judgments, was entitled to recognition.

---

[633] *Showlag v Mansour* [1995] 1 AC 431; *Phillips v Avena* [2005] EWHC 3333 (Ch). *Res judicata* and its application to foreign judgments is dealt with in detail by Barnett (ch 2, fn 196).

[634] See *DSV Silo und Verwaltungsgesellschaft mbH v Owners of the Sennar ('The Sennar') (No 2)* [1985] 1 WLR 490; *Carl Zeiss Stiftung v Rayner & Keeler Ltd* [1967] 1 AC 853, [1966] 5 WLUK 63. See also Barnett (ch 2 fn 196).

[635] *DSV Silo und Verwaltungsgesellschaft mbH v Owners of the Sennar; ('The Sennar') (No 2)* (n 634).

[636] *Phillips v Avena* [2005] EWHC 3333 (Ch).

[637] *Showlag v Mansour* [1995] 1 AC 431.

VI. Other Sundry Matters

Recognition and enforcement are treated separately under the model law. Recognition of the judgment appears to be the major hurdle which a judgment creditor needs to surmount. Once a judgment is entitled to recognition, it goes without saying that it is enforceable, even though the drafters used the word 'may', suggesting that it is discretionary.[638] This should not be a problem considering that the policy objective of the model law is liberalising foreign judgments' recognition and enforcement.[639]

Enforcement of money and non-money judgments are treated separately as well. For non-money judgments, the court addressed is given wider powers to amend the foreign judgments/orders in such a way that they could become enforceable in the receiving State. The law provides that a court addressed may:

(a) make an order that the judgment be modified as may be required to make it enforceable in [...], unless the judgment is not susceptible of being so modified;

(b) make an order stipulating the procedure to be used in enforcing the judgment.[640]

This provision allows the court addressed to adapt the non-money judgment to such an extent that will make it enforceable in the receiving State. For instance, if the remedy is not available in the receiving State, the court addressed may modify the order by granting a relief which closely reflects the one granted by the foreign judgment. The criteria set out by the Canadian courts in *Pro Swing Inc v Elta Golf Inc*[641] and *Dish v Shava*[642] are recommended. The most important conditions are that the terms of the order should be clear and specific, and the enforcement of the order should not be unduly burdensome to the court addressed. This provision is an improvement on the Hague Judgments Convention, which allows the recognition of final non-money judgments but without any guidance on how a court addressed may deal with the judgments, especially in cases where such reliefs are not available in the receiving State.

Registration of a judgment can only be set aside where the foreign court lacks jurisdiction, as spelt out under section 5, or where such a judgment is not enforceable under the model law (such as any violation of section 6), and where the judgment has been satisfied or is not enforceable in the State of origin.[643] Enforcement proceedings may be stayed, upon terms to be stipulated by the court addressed, if an appeal is pending in the State of origin or the time within which such an appeal may be made has not expired.[644]

---

[638] Section 7 CML.
[639] Perhaps, 'may' could be changed to 'shall' in implementing legislation.
[640] Section 16.
[641] 2006 SCC 52.
[642] *Dish v Shava*, 2018 ONSC 2867.
[643] Section 12(2).
[644] Section 13.

VII. Conclusion

This chapter examines in detail the CML on the Recognition and Enforcement of Foreign Judgments (2017). In line with the theory of pragmatism espoused in Chapter three above, the model law is analysed against the background of legal certainty, efficiency, fairness and justice, using practical experience, and comparative and empirical methodologies. The analysis notes the improvements in the model law as a significant attempt to modernise the Commonwealth judgments enforcement scheme, bringing it closer to the Hague Judgments Convention and other modern regional and bilateral treaties.

It is indisputable that the policy objective of the model law fits into the pragmatic theory. The abolition of reciprocity, provision of extended jurisdictional filters, and a general prohibition of the review of foreign judgments except in limited cases, all emphasise the policy of finality of litigation and respect for the integrity of foreign courts and their decisions. In this way, it prioritises private interests over those of the State and offers more certainty and predictability to litigants, who can make strategic decisions on where to sue with an assurance that their judgments will be enforceable. Besides, the liberalised regime, which admits judgments from every country, including money and non-money judgments, will bring about efficiency because it will save litigants time and the extra cost of having to file a fresh action to get such judgments enforced.

Nevertheless, it is observed that many of the jurisdictional filters appear to be deficient in drafting, as they fail to take care of some of the practical problems that have been identified in the Commonwealth jurisprudence and that of other States. The simplistic,[645] or in some cases, overly broad[646] drafting approach adopted by the drafters may produce some uncertainties which could have been avoided.

Conclusively, the model law represents an improved Commonwealth judgments enforcement scheme. It is significantly different from the 1922/1933 statutes in many respects. It will be a boost to the emerging global judgments liberalisation. Private litigants, especially judgment creditors, should find this simple and efficient framework more useful than the extant regimes. Above all, it is yet to be seen, how the Commonwealth Secretariat intends to ensure that Member States whose laws still replicate the 1920/1933 statutes adopt the new model law.

---

[645] For instance, s 5(1)(g) on contract jurisdiction.
[646] For instance, s 5(1)(k) on products and services liability.

PART III

Hague Conventions

6

The Hague Judgments Project: Pre-2019 Attempts

I. Introduction

Ralf Michaels recalls that Savigny's dream of convergence of law under the bond of Christianity never materialised because Christian nations do not agree on relevant issues.[647] This is as true today as it was in the past. States are of diverse socio-political and legal backgrounds. Their worldviews about the role of the State, the functions of law, the role of the courts, and the standards of justice, amongst other things, differ. Narrowing the issue down to recognition and enforcement of foreign judgments, the case of punitive judgments readily comes to mind. While the US and the United Kingdom have a shared legal history and culture, they differ on the acceptability of punitive damages. While a court in the US may award punitive damages, such awards are considered to be against the public policy of the United Kingdom.[648] In *SAS Institute Inc v World Programming Ltd*,[649] the English commercial court went as far as holding that neither a US award of treble damages nor its main compensatory part is enforceable. The position is similar in several European States.[650] Assumption of jurisdiction is another good example. The US concept of personal jurisdiction is informed by the Due Process Clause of the Fourteenth Amendment.[651] Even though the concept of 'due process' has its roots in English statutes,[652] it has acquired a unique interpretation and understanding in the US.

---

[647] Ralf Michaels, 'Globalizing Savigny? The State in Savigny's Private International Law and the Challenge from Europeanization and Globalization' in Michael Stolleis and Wolfgang Streeck (eds), *Aktuelle Fragen zu politischer und rechtlicher Steuerung im Kontext der Globalisierung* (Nomos 2007) 139.

[648] See *SAS Institute Inc v World Programming Ltd* [2018] EWHC 3452 (Comm); *JSC VTB v Skurikhin* (n 649), *Service Temps Inc v MacLeod* (n 649).

[649] [2018] EWHC 3452 (Comm). See also *JSC VTB v Skurikhin* [2014] EWHC 271 (Comm) para 42, *Service Temps Inc v MacLeod* [2013] CSOH 162.

[650] Cedric Vanleenhove, 'The Enforcement of American Punitive Damages in the European Union', *Punitive Damages in Private International Law* (Intersentia 2016).

[651] The Fourteenth Amendment states that no state shall 'deprive any person of life, liberty or property, without due process of law'. For an analysis of its origin in the American jurisprudence, see Ronald A Brand, 'Due Process, Jurisdiction and a Hague Judgments Convention' (1999) 60 *University of Pittsburgh Law Review* 661.

[652] Ibid, 664.

The divergences in law, judicial approach, the standard of justice, and States' interests and values make it a policy question what kind of foreign judgment should be recognised and enforced by a court addressed. For international litigants, the divergences create legal uncertainties which further increase litigation and enforcement risks respectively.[653] One pragmatic way of addressing this concern requires that States should cooperate to find a balance between these diverse and competing standards, policies, interests and values. One pragmatic solution is the availability of a multilateral platform where States' representatives can carry out painstaking negotiations on different aspects of judgments recognition laws with a view to setting acceptable global standards for judgments, acceptable connections between courts and disputes and other criteria that foreign judgments should meet. Such a platform allows States to exchange views on their differences and to offer compromises which would lead to harmonisation.

Pragmatism is not limited to addressing practical legal problems being faced by cross-border litigants; it also touches on the modalities that can deliver a judgments framework that is acceptable, and implementable, by the vast majority of States. Therefore, while it is desirable to focus on the practical problems confronting litigants, it is also imperative that the resulting framework is acceptable globally. Otherwise, what would be offered is a very beautiful judgments convention that addresses all, or most of the challenges but which only a few States are ready to ratify. The 1971 Hague Judgments Convention is a good example.

The first objective of this chapter is to examine the historical background to previous international harmonisation attempts, their pitfalls and the build-up to the 2019 Hague Judgments Convention. This historical background is necessary for a better understanding of the current state of play, and the pragmatism of having a minimum harmonisation approach as adopted in the Hague Convention on Choice of Court Agreements (HCCA) and the 2019 Judgments Convention. The chapter will devote some time to the HCCA, which is part of the history of the 2019 Judgments Convention. It is not the aim of the chapter to fully discuss the articles of the HCCA, as that has already been done by some learned writers.[654] However, it is imperative to consider the key aspects of the Convention – prorogation, derogation and enforcement – and the emerging case law on the HCCA, which will be a contribution to the existing literature on the subject. Besides, prorogation and derogation are inextricably linked with enforcement, and the latter cannot be meaningfully discussed without the former. The second objective is to demonstrate why States should adopt the HCCA together with

---

[653] Richard Fentiman (ch 1, fn 25) 6–7.

[654] Ronald A Brand and Paul Herrup, *The 2005 Hague Convention on Choice of Court Agreements : Commentary and Documents* (Cambridge University Press 2008); Trevor C Hartley, *Choice-of-Court Agreements under the European and International Instruments: The Revised Brussels I Regulation, the Lugano Convention, and the Hague Convention* (OUP 2013); Beaumont, 'Hague Choice of Court Agreements Convention 2005: Background, Negotiations, Analysis and Current Status' (ch 1, fn 50).

the sister Convention (2019 Judgments Convention) as a package deal. The HCCA is the first fruit of the Judgments Project and compliments the Judgments Convention. An insight into the relationship between them is therefore desirable.

II. International Harmonisation of Foreign Judgments Laws

The challenges of recognition and enforcement of foreign judgments became prominent in the eighteenth century when the concepts of sovereignty and territorialism held sway in Continental Europe. Many States were opposed to foreign influence and this had a negative impact on the circulation of foreign judgments because judgments were considered as sovereign acts. Hard borders did not stop cross-border trade, commerce and other social engagements. Rather, these activities were increased by the Industrial Revolution and the advancement in communications and transportation of goods and persons.

One of the consequences of the post-Westphalian system is that each State has an exclusive adjudicatory, legislative and judicial jurisdiction over its territory. This means that a State can exercise direct jurisdiction on its soil as it deems fit, and can determine what effect, if any, to give to a foreign judgment. This arrangement led to divergent national approaches to the questions of jurisdiction and judgments. The diversity of laws posed some challenges to cross-border litigants who in many cases were unable to enforce judgments abroad as a result of numerous obstacles that were prevalent in most legal systems.

This situation troubled some of the leading scholars of that time. The responses from leading theorists such as Huber and Savigny were not specifically targeted at foreign judgments, although, some aspects of their postulations may be extended to foreign judgments. For instance, Huber's comity supports the recognition of foreign judgments and Savigny's seat of legal relations is useful for international jurisdiction rules. However, the complexities of the ever-evolving world, and the tendencies of States to act out of self-interest required that more needed to be done to bring about harmonisation, legal certainty and mutual trust which remain necessary for the progressive development of judgments recognition laws and an improved solution to the myriads of problems affecting jurisdiction and foreign judgments.

A. *Institut de Droit International* (IDI)

The first multilateral attempt to harmonise rules of jurisdiction and judgments enforcement was made by IDI. IDI was established in 1873 in Ghent, Belgium by leading European international law scholars who craved a professional and non-governmental body to be dedicated to the progressive development of international law.[655] At its Paris Session in 1878, where TMC Asser served as Rapporteur, it proposed certain recommendations, which were contained in a resolution adopted by the body.[656] The body was of the view that proper harmonisation would be best achieved through a diplomatic conference among States whose judiciaries were ready to present sufficient guarantees for foreign judgments.[657] It further recommended that a judgments convention should lay down uniform rules on key aspects of judgments recognition law, with minimum procedural formalities which foreign judgments must meet.[658] Draft Principles were concluded at the Vienna Session in 1924[659] as a template that could be adopted by States for bilateral treaties. There is no record that the Draft Principles were adopted by any State. It can be argued that the drawback in the IDI's attempt is the absence of States' support, which is of great importance in any exercise aimed at harmonising judgments recognition rules.

B. International Law Association (ILA)

The ILA was formed in 1873 in Brussels as a non-governmental international consultative body for the study and development of public and private international law.[660] Unlike the IDI, the ILA's founding members included distinguished lawyers from the United States, Canada, and the United Kingdom. The body was formed for the harmonisation of the conflicting application of national laws, especially in the area of commercial and maritime law.[661] To put it in the words of the secretaries of the first conference, the main objective of their activity was 'the minimizing of occasions for international friction and international disputes by the assimilation of the laws and practice of the different States'.[662] One of the earliest successes it recorded was the wide acceptance and ratification of its Principle of Arbitration as a means of settling international disputes by national legislatures.[663]

The ILA has had enforcement of foreign judgments on its agenda as far back as 1878 when Dr Hovv from Amsterdam moved that a *projet de loi* for the unification

---

[655] Martti Koskennjemi, 'Gustave Rolin-Jaequemyns and the Establishment of the Institut de Droit International (1873)' (2004) 37 *Revue Belge de Droit International* 5; Joseph G Alexander and George G Phillimore, 'Preface' (1873) 1 *International Law Association Reports of Conferences* iii, iv.

[656] Institut de Droit International, 'Exécution Des Jugements' (1878) <http://www.idi-iil.org/app/uploads/2017/06/1878_paris_01_fr.pdf> accessed 18 July 2019.

[657] See Art 1.

[658] See Art 2.

[659] Institut de Droit International, 'Autorité et Exécution des Jugements Étrangers' (1924) <http://www.idi-iil.org/app/uploads/2017/06/1924_vien_03_fr.pdf> accessed 18 July 2019.

[660] See Torsten Stein, 'International Law Association (ILA)', *Max Planck Encyclopedia of Public International Law* (OUP 2015).

[661] Joseph G Alexander and George G Phillimore (n 655) xi.

[662] Ibid.

[663] Ibid, ix.

of law and practice of judgments recognition and enforcement be considered.[664] A committee of eminent scholars, including the likes of FT Piggott, Alderson Foote QC, and Mr TMC Asser, was formed to consider appropriate rules that could form the basis of a judgments convention. The committee did painstaking work, in a very pragmatic and methodical way.[665] It carried out a comparative inquiry on the subject matter in various jurisdictions by considering several scholarly works, the existing bilateral treaties between States, and the discussions at various conferences.[666] A closer look at the Foreign Judgments Committee Report of the Proceedings of the Nineteenth and Twentieth Conferences respectively reveals that the conundrums being faced today at The Hague are not new. The questions have always revolved around acceptable bases for a foreign court's jurisdiction, appropriate legal terminology (choice of words) and the degree of harmonisation necessary for an efficient global regime.[667]

The ILA's recommendations were neither considered by national legislatures nor did they form the basis of any global convention. Several reasons could be offered for this failure which further underscore the importance of pragmatism in any global work on jurisdiction and judgments. The first shortcoming observed from the reports is that the proposed rules were drafted by the English section of the drafting committee. Several members from other European States criticised the rules, which were said to be rooted in English law.[668] They also doubted the usefulness of a judgments convention which excluded direct jurisdiction rules. The other major shortcoming is the fact that the activities of the ILA were not backed by sovereign States. Although the Italian government, through Mancini, at one point offered to sponsor a diplomatic conference and indeed invited other States accordingly, the conference did not happen due to the outbreak of cholera in northern Italy in 1885.[669] No State showed an interest in the ILA's conferences afterwards. As Dr Arthur Kuhn, the American representative rightly notes, an unofficial body can hardly prepare rules for States' adoption in delicate areas of law such as jurisdiction and judgments because those matters implicate States' sovereignty.[670] Be that as it may, the ILA concluded a model law in 1960, which was closely similar in structural design to the 2019 Judgments Convention. It provided for a simple

---

[664] 'Seventh Annual Conference' (1879) 7 *Association for the Reform & Codification of the Law of Nations Reports of Conferences* 1, 121.

[665] For instance, questions on jurisdictional bases and other areas of judgments enforcement law were posed to experts from Spain, France, Germany, Russia and Holland amongst others. See 'Foreign Judgment' (1880) 8 *Association for the Reform & Codification Law of Nations Reports of Conferences* 175, 176.

[666] 'Seventh Annual Conference' (n 664) 215.

[667] International Law Association, 'Foreign Judgments', *Report of the Twentieth Annual Conference* (Williams Clowes and Sons Ltd 1901).

[668] James Paul Govare, 'Convention Internationale Pour l'Execution Des Jugements Etrangers' (1924) 33 *International Law Association Reports of Conferences* 169, 193.

[669] FJ Tomkins, 'Execution of Foreign Judgments', *Association for the Reform and Codification of Law of Nations: Report of the Thirteenth Conference* (1887) 169; HCCH, 'Annual Report 2018' (2019) 15.

[670] James Paul Govare (n 668) 204.

framework for judgments recognition, with minimum harmonisation of indirect jurisdictional bases, prohibiting any exercise of jurisdiction contrary to express agreement, and giving States the latitude to go beyond the jurisdictional bases agreed upon.[671]

C. Hague Conference on Private International Law (HCPIL/HCCH)

In February 1874, Mr Gericke on behalf of the government of the Netherlands sent a memorandum to the governments of the United States, Germany, UK, Austria, Belgium, France and Italy for the establishment of a diplomatic conference on jurisdiction and enforcement of foreign judgments. He suggested that there was a dire need for an 'international commission whose duty it should be to draw up a body of rules which the governments interested should pledge themselves to introduce into their legislation or to follow in their treaties'.[672] This move did not materialise until TMC Asser successfully persuaded the Dutch government to hold the first diplomatic conference in 1893.[673] It will be recalled that one of the shortcomings that were identified in the activities of the IDI and the ILA was the absence of political backing from States. It was, therefore, a wise move that any further activity in this area should be States driven. HCPIL is the oldest inter-governmental body with a 'legislative mission' on the harmonisation or unification of private international law.[674] It became a permanent organisation when its Statute came into force in 1955. Although it started as a European body, the Conference began to have a global outlook when Japan (1955),[675] and common law countries like the United Kingdom (1955), United States (1964) and Canada (1968) joined. Currently, it has 82 Member States and 1 Regional Economic Integration Organisation (REIO).[676] It remains the only expert international body with a high degree of competence and acceptability whose objectives exclusively focus on the development of all aspects of private international law.

Enforcement of judgments was not a major agenda item for HCPIL in its first four conferences, held in 1893, 1894, 1900 and 1904 respectively. The Conference

---

[671] 'Enforcement of Foreign Judgments' (1960) 49 *International Law Association Reports of Conferences* 290, 310–12. See also the updated version of the model law at 'Enforcement of Foreign Judgments' (1962) 50 *International Law Association Reports of Conferences* 491, 492–95.

[672] For the text of the memorandum sent to the government of the United States, see 'Papers Relating to the Foreign Relations of the United States Transmitted to Congress with the Annual Message of the President', *Foreign Relations of the United States (FRUS)* (1874).

[673] Hans Van Loon, 'The Global Horizon of Private International Law', *Recueil des Cours* vol 380 (Brill Nijhoff 2016) 27.

[674] Hans Van Loon, 'The Hague Conference on Private International Law: Asser's Vision and an Evolving Mission' (2007) 2 *Hague Justice Journal* 1, 1–2.

[675] Initially as an observer in 1904.

[676] See HCCH, 'Status Table' (*Statute of the Hague Conference on Private International Law*) <https://www.hcch.net/en/instruments/conventions/status-table/?cid=29> accessed 13 June 2019.

felt that matrimonial (eg, marriages and succession) and civil procedure (eg, legalisation of documents and taking of evidence) issues were of utmost priority.[677] Its activities were severely affected by the First and Second World Wars. Hence, no significant result was achieved until the Seventh Session in 1951 when more States joined the Conference and negotiations on various conventions resumed.[678] Jurisdiction and enforcement of foreign judgments came to the front burner at the Eighth Session in 1956 and formed a key part of the discussions at the Ninth (1960),[679] Tenth (1966),[680] Extraordinary (1966)[681] and Eleventh (1968)[682] Sessions. It concluded the first judgments convention in 1971. The failure of that convention necessitated the search for a new one, which began in 1992. It produced a Convention on Choice of Court Agreements in 2005 (HCCA) and a brand-new judgments convention in 2019.

III. HCPIL: History of the Hague Judgments Project

A. 1971 Judgments Convention

HCPIL did record some achievements from the first four conferences it had, especially in the area of civil procedure. The body ventured into civil and commercial matters amongst others after the World Wars.[683] Between 1954 and 1956, no fewer than three conventions were concluded on international sales of goods and one on the recognition of the legal personality of foreign companies.[684]

At the Ninth Session, several proposals were submitted on recognition and enforcement of foreign judgments.[685] Austria proposed that the 1958 Convention

---

[677] Simeon E Baldwin, 'The Comparative Results, in the Advancement of Private International Law, of the Montevideo Congress of 1888–9 and the Hague Conferences of 1893, 1894, 1900, and 1904' (1905) 2 *Proceedings of the American Political Science Association* 73, 77.

[678] Loon (n 674) 5; ML Saunders, 'The Hague Conference on Private International Law' (1966) 2 *Australian Yearbook of International Law* 115, 115–16.

[679] See Kurt H Nadelmann and GAL Droz, 'The Hague Conference on Private International Law Ninth Session' (1960) 9 *American Journal of Comparative Law* 583.

[680] Kurt H Nadelmann and Willis LM Reese, 'The Tenth Session of the Hague Conference on Private International Law' (1964) 13 *The American Journal of Comparative Law* 612.

[681] Kurt H Nadelmann and Arthur T von Mehren, 'The Extraordinary Session of the Hague Conference on Private International Law' (1966) 60 *American Journal of International Law* 803.

[682] Philip W Amram, 'Report on the Eleventh Session of the Hague Conference on Private International Law' (1969) 63 *The American Journal of International Law* 521.

[683] Kurt H Nadelmann and Willis LM Reese, 'The American Proposal at the Hague Conference on Private International Law to Use the Method of Uniform Laws' (1958) 7 *The American Journal of Comparative Law* 239.

[684] See HCCH, 'Conventions, Protocols and Principles': <https://www.hcch.net/en/instruments/conventions> accessed 13 June 2019.

[685] There was an earlier effort at the Fifth Session in 1925, which only led to a draft convention that could serve as a basis for bilateral treaties. See A Droz and Adair Dyer, 'The Hague Conference and the

on the Jurisdiction of the Selected Forum in the Case of International Sales of Goods[686] could be expanded beyond the issue of jurisdiction. Belgium proposed a general convention on recognition and enforcement of foreign judgments. Similarly, the Council of Europe proposed a general judgments convention, while the ILA proposed a model law premised on its 1960 draft.[687] Following these proposals, the Conference asked the Permanent Bureau to consider the desirability and feasibility of a convention on recognition and enforcement of judgments.

The first set of issues that confronted the Conference was the best approach for the harmonisation of the diverse private international rules. This issue was principally raised by the United States delegates, who were of the view that because of the knotty issues surrounding the objectives of the Conference, model laws would be a pragmatic option due to the flexibilities they offer.[688] They also thought that a model law could easily be adapted by national legislatures to align with peculiar legal cultures and constitutional requirements. This view was supported by the United Kingdom. The Conference decided otherwise. One cannot but agree with the decision to retain the diplomatic nature of the Conference.[689] It is essential to get States to be more committed to the activities of HCPIL and deliver conventions which bind States to act uniformly. It will also help to drive HCPIL's membership. There are other numerous advantages that conventions have over model laws and this is more obvious in a subject matter such as jurisdiction and judgments where states would naturally want to act out of self-interest unless restricted by positive mandatory rules. In addition, legal certainty, and predictability of results for private international litigants are another focus of any harmonisation project. That certainty and predictability can only be better achieved by mutually agreed rules which apply across the board with little or no variations. Having decided on the method of harmonisation,[690] two other critical issues emerged for deliberation. One was the type of convention to be negotiated and the other was how to deal with judgments from unfriendly States and States with inexperienced or corrupt judiciary. These two issues were germane in the 1960s when the atmosphere was still tense following the bitter experiences of the World Wars. It was also an era of decolonisation when many third world countries' judiciaries were still cutting their teeth in legal scholarship.

Main Issues of Private International Law for the Eighties' (1981) 3 *Northwestern Journal of International Law & Business* 155, 176.

[686] Signed by Austria, Belgium, Germany and Greece but never ratified by any of them. See <https://www.hcch.net/en/instruments/conventions/status-table/?cid=34> accessed 13 July 2019.

[687] RH Graveson, 'The Ninth Hague Conference of Private International Law' (1961) 10 *International and Comparative Law Quarterly* 18, 27.

[688] Nadelmann and Reese (n 680).

[689] Ibid.

[690] While the Conference resolved to adopt a convention, it was also agreed that the text of the convention would be circulated in the form of a model law which can be used as a basis for uniform legislation in countries like the United States and Canada. See JG Castel, 'Canada and the Hague Conference on Private International Law : 1893–1967' (1967) 1 *Canadian Bar Review* 1, 17.

The 1971 Hague Convention on Foreign Judgments in Civil and Commercial Matters was concluded at an extraordinary session in April 1966. The analysis of the Convention will not be considered because it would serve no useful purpose here. However, it is worth mentioning that the two major issues identified above were largely responsible for the failure of the Convention. On judgments from unfriendly States or inexperienced and corrupt judiciaries, the delegates resolved to have a multilateral convention which would only operate by way of bilateralisation.[691] In essence, States are required to conclude a separate bilateral agreement with one another for the Convention to become effective between them.[692] This complex version of bilateralisation has not only created a complex and convoluted regime, but it was also an albatross that has worked against global acceptance of the Convention.

A more daunting task for the Conference was the reconciliation of the problem surrounding jurisdictionally improper fora. The 1971 Convention is a simple convention that stipulates minimum recognition requirements including the rules of indirect jurisdiction. When the negotiations were almost concluded, the six EEC States proposed a draft convention on jurisdiction and recognition of judgments (a double convention). The draft permitted the use of improper jurisdictional grounds such as tag jurisdiction,[693] nationality, presence of assets amongst others, on defendants from third States. This discrimination generated a heated debate at the Hague Conference since residents of many Member States, including the United States and the United Kingdom, would be adversely affected. The delegates moved to block this discrimination. Following a request from the United States and the United Kingdom, a Special Commission was convened to draft a Supplementary Protocol, which black-listed (prohibited) most of the improper jurisdictional grounds.[694] It was also agreed that both instruments should be signed together.

The 1971 Judgments Convention entered into force on 20 August 1979 when it became effective in the Netherlands and Cyprus. It was also ratified by Portugal (1983) and Kuwait (2002) and acceded to by Albania (2010).[695] While most States did not show interest in the Convention, there has also been no evidence of bilateralisation among the five signatories to the Convention. As captured by Professor Ronald Brand, the Convention 'remains useful only as an academic text'.[696]

---

[691] Article 21.

[692] Graveson (n 687) 28; Philip W Amram, 'Uniform Legislation as an Effective Alternative to the Treaty Technique' (1960) 54 *Proceedings of the American Society of International Law at its Annual Meeting (1921–1969)* 62, 92.

[693] An exercise of jurisdiction based on the service of summons on an out-of-State defendant who was present within the jurisdiction of the court. It is otherwise referred to as transient jurisdiction.

[694] Saunders (n 678) 125–27.

[695] HCCH, 'Status Table: Convention of 1 February 1971 on the Recognition and Enforcement of Foreign Judgments in Civil and Commercial Matters': <https://www.hcch.net/en/instruments/conventions/status-table/?cid=78> accessed 18 June 2019.

[696] Ronald A Brand, 'New Challenges in the Recognition and Enforcement of Judgments' (2018) *University of Pittsburgh Legal Studies Research Paper No 2018–29*, 35.

The takeout from the 1971 Judgments Convention is that a global judgments convention is characteristically different from those of bilateral and regional conventions. At a global level, States' policies and interests differ more. More time, and more importantly, extensive negotiations may be required to trade off these competing policies and interests. The 1971 Convention was proposed at the Tenth Session in 1964 and hurriedly concluded at the Extraordinary Session in 1966 even though the issue of improper jurisdictional grounds only surfaced at the Extraordinary Session. It should not surprise anyone that Germany and France abstained from voting on the recommendations that require Member States to sign the Convention and the Supplementary Protocol together.[697] Thus, the Convention cannot be said to have emerged from a truly consensual process.

B. The Hague Judgments Project

There was a lull after the conclusion of the 1971 Judgments Convention for about two decades. It was an era of the second and third wave of globalisation,[698] which ushered in burgeoning global trade, computerisation and global connectivity. These developments necessitated increased cross-border litigation and thus the much-needed international cooperation to address the challenges of improper jurisdictional grounds and enforcement of foreign judgments. In 1992, these realities, amongst other things, possibly pushed the US to request HCPIL to take up a judgments project once again. In a letter from Edwin D Williamson, a Legal Advisor in the US Department of State, to the Secretary-General of the Hague Conference, the US proposed a single convention thus:

> The United States would like to propose that The Hague Conference resume work in the field of recognition and enforcement of judgments with a view to preparing a single convention to which Hague Conference Member States and other countries might become parties and that would enter into force only between ratifying or acceding States that agree that it should enter into force as between them.[699]

Having suggested a single convention, the letter went further to make an innovative suggestion for what would later be known as a mixed convention. To lay bare the rationale for the second proposal, the relevant part is reproduced here:

> While taking account of the 1971 Hague Convention, we would propose that The Hague Conference build on the Brussels and Lugano Conventions in seeking to achieve a convention that is capable of meeting the needs of and being broadly accepted by the

---

[697] Kurt H Nadelmann, 'The Common Market Judgments Convention and a Hague Conference Recommendation : What Steps Next ?' (1969) 82 *Harvard Law Review* 1282, 1284.

[698] Peter Vanham, 'A Brief History of Globalization' (2019): <https://www.weforum.org/agenda/2019/01/how-globalization-4-0-fits-into-the-history-of-globalization/> accessed 18 June 2019.

[699] A copy of the letter is available at <https://2009-2017.state.gov/documents/organization/65973.pdf> (accessed 18 June 2019).

larger community represented by the Member States of The Hague Conference. For example, it appears that it might be possible to accept certain of the bases of jurisdiction and bases for recognition and enforcement of judgments set out in the Brussels and Lugano Conventions and thereby make provision for a generally accepted system for use in Europe and beyond. However, other aspects of these Conventions may not be so broadly acceptable and would need change to accommodate the needs and preferences of countries from other regions of the world than Western Europe. It seems to us that we need not necessarily choose between a *traité simple*, dealing essentially only with those judgments that are entitled to recognition and enforcement in party States, and a *traité double* also dealing with permissible bases of jurisdiction for litigation involving persons or entities habitually resident in party States. We believe that there should be consideration of the possibility for party States to utilize jurisdictional bases for litigation that are not designated as permissible or exorbitant by the convention. So long as such jurisdictional bases are not excluded as exorbitant, judgments based on them would not be entitled to recognition and enforcement under the convention, but party States would remain free to recognize and enforce them under their general law.

It is glaring from the proposals that the hurriedly concluded discussions on improper jurisdictional grounds at the Extraordinary Session in 1966 would reappear. This is further confirmed by the response of the Permanent Bureau to the US proposal, where it was noted that a simple convention like the 1971 Convention might be a starting point, while other convention formats – double and mixed – would also be on the table.[700]

A Special Commission on General Affairs and Policy deliberated on the US proposal in June 1992. It recommended that a Working Group of experts on judicial jurisdiction be set up to report their findings to the Seventeenth Session.[701] The Working Group favoured a double convention but could not achieve consensus on some of the jurisdictional grounds to be excluded especially tag jurisdiction and 'doing business'.[702] Several meetings were held between 1992 and 1996 to finetune the areas of disagreement. Thereafter, a Special Commission met between 1997 and 1999 to prepare a preliminary draft convention on jurisdiction and judgments. The final product was more of a double convention than mixed. It stipulates the required bases (the white list), the prohibited bases (the black list) and undefined permissible bases (jurisdiction under national law not prohibited under the convention).[703]

This effort came to nought in June 2001 when the Diplomatic Conference failed to reach consensus on several key issues contained in the draft convention. Those issues included acceptable jurisdictional bases for internet and e-commerce

---

[700] HCCH, 'Some Reflections of the Permanent Bureau on a General Convention on Enforcement of Judgments', *Preliminary Doc No 17 of May 1992 in Proceedings of the Seventeenth Session* (1993).

[701] HCCH, 'Conclusions of the Special Commission of June 1992 on General Affairs and Policy of the Conference', *Preliminary Doc No 18 of August 1992 in Proceedings of the Seventeenth Session* (1993) 253.

[702] HCCH, 'Conclusions of the Working Group Meeting on Enforcement of Judgments', *Preliminary Doc No 19 of November 1992 in Proceedings of the Seventeenth Session* (1993), 261.

[703] See Chapter II and Articles 17 and 18 of the 1999 Preliminary Draft Convention on Jurisdiction and Foreign Judgments in Civil and Commercial Matters.

disputes, intellectual property, consumer and employment contracts. In addition, no consensus was achieved for activity-based jurisdiction, bilateralisation and the relationship between the convention and other regional instruments such as the Brussels/Lugano Convention.[704]

The major drawback at this first exercise was an attempt to push a Brussels-tailored convention at the global level. It was apparent that the majority of members of the Special Commission preferred a 'classical double convention' and the only difference between the draft convention and a classical double convention was Article 17 which permitted Contracting States to assume jurisdiction as available under their respective national laws. Apart from this, the convention sought to add too many subject matters, such as intellectual property, internet and e-commerce, at a time when the law was still evolving in many States. Again, this is further evidence of the EU-centric nature of the draft.

The collapse of the first attempt has also been attributed to the US/EU divide, or the contrasting positions of the civil and common law regimes broadly speaking. As Janet Walker cautions, this does not mean that other Member States of the Hague Conference have no independent views about the issues tabled for consideration.[705] A few examples of these issues can be cited. There was a stalemate on personal and activity-based jurisdictional grounds. The US due process requirement stipulates that a court cannot assume jurisdiction over a non-resident defendant unless he maintains some minimum contacts with the forum. This is contrasted with the EU approach where a single transaction with a State is a sufficient link between that State and the dispute. In the same vein, while the US and other common law systems have consistently affirmed tag jurisdiction as a sufficient link, it is considered an exorbitant ground by most Hague Conference Member States especially the EU delegates. Professor Ronald Brand rightly indicates that the US negotiators had no discretion on these issues because the convention addresses direct jurisdictional grounds, the text of which violates the US Constitution.[706] In all, the Diplomatic Conference agreed that the draft was too ambitious.

A second attempt was made between 2002 and 2005. Allan Phillip of Denmark has been credited for sounding a note of caution on the over-ambitious 1999 draft convention and the need to work on a moderate project that would command global acceptance.[707] The informal Working Group, which he chaired, suggested a convention focusing on choice of court agreements. The Group adopted a

---

[704] HCCH, 'Some Reflections on the Present State of Negotiations on the Judgments Project in the Context of the Future Work Programme of the Conference', *Preliminary Doc No 16 of February 2002* (2002) 5.

[705] Janet Walker, 'Canada's Position on a Multilateral Judgments Convention' in C Carmody, Y Iwasawa and S Rhodes (eds), *Trilateral Perspectives on International Legal Issues: Conflict and Coherence* (3rd edn American Society of International Law 2003) 127, 129; Beaumont, 'A United Kingdom Perspective On the Proposed Hague Judgments Convention' (ch 2, fn 162).

[706] Brand, 'Due Process, Jurisdiction and a Hague Judgments Convention' (n 651) 702.

[707] Beaumont, 'Hague Choice of Court Agreements Convention 2005: Background, Negotiations, Analysis and Current Status' (ch 1, fn 50) 130–31.

'bottom-up' approach, which allowed the delegates to build upon areas where consensus had emerged.[708] The Group met between 2002 and 2003, examined areas of consensus from previous works and decided to focus on choice of court agreements in B2B cases because of their significance to cross-border transactions. The Special Commission on General Affairs and Policy overwhelmingly supported the recommendation and, therefore, a Special Commission was constituted to work on a draft convention. The draft convention was finalised and adopted at a Diplomatic Conference in 2005. Thus, the Hague Convention of 30 June 2005 on Choice of Court Agreements (HCCA) became the first fruit of the Hague Judgments Project.

In 2010, the Permanent Bureau invited the Council on General Affairs and Policy to consider the case for the resumption of works on the Judgments Project. This is dubbed as the third attempt. The Council accepted the proposal but deferred the work to such time as the HCCA entered into force.[709] It eventually gave a greenlight in 2011 provided that the future work would not hinder the promotion of the HCCA. A Working Group was constituted, and they had several meetings between 2013 and 2015. A Proposed Draft Text was concluded and forwarded to the Permanent Bureau and the same was reported to the Council on General Affairs and Policy in 2015.[710] A Special Commission was convened in June 2016 to prepare a preliminary draft convention. The Commission met between June 2016 and May 2018. The 2018 draft convention was considered and adopted at a Diplomatic Conference in June/July 2019 with some modifications. A brand-new convention was birthed on 2 July 2019 and Uruguay became the first signatory to the Convention on the same day.

IV. HCCA

A. Introduction

The HCCA is the first fruit of the Hague Judgments Project. The Convention came into force on 1 October 2015 when the EU, on behalf of 27 Member States, ratified it. Also, it has been ratified by Denmark, Mexico, Montenegro and Singapore. It has been signed but is yet to be ratified by the United States, Ukraine and China. Although the Convention came into force 10 years after its negotiation, this is not unusual for a typical Hague convention. What is more appealing is that there is a growing interest among States to join the Convention. For instance, in 2016, the Australian Parliament's Joint Standing Committee on Treaties recommended the ratification of the Convention and proposed that an International

---

[708] HCCH, 'Report on the First Meeting of the Informal Working Group on the Judgments Project of October 2002', *Preliminary Doc No 20 of November 2002* (2002) 5.

[709] HCCH, 'Council on General Affairs and Policy of the Conference (7–9 April 2010): Conclusions and Recommendations Adopted by the Council' (2010).

[710] HCCH, 'Ongoing Work in the Area of Judgments', *Preliminary Doc No 7B of January 2016*.

Civil Law Act be enacted for its implementation.[711] While Canada is yet to sign the Convention, the Canadian Uniform Law Conference has adopted legislation for its nationwide implementation.[712] In 2017, Ontario enacted the Burden Reduction Act, 2017 to reduce regulatory burdens on businesses. Schedule 4 of the Act contains new legislation – the International Choice of Court Agreements Convention Act, 2017 – making it the first province in Canada to domesticate the HCCA.[713] Saskatchewan followed suit in 2018 by enacting the Choice of Court Agreements (Hague Convention Implementation) Act.[714] In the same vein, Russia, Brazil, Tunisia, New Zealand, Argentina and Costa Rica are considering joining the Convention.[715] This is an attestation of the likelihood of more successes to be recorded for this Convention.

The Convention has been described as a game-changer.[716] The reason is not farfetched. It offers the global community an additional layer of protection and enforcement of international contracts because it places courts' judgments on a par with arbitral awards in terms of the enforcement mechanism. Thus, exclusive choice of court agreements in contracts should be chosen as often as arbitration agreements with the growing ratification or adoption of the HCCA. If the acceptability grows, as expected, it can arguably change the tide of international commercial litigation, as parties may be inclined to a court-based resolution because of the legal certainty of enforcement of choice of court agreements[717] and also the added advantage of appealability of court decisions.[718] Evidence from the American Bar Association already suggests that 70 per cent of their respondents in a survey conducted on this subject matter indicate that they would be 'more willing to designate litigation instead of arbitration' in their contracts.[719]

---

[711] Joint Standing Committee on Treaties, Parliament of the Commonwealth of Australia, 'Report 166: Implementation Procedures for Airworthiness-USA; Convention on Choice of Courts-Accession; GATT Schedule of Concessions-Amendment; Radio Regulations-Partical Revision' (2016) 17–21. See <https://www.ulcc.ca/en/uniform-acts-new-order/current-uniform-acts/645-hague-convention-choice-of-court/1404-hague-convention-on-choice-of-court-agreements-act>.

[712] See <https://www.ulcc.ca/en/uniform-acts-new-order/current-uniform-acts/645-hague-convention-choice-of-court/1404-hague-convention-on-choice-of-court-agreements-act>.

[713] The Bill received Royal Assent on 22 March 2017. The text is available at <https://www.ontario.ca/laws/statute/17i02a>.

[714] S.S. 2018, c. C-10.2, Gazette Vol 115:22 (31 May 2019). The text is available at: <http://canlii.ca/t/53g0b>.

[715] Frank Poon, 'The Hague Choice of Court Convention and the Current Judgment Project', *UNCITRAL Judicial Summit* (2017) <http://uncitralrcap.org/wp-content/uploads/2018/03/10.13-Judicial-Conference-slides-Session-4.pdf> accessed 24 June 2019.

[716] Sundaresh Menon, 'International Commercial Courts: Towards a Transnational System of Dispute Resolution', *Opening Lecture for the DIFC Courts Lecture Series 2015* (2015) 36.

[717] Marta Pertegás, 'The Brussels I Regulation and the Hague Convention on Choice of Court Agreements' (2010) 11 *ERA Forum* 19.

[718] Rachel Elliott, 'The Hague Convention on Choice of Court Agreements – Will It Be a Game Changer for International Litigation?', *European Law Firm* (19 April 2016) <https://www.european-law-firm.com/news/the-hague-convention-on-choice-of-court-agreements-will-it-be-a-game-changer-for-international-litigation> accessed 24 June 2019.

[719] American Bar Association, 'Hague Choice of Court Agreement: Recommendation' (2006) <https://www.americanbar.org/content/dam/aba/migrated/intlaw/policy/investment/hcca0806.pdf> accessed 24 June 2019.

B. Pragmatism in its Making

Pragmatism in a global judgments enforcement scheme entails two basic things. First is the appreciation of the practical problems to be solved and the need to prioritise justice, efficiency and legal certainty as each case may dictate. Second, in a global context, there is a need for some elements of realism. 'Realism' in this context is used literally and denotes the need to take account of States' policies, interests and their likelihood of ratifying the proposed rules. Thus, two practicalities are being considered here: the need for a convention that addresses practical legal problems faced by cross-border litigants; and also the global acceptability of the Convention. Where either or both of these two practicalities are taken for granted, two results are readily expected: a convention with no practical utility, and/or a merely fanciful piece of legislation, which does not command global respect and acceptance.

The HCCA's principal focus is to provide a global mechanism for the enforcement of foreign judgments arising from an exclusive choice of court agreement. Before 2015 when the Convention came into force, the 1958 New York Convention on enforcement of arbitral awards was the only available framework. While the New York Convention has achieved tremendous success, there are still many gaps to be filled. International arbitration is relatively expensive and may not be affordable to 'middle-class litigants'[720] both individual and corporate. Arguably, micro, small and medium-sized enterprises (MSMEs) and many other groups of litigants may need an alternative regime for enforcement of choice of court agreements. The 2018 International Arbitration Survey from Queen Mary University of London School of International Arbitration reiterates that cost is arbitration's worst feature.[721] Other compelling reasons may make choice of court agreements attractive in cross-border transactions. These include the fact that some disputes are not arbitrable, lack of a good case management system and lack of speed by arbitrators, limited powers to grant interim reliefs, discovery and other pre-trial remedies, non-appealability of awards, and unnecessary interventions from national courts.[722] Therefore, there is no gainsaying that the HCCA would not only address these specific challenges, it would also provide legal certainty amid the divergent national laws and policies on exclusive choice of court agreements.

(i) Consensual Method

The first pragmatic approach adopted by the Working Group was to build the Convention from simple matters where consensus already existed amongst States.

---

[720] Teitz (ch 3, fn 304) 544.
[721] Queen Mary University of London, '2018 International Arbitration Survey: The Evolution of International Arbitration' (2018) <http://www.arbitration.qmul.ac.uk/media/arbitration/docs/2018-International-Arbitration-Survey-report.pdf> accessed 18 July 2019.
[722] Ibid.

The overall framework provides for harmonisation of the rules on jurisdiction and recognition and enforcement of judgments only for the core area of 'exclusive' choice of court agreements. Even here the Convention does not stop States from exercising direct and exclusive jurisdiction based on a choice of court agreement that does not meet the formal validity requirements in the Convention, eg an oral agreement based on a commercial usage in that trade or upon previous practice between the parties to the agreement; but other Contracting States do not have any duty to decline jurisdiction in favour of the chosen court or to recognise and enforce the judgment from the chosen court. The utility of this approach is that consensus could more easily be achieved on a narrowed theme of exclusive choice of court agreements, while an individual State or a group of interested States might go beyond the benchmark set out by the Convention. For instance, Article 22 provides for reciprocal enforcement of non-exclusive choice of court agreements. Similarly, under Article 26, the Convention does not affect existing or future treaty obligations that may be created between or among Contracting States. The adoption of a consensual approach was not only useful in the preparation of the Convention, but also the negotiation process. It was a confirmation that Member States overwhelmingly supported the Convention, and this could be a boost for wide ratification. The Hague Conference changed from majority voting to a consensual method in 2007[723] and this has been applied to all conventions negotiated from that year. This is quite different from the mechanism adopted for the failed 1971 Convention and the Supplementary Protocol, which were pushed through by majority votes.

(ii) Bottom-Up Approach

Different approaches have been used in the past to draw up judgments conventions. While no hard and fast rule can be stipulated, experience has shown that a successful global judgments convention requires a thoughtful and meticulous method. For the HCCA, the Working Group did not proceed with any preconceived list of items or evolve a draft by strict adherence to formalistic doctrines. It began by breaking down previous works into pieces, with a view to identifying the core areas where consensus had emerged. Then, other possible additions were considered. It achieved this task by considering the 'what if' questions. This enabled the Working Group and the Special Commission to focus on an item and

---

[723] The Statute of the Hague Conference was amended in 2005 at the Twentieth Session and became effective on 1 January 2007. Article 8(2) now provides that 'The Sessions, Council and Special Commissions shall, to the furthest extent possible, operate on the basis of consensus'. For what consensus means at HCPIL and the politicking which led to it, see Hartley, *Choice-of-Court Agreements under the European and International Instruments: The Revised Brussels I Regulation, the Lugano Convention, and the Hague Convention* (n 654) 20–21; Brand and Herrup (n 654) 9–10; Beaumont, 'Reflections on the Relevance of Public International Law to Private International Law Treaty Making' (ch 1, fn 58) 55–61.

the consequences of its addition or removal for the overall architecture and scope of the Convention. It started from ground zero and populated the list item-by-item, subject-by-subject. Thus, even though consensus appeared to have been reached on some jurisdictional bases such as residence and submission in the previous works, they were eventually dropped from the scope of the Convention because of the complexities they might bring, which would affect the secure foundation of the Convention. The 'what if's also brought in declarations and other flexibilities which paved the way for consensus on the key areas like Articles 1, 4, 5 and 8. Although this approach led to a narrow Convention, this seeming drawback was remedied by providing an in-built mechanism (eg Articles 22 and 26) for advancing its frontiers among willing States as more consensus might be available in the future. Also, the Convention is complementary to the 2019 Judgments Convention. Therefore, whatever cannot be covered by the HCCA can be covered by the broader 2019 Convention.

(iii) Flexibility

One other characteristic of the HCCA is its flexibility. This is connected with the move to accommodate divergent interests of Member States, especially in the context of a convention dealing with direct jurisdictional grounds. The utility of this approach is that many incongruent views can be aggregated, and divergent positions can be harmonised or avoided altogether while not undermining the substance of the Convention. The drafters made use of reservations and declarations to achieve this objective. For instance, Article 19 permits a State to make a declaration that its courts may decline jurisdiction if there is no practical connection between the State and the dispute and its parties.[724] This negates the obligation created under Article 5 which vests exclusive jurisdiction in the chosen court. Conversely, Article 20 also allows the State not to recognise a foreign judgment where the only connection between the transaction and the State of origin is the choice of court agreement. These exceptions were created to please States such as China whose civil procedure laws require their courts to disregard jurisdictional agreements nominating courts that have no real and practical connections to the dispute.[725]

---

[724] The other condition for Article 17 to apply is that the parties and other relevant elements are connected to the requested State. For declarations and reservations under the HCCA, see the extensive discussion in Beaumont, 'Hague Choice of Court Agreements Convention 2005: Background, Negotiations, Analysis and Current Status' (ch 1, fn 50).

[725] Sadly, China now applies the rule to foreign courts only. See Peng Xianwei, 'Choice of Court Agreement and the Practical Connection Principle: A Comment on the Chinese Supreme Court's Civil Ruling Regarding the "Hero" Online Game Jurisdiction Dispute Case' (2013) (3) *Journal of Business Law* 317, 318; Yong Gan, 'Jurisdiction Agreements in Chinese Conflict of Laws: Searching for Ways to Implement the Hague Convention on Choice of Court Agreements in China' (2018) 14 *Journal of Private International Law* 295, 304–6. Gan notes that by judicial practice, the requirement of an actual connection has been dropped for agreements nominating Chinese courts but retained for foreign courts. Thus, a Chinese court would exercise jurisdiction even if it had no connection with the dispute. On the other hand, it would disregard a similar agreement if it were in favour of a foreign court.

Flexibility is also observed in the treatment of judgments from designated non-exclusive courts. Article 22 provides for possible enforcement of those judgments on a reciprocal basis. The utility of this provision is that it removes the logjam that would have been created in negotiating jurisdictional requirements for non-exclusive choice of court agreements, attendant parallel litigation, and the debacle of setting *forum non conveniens* and *lis pendens* rules.[726] One can add Article 21 to the list. This allows States that have a 'strong interest' in not applying the Convention to specific issues to exclude such issues by declaration. Examples of such interests that have been identified by writers include insurance contracts (for the EU and Denmark), foreign joint-venture agreements (China), franchise contracts (US), and asbestos cases (Canada).[727] Richard Garnett wonders whether this would not become a Trojan horse, which may render the Convention a 'hollow shell'. Brand and Herrup seem to have a similar view. One cannot but concede that this seems to be the natural implication of Article 21, even though such a path could undermine the overall utility of the Convention. However, a purposive interpretation which limits the use of Article 21 to 'strong interests' on some specific matters, and not as a substitute for Article 2 (exclusions from the scope of the Convention) as argued by Beaumont, seems more pragmatic.[728] Be that as it may, that flexibility is a necessary evil as Member States were faced with a choice of another stalemate, or to achieve a moderate success by trading off some few specific matters, which may merely be ancillary to Article 2. Professor Paul Beaumont's insights on what transpired during the negotiations buttress this point. He notes that the US delegation at the Special Commission was ready to block a consensus if the Convention would not permit the kind of flexibility that would allow the US Senate to have some discretion in the way the Convention would be applied in the US.[729] Of all the Contracting Parties, only Denmark, the EU and the United Kingdom have made declarations (under Article 21) which limit the application of the Convention to certain types of insurance contracts.[730] Singapore, Montenegro and Mexico have made no declaration. This may well mean that the problem is unduly exaggerated.

The flexibilities represent the pragmatism of the HCCA. Although, it may not be as watertight as the New York Convention due to the exclusion of more subject matters – including consumer and employment contracts – and making available more defences against recognition, the creativity of the drafters enabled the negotiators to achieve consensus on many aspects of the Convention.[731] It would have been another failure without such flexibilities.

---

[726] Trevor Hartley and Masato Dogauchi, Explanatory Report: HCCA (ch 5, fn 442) 57.

[727] See Richard Garnett, 'The Hague Choice of Court Convention: Magnum Opus or Much Ado About Nothing?' (2009) 5 *Journal of Private International Law* 161, 179; Beaumont, 'Hague Choice of Court Agreements Convention 2005: Background, Negotiations, Analysis and Current Status' (ch 1, fn 50) 150.

[728] Beaumont (ch 1, fn 50) 150–54.

[729] Ibid, 152.

[730] See Paul Beaumont, 'The Revived Judgments Project in The Hague' (2014) 4 *Nederlands Internationaal Privaatrecht* 532, 532–39.

[731] Teitz (ch 3, fn 304) 552–53.

C. Prorogation

The principal aim of the HCCA is to create legal certainty for choice of court agreements with a maximum guarantee that resulting judgments from chosen courts are widely circulated. The law has never been straightforward in this area. Historically, courts often guard their jurisdiction jealously and view with concern any attempt by private litigants to oust their jurisdiction.[732] In recent times, however, party autonomy has triumphed and courts, globally, have enforced choice of court agreements in most cases.[733] The difficulty lies in the different approaches adopted by national courts, and the attending frustration on parties who often need to litigate on venue despite the existence of a preferred choice.

The debate goes beyond whether jurisdiction agreements are exclusive or not exclusive. Even where an exclusive choice has been made, there is no guarantee that the chosen court would not decline jurisdiction, especially in Anglo-American jurisdictions where courts can stay proceedings because of the doctrine of *forum non conveniens* (FNC) and other policy considerations.[734] As Hill and Chong rightly note, it cannot be assumed that jurisdiction agreements will be enforced as a matter of course.[735] For instance, the Canadian Supreme Court has been going forth and back on what constitutes 'strong cause' that may warrant a chosen court to decline jurisdiction or stay proceedings. Between 2003 and 2017, it handed down no fewer than three decisions on what constitutes a 'strong cause', whether the test stands alone, or is an aspect of the FNC test, and whether the 'strong cause' test is applied first and then the FNC test when necessary.[736] Brand and Jablonski narrate a similar experience in the US on how the federal circuit courts are split on how and when to apply the *Bremen* and FNC tests to choice of court agreements.[737] The same problem has been observed in Singapore. Professor Tiong Min Yeo, analysing the judicial practice in Singapore, notes that the standards of the 'strong cause' test have varied over the years.[738] In some cases, foreign jurisdiction clauses have been disregarded simply because the claimant argued that the defendant has no merit to the defence. These varied approaches create uncertainties and will

---

[732] Hartley, *Choice-of-Court Agreements under the European and International Instruments: The Revised Brussels I Regulation, the Lugano Convention, and the Hague Convention* (n 654) 6–10; Ronald A Brand and Scott R Jablonski, *Forum Non Conveniens: History, Global Practice, and Future under the Hague Convention on Choice of Court Agreements* (Oxford University Press 2007) 185–86.

[733] Christa Roodt, 'Venue in Transnational Litigation: Party Autonomy Adds New Impetus to the "Judgment Project"' (2006) 16 *South African Mercantile Law Journal* 13, 20–21.

[734] Brand and Jablonski (n 732) 194.

[735] Hill and Chong (ch 5, fn 562) 316.

[736] These cases are *ZI Pompey Industrie v Ecu-Line NV* [2003] 1 SCR 450; *Teck Cominco Metals Ltd v Lloyd's Underwriters* [2009] 1 SCR 321, and *Douez v Facebook* [2017] 1 SCR 751. They are discussed by Geneviève Saumier, 'Has the CJPTA Readied Canada for the Hague Choice of Court Convention?' (2018) 55 *Osgoode Hall Law Journal* 141.

[737] Brand and Jablonski (n 732) 198–203.

[738] Tiong Min Yeo, 'The Choice of Court Agreement: Perils of the Midnight Clause', *12th Yong Pung How Professorship of Law Lecture* (22 May 2019, Singapore Management University).

ultimately lead to increased litigation risk, and a less efficient cross-border dispute settlement regime.[739]

Article 5 of the HCCA brings the much-needed legal certainty to this important area of international commercial litigation. The basic rule under the Convention is that the court of a Contracting State chosen by parties has exclusive jurisdiction over the dispute unless the agreement is null and void under the law of that State. Article 5(2) requires the chosen court not to entertain requests for a stay of proceedings on the ground of *forum non conveniens* or *lis pendens*. It further provides in Article 3(b) that 'a choice of court agreement which designates the courts of one Contracting State or one or more specific courts of one Contracting State shall be deemed to be exclusive unless the parties have expressly provided otherwise'. A practical illustration is the case of *M v V*,[740] where the English High Court declined jurisdiction to hear an application for maintenance because the parties had chosen to resolve their dispute in France. This is notwithstanding that both parties were resident in England at the relevant time.

The above provisions solve two major practical problems affecting choice of court agreements. These problems have often been the subject of preliminary litigation before the substantive disputes are heard. In many cases, they are argued up to the apex courts, as seen in some of the cases from the common law countries mentioned above. One of the problems is whether a chosen court can stay proceedings or decline jurisdiction in favour of a non-chosen court and under what conditions would such a stay be entertained. This position is now harmonised in the Convention, with a seemingly straightforward rule that party autonomy must prevail, and a chosen court must hear the dispute, except where the agreement is invalid under its law. This, to a large extent, would solve the problems created by forum shopping and the challenges of establishing FNC guidelines, as seen in the Canadian and other common law cases, or the challenge of setting priority rule for *lis pendens*, as seen in *Erich Gasser*[741] and other pre-Brussels Ia cases.[742]

The second problem is the harmonised position on the presumption of exclusivity. Again, the problem is more prevalent in the common law jurisdictions,[743] where the preponderance of case law authorities presumes non-exclusivity in

---

[739] Fentiman (ch 1, fn 25) 42–43.

[740] *M v V* [2010] EWHC 1453 (Fam). Although the decision was given in the context of the Brussels I Regulation.

[741] Case C-16/02 *Erich Gasser GmbH v MISAT Srl*, ECLI:EU:C:2003:657. Ahmed and Beaumont have rightly noted that the Article 6 exceptions are an apparent tolerance of possible parallel proceedings. See Mukarrum Ahmed and Paul Beaumont, 'Exclusive Choice of Court Agreements: Some Issues on the Hague Convention on Choice of Court Agreements and Its Relationship with the Brussels I Recast Especially Anti-Suit Injunctions, Concurrent Proceedings and the Implications of BREXIT' (2017) 13 *Journal of Private International Law* 386, 396.

[742] The *Gasser* problem has been rectified by Article 31 of Brussels Ia, which requires a non-chosen court to, *suo motu*, stay proceedings until the chosen court has ruled that it has no jurisdiction.

[743] Brand and Jablonski (n 732) 197–98. However, some civil law systems such as China have been found to exercise jurisdiction one way or the other where a jurisdiction agreement did not contain the word 'exclusive'. See Gan (n 725) 300.

jurisdictional agreements unless the word 'exclusive' is specifically used by parties. Some authorities went as far as denying any fixed meaning to either 'exclusive' or 'non-exclusive'. In *BNP Paribas SA v Anchorage Capital Europe LLP*, Males J was of the view that:

> the terms 'exclusive' and 'nonexclusive' themselves are merely convenient labels … I prefer to ask the question whether the commencement and pursuit of the foreign proceedings in question are things which a party has promised not to do.[744]

This approach creates uncertainties, as parties will not be able to ascertain the venue for litigation until the point is subjected to a preliminary judicial interpretation.

The presumption of exclusivity seems to be in harmony with business common sense. The essence of choosing a court is primarily to have that court adjudicate the dispute arising from the transaction. The express choice ordinarily negates any intention of litigation in a different jurisdiction(s). Adding 'exclusive' appears to be a reinforcement of the parties' choice. What is clear is that in a few cases where they do not intend exclusivity, it is often demonstrated with clear words such as *'the issuer hereby submits to the non-exclusive jurisdiction of the English courts'*[745] or the *'Lessor shall not be prevented from taking proceedings relating to any dispute or claim as aforesaid in any other courts with jurisdiction'.*[746] It is therefore pragmatic, for legal certainty, that the presumption should be that a nominated court has exclusive jurisdiction unless parties specifically opt-out by using 'non-exclusive' or provide an alternative venue(s) as shown above. This would cover the vast majority of cases. The application of this provision should not pose any problem, as national courts have maintained a similar attitude in support of arbitration proceedings. Today, a reference to arbitration with or without the word 'exclusive' means that parties have agreed to arbitrate, and most courts would compel them to honour that choice.[747] There is no practical benefit in treating a choice of court agreement differently from that of arbitration.

The restrictive scope of the Convention has been criticised by some commentators. Professor Adrian Briggs wonders why non-exclusive jurisdiction agreements are excluded from the scope of the Convention.[748] Dammann and Hansmann also argue against the restriction of the Convention to international cases because that prevents parties from avoiding corrupt and inefficient judiciaries.[749] Dammann

---

[744] *BNP Paribas SA v Anchorage Capital Europe LLP* [2013] EWHC 3073 (Comm), para 88.

[745] *China Export & Credit Insurance Corporation v Emerald Energy Resources Limited* [2018] EWHC 1503 (Comm).

[746] *AeroSale 25362 Aviation Ltd v Med-View Airline Plc* [2017] 9 WLUK 247.

[747] See Stewart R Shackleton, 'Annual Review of English Judicial Decisions on Arbitration – 2000' [2001] *International Arbitration Law Review* 178, 183 (noting that an English court would refer parties to arbitration even if it is just a 'fragmentary contractual provision containing only the brief mention: "arbitration in London"').

[748] Adrian Briggs, Agreements on Jurisdiction and Choice of Law (Oxford University Press 2008) chapter 13, 528.

[749] Jens Dammann and Henry Hansmann, 'Globalizing Commercial Litigation' (2008) 94 *Cornell Law Review* 1, 3–4.

and Hansmann's argument merits a closer examination. There may indeed be genuine cases where parties intend to have their dispute resolved by foreign courts as against their home courts. It is not in all cases that parties do attempt to avoid forum law. They may opt for a foreign court because of its expertise or effective case management system, which may not be available in their home State. They may prefer a foreign court because its decisions are enforceable globally or simply because of the presence of the assets of one or both parties in the foreign jurisdiction.[750] Some provisions of the Convention can take care of cases of avoidance of forum law, which is the only plausible reason why a State may not want to enforce a foreign jurisdiction agreement.[751] Therefore, there is no serious justification for excluding choice of court agreements solely because a wholly domestic contract contains a foreign jurisdiction clause. This is one of the shortcomings of the Convention.

For non-exclusive and other asymmetric clauses, two problems would be created if they were to be retained under the Convention. One is how to distinguish cases where two nominated courts are exclusive and where they are non-exclusive. Let's consider these examples:

'Any dispute relating to the interpretation, conclusion, performance or termination of this contract or otherwise relating to it shall be within the competence of the Court of Turin or London' (CL1)

'Any dispute relating to the interpretation, conclusion, performance or termination of this contract or otherwise relating to it shall be within the competence of the Italian court by the Lessor or the English Court by the Lessee' (CL2)

Most courts would interpret CL1 as non-exclusive and that is supported by the simple presumptive rule of the Convention, which says nominating the court of a Contracting State is exclusive, and by extension, a nomination of two or more courts is non-exclusive. There is no major difference between CL1 and CL2 other than stipulating who is to sue in Italy and who is to sue in England. Brooke Marshall makes a good attempt to bring in asymmetric jurisdiction clauses, especially a *Rothschild* clause (whereby one party is given a greater choice of possible forums than the other(s)) within the purview of the Convention and offers five different ways in which such clauses can become exclusive for the purpose of the Convention.[752] The reality is that those clauses cannot fit within the definition of

---

[750] Tiong Min Yeo (n 738).

[751] For instance, Article 9(b) and (e); incapacity and public policy. This can be the case where the law of the receiving State has a strong policy, evidenced by specific mandatory statutes, of having such a dispute litigated in the State. See also Tiong Min Yeo, 'Hague Convention on Choice of Court Agreements 2005: A Singapore Perspective' (2015) 114 *Journal of International Law and Diplomacy* 50, 55.

[752] Brooke Marshall, 'The 2005 Hague Convention: A Panacea for Non-Exclusive Asymmetric Jurisdiction Agreements Too?' in Michael Douglas and others (eds), *Commercial Issues in Private International Law: A Common Law Perspective* (Hart Publishing 2019) 100–113. The English courts have also held that such clauses are exclusive, although within the context of Brussels Ia. See *Etihad Airways PJSC v Prof Dr Lucas Flother* [2020] EWCA Civ 1707; *Commerzbank Aktiengesellschaft v Liquimar Tankers Management* [2017] EWHC 161 (Comm).

'exclusive' under the Convention simply because by their nature, and in whatever variant they come, parties have indicated the option of suing in at least two different courts. It then means the Convention will have to deal with different drafting styles and strategies used by drafters now or those to be invented in the future. The end product will be that any nominated court, whether expressly mentioned or unilaterally decided by a party, can potentially exercise jurisdiction. This will water down the effectiveness of the Convention assuming it will be accepted by States.

The other challenge is that it fully throws open the problem of parallel litigation and the need for rules governing such proceedings. This has been greatly reduced under the current regime by limiting such possibility to only exceptional cases.[753] In a global context, it is pragmatic that those cases remain as non-exclusive. Article 22 can take care of a *Rothschild* clause and other non-exclusive clauses. One can be optimistic that with the emerging trend in judicial cooperation, States would take the benefit of the Article and move beyond the frontiers of the Convention. The 2019 Judgments Convention can also accommodate all of these cases.[754] Thus, it is sensible that States should adopt the two Conventions as a whole package.

D. Derogation

The Convention has been described as a classical mixed convention[755] with a special focus on exclusive choice of court agreements. This implies that not only does it stipulate a direct jurisdictional ground for a court of origin, but it also prohibits it from exercising jurisdiction in particular circumstances. Article 6 provides that a non-chosen court shall suspend or dismiss proceedings to which an exclusive jurisdiction agreement applies. It has been mentioned earlier that for a jurisdiction agreement to come under this convention, it has to nominate the court(s) of a Contracting State. *Ab initio*, only the nominated court can exercise valid jurisdiction over the dispute, broadly speaking. Therefore, other Contracting States' courts must decline jurisdiction or suspend their proceedings. The Convention leaves no discretion in this regard and it does not matter that the non-chosen court is first seised. Article 6 discountenances *forum non conveniens* or *lis pendens* arguments.[756] This adds a great value to the Convention as it provides much more certainty for litigants. On this note, the Convention departs from the prevailing national law and judicial practice of many States, both common and civil law. The Article 6 solution also radically differed from the Brussels I regime until the

---

[753] Ahmed and Beaumont (n 741) 395; Trevor Hartley and Masato Dogauchi, Explanatory Report: HCCA (ch 5, fn 442) 61.

[754] See Article 5(1)(m) and Beaumont's Series Editor's Preface in Douglas et al (n 752).

[755] See Beaumont, 'Hague Choice of Court Agreements Convention 2005: Background, Negotiations, Analysis and Current Status' (ch 1, fn 50) 134.

[756] Hartley, *Choice-of-Court Agreements under the European and International Instruments: The Revised Brussels I Regulation, the Lugano Convention, and the Hague Convention* (n 654) 231–32.

latter was recast in Brussels Ia to work in harmony with the Convention: indeed Brussels Ia goes further, as the non-chosen court has to suspend its proceedings (no exceptions, unlike Article 6) as soon as the chosen court is seised of the case until the chosen court decides on its jurisdiction.

The flexibility comes in through the exceptions created under Article 6. These exceptions permit a non-chosen court of a Contracting State to assume jurisdiction only in five situations. These are:

a)   the agreement is null and void under the law of the State of the chosen court;
b)   a party lacked the capacity to conclude the agreement under the law of the State of the court seised;
c)   giving effect to the agreement would lead to a manifest injustice or would be manifestly contrary to the public policy of the State of the court seised;
d)   for exceptional reasons beyond the control of the parties, the agreement cannot reasonably be performed;
e)   the chosen court has decided not to hear the case.

The Explanatory Report highlights the relationship between these clauses and those of the New York Convention. It maintains that they largely serve the same purpose, but HCCA offers more clarity by stipulating the choice of applicable law for determining 'null and void' and 'incapacity'. What seems not to be right in the Report concerning Article 6(a) is that it suggests that a court seised but not chosen can exercise jurisdiction on the ground that a jurisdiction agreement is null and void, although it 'will not be applying its own law' to resolve the issue.[757] This interpretation poses a danger as parties can use it to indulge in unnecessary preliminary litigation over forum. If parties had chosen a court, that court ought to have exclusive jurisdiction to determine the validity of the agreement and, furthermore, it is the best court for interpreting its laws. There is no convincing reason why a chosen court should be avoided for a non-chosen court on the question of the validity of the choice of court agreement. Although Brand and Herrup suggest that Article 6 does not create jurisdiction in the court seised – which supports the position being canvassed –, their position seems to contradict that of the Hartley and Dogauchi Report as mentioned above.[758] However, Brand and Herrup later agreed that those exceptions under Article 6 'allow a court not chosen in an exclusive choice of court agreement to exercise jurisdiction'[759] and they did call these grounds 'alternative jurisdiction'.[760] These alternative jurisdictional grounds, especially Article 6(a)–(c), may undermine the effectiveness of the HCCA. Parties can frequently use them to bring frivolous suits in their preferred jurisdictions in breach of the jurisdiction agreement. Since judgments based on

---

[757] This assumption is confirmed in another work of one of the Rapporteurs, Professor Trevor Hartley where he discusses *renvoi* under the Choice of Court Agreement. See Hartley (n 654) 169. Brand and Herrup share a similar view. See Brand and Herrup (n 654) 81.
[758] Brand and Herrup (n 654) 88.
[759] Ibid, 89.
[760] Ibid.

Article 6 jurisdictional grounds are not enforceable under the Convention, their use is doubtful. A better arrangement would have been that a non-chosen court should only assume jurisdiction if the chosen court had decided that the agreement is invalid. Article 6(a) and (b) for instance would have been needless or, at best, merged with Article 6(e) to read that the chosen court had 'ruled that the agreement is null and void and decided not to hear the case'. This would, at least, save some cost at the litigation stage as parties could expect that any question relating to the nullity and incapacity should only be settled by the chosen court. These grounds are already available as refusal grounds under Article 9 and can take care of cases where the chosen court has improperly addressed the questions.

It is noted from the Explanatory Report that the exception under Article 6(a) in particular may be necessary for third party proceedings or joinder of parties who are bound by a jurisdiction agreement to a dispute before a non-chosen court. To cite the example given in the Report, A sues B, a car dealer in Canada for product liability. B applies to join C the manufacturer, in breach of a jurisdiction agreement between B and C in favour of England. Assuming England and Canada are Contracting States, the Canadian court is expected to decline jurisdiction under Article 6. B may allege that the agreement with C is null and void, which means the Canadian court must determine that question under Article 6(a). Be that as it may, the Canadian court could as well suspend proceedings to allow the English court to determine the question. Is it, then, justifiable to create alternative jurisdictional grounds because of third parties' proceedings? Can't the same result be achieved under Article 6(e)? Will it not lead to a waste of judicial resources that any litigant can simply ignore a jurisdiction agreement by proceeding straight to a non-chosen court to argue that the agreement is a nullity under the law of the chosen court?

The public policy and incapability of enforcement may be accepted as exceptional situations under which courts of Contracting States could assume jurisdiction contrary to the forum agreed by the parties. The exceptions ought to be limited to those rare circumstances. Otherwise, parallel proceedings in the chosen court and other non-chosen courts may become rampant since parties can easily allege nullity, incapacity and injustice. Such grounds should only be raised at enforcement proceedings to enhance the effectiveness of the Convention and prevent 'abusive litigation tactics'.[761]

The other shortcoming that is observed under Article 6 is that for the acceptable rare cases – eg public policy – the Convention fails to provide clear rules that would coordinate proceedings between the chosen court and the non-chosen court that is assuming jurisdiction on exceptional grounds. Assuming A, an English company, contracted with B, a Chinese company, and the parties nominated the English court as the venue for litigation. A filed a lawsuit in England as agreed and B also filed another suit in China on the ground of 'manifest injustice'. Both courts

---

[761] This approach is similar to the French judicial practice. See the Opinion of the Advocate General Wathelet in Case C-536/13 'Gazprom' OAO v Lietuvos Respublika, ECLI:EU:C:2014:2414.

may affirm jurisdiction under Articles 5 and 6 respectively. Sadly, the Convention provides no solution to this problem at the litigation stage. The problem may be carried over to the enforcement stage, especially if the second litigation was meant to pre-empt enforcement in China. This can create clashes and mistrust among Contracting States and invariably affects the expected mutual cooperation and understanding amongst them.

E. Enforcement

The Convention guarantees enforcement of judgments rendered by courts exclusively chosen by parties, save in the context of very limited permissible grounds for refusal. It explicitly prohibits any review of the merits of the foreign judgment, and the court addressed is bound by the findings of fact of the court of origin concerning its jurisdiction.[762] The permissible grounds for refusal of recognition are enumerated under Article 9(a)-(e). These are cases where the judgment was obtained from a proceeding which breached natural justice and due process, was obtained by fraud in connection with a matter of procedure, violates some fundamental policy of the court addressed, and where the judgment is inconsistent with a previous judgment rendered between the parties either by the court addressed or the courts of other Contracting States. Interestingly, nullity of the agreement (under the law of the chosen court) and incapacity of any party under the law of the court addressed are also grounds for refusal. It makes more sense that those issues be raised in either the chosen court or the court addressed at the enforcement stage, as earlier argued.

The likely problem that may arise from the application of Articles 8 and 9 (recognition and enforcement) is the seeming complexity of exclusion and inclusion of 'international cases'. On the one hand, Article 1(2) states that the Convention applies to international cases and a case is international unless the parties and the other relevant elements of the dispute are connected only to the home State. Put differently, the Convention does not apply to wholly domestic cases. For enforcement purposes, Article 1(3) says a case is international provided it is a judgment from another Contracting State. Thus, a wholly domestic case which is excluded under Article 1(2) becomes admissible under Article 1(3) at the enforcement stage. To illustrate this problem, the example offered by Professor Trevor Hartley will be used. A case is wholly connected to England, but the parties nominate the court of another Contracting State. By Article 1(2) this case is not covered by the Convention, and the English court can assume jurisdiction even if a parallel proceeding is going on in the chosen State. However, once a judgment is given by the chosen court, Article 1(3) says an enforcement proceeding can be brought in England and by Article 8, the English court is obliged to recognise the

---

[762] Article 8(2). However, this does not apply to a default judgment.

judgment as it is now an 'international case'. Although Professor Hartley submits that the imminent conflicting judgments may be settled by Article 9(f), which provides that a court may not recognise a foreign judgment that is inconsistent with a judgment already given in the requested State, what the distinguished author did not address is the situation where it was the foreign judgment that was rendered first.[763] Will an English court discontinue its proceedings once a foreign judgment has been rendered in a case that is wholly connected with England and especially when the English court was first seised? At the jurisdictional stage, can the English court issue an anti-suit injunction against the other Contracting State because the case is not covered by the Convention? What if the foreign judgment was obtained in breach of the anti-suit injunction? If the two judgments are before a third Contracting State and the English judgment was first in time, will that not qualify as a ground on which to refuse the judgment from the chosen court? Will this not jeopardise the 'partial' mutual trust established by the Convention?

F. Case Law

One of the factors that can guarantee the effectiveness of choice of court agreements is a uniform interpretation of the Convention. Uniform interpretation will enhance legal certainty and make the job of practitioners easier in rendering advice to their clients who need to make informed decisions concerning their international transactions. Article 23 requires courts, when interpreting the Convention, to have regard to 'its international character and to the need to promote uniformity in its application'. This can be a daunting task given the fact that there is no supranational court such as the CJEU that can give a definitive interpretation of the text and given also the tendency of 'home-ward' interpretations by national courts.

A possible solution is for national courts to give deference to the Explanatory Report as much as practicable. The Report ought to be the first point of call when courts are faced with the interpretation of the Convention. While interpretation may be influenced by domestic law and policy, national courts need to bear in mind that they are dealing with an international treaty, even though for most States, the treaty will have been domesticated by a specific statute. The Report gives the background to, and the consensual interpretation and understanding of every article of the Convention both at the drafting stages and at the Diplomatic Conference. It is desirable that an autonomous interpretation of concepts and expressions is pursued by considering the objectives of the Convention and its international character. Thus, the Explanatory Report, the *travaux préparatoires*, and other relevant guides that may be made available by the Hague Conference and the interpretations derivable from other relevant Hague conventions should

---

[763] Hartley, *Choice-of-Court Agreements under the European and International Instruments: The Revised Brussels I Regulation, the Lugano Convention, and the Hague Convention* (n 654) 100–102.

be strictly adhered to unless those sources do not directly address the issue under consideration.[764] In the case of the latter, comparative jurisprudence can be a very useful tool for national courts. It has already been demonstrated in Chapter three how it fosters a mutual understanding of the concept of reciprocity in some States. Today, China, Israel, and Germany have moved from strict reciprocity to 'assumed' reciprocity for judgments from non-treaty States.[765] Uniform results could be achieved, for situations not specifically covered by the Explanatory Report, by working out solutions which will work in harmony with judgments rendered in other Contracting States.

Singapore recorded the first decided case under the Convention with a ruling delivered on 19 June 2018 in *Ermgassen & Co Limited v Sixcap Financials Pte Limited*.[766] The Convention was domesticated by a Choice of Court Agreements Act[767] passed by the Singaporean parliament on 14 April 2016. In this case, sometime in July 2016, Sixcap Financials Pte Limited engaged the claimant for financial advice and other related professional services. The engagement letter states that 'Ermgassen & Co and the Client irrevocably submit to the exclusive jurisdiction of the English courts to settle any disputes in connection with any matter arising out of the Engagement Letter and/or these Terms of Engagement.' The claimant took out a writ against the defendant in England for unpaid invoices issued to the latter. A judgment for €1,013,536.48 including £38,635 costs was obtained. The claimant applied for the enforcement of the judgment sum and costs in Singapore where the defendant was registered.

The court enforced the judgment under the Choice of Court Agreements Act, being a judgment from one of the Contracting States. It determined that the UK is a Contracting State, the case was an 'international case' and none of the refusal grounds was applicable. In arriving at these conclusions, the court relied extensively on the Hartley and Dogauchi Explanatory Report.

Two interesting issues came up in this decision. One was the risk of divergent interpretation of undefined terms and the other was the relationship between the harmonised rules of the Convention and certain gaps that are left to be filled by national law. Article 13(1) of the Convention provides:

Article 13 – Documents to be produced

(1) The party seeking recognition or applying for enforcement shall produce:

a) a complete and certified copy of the judgment …
c) if the judgment was given by default, the original or a certified copy of a document establishing that the document which instituted the proceedings or an equivalent document was notified to the defaulting party

---

[764] Brand and Herrup (n 654) 27–32.
[765] See Chapter 3, section VI.C.
[766] *Ermgassen & Co Limited v Sixcap Financials Pte Limited* [2018] SGHCR 8.
[767] Cap 39A, Choice of Court Agreements Act 2017 Rev Ed.

Ermgassen did not attach a 'complete and certified copy of the judgment'. Rather, the relevant document it exhibited was an enrolled order by Senior Master Fontaine of the High Court of Justice of England & Wales ('the Summary Judgment Order'). Besides, it was observed that there was no specific document 'establishing that the document which instituted the proceedings, or an equivalent document was notified to the defaulting party' amongst the documents that the company supplied to the court.

In resolving these two issues, the Singapore High Court held that service could be presumed from the Senior Master's Order and thus the judgment was not given by default. The Court opined (at paragraph 22 of its judgment) that:

> the Plaintiff states in its supporting affidavit that although neither the Defendant nor its solicitors appeared at the hearing of the Summary Judgment Application, the Senior Master heard the Plaintiff's counsel on that application before granting it. I find that the Plaintiff's averment in this regard is supported on the face of the Summary Judgment Order where its preamble states, *inter alia*, 'AND UPON HEARING Counsel for the Claimant ...'

The Court went further to justify this conclusion, quoting the Hartley and Dogauchi Report thus:

> '... Article 13(1)(c) requires documentary evidence that the defendant was notified, but this applies only in the case of a default judgment. *In other cases, it is assumed that the defendant was notified unless he or she produces evidence to the contrary.* ... [emphasis added]'.

The Court dispensed with the failure to produce a complete and certified copy of the judgment as required by the Convention. While noting that the company could have done better, it was the considered view of the Court (at paragraph 24) that the omission was not fatal to the case because:

> The Hartley/Dogauchi Report (at [211]) clarifies that, notwithstanding Article 13(1) of the Hague Convention requiring the production of certain documents in an application for the recognition or enforcement of a foreign judgment, '[t]he law of the requested State determines the consequences of failure to produce the required documents'. This suggests that the failure to produce a required document is not envisaged to be invariably fatal in all cases.
>
> ... I further find this view to be consistent with the guidance provided in the Hartley/Dogauchi Report (at [211]) which highlights that '[e]xcessive formalism should ... be avoided: if the judgment-debtor was not prejudiced, the judgment-creditor should be allowed to rectify omissions'.

First, the approach of the Singaporean court gives an assurance that national courts are likely to be influenced by the Explanatory Report. It is hoped that other courts will follow suit. The decision also demonstrates that a court addressed may misconstrue terms and concepts that are defined neither by the Convention nor the Explanatory Report. In this instance, there is no clue from the Convention and the Report on what 'default judgment' means. A default judgment could be a judgment in default of appearance or in default of defence. In the case under review, it was a case of default of appearance and defence. The Singaporean court concluded that it was a judgment on the merits because the applicant's counsel 'was heard'. However, there is no evidence on record to show whether the hearing in the High Court of England & Wales was just one for moving the application simpliciter or whether the applicant argued the case on merits and led evidence in support. One can hazard a guess that it was the former. Does this make such judgment to be on the merits? The error committed here led the Court to misconstrue the Explanatory Report on Article 13(1)(c) which says, 'in other cases, it is assumed that the defendant was notified unless he or she produces evidence to the contrary'. Thus, because it was not a default judgment, service was presumed, and the applicant need not produce any document to show proper service. The error was, however, cured by reference to the overall objective of the Convention which advises against excessive formalism. The second point to be noted here is that the Explanatory Report states that national law determines the consequence of non-compliance with Article 13. The Court, in this instance, decided the consequence based on the overall objective of the Convention and not what effect such non-compliance would have under Singaporean law. Neither the Choice of Court Agreements Act nor Order 111 of the Singapore Rules of Court provides any penalty for non-compliance. Thus, it makes sense for the Court to have recourse to the Convention in filling this gap.

The Convention has also been engaged in passing in a few other cases. The CJEU was asked in *Hőszig Kft v Alstom Power Thermal Services*[768] to give a preliminary ruling on the issues of consent, an improper designation of a chosen court and the law that determines the substantial validity of jurisdiction agreements as contained in Article 25 of Brussels Ia. It is cheering to know that courts, especially a supranational court like the CJEU, are having recourse to the Hague Convention and its Explanatory Report as guidance or at least seeing the need to maintain an interpretative approach that aligns with the Hague framework. Advocate General Szpunar advised the CJEU as follows in his Opinion:

> The main reason why the wording cited above has been added to what is now art.25(1) of Regulation 1215/2012 is, in my view, to align that article to the text of art.5 of the Hague Convention on Choice of Court Agreements, which entered into force on 1 October 2015 … The Union is both a member of the Hague Conference on Private International Law and a contracting party to the Hague Convention on Choice of Court Agreements. Given that the area covered by the Convention falls within an area where the Union has, by virtue of Regulations 44/2001 and 1215/2012, exercised its competence, there is an interest in maximum alignment of the Convention and the system established by the Union in those regulations. More generally, by virtue of art.3(b) of the 2005 Hague Convention, a choice of courts agreement which designates the courts of one Contracting State or one or more specific courts of one Contracting State is to be

---

[768] Case C-222/15 *Hőszig Kft v Alstom Power Thermal Services*, ECLI:EU:C:2016:525.

deemed to be exclusive unless the parties have expressly provided otherwise. Moreover, as the Commission rightly points out, the explanatory report on the Convention specifically addresses the question of an agreement referring to courts of a State in general or to one or more specific courts in a State[769]

In *Gulf International Bank BSC v Aldwood*,[770] the reciprocal nature of the HCCA was affirmed *per obiter*. The High Court noted that the Convention has no role to play in deciding whether an English court should assume or decline jurisdiction based on an exclusive jurisdiction clause in favour of the Kingdom of Saudi Arabia, since the latter is not a party to the HCCA. In *Commerzbank Aktiengesellschaft v Liquimar Tankers Management Inc*,[771] the Court considered the nature and effect of asymmetric choice of court agreements and whether it ought to grant a stay of proceedings under Article 31(2) of Brussels Ia. In this case, Liquimar, in breach of an agreement to sue in England, commenced an action against the Bank in Greece. It asked the English High Court, which was the second seised, to stay the proceedings. It argued that asymmetric jurisdiction should not be treated as conferring exclusive jurisdiction on the English courts, and called in aid the provisions of the Hague Convention and the need for the court to interpret Article 31(2) of Brussels Ia in harmony with the former.

The English court noted that there is no EU jurisprudence on this point and thus carried out a comparative inquiry on the nature of asymmetric clauses under English law, civil law, and the Hague Convention. Mr Justice Cranston considered the views of the Explanatory Report on asymmetric jurisdiction clauses amongst other issues.[772] The Court, however, made some comments which flag up the likelihood that some courts may jettison the views expressed in the Explanatory Report. Cranston J's views on the relationship between the Brussels regime and the Hague Convention and possible construction of asymmetric clauses under the latter are as follows:

> [71] The Hague Convention, in my view, offers no assistance in the characterisation of asymmetric jurisdiction clauses under Article 31(2) of Brussels 1 Recast. There is no reference to the Hague Convention in Brussels 1 Recast, although the drafting of both occurred in tandem and Council Decision 2014/887/EU referred to ensuring coherence between the rules of the EU on the choice of court in civil and commercial matters and those of the Hague Convention.

> [72] While there is an overlap between the two instruments, however, there are important divergences …

> [73] Further, there is a definition of exclusive jurisdiction clauses in Article 3(a) of the Hague Convention, whereas there is no definition in Brussels 1 Recast. The reporters record that the Diplomatic Session adopting the Hague Convention accepted that the

---

[769] Paras 49–51 of AG Szpunar's Opinion, ECLI:EU:C:2016:224.
[770] *Gulf International Bank BSC v Aldwood* [2019] EWHC 1666 (QB).
[771] [2017] EWHC 161 (Comm). See also *Etihad Airways PJSC v Prof Dr Lucas Flother* [2020] EWCA Civ 1707; *Punjab National Bank (International) Ltd v Srinivasan & Others* [2019] EWHC 3495 (Ch).
[772] [2017] EWHC 161 (Comm) paras 37–39.

definition in Article 3(a) did not extend to asymmetric jurisdiction clauses, something the reporters themselves do not seem to have regarded as clear.

[74] *There are good arguments in my view that the words of the definition of exclusive jurisdiction clauses in Article 3(a) of the Hague Convention cover asymmetric jurisdiction clauses.* For present purposes, however, there is no need to reach a concluded view on the ambit of the definition. Even if it were to be read as excluding asymmetric jurisdiction clauses, however, that in my view is of no assistance as to the quite separate issue of their characterisation under Article 31(2) of Brussels 1 Recast (emphasis added).

Although Mr Justice Cranston did not reach any considered view on this point, his remarks do raise a concern that national courts might want to construe certain provisions of the Convention contrary to the views expressed at The Hague. This approach should be discouraged and is one of the ways *not* to deal with the Convention.

The Convention has also been engaged in Greece. Apostolos Anthimos reported a decision of the Piraeus Court of First Instance concerning the applicability or otherwise of the Convention on a choice of court agreement which read thus:[773]

The contract is governed by English law; the contracting parties accept the exclusive jurisdiction of English courts for the resolution of any dispute related to the present contract.[774]

It was reported that the Court confirmed that the subject matter falls within the scope of the Convention and the agreement was signed after the Convention came into force. However, after analysing the clause, the Court concluded that it was asymmetric and thus not enforceable under the Convention. While we agree with the Court that asymmetric clauses do not fall within the scope of the Convention, the above clause is not asymmetric. It is on this note that we agree with Anthimos's criticism of this decision.

G. The HCCA and the Judgments Convention: A Package Deal

The HCCA is designed to provide legal certainty and predictability for jurisdiction agreements. Like the New York Convention, cross-border litigants need a simple and efficient international framework that gives maximum effect to choice of court agreements. Ultimately, its success can only be guaranteed if it is widely adopted by States and national courts pay due regard to the international nature of the Convention in their interpretative function.

---

[773] Apostolos Anthimos, 'First contact of Greek courts with the 2005 Hague Choice of Court Convention': <https://conflictoflaws.net/2020/first-contact-of-greek-courts-with-the-2005-hague-choice-of-court-convention/> accessed on 12 November 2020.
[774] Translation is supplied by Apostolos Anthimos.

In line with the pragmatic model being proposed in this book, the negotiators have placed more emphasis on predictability by offering litigants clear rules that can assist them in making strategic decisions concerning their contracts. Other than Article 6 that imports some flexible rules that can potentially disturb the maximum enforcement of jurisdiction agreements, courts are also clear as to what is expected of them where parties settled for a particular jurisdiction for dispute settlement. By and large, the combination of the HCCA and the New York Convention is a good package for resolving international litigation arising from cross-border trade and commerce.

The HCCA leaves out non-exclusive jurisdiction agreements and asymmetric clauses, which are very popular in international finance contracts. Although Article 22 allows States to go beyond the frontiers of the Convention by making reciprocal declarations for the enforcement of these clauses, no State has done that to date. The other opportunity for this is the sister Judgments Convention. It makes more sense for States to join both Conventions so that the existing gaps (eg the excluded matters or other types of jurisdiction clauses) may be filled up. London is a hub for international commercial litigation and some EU States[775] (France, the Netherlands, Belgium, and Germany), Singapore[776] and China[777] have equally established international commercial courts. Litigants are worried whether their choice of the English courts (or other emerging courts in France, Germany, China and elsewhere) will be enforced. The most effective solution will be for States (UK, EU and others) to ratify or accede to both the HCCA and the Judgments Convention which have now harmonised the rules on exclusive and non-exclusive agreements (including asymmetric clauses).

V. Conclusion

Jurisdiction and foreign judgments are synonymous with a direct exercise of State power. This characteristic differentiates them from other aspects of private international law. Both concepts implicate not only legal policies but also socio-economic and political considerations. Any convention on these two subjects must navigate a web of legal, economic and political vagaries. The task is more daunting if a convention seeks to combine both subjects in a global project. The complexities

---

[775] See Georgia Antonopoulou and Xandra Kramer, 'The International Business Courts saga continued: NCC First Judgment – BIBC Proposal unplugged', available at: <https://conflictoflaws.net/2019/the-international-business-courts-saga-continued-ncc-first-judgment-bibc-proposal-unplugged/> (accessed 22 December 2020).

[776] Stephen Chong, 'Singapore International Commercial Court: A New Opening in a Forked Path' (Speech delivered by Justice Steven Chong at the British Maritime Law Association Lecture and Dinner in London, 15 October 2015): <https://www.supremecourt.gov.sg/Data/Editor/Documents/J%20Steven%20Chong%20Speeches/The%20SICC%20-%20A%20New%20Opening%20in%20a%20Forked%20Parth%20-%20London%20(21.10.15).pdf> (accessed 22 December 2020).

[777] <http://cicc.court.gov.cn/html/1/219/index.html> (accessed 22 December 2020).

arising from aggregating the divergent legal traditions and concepts, incongruent States' interests and values have worked against every attempt at negotiating a judgments convention for decades.

This chapter examines the historical background to international harmonisation of judgments laws, taking it as far back as 1873 when the first attempt was made by the *Institut* to discuss the harmonisation of divergent judgments recognition and enforcement laws and practices. The discussions of the *Institut*, followed by the brilliant works of the International Law Association, demonstrated that a global judgments convention is an onerous but surmountable task. No wonder the first convention negotiated by the Hague Conference on Private International Law failed and the subsequent attempts required painstaking negotiations that lasted for nearly three decades.

The history of the 2019 Judgments Convention, whose text will be considered in the next chapter, teaches exactly what pragmatism means in private international law and why it is a preferred approach that can deliver results in situations where harmonisation of knotty areas is desired. One lesson to be learned from this historical piece is the primacy and effectiveness of conventions as a tool of harmonisation, especially for areas touching on jurisdiction and judgments. Conventions require specific commitments from States both in the process of negotiation, ratification and implementation. The ILA Draft Convention, for instance, could not get the attention of States because the move did not come from them and neither were they part of the process. This can be contrasted with the diplomatic nature of the Hague Conference and the commitment of its Member States right from when the United States initiated the move for the global judgments convention in 1992.

The difference in the making of the 1971 Judgments Convention and the HCCA is also an illustration of how pragmatism works in practice. The bottom-up approach used in building the HCCA, and the flexibilities used to achieve consensus on seemingly irreconcilable issues are the magical tools that ensured that the HCCA was successfully midwifed. Otherwise, the draft could have become another miscarriage like the 1999 Draft Convention or at best, a stillbirth like the 1971 Judgments Convention. The mix-and-match approach also deserves to be mentioned. A practical application is Article 6, which provides harmonised grounds upon which a non-chosen court will not be obliged to decline jurisdiction in favour of a chosen court. The result gives an autonomous solution which arguably has more practical utility than those offered by common law and civil law traditions. The 1971 Judgments Convention and the attempts at a new convention between 1992 and 2001 were not entirely wasted efforts. They provide a pool of experiences from which future works in this area, including direct jurisdiction, could be handled.

Lastly, the HCCA is designed to be narrow to ensure effectiveness and the requisite legal certainty for jurisdiction agreements. The Convention is designed to complement the 2019 Judgments Convention. States should join both conventions in order to have a comprehensive framework for foreign judgments and to aid the global judgments liberalisation agenda.

7

2019 Hague Judgments Convention

I. Introduction

It was a blissful atmosphere in the Great Hall of Justice when the 2019 Hague Judgments Convention was adopted on 2 July 2019. This was not unexpected. It had taken 27 years of intensive formal and informal negotiations and brainstorming to deliver the Convention. It is of great significance to anyone who is familiar with the extensive literature on the Hague Judgments Project. Many have wondered whether the Convention would ever be delivered. While some writers were pessimistic, others offered different suggestions on how it could be achieved. A reflection on the past efforts will drive home this point. Professor Arthur T von Mehren, in a seminal article written in 2000, enthusiastically asked: 'Can the Hague Conference Project Succeed?'.[778] Linda Silberman wondered: 'Will the Proposed Hague Judgments Convention be Stalled?'.[779] Yoav Oestreicher painted a rather gloomy picture when he noted: 'We're on a Road to Nowhere'.[780] Amidst these rhetorical questions, other scholars offered different national perspectives on the failed 1999 Draft Convention. Paul Beaumont examined it from a United Kingdom perspective;[781] Masato Dogauchi gave a perspective from the perspective of Japan;[782] Linda Silberman gave a US perspective;[783] Louise Lussier gave a Canadian perspective,[784] and David Goddard[785] also considered it from the Pacific viewpoint. Indisputably, the Judgments Project remains one of the most intellectually engaging exercises ever carried out by the Hague Conference.[786]

---

[778] Von Mehren (ch 1, fn 56).

[779] Linda Silberman, 'Comparative Jurisdiction in the International Context: Will the Proposed Hague Judgements Convention Be Stalled?' (2002) 52 *DePaul Law Review* 319.

[780] Yoav Oestreicher, '"We're on a Road to Nowhere" – Reasons for the Continuing Failure to Regulate Recognition and Enforcement of Foreign Judgments' (2008) 42 *The International Lawyer* 59.

[781] Beaumont, 'A United Kingdom Perspective On the Proposed Hague Judgments Convention' (ch 2, fn 162).

[782] Masato Dogauchi, 'The Hague Draft Convention from the Perspective of Japan', *Seminar on the Draft Convention on Jurisdiction and Foreign Judgments in Civil and Commercial Matters Organised by Union International des Avocats* (20–21 April 2001, Edinburgh).

[783] Linda Silberman, 'Can the Hague Judgments Project Be Saved?: A Perspective from the United States' in John J Barceló and Kevin M Clermont (eds), *A Global Law of Jurisdiction and Judgments: Lessons from the Hague* (Kluwer Law 2002).

[784] Louise Lussier, 'A Canadian Perspective' (1998) 24 *Brooklyn Journal of International Law* 31.

[785] David Goddard, 'Rethinking the Hague Judgments Convention: A Pacific Perspective' (2001) 3 *Yearbook of Priv Int'l L* 27.

[786] The HCCH has listed on its website over 270 scholarly publications on the Hague Judgments Project since 1992.

The Convention promises a great deal of relief to international litigants and their counsel if it is widely ratified by States. One of the major challenges judgment creditors face is how to enforce judgments against absconding defendants who can easily move their assets across borders. With a global judgments convention which ensures that judgments are widely circulated, judgment creditors will not only have access to justice but will be getting 'access to practical justice'[787] because their judgments will be given effect to globally. Another objective of the Convention is the enhancement of the accessibility of judgment enforcement laws through the harmonisation of divergent national laws. Lawyers can offer legal advice to litigants by examining the harmonised rules, which have set out the requirements that will guarantee a global circulation of judgments. Closely related to this point is that the Convention provides legal certainty and predictability of the rules governing foreign courts' jurisdiction and the grounds for refusal of recognition. Legal certainty and predictability of rules will mitigate both litigation risk and enforcement risk. Litigants should now be able to make strategic decisions on where to sue, when to participate or avoid certain proceedings, the circumstances that can make judgments circulate and the limited grounds for attacking foreign judgments. The kind of bad decisions that judgment debtors made in *Beals v Saldanha*[788] and, recently, in *Midbrook Flowerbulbs Holland BV v Holland America Bulb Farms*[789] can be largely reduced. It is also hoped that with the limited global harmonisation, the Convention, together with the HCCA, will boost global trade and investment, since litigation and enforcement risks have been greatly reduced.[790]

The Convention addresses only recognition and enforcement of foreign judgments. It sets out what qualifies as a substantial connection between a foreign court and an underlying dispute. The framework is built on the idea of qualified mutual trust among the Contracting States. By this scheme, a judgment rendered by the court of a Contracting State is enforceable in other Contracting States without any need for reviewing the merits of the judgment. The major task for the court addressed is to examine the judgment to ascertain that it meets the jurisdictional requirements of the Convention and that none of the grounds for non-recognition applies. The court addressed is then obliged to enforce the judgment accordingly.

This aim of this chapter is to critically analyse the 2019 Judgments Convention. It examines the pragmatism in the negotiation of the Convention, the extent to which it addresses the challenges facing cross-border litigants and the likelihood of its acceptance by most States. The analysis mainly focuses on the key aspects of the Convention: scope, jurisdictional connections and refusal grounds. The analysis is restricted to these areas for two main reasons: one, these are the main subjects

---

[787] David Goddard (ch 1, fn 27) 476.
[788] *Beals v Saldanha* [2003] 3 SCR 416.
[789] *Midbrook Flowerbulbs Holland BV v Holland America Bulb Farms* 874 F.3d 604 (9th Cir. 2017). In this case, a debtor abandoned proceedings after the trial court denied his motion on jurisdiction. Unfortunately, the court addressed ruled that the judgment was enforceable.
[790] David Goddard (ch 1. fn 27) 476.

that affect the practical needs of litigants; two, the other issues – which are largely procedural matters and the relationship between the Convention and other instruments – cannot be accommodated for want of space.

The analyses of the relevant Articles are carried out from a comparative perspective using relevant cases and statutes from leading jurisdictions such as the UK, the US, the EU, amongst others. The Garcimartín and Saumier Revised Explanatory Report[791] (the Report) is also relied upon in this assessment even though it was written based on the 2018 draft.

II. Pragmatism in the Negotiation of the Convention

A. General Approach

In Chapters three, four and five of this book, the concept of pragmatism in private international law, particularly in judgments recognition and enforcement, has been laid out. At the risk of being repetitive, a global judgments enforcement scheme should identify clear connections between a State of origin and an underlying dispute and appropriate procedural standards that foreign judgments must meet. These two issues are the gravamen of most of the objections raised in enforcement proceedings. If judgments must circulate freely, States must focus on these two practical problems by proposing certain minimum standards of procedural justice and acceptable jurisdictional links. In such a scheme, all that is required for a court addressed is to verify that the judgment meets those global standards.

The next question is how to deliver the desired framework on a multilateral platform whose membership comprises States from diverse legal, cultural, economic and political backgrounds. This reality was not lost on the Hague Conference. Indeed, the practicalities were noted right from the onset. In preparing the Proposed Draft Text, these realities informed the general approach of the Working Group and the Special Commission. The Permanent Bureau mentions that:

> The Working Group proceeded on the basis that the future Convention should contain *an efficient system* for the recognition and enforcement of foreign judgments in civil and commercial matters, *one that will provide for circulation of judgments in circumstances that the Working Group considered uncontroversial* (emphasis added).[792]

---

[791] For the final report, see Francisco Garcimartín and Geneviève Saumier, Explanatory Report on the Convention of 2 July 2019 on the Recognition and Enforcement of Foreign Judgments in Civil or Commercial Matters (HCCH 2019 Judgments Convention) (HCCH, 2020). Electronic copy is available at https://assets.hcch.net/docs/a1b0b0fc-95b1-4544-935b-b842534a120f.pdf (Accessed 12 June 2021).

[792] HCCH, 'Explanatory Note Providing Background on the Proposed Draft Text and Identifying Outstanding Issues: Preliminary Document No 2 of April 2016 for the Attention of the Special Commission of June 2016 on the Recognition and Enforcement of Foreign Judgments' (2016).

David Goddard puts the above statement in context. He recalls that the general approach adopted by the Special Commission at the drafting stage was to ask the participants: 'is it reasonable for this judgment to be recognised and enforced?',[793] thus, focusing on the reasonability of jurisdictional connections and objections to enforcement. The drafters narrowed down the discussions to scenarios that would reasonably align with the divergent laws and policies of Hague Conference Member States when drafting the Convention.

B. Minimum Harmonisation

Judgments recognition and enforcement regimes are of different standards across the globe. In the Anglo-American jurisdictions, the courts are liberal and often enforce foreign judgments. While many Commonwealth States apply a simple registration system to foreign judgments on a reciprocal basis, there is a window for common law action on judgments from non-reciprocating States. Theoretically, all foreign judgments are enforceable one way or the other under the Anglo-American systems. The major drawbacks under Anglo-American systems are the restrictive concept of international jurisdiction and the review of the merits of foreign judgments through certain defences. On the other side of the spectrum are some civil law countries, which enforce foreign judgments only from those countries that they have treaty relations with. While some other civil law jurisdictions enforce foreign judgments based on reciprocity, a few others are willing to do so on more liberal terms.[794]

The beauty of the 2019 Judgments Convention is that it strikes a balance between the supposedly liberal regimes and those that are less receptive to foreign judgments. It sets up a minimum harmonisation of the divergent rules and standards that apply in various jurisdictions. With this approach, a qualified mutual trust, which should enable judgments to circulate globally, is created. Also, it upgrades and brings up to date the judgment enforcement rules of many States whose extant laws are considered too restrictive. For the liberal States and others with sophisticated judgments schemes, the Convention only sets a 'floor' and not a 'ceiling'.[795] It allows for the continuous development of their laws because judgments that cannot circulate under the Convention may still be enforceable under national laws.

The minimum harmonisation approach has also helped to gauge the degree of harmonisation necessary for an efficient global framework. This enabled the drafters and negotiators to avoid delicate areas where it would be practically impossible to get consensus. Therefore, the overall framework of the Convention is that it

---

[793] David Goddard (ch 1, fn 27) 480.
[794] Arthur T von Mehren and Donald T Trautman (ch 1, fn 78).
[795] David Goddard (ch 1, fn 27) 474.

sets acceptable minimum jurisdictional and procedural standards for foreign judgments with the possibility of enforcement under the Convention,[796] national laws[797] or other bilateral and multilateral treaties.[798]

C. Mix-and-Match Approach

The text of the Convention is different, in varying degrees, from those of national laws, bilateral and regional treaties. This is expected because a global convention needs to aggregate the non-congruent interests of Contracting States to command a global acceptance and the text must also be as succinct as possible in order to achieve uniform interpretation. Generally, the text does not follow any particular legal order, whether common or civil law. Rather, it contains a mixture of ideas from both systems and, in some cases; specific concepts were borrowed from some national laws. For example, the jurisdictional connection for contract disputes adopts some terminologies that are peculiar to some legal systems. Article 5(1)(g) provides that:

> A judgment is eligible for recognition and enforcement if one of the following requirements is met –
>
> ...
>
> (g) the judgment ruled on a contractual obligation and it was given by a court of the State in which performance of that obligation took place, or should have taken place, in accordance with
>
> (i)   the agreement of the parties, or
>
> (ii) the law applicable to the contract, in the absence of an agreed place of performance,
>
> unless the activities of the defendant in relation to the transaction clearly did not constitute a purposeful and substantial connection to that State;

The proviso 'purposeful and substantial connection' is a combination of 'purposeful availment' as developed by the US Supreme Court,[799] and 'real and substantial' connection of the Canadian Supreme Court.[800] That phrase was not found previously in any bilateral or multilateral treaty. It is neither used in common law nor civil law courts. However, the proviso is necessary to meet the due process requirement of the United States Constitution. Otherwise, the US, which is a major

---

[796] Art 4.

[797] Art 15.

[798] Art 23.

[799] See *Asahi Metal Industry Co v Superior Court*, 480 US 102, 106 (1987).

[800] *Beals v Saldanha* (n 788). See also Ronald A Brand and Cristina M Mariottini, 'Note on the concept of "Purposeful and Substantial Connection" in Article 5(1)(g) and 5(1)(n)(ii) of the February 2017 draft Convention' Preliminary Doc No 6 of September 2017 for the attention of the Third Meeting of the Special Commission on the Recognition and Enforcement of Foreign Judgments (13–17 November 2017).

destination for foreign judgments, would have been shut out since the draft would potentially violate its Constitution. The US delegates could also have blocked any consensus on the final Convention without this proviso, as learnt from the HCCA experience.[801]

It is also observed that the meaning of 'place of performance' in subparagraph 5(1)(g) is different from the Brussels regime, common law and civil law as well. There is also the case of enforcement of *transactions judiciaires* (judicial settlements) which is a concept that is well known to civil law systems. Other examples can be seen from the way the jurisdictional grounds are worded, with provisos or explanations which seek to address some problems being experienced in extant judgments recognition laws either at the national or regional level.[802]

D. Consensus and Flexibilities

Consensus is more desirable in a broader judgments convention because it covers a wide range of subjects from contract to tort, trust, property and others. It ensures that only the subject matters that are less controversial fall within the scope of the Convention and that the text largely aligns with the fundamental legal order of most States. Were it not for the consensual approach, some Member States, eg the EU States, may use a bloc vote to push certain items which do not command the support of other key States. For instance, in the 2016 and 2017 drafts, the Working Group and Special Commission were optimistic that intellectual property would be approved at the Diplomatic Conference. It is well known that some developed countries, where many of these IP rights, especially patents, are registered, favoured the inclusion of IP judgments in a global convention.[803] However, the major objection came from the US whose IP stakeholders persuaded the US government and others, such as Australia and Canada, to oppose the inclusion of IP.[804] The EU later proposed an amendment which would restrict the scope to copyright and related matters. This move failed at the Diplomatic Conference, as consensus could not be achieved on any aspect of IP judgments.[805] Some might argue that consensus has led to the exclusion of some important subject matters. While this is true, such exclusions were dictated by the reality of finalising a convention that would be acceptable to most States since the Convention is meant to be global and not just transatlantic. Moreover, as previously mentioned, the Convention does not stop States from enforcing judgments arising from excluded matters under their

---

[801] Beaumont (ch 1, fn 50) 150–54.

[802] See for instance, Art 5(1)(l); Art 5(1)(m); Art 5(2).

[803] Lundstedt (ch1, fn 60) 934.

[804] 'EU/US Disagreements Highlighted as USPTO Rejects Inclusion of Intellectual Property in Hague Convention' (*World Trademark Review*): <https://www.worldtrademarkreview.com/government-policy/euus-disagreements-highlighted-uspto-rejects-inclusion-intellectual-property> accessed 8 November 2019.

[805] Lundstedt (ch 1, fn 60).

national laws. They are only not *required* to enforce those judgments under the Convention. It is a clever way of removing the hurdles and dumping them at the doorstep of States to deal with in the manner they deem fit under their respective national laws.

In addition to a consensual approach, the Convention adopts the same kind of flexibilities as the HCCA. It permits States to make declarations not to enforce foreign judgments concerning wholly domestic cases.[806] Article 18 permits States that have a 'strong interest' in not applying the Convention to specific matters to do so by declaration. Article 19 permits a State to declare that it will not apply the Convention to a dispute in which the State or its agencies are a party. As explained in Chapter six, the purpose of these declarations is to incentivise as many States as possible to join the Convention. Thus, it is sensible to relax the obligations created by the Convention, especially, in sensitive areas that may prevent States from ratifying or acceding to the Convention.

III. Scope and Exclusions

Unlike the narrow theme of the HCCA, the Judgments Convention applies to all judgments rendered in civil and commercial cases save those matters that are expressly excluded by Article 2(1).[807] 'Civil and Commercial matters' is a regular phrase in the Hague conventions and other bilateral and regional judgments treaties. For a multilateral judgments convention, what do 'civil' and 'commercial' mean bearing in mind that their meaning may differ under national laws?[808] The draft Explanatory Report notes that the concept must be given an autonomous meaning by reference to the objectives of the Convention and its international character.[809] This approach is consistent with the views expressed in the Hartley and Dogauchi Report concerning the HCCA[810] and also by other legal commentators such as Burkhard Hess and Cristian Oro Martinez.[811] The Explanatory Report goes on to emphasise that they are used to broadly distinguish between private and public law and as such:

> it is necessary to identify the legal relationship between the parties to the dispute and to examine the legal basis of the action brought before the court of origin to establish whether the judgment relates to civil or commercial matters.[812]

---

[806] Art 17, Judgments Convention.

[807] And arguably, those that may be excluded by declarations under Art 19.

[808] For discussions on the various approaches under Hague instruments and EU law, see Burkhard Hess and Cristian Oro Martinez, 'Civil and Commercial Matters' in Jürgen Basedow and others (eds), *Encyclopedia of Private International Law* (Edward Elgar Publishing 2017) 346.

[809] Garcimartín and Saumier (n 791) para 8.

[810] Trevor Hartley and Masato Dogauchi (ch 5, fn 442) para 49.

[811] Hess and Martinez (n 808) 347.

[812] Ibid. This broader interpretation has been favoured by the Special Commission in their assessment of the operations of other Hague Conventions. See Permanent Bureau of the Hague Conference

This distinction reflects the meaning of the concept of 'civil and commercial' in the CJEU jurisprudence. It can be argued that the Report basically adopts the position of the CJEU. In *Pula Parking d.o.o. v Sven Klaus Tederahn*,[813] the CJEU notes that:

> In accordance with the Court's settled case-law, in order to ensure, as far as possible, that the rights and obligations which derive from that regulation for the Member States and the persons to whom it applies are equal and uniform, the concept of 'civil and commercial matters' should not be interpreted as a mere reference to the internal law of one or other of the States concerned. That concept must be regarded as an autonomous concept to be interpreted by reference, first, to the objectives and scheme of that regulation and, second, to the general principles which stem from the corpus of the national legal systems ... In order to determine whether a matter falls within the scope of Regulation No 1215/2012, it is necessary to identify the legal relationship between the parties to the dispute and to examine the basis and the detailed rules governing the bringing of the action.[814]

It is imperative to stress this distinction because 'civil law' is broadly known in the common law jurisdictions to include any dispute that is not criminal in nature.[815] This broad understanding may include some public law matters such as constitutional, administrative and tax law matters. However, these issues are understood to be public law matters and not civil (ie private) in major European legal systems, as noted in one of the Permanent Bureau's preliminary documents on the 2016 draft of the Convention.[816] Therefore, the appropriate classification under common law that aligns with the objectives of the Convention is the private and public law classification. Considering the objectives of the Convention, the views expressed in the Explanatory Report, and those of the European and English courts, the autonomous meaning to be derived for civil and commercial matters is that they broadly cover private law disputes that do not involve the exercise of State powers or enforcement of public laws. This is further buttressed by the exclusion of public laws general from the scope of the Convention.

While the 'civil and commercial matters' concept may not pose any difficulty in most cases, the same cannot be said for some hybrid or borderline cases where the line between a public and private claim is blurred. This will likely arise in cases of private enforcement of public laws. For such hybrid cases, the only clue from the Report is that courts should consider the 'legal relationship between the

---

on Private International and Law, *Practical Handbook on the Operation of the Hague Convention of 15 November 1965 on the Service Abroad of Judicial and Extrajudicial Documents in Civil or Commercial Matters* (Wilson & Lafleur 2006), cited by Hess and Martinez (n 808) 350. The approach is recommended for the Judgments Convention since it has enumerated certain excluded matters.

[813] Case C-551/15 *Pula Parking d.o.o. v Sven Klaus Tederahn*, ECLI:EU:C:2017:193.

[814] Ibid, paras 33 and 34.

[815] Gary Slapper and David Kelly, *The English Legal System* (14th edn, Routledge 2017) 8.

[816] HCCH, 'Note on Article 1(1) of the 2016 Preliminary Draft Convention and the term "Civil or Commercial Matters"', *Preliminary Document No 4 of December 2016 for the Attention of the Special Commission of February 2017 on the Recognition and Enforcement of Foreign Judgments* (HCCH 2016) <https://assets.hcch.net/docs/9be83162-a32b-457c-8232-16748c841789.pdf> accessed 29 May 2020.

parties' and the 'legal basis for the action'. *Pula Parking d.o.o. v Sven Klaus Tederah* illustrates the ambiguity that may arise from these kinds of actions. In this case, Pula Parking d.o.o., a company owned by the town of Pula (Croatia), administers, supervises, cleans and maintains public parking spaces. It also collects parking fees and tickets from those who park without paying the parking fees. Mr Tederahn, a German resident, was ticketed for parking without a ticket. He was required to pay the ticket within eight days, after which interest would accrue. The CJEU was asked to deliver a ruling whether the judgment obtained by the parking company related to a civil matter and thus came within the scope of Regulation (EU) No 1215/2012. Applying the reasoning quoted above, the Court ruled that the case fell within the 'civil or commercial' concept. It noted that the unpaid parking debt was contractual in nature (the legal basis of the claim); the purpose of the recovery action was to safeguard private interests; the fine was a consideration for service rendered; and Pula Parking was not exercising any public powers (private law relationship). While the CJEU decision is sound, it is not out of place to think that courts elsewhere may not characterise the ticketing service by Pula as contractual in nature. Be that as it may, the objective of the Convention is to enforce private rights as against public laws.

The last paragraph takes us to the first set of excluded matters. Enforcement of foreign public laws – revenue law, criminal law and other administrative/public law – are usually prohibited by national laws except where there is a special treaty to that effect.[817] They remain excluded under the Convention. According to the Explanatory Report, the exclusion covers cases where one of the parties, usually a State, is exercising public powers to punish a person for conduct proscribed by criminal law or to enforce public revenue laws. A good example is *Re State of Norway's Application*,[818] where the substance of the proceedings was to recover inheritance taxes from the estate of a deceased Norwegian citizen. Although the House of Lords ruled that the action was civil, not criminal, such a judgment is outside the scope of the 2019 Convention because it amounts to an enforcement of public revenue law. The relevant factors which take a foreign judgment out of the scope of the Convention are that the foreign law or penalty is enforced by a State or its agents, and the benefit (judgment sum) accrues to that State. An Ontario court demonstrated this point in *AAA Entertainment v Cinemavault Releasing International*.[819] In this case, Cinemavault opposed the penalty imposed by an Amsterdam court for failure to comply with the judgment. The court addressed held that a judicially imposed penalty did not violate Ontario public policy because it was not penal in nature. The court reasoned that the action was commercial, the penalty did not create any obligation to the foreign State but was

---

[817] Lawrence Collins, 'Professor Lowenfeld and the Enforcement of Foreign Public Law' (2009) 42 *International Law and Politics* 125, 150.
[818] *Re State of Norway's Application* [1990] 1 AC 723.
[819] *AAA Entertainment v Cinemavault Releasing International*, 2017 ONSC 100.

meant to encourage compliance with the court order and the penalty was in favour of the judgment creditor. This case fits what the Report describes as a monetary penalty being a conditional obligation to encourage compliance.[820] In *Chase Manhattan Bank, NA v Hoffman*,[821] a US court also ruled that a Belgian judgment, which awarded a civil remedy even though the substantive proceeding was criminal in nature, was enforceable. The court noted that 'the judgment was remedial: it afforded a private remedy rather than punished an offense against the public justice of Belgium. Moreover, the benefit of the judgment accrued in its particulars to the private party plaintiff, not the state'.[822] The US Court of Appeal gave a similar decision in *Hyundai Securities Co Ltd v Ik Chi Lee*.[823] These decisions align with what obtains in other common and civil law jurisdictions.[824]

Antitrust judgments are excluded largely because they often involve the enforcement of public laws by regulatory agencies. The Diplomatic Session was able to secure a historic compromise that brought private antitrust actions – follow-on cases – relating to cartels within the scope of the Convention. The Explanatory Report suggests that the Convention should apply where a government agency acts on behalf of private parties like investors or customers without exercising 'extraordinary powers or privileges'. It is unclear what the authors meant by 'extraordinary powers', but it can be assumed that this is nothing more than the usual governmental or regulatory powers. Professor Beaumont opined that a strict construction of 'governmental powers' would mean that antitrust actions by government agencies on behalf of private parties constitute an exercise of public powers and as such do not fall under 'civil and commercial'.[825] Professor Hess and Martinez hold a similar position.[826] While this view is unassailable, it is suggested that where a regulatory agency acts on behalf of private parties and the private parties are exclusively the beneficiaries of the reliefs (eg monetary) in those actions, such a case should fall under 'civil and commercial' matters. A close example is *United States Securities and Exchange Commission v Manterfield*,[827] where SEC sued on behalf of the victims of a fraudulent scheme and intended to obtain orders which would require that the proceeds be returned to the investors.

Considering this qualification, the scholarly views mentioned above and the principles that have been established under *Pula Parking d.o.o.* and *Hyundai Securities Co*, it is opined that the Convention will apply to antitrust follow-on cases relating to cartels. Such cases are becoming increasingly popular in

---

[820] Garcimartín and Saumier (n 791) para 83–84.
[821] *Chase Manhattan Bank, NA v Hoffman* 665 F.Supp. 73 (D.Mass.1987).
[822] Ibid, 76.
[823] *Hyundai Securities Co Ltd v Ik Chi Lee*, 232 Cal. App. 4th 1379 (Cal. Ct. App. 2015).
[824] Collins, 'Professor Lowenfeld and the Enforcement of Foreign Public Law' (n 817).
[825] Paul R Beaumont, 'Judgments Convention: Application to Governments' (2020) 67 *Netherlands International Law Review* 121, 126.
[826] Hess and Martinez (n 808) 357.
[827] *United States Securities and Exchange Commission v Manterfield* [2009] EWCA Civ 27.

several European States.[828] For instance, in 2015 the United Kingdom enacted the Consumer Rights Act to expand the jurisdiction of its Competition Appeal Tribunal to hear 'standalone' claims which did not arise from infringement decisions.[829] Thus, the judgments from such standalone claims and follow-on cases arising from prior infringement decisions are enforceable under the Convention because they are brought by private litigants inter se, and they are remedial in nature, benefitting private litigants and not public authorities.

Some items are excluded from the scope of the Convention because there are Hague Conventions or other specialised multilateral conventions that have already addressed the matters. These subject matters are family law and succession; insolvency and analogous matters; carriage of passengers and goods; transboundary marine pollution and marine pollution in areas beyond national jurisdiction; liability for nuclear damage; the validity of entries in public registers; arbitration and related proceedings; and some antitrust (competition) matters – notably abuse of a dominant position.[830] Arbitration and antitrust matters are perhaps the most important heads here because they are a key aspect of international commercial disputes. Arbitration is excluded because there is a comprehensive international framework for the enforcement of arbitral awards, ie the New York Convention. The Convention is one of the most successful international treaties, with the Maldives becoming the 161st Contracting State on 17 September 2019.[831]

The third category of exclusions involves those matters where the fundamental differences in the laws of Contracting States make it impossible to achieve any consensus. This affects defamation, privacy and intellectual property (IP) judgments. Defamation and privacy are constitutional issues in many States and the level of protection differs considerably. For instance, because the US Constitution guarantees free speech, judgments from States whose protection of free speech is not up to the standard guaranteed by the US law will be contrary to US public policy and, thus, unenforceable.[832] For IP judgments, the United States, Australia and Canada did not support inclusion in the Convention because of serious objections from their stakeholders.

A matter is not excluded simply because a State is a party to a dispute. If the substance of the dispute falls within the scope of the Convention, then the

---

[828] Pier Luigi Parcu, Giorgio Monti and Marco Botta (eds), *Private Enforcement of EU Competition Law: The Impact of the Damages Directive* (Edward Elgar Publishing 2018); Thomas Thiede, 'Fine to Follow-on? Private Anti-Trust Actions in European Law' (2017) 5 *China-EU Law Journal* 233, 236.

[829] Slaughter and May, 'Private Enforcement of Competition Law in the UK' (2017): <https://www.slaughterandmay.com/media/2534704/private-enforcement-of-competition-law-in-the-uk.pdf> accessed 10 August 2019.

[830] Art 1, Judgments Convention.

[831] See <http://www.newyorkconvention.org/countries> accessed 28 January 2020.

[832] See John F Coyle, 'The SPEECH Act and the Enforcement of Foreign Libel Judgments in the United States' (2017) 18 *Yearbook of Private International Law* 245 (discussing *Trout Point Lodge, Ltd v Handshoe*, 729 F.3d 481 (5th Cir. 2013) and other cases where foreign libel judgments were denied recognition).

Convention applies. The Convention must be read together with the doctrine of sovereign immunity under national and international law. Broadly put, States can only be impleaded where the underlying dispute involves a commercial activity,[833] and they are thereby exercising the power of a private citizen.[834] In *Servaas Inc v Republic of Iraq*,[835] the US Court of Appeal held that in an enforcement action, what the court considers is the underlying conduct that gave rise to the foreign judgment. It went further to cite *International Housing Ltd v Rafidain Bank Iraq*,[836] where Iraq's contract for the purchase of goods, services and technology was held to be a civil and commercial matter. In March 2019, a Luxembourgish court declined to enforce a $6 billion US judgment awarded against Iran over its role in the 9/11 terrorist attack. Iran successfully pleaded that there is no terrorism exception to sovereign immunity under international law.[837] Therefore, the US court had no international jurisdiction, since the underlying dispute was not a commercial activity. In *NML Capital Ltd v Argentina*,[838] non-payment of bonds was held to be a commercial transaction and because the contract contained a jurisdiction agreement, the State of Argentina had submitted by contract and thereby waived its jurisdictional immunity. This case must be distinguished from unilateral sovereign debt restructuring cases which are a non-civil and commercial matter that is expressly excluded from the scope of the Convention for clarity and to reassure concerned States such as Argentina. These are non-civil and commercial because a State uses its sovereign powers to impose a 'haircut' on lenders, by paying them a lesser amount or nothing.[839]

Apart from jurisdictional immunity, States may avail themselves of the immunity against execution. A foreign court might have properly exercised jurisdiction and yet the judgment may not be enforceable against the foreign sovereign. In *AIC Limited v Federal Government of Nigeria*,[840] the English High Court held that enforcement proceedings do not fall within the 'commercial transaction' exception and States are entitled to raise immunity against an enforcement proceeding. This represents the position under the Administration of Justice Act 1920 and

---

[833] Some States, notably Argentina, insisted that sovereign debt restructuring – which is a clear exercise of public power – be specifically excluded from the scope of the Convention. See Art 2(1)(q).

[834] See also the United Nations Convention on Jurisdictional Immunities of States and Their Property, New York, 2 December 2004. Signatories: 28; Parties: 22; not yet in force.

[835] *Servaas Inc v Republic of Iraq*, 653 Fed. Appx. 22 (2d Cir. 2011).

[836] *International Housing Ltd v Rafidain Bank Iraq* 893 F.2d 8, 11–12 (2d Cir. 1989).

[837] The judgment is available at <https://justice.public.lu/dam-assets/fr/actualites/2019/Jgt20190327-exequatur-anonyme.pdf>. It was analysed by Professor Hess in B Hess, 'Not a Simple Footnote: 9/11 Litigation in the Civil Courts of Luxembourg' (2019) 5 *Praxis des Internationalen Privat- und Verfahrensrechts*.

[838] *NML Capital Ltd v Argentina* [2011] UKSC 31. This principle also applies where the State has agreed to resolve the underlying dispute by arbitration. See *Tsavliris Salvage (International) Ltd v The Grain Board of Iraq* [2008] EWHC 612 (Comm).

[839] For some CJEU cases on sovereign debt restructuring, see Sebastian Grund and Mikael Stenstrom, 'A Sovereign Debt Restructuring Framework for the Euro Area' (2019) 42 *Fordham International Law Journal* 795, 829–34.

[840] *AIC Limited v Federal Government of Nigeria* [2003] EWHC 1357 (QB).

the Foreign Judgments (Reciprocal Enforcement) Act 1933. It contrasts with the US approach where the underlying transaction that led to the judgment is what a court addressed considers, and not the enforcement action. Recently, the English position has aligned with that of the US. The UK Supreme Court reversed *AIC Limited* in *NML Capital Limited v Republic of Argentina*,[841] holding that the State Immunity Act 1978 altered the 1920 and 1933 Acts by incorporating the restrictive approach to sovereign immunity. With the enactment of the State Immunity Act 1978, there is no immunity to an enforcement proceeding if the underlying contract relates to a commercial activity. This same approach was adopted by the Canadian Supreme Court in *Kuwait Airways Corp v Iraq*.[842]

IV. International Jurisdiction

International jurisdiction is the bedrock of judgments recognition and enforcement frameworks and often determines their effectiveness or otherwise. Regulating jurisdiction of courts at the international level has always been an onerous task because jurisdiction itself is considered as an exercise of sovereignty. A State's exercise of jurisdiction may be driven by legal and extra-legal norms. To that extent, it is extremely difficult to regulate how foreign courts should exercise direct jurisdiction. Whether the assumption of jurisdiction is acceptable or not is also the prerogative of the court addressed. The 9/11 litigation in the US is a good example. In 2016, the US Congress enacted the Justice Against Sponsors of Terrorism Act (JASTA) to enable 9/11 victims to pursue claims against Saudi Arabia, Iran and other States that covertly or overtly supported the terrorists. While no State can dictate how US courts should exercise jurisdiction, due to the principle of independence and non-interference, a receiving State is equally at liberty to determine whether that jurisdictional basis is acceptable or not. When the judgments came before the Luxembourgish court for enforcement, the latter did not accept that the US court had rightly assumed jurisdiction. It is therefore desirable for legal certainty and predictability that States should agree on acceptable connections between foreign courts and disputes/parties. This is the objective of Articles 5 and 6 of the Convention.

From extant recognition practices, there are at least three approaches to determining the propriety of foreign courts' jurisdiction. This is a semblance of what Professor Arthur von Mehren described as a unilateral and bilateral theory of the source of jurisdictional requirements.[843] In some States, such as Anglo-American jurisdictions, the law of the receiving State is the source of the jurisdictional

---

[841] [2011] UKSC 31.
[842] *Kuwait Airways Corp v Iraq* [2010] 2 SCR 571.
[843] Arthur T von Mehren, 'Recognition and Enforcement of Foreign Judgments – General Theory and the Role of Jurisdictional Requirements', *Recueil Des Cours* (Martinus Nijhoff Publishers 2002) 56–57; Cuniberti (n 20) 298.

requirement for foreign judgments. In other words, a foreign judgment is only entitled to recognition if it meets the jurisdictional connections deemed appropriate by the receiving State. It is not enough that the court addressed would have exercised jurisdiction under the same circumstance. A second category is States like Germany where a foreign judgment can be recognised based on jurisdictional reciprocity. In these States, the foreign court's jurisdiction is valid where a similar jurisdictional ground exists in the forum. The third category represents States like Canada where jurisdictional grounds are determined, not by a strict adherence to the law of the State of origin or receiving State but largely by the reasonableness and the degree of connection between the court and the dispute.

At the Working Group, these three approaches were considered. For instance, Professor Ronald Brand argued for a simple non-discriminative jurisdictional reciprocity rule. Hence, rather than having a long list of specific jurisdictional grounds, a judgment should circulate if the foreign court's jurisdictional basis is available under the law of the receiving State. He maintained that an enumerated list may become outdated as time passes by.[844] It is opined that the Working Group rightly rejected this approach as it will greatly diminish harmonisation, legal certainty and predictability which are the principal objectives of the Convention. The Convention does not follow any of the national approaches, strictly speaking. Rather, what it does is to set out a list of acceptable connections that guarantees the circulation of judgments in Contracting States. Of course, to some extent, the Convention also considers the fears of Professor Brand and that has been taken care of by giving States the liberty to enforce judgments that meet jurisdictional requirements approved by national law in so far as the enforcement will not violate the obligation imposed under Article 6 of the Convention. The jurisdictional requirements under Articles 5 and 6 will be examined hereunder.

A. Habitual Residence (Natural and Juristic Persons)

Article 5(1) reads:

> A judgment is eligible for recognition and enforcement if one of the following requirements is met –
>
> (a) the person against whom recognition or enforcement is sought was habitually resident in the State of origin at the time that person became a party to the proceedings in the court of origin;
>
> (b) the natural person against whom recognition or enforcement is sought had their principal place of business in the State of origin at the time that person became a party to the proceedings in the court of origin and the claim on which the judgment is based arose out of the activities of that business;

---

[844] Ronald A Brand, 'The Circulation of Judgments Under the Draft Hague Judgments Convention' (2019) *Working Paper No. 2019-02.*

The first jurisdictional requirement listed by the Convention is habitual residence. A judgment debtor's habitual residence is a general jurisdiction ground and the courts of that State can entertain any claim against the defendant irrespective of where the cause of action arose. The concept of habitual residence is widely used in Hague conventions, regional treaties and national laws.[845] It is rooted in the civil law tradition as illustrated by the maxim: *actor sequitur forum rei*. Habitual residence also conforms with the doctrines of territoriality as the legal foundation of jurisdiction. Likewise, it is always just and convenient for the defendant to be answerable to claims sought against him in his country of abode.

The Convention defines 'habitual residence' for non-natural persons in the same way as 'residence' is defined in the HCCA.[846] The editors of Dicey & Morris note that it has been a deliberate policy of the Hague Conference not to define 'habitual residence' for natural persons so that it is not mechanically applied, which may eventually lead to unjust results.[847] This explanation seems plausible considering the controversies surrounding its application in family law conventions where it has been mostly engaged. Perhaps the same justification may be offered for the new approach adopted by this Convention: offering a definition for corporate entities but not for natural persons.

Habitual residence of natural persons has been well addressed in family law disputes, notably abduction and custody cases. According to various rulings that have been issued by the CJEU, habitual residence is the place where a party has established his stable centre of interests, and in determining the stable centre of interests, the court is expected to consider the aims and objectives of the particular legislation concerned.[848] This understanding can be applied to civil and commercial matters. Habitual residence, as against mere residence, suggests that a defendant must be resident in fact, *and for settled purposes* in the State of origin at the time when an action was instituted against him. Put differently, the judgment debtor should maintain some family or social relationship in that jurisdiction or regularly stay there even though he may be absent for some time. The CJEU's guidance aligns with the views expressed in the draft Explanatory Report that it 'is a general rule based on the idea of the "natural" or "home state" forum'[849] and that 'it … expresses a close connection between a person and his or her socio-economic environment'.[850]

---

[845] Pippa Rogerson, 'Habitual Residence: The New Domicile?' (2000) 49 *International & Comparative Law Quarterly* 86, 86–87.

[846] Article 3(2) of the Convention approves four connections for the habitual residence of corporations. They are: the statutory seat, the State under whose law it was formed, the place of central administration, and where it has its principal place of business.

[847] Lord Collins of Mapesbury and others, *Dicey, Morris and Collins on the Conflict of Laws* (n 72) para 6-123.

[848] Several of such cases are analysed in *Marinos v Marinos* [2007] EWHC 2047 (Fam).

[849] Garcimartín and Saumier (n 791) para 147.

[850] Ibid, para 150.

These views suggest that habitual residence will be decided based on some fact-specific inquiries. Where the habitual residence of a natural person judgment debtor is in issue, a court addressed needs to examine all relevant facts to determine whether the State of origin can be described as the debtor's home. This is where the problem lies. The experience from sister conventions dictates that habitual residence for individuals needs some clarification. Although we are not dealing with children or immigrants seeking benefits, the habitual residence of judgment debtors can also be problematic in some cases. The reason is obvious. In the Anglo-American jurisdictions for instance, habitual residence may be interpreted to mean something akin to domicile, or ordinary residence, or something in between, since they are all based on the connection of the defendant with a given territory.[851] Any connection more than mere presence may suffice, since the objective of Article 5(1)(a) is to establish general jurisdiction. In essence, a natural person who has many residences can be sued in any of his residences and such a person should not escape civil jurisdiction simply because a claimant cannot determine which of the residences is strong enough to be habitual. The ultimate decision of the degree of habitation that amounts to habitual residence, in the absence of an autonomous definition offered by the Convention, will depend on the assessment of the court addressed. A finding of fact on habitual residence by the State of origin may not bind a court addressed. Thus, a limited review may be expected if the fact is contested by the judgment debtor. Habitual residence for corporate defendants has already been defined by Article 3(2) to include the place of incorporation, central administration or principal place of business.

A few cases can be used to illustrate what may or may not qualify as 'habitual residence' for the purpose of the Judgments Convention. In the Scottish case of *Zigal v Buchanan*,[852] the judgment debtor resided in an apartment in Hong Kong while executing some business there. Residence was rightly established in that case because what is required under common law is ordinary residence or presence. For this Convention, it may be argued that he was habitually resident in Hong Kong at the relevant time, considering the length of his stay and his business activities in the State. In *Suzhou Haishun Investment Management Co Ltd v Zhao & Others*,[853] an Australian court found that a judgment debtor was resident in China based on the Chinese 'hukou system' which mandates all Chinese persons to maintain a registered address in China. It is doubtful whether such residence will

---

[851] In *R v Barnet London Borough Council* [1982] UKHL 14, both the Court of Appeal and House of Lords used ordinary residence to explain habitual residence, invariably suggesting that there is no difference between the two concepts. *Kapur v Kapur* [1984] FLR 920 holds that habitual residence means ordinary residence. In *Re Bates (Minor)* [1989] 2 WLUK 293, Waite J, following *Kapur*, categorically states that 'there is no real distinction between ordinary residence and habitual residence'.

[852] *Zigal v Buchanan* [2019] CSIH 16. More details are reported in the first instance decision at [2018] CSOH 94.

[853] *Suzhou Haishun Investment Management Co Ltd v Zhao & Others* [2019] VSC 110.

qualify as habitual residence under the Convention, especially, if the defendant can establish that he is not in fact living in China. In this case, it was alleged that the debtor had left China before the commencement of the action with no intention to return. 'Habitual residence' cannot be found based on nationality or citizenship simpliciter.[854] Otherwise, in extreme cases, it might be erroneously stretched to cover a defendant who has assets within the jurisdiction even though he does not live there.

B. Natural Persons' Principal Place of Business

Article 5(1)(b) vests jurisdiction in a State where natural persons have their principal place of business. This head of jurisdiction is targeted at natural persons who are in business. Since these businesses often have no separate legal personality, the proprietors or partners are usually sued as the alter ego.[855] This appears to be the first judgment enforcement framework that provides a distinct head of jurisdiction for non-corporate defendants. It is only presumed in other instruments from what is usually referred to as 'doing business' jurisdiction. The specific provision provides more clarity and certainty in this regard.

Article 5(1)(b) does not qualify that judgment should relate to disputes arising from the activities of the defendant's business *in the State of origin*. The paragraph, therefore, vests a limited general jurisdiction in the court of the State where the principal place of the business is located. For enforcement purposes, that State has a real and substantial connection with all business activities carried out in that State. For instance, Mr A is habitually resident in France but operates a thriving retail business in Luxembourg. He retains the services of an accounting firm in Germany. Mr A is indebted to Mr B in Luxembourg for some personal items he bought in Luxembourg, and also has some unpaid invoices issued by the accounting firm in Germany. From this scenario, both Mr B and the firm can sue Mr A in France (Article 5(1)(a)) and the judgment will circulate under the Convention. The firm can also proceed against Mr A in Luxembourg under Article 5(1)(b) because that is the principal place of the business. The judgment issued in those proceedings will also circulate under the Convention. Concerning personal items bought in Luxembourg, that will not fall under the scope of Article 5(1)(b) because it has nothing to do with the business.

---

[854] The Australian courts are particularly well known to have applied citizenship as a ground for international jurisdiction. See *Liu v Ma & Another* [2017] VSC 810; *Independent Trustee Services Ltd v Morris* [2010] NSWSC 1218.

[855] See for instance, *Blohn v Desser* [1962] 2 QB 116 where a judgment was obtained against a partnership in Australia. However, the enforcement action failed in England partly because the defendant was not named in the foreign proceedings and as such the judgment could not be enforced against her personally even though she was a sleeping partner in the firm.

C. Claimant/Counterclaimant

Article 5(1) continues:

> (c)   the person against whom recognition or enforcement is sought is the person that brought the claim, other than a counterclaim, on which the judgment is based
>
> ...
>
> (l)   the judgment ruled on a counterclaim –
>
> > (i)   to the extent that it was in favour of the counterclaimant, provided that the counterclaim arose out of the same transaction or occurrence as the claim; or
> >
> > (ii)   to the extent that it was against the counterclaimant, unless the law of the State of origin required the counterclaim to be filed in order to avoid preclusion;

This ground is very straight forward and is found in almost all national laws and other bilateral and regional judgment enforcement treaties. Where a claimant (not as a counterclaimant) files an action in court, by his conduct he has clothed the court with jurisdiction even if none existed in the first place. It is a simple case of *volenti non fit injuria*. He cannot turn around to dispute the jurisdiction of the court if things do not go well for him. Thus, a foreign court chosen by a claimant has sufficient connection with the dispute submitted to it by the claimant. This will mostly apply where a claimant's case is dismissed, and the defendant wishes to rely on the dismissal either in a subsequent case filed by the claimant, where cost/damages was awarded against the claimant or in other cases where the earlier judgment will be relevant for the defendant's case. For instance, Mr A, who is resident in China, enters into a contract with B Ltd, a company registered in the United Kingdom, for the delivery of some goods to B Ltd in England. The contract was executed in England, to be delivered in England and payment was also to be made in England. There was a dispute concerning the quality of the items delivered and whether B Ltd was entitled to full payment. B Ltd sued in China. The Chinese court held that B Ltd was not liable for any outstanding amount. Not being satisfied with the judgment, B Ltd took out a summons in England against Mr A for the recovery of the outstanding payment. If the United Kingdom and China are parties to the Convention, the Chinese judgment will be entitled to recognition in the English proceedings. B Ltd cannot argue that China has no connection with the dispute because, by Article 5(1)(c), a judgment given by a court chosen by a claimant will freely circulate under the Convention.

The other aspect of this ground concerns judgments arising from counterclaims. In most national civil procedure laws, a counterclaim is a self-standing suit and it survives even if the main suit has been struck out. A counterclaimant who was the defendant in the main suit is deemed to have chosen the court concerning the claims he puts forward in the counterclaim. This gives the trial court a substantial connection. For instance, in *GFH Capital Ltd v Haigh*,[856] the English

---

[856] *GFH Capital Ltd v Haigh* [2020] EWHC 1269 (Comm).

High Court enforced a DIFC judgment (through summary judgment procedure) because Haigh had defended the claim before the Dubai court and advanced a positive counterclaim. His attempt to challenge the jurisdiction of the DIFC failed.

The conditions for the application of subparagraph (l)(i) is that if the judgment favours the counterclaimant, a connection is only established where the issues raised arose out of the same transaction as the main suit. What this means is that the debtor would not be deemed to have submitted to jurisdiction with regards to any new issue raised in the counterclaim, which was not connected to the main claim or the underlying transaction. The phrase 'transaction or occurrence' suggests that the main claim and counterclaim need not necessarily be contractual. What matters is whether they are sufficiently related that justice and expediency require that they should be tried together. Thus, the main claim and the counterclaim will be deemed to be connected if they have a common origin, ie they are both based on the same facts, irrespective of whether one is tort and the other is contract, for instance. This is the approach of the CJEU in *Petronas Lubricants Italy SpA v Livio Guida*[857] and the Commonwealth courts will treat it the same way.[858]

On the other hand, if the counterclaimant lost, then we need to inquire whether he was mandated by the law of the State of origin to present the counterclaim. Where that is the case, then the judgment will not circulate under the Convention because he did not voluntarily present the counterclaim. However, where he was not mandated to present a counterclaim, but he did and lost, then he is no better than a claimant under Article 5(1)(c). The provisions of the Convention regarding counterclaims are more restrictive compared to those of national laws and regional treaties, which make no distinction between cases where the judgment favours the counterclaimant or otherwise. This is an appreciable improvement and offers more clarity than extant instruments.

D. 'Branch Jurisdiction'

Article 5(1)(d) reads

> (d)   the defendant maintained a branch, agency, or other establishment without separate legal personality in the State of origin at the time that person became a party to the proceedings in the court of origin, and the claim on which the judgment is based arose out of the activities of that branch, agency, or establishment;

This head of jurisdiction concerns a defendant who does business in foreign jurisdictions through branches, agents or other establishments. It often applies to corporate defendants but because the subparagraph gives no such limitation, it

---

[857] Case C-1/17 *Petronas Lubricants Italy SpA v Livio Guida*, ECLI:EU:C:2018:478.
[858] *Stoke v Taylor* (1880) 5 QBD 569; *Lion Creek Properties, Ltd, LLP v Sorobey*, 2014 ABQB 405 (CanLII); *Skaggs Companies Inc v Mega Technical Holdings Ltd*, 2000 ABQB 480 (CanLII).

can also apply to individuals, partnerships and other unincorporated associations. The ground is similar in substance to Article 7(5) of Brussels Ia and Article 5(1) of the CML.

Before examining 'branch jurisdiction', it is imperative to point out one significant proviso in this draft which differentiates it from others that are mentioned above. The Convention requires that a defendant, be it individual or corporate, should be carrying on or doing business 'without separate legal personality in the State of origin'. This limitation excludes subsidiaries and other local representatives of foreign defendants that are established under the laws of the State of origin. The Explanatory Report does not give any hint concerning this limitation. This would have aided a better understanding of the subparagraph, since such limitation is hardly known outside the Brussels Ia framework.[859] It can be argued that the limitation seeks to address the controversies surrounding jurisdiction over foreign corporations, the legitimate use of corporate personality and the enforcement of judgments obtained against subsidiaries on assets of foreign principals. These issues have been considered in *Adams v Cape Industries*[860] and *Yaiguaje v Chevron Corporation*.[861] In *Adams*, the English court considered the propriety of the assertion of jurisdiction over Cape Industries Plc by a US court based on the activities of its US subsidiaries. In *Chevron*, an Ontario Court of Appeal had to decide whether it was appropriate to enforce an Ecuadorian judgment obtained against Chevron Corporation over Chevron Canada assets. Both cases failed on the strength of the doctrine of corporate legal personality. The Convention aligns with the position of the English and Canadian courts and this provides more clarity on this issue. Thus, where a defendant does business in a State of origin through another company formed under the law of the State of origin, a judgment issued against the defendant for transactions conducted by its subsidiary in the State of origin will not circulate under the Convention against the defendant, because Article 5(1)(d) requires that the parent company should have transacted directly or through an unincorporated entity.

Having said that, what does it mean for a judgment debtor to maintain a 'branch', an 'agency' or 'other establishment' in a State of origin? Does it mean that the judgment debtor must open and maintain a branch office in its name? Can the judgment debtor act through another unincorporated entity like a firm? Can the judgment debtor act through an individual who may or may not have an office? These questions are necessary because of the differences between the text of the Convention and other instruments. For instance, the CML version provides that 'the judgment debtor, being a defendant in the court of the state of origin, had an

---

[859] While this limitation is not expressly stated in Art 7(5) of Brussels Ia (and its predecessors), it has been incorporated through the CJEU case law. See Case C-212/97 *Centros Ltd v Erhvervs-og Selskabsstyrelsen*, ECLI:EU:C:1999:126; Case C-154/11 *Mahamdia v People's Democratic Republic of Algeria*, ECLI:EU:C:2012:491.
[860] [1990] Ch 433 (ch 1, fn 28) 518 (CA).
[861] *Yaiguaje v Chevron Corporation*, 2018 ONCA 472.

office or place of business …'. The English courts have interpreted 'had an office' and 'place of business' to mean that a defendant should be carrying on business in a foreign country at a definite location or through 'a resident agent with power to contract'.[862] In *Littauer Glove Corp v FW Millington*,[863] it was held that an English company was not carrying on business and, therefore did not have a branch in the US simply because its employee transacted business on its behalf in the US in a hotel room. Salter J noted that the employee was merely a commercial traveller on a tour. Similarly, in *Vogel v R and A Kohnstamm Ltd*,[864] it was held that the defendant company was not carrying on business in Israel even though it sold leather skins to the claimant through one Mr Kornbluth who had an office in Tel Aviv. The court refused the enforcement of the Israeli judgment granted against the defendant because it did not have an office in Israel and all correspondence was exchanged through the defendant's office in England. Thus, the foreign agent was only an intermediary between customers and the defendant.

The English cases are very much similar to the position of the CJEU. In *Ahmed Mahamdia v People's Democratic Republic of Algeria*,[865] the CJEU held that:

> First, the concept of 'branch', 'agency' or 'other establishment' implies a centre of operations which has the appearance of permanency, such as the extension of a parent body. It must have a management and be materially equipped to negotiate business with third parties, so that they do not have to deal directly with the parent body.[866]

The first part of the excerpt agrees with *Littauer* and *Vogel*. It can be summarised that the 'branch', 'agency' or 'establishment' must be a fixed place of business for the principal/parent company to be regarded as doing business in the State of origin. The second part, which speaks about having a management and being sufficiently equipped to transact business on behalf of the parent company also supports the English cases. Thus, the parent company may simply open a branch in its name in the State of origin (ie an extension of the parent company) or act through a separate firm or other non-juristic establishments that can bind it in contract. A good example is the case of *Saccharin Corp Ltd v Chemische Fabrik von Heyden Aktiengesellschaft*[867] where one Mr EW Blasius was appointed as a sole agent for the defendant German corporation. He maintained an office in England and transacted business on behalf of the defendant there.

This analysis will not be complete without examining how this head of jurisdiction impacts US law. American jurisdiction law has been going through a refining process to respond to the criticisms from both within and outside the US. While the details of the rules cannot be presented here, it suffices to say that this head of

---

[862] *Adams* [1990] Ch. 433, 476.
[863] *Littauer Glove Corp v FW Millington* (1928) 44 TLR 746.
[864] *Vogel v R and A Kohnstamm Ltd* [1973] QB 133.
[865] C-154/11 (n 859) para 48.
[866] Ibid.
[867] *Saccharin Corp Ltd v Chemische Fabrik von Heyden Aktiengesellschaft* [1911] 2 KB 516.

jurisdiction is in line with the US concept of specific personal jurisdiction. The US Supreme Court has emphasised that specific personal jurisdiction cannot be exercised over a foreign defendant unless there is sufficient connection between the forum and the defendant. Thus, where a defendant maintains a branch or agency as explained above in a particular State, that will be a sufficient connection between the State and the defendant. The existence of such a branch will satisfy the due process and minimum contact requirements to give rise to specific personal jurisdiction for the transactions carried out through the branch.[868] For instance, in *McIntyre Machinery, Ltd v Nicastro*,[869] the US Supreme Court clarified that a New Jersey court could not exercise specific jurisdiction over McIntyre because the company did not sell its machines to buyers in the state, did not have any office or property there, and the distributor was an independent company not under the control of McIntyre.

E. Consent/Submission

Article 5(1) continues:

(e) the defendant expressly consented to the jurisdiction of the court of origin in the course of the proceedings in which the judgment was given;

(f) the defendant argued on the merits before the court of origin without contesting jurisdiction within the timeframe provided in the law of the State of origin, unless it is evident that an objection to jurisdiction or to the exercise of jurisdiction would not have succeeded under that law;

A State of origin has a substantial connection to a dispute if the judgment debtor consented to the jurisdiction of its court. A defendant may consent to the jurisdiction of the court of the State of origin in several ways. This can be by filing a claim/counterclaim, unconditionally appearing to a summons, submission by contract (exclusive and non-exclusive jurisdiction agreement) or arguing the merits of the case. Article 5(1)(e) deals with the consent expressly given 'in the course of the proceedings'. The comments of the International Bar Association (IBA) on the 2016 draft of the Convention shed some light on why the Special Commission opted for express consent and only such consent that was given 'in the course of the proceedings'.[870] In line with the objective of setting bright-line rules which can

---

[868] *International Shoe Co v Washington*, 326 US 310 (1945).

[869] *McIntyre Machinery, Ltd v Nicastro* 564 US 873 (2011). A caveat is necessary on *Mcintyre*. The case also noted that a foreign corporation may be subjected to specific jurisdiction even without having a branch or agent. The court opined that such defendants could do so by sending their goods rather than agents. This is where the 'stream of commerce' and 'purposeful availment' analysis comes in. This aspect of the decision is more relevant to Art 5(1)(g) of the Convention.

[870] International Bar Association, 'Report of the International Bar Association (IBA) on the 2016 Preliminary Draft Convention', *Information Document No 8 of February 2017 for the attention of the Special Commission of February 2017 on the Recognition and Enforcement of Foreign Judgments* (HCCH 2017) <https://assets.hcch.net/docs/03311845-08cd-4048-953b-285914e44e25.pdf> accessed 30 May 2020.

guide litigants in making informed decisions on where to sue and when to defend proceedings and not, it was thought to be desirable to let defendants be aware that they are making a voluntary decision to submit to the jurisdiction of the foreign court. Thus, they should not be tricked into consenting to be sued in a jurisdiction by would-be plaintiffs.

The draft Explanatory Report mentions that this type of consent may not be known in all procedural systems.[871] This is true, at least, for most common law jurisdictions. A defendant either enters a conditional or unconditional appearance to a summons. The nature of the memorandum of appearance determines whether he submits voluntarily or otherwise. There is no known procedure for a defendant, orally or in writing, to give express consent to jurisdiction. However, such a procedure may exist elsewhere. Be that as it may, a judgment will circulate under this head of jurisdiction if the defendant, orally or in writing, either by himself or through his counsel, consents to the jurisdiction of the court.

The next question is how is consent determined? The draft Explanatory Report states that the court addressed is not examining whether the foreign court had properly exercised direct jurisdiction according to the foreign court's law. It does not state whether such assessment should be determined by the law of the receiving State. The preferable approach is that consent should be determined autonomously. Express consent should be determined by examining the relevant facts or conduct of the defendant, whether acting alone or through counsel, to ascertain whether it could be reasonable to say that he accepts that the case against him should be tried by that court. Thus, a defendant who files a memorandum of appearance should be deemed to have expressly consented to the jurisdiction of the court, since that consent can be inferred from the pleadings. Situations where the defendant defends himself in court and makes that intention known in open court should not pose any problem.

The contentious part has always been subparagraph (f), which deals with submission or implied consent or 'tacit prorogation', as variously described by Professor Geneviève Saumier.[872] Here, submission is implied from the conduct of the defendant: arguing to the merits of the case. The ambiguities have been noted in Chapter five above while discussing the concept of submission under the CML. A typical problem concerning submission arose in *CE Design Ltd v HealthCraft Products Inc.*[873] In this case, the judgment debtor abandoned proceedings in Canada after it lost the motion challenging the jurisdiction of the court. It opposed the enforcement of the judgment in the United States for want of jurisdiction. An Appellate Court of Illinois ruled that *res judicata* applied and the judgment debtor would not be able to re-litigate the matter. The issue is compounded where

---

[871] Garcimartín and Saumier (n 791) para 171.
[872] Geneviève Saumier, 'Submission as a Jurisdictional Basis and the HCCH 2019 Judgments Convention' (2020) 67 *Netherlands International Law Review* 49, 50–51.
[873] *CE Design Ltd v HealthCraft Products Inc*, 79 N.E.3d 325 (Ill. App. Ct. 2017).

a defendant (who is not represented) exchanges letters with the court protesting jurisdiction and explaining his side of the case in a layman's way.[874]

Professor Geneviève Saumier notes the divergence in the assessment of conduct that amounts to submission under national laws, and how the procedural law of the foreign court might be relevant even though the assessment is guided at the enforcement stage by the law of the State addressed.[875] The IBA report also indicates the complexities that lie in striking a balance between debtors who genuinely contest the jurisdiction of foreign courts and those who, without any strong arguable case, might nevertheless raise objections to be able to raise it as a ground at the enforcement stage.[876] The Convention's approach is to go for a narrow concept of submission. By the standard set by subparagraph (f), submission exists only where the defendant argues on the merits of the case without raising any objection within the timeframe permitted by the law of the State of origin. Submission will also occur if the defendant appears and does not raise *forum non conveniens* if that has a chance of succeeding. Anything short of a prompt motion challenging jurisdiction will be regarded as submission. However, where the defendant did not bother to object simply because such objections are not allowed by the law of the State of origin or are routinely dismissed by its courts, submission will not be implied. Thus, *CE Design Ltd v HealthCraft Products Inc* should be decided differently if it was decided under the rules of indirect jurisdiction provided for by the Convention.

As rightly noted by Professor Geneviève Saumier, judgment debtors must be wary that what does not amount to submission under the Convention may nevertheless be valid under national laws. Their chances may well depend on whether Contracting States will stick to the standards set by the Convention (which may likely be the case) or have recourse to a possibly broader concept of submission under national laws.

F. Contractual Obligations

Article 5(1) continues:

(g)   the judgment ruled on a contractual obligation and it was given by a court of the State in which performance of that obligation took place, or should have taken place, in accordance with –

(i)   the agreement of the parties, or

(ii)   the law applicable to the contract, in the absence of an agreed place of performance,

unless the activities of the defendant in relation to the transaction clearly did not constitute a purposeful and substantial connection to that State;

---

[874] *Von Wyl v Engeler* [1998] 3 NZLR 416; *De Santis v Russo* [2001] QCA 457.
[875] Saumier (n 872) 52–55.
[876] International Bar Association (n 870) 25–26.

This head of jurisdiction is very important because it will likely be one of the most often engaged connections. In line with modern trends, the State of origin has a substantial connection if it is the State where the performance of the obligation in question took place or was meant to take place. A cursory look at the provision reveals that it is unique and slightly different from those of national laws and regional treaties. It blends part of the Brussels Ia solution with an adaptation of the US concept of 'purposeful availment'. Like other special jurisdictional grounds, a contract ground was only recently introduced in the CML. A contract ground does not exist in the extant Commonwealth judgments schemes. This mix-and-match approach of Article 5(1)(g) gives a unique solution. However, as the subsequent analysis reveals, the solution might not be better than turning the Brussels Ia contract jurisdiction rule into an indirect rule, but that was not an option because it was not acceptable to the US for due process reasons. Thus, some of the already identified challenges may persist.[877]

The first task is to determine what obligation does Article 5(1)(g) refer to. The Convention mentions 'that obligation' as against Brussels's 'the obligation in question'. A purposive interpretation of the Convention should mean that 'that obligation' refers to 'the obligation in question', ie the obligation that the court of origin ruled upon in its judgment.[878] The Convention thus adopts a similar approach to the direct rule of jurisdiction in Article 7(1)(a) of Brussels Ia, as derived from the Brussels Convention, but adapts it to be an indirect rule to be applied at the recognition and enforcement stage. The objective of this approach is to ensure that the court giving the contractual ruling had a significant connection with the contractual dispute by being the place of performance of the aspect of the contract that the court ruled upon. The controversies that come up when courts are applying Article 7(1)(a) of Brussels Ia as a direct jurisdiction rule – eg identifying the principal obligation in complex contracts which involve several obligations and then giving jurisdiction over all the contractual issues in dispute to the courts of the place of performance of that obligation, or splitting the jurisdiction in cases with different places of performance when there are equal obligations like *Leathertex v Bodetex* – are not addressed in the 2019 Convention.[879] What will be of interest to a court addressed in the approach adopted under this Convention is whether the obligation upon which the foreign judgment ruled was, or ought

---

[877] See Beaumont, Danov, Trimmings and Yuksel, *Cross-Border Litigation in Europe* (ch 1, fn 40) 499–584.

[878] The foundation for this solution was laid by the CJEU's decision in Case 14/76 *A De Bloos, SPRL v Société en commandite par actions Bouyer*, ECLI:EU:C:1976:134 Before then, there used to be some controversy as to whether the relevant obligation is the obligation in question or the characteristic obligation. See Claude Witz, 'The Place of Performance of the Obligation to Pay the Price: Art. 57 CISG' (2005) 25 *Journal of Law and Commerce* 325, 326–28. Professor Jonathan Hill has, however, criticised this solution because it may lead to the allocation of jurisdiction to a court that has the weakest or no connection to the dispute. See Jonathan Hill, 'Jurisdiction in Matters Relating to a Contract under the Brussels Convention' (1995) 44 *The International and Comparative Law Quarterly* 591, 600–601.

[879] Case C-420/97 *Leathertex Divisione Sintetici SpA v Bodetex BVBA*, ECLI:EU:C:1999:483.

to have been, performed in the State of origin and nothing more. This is simple, straightforward and more pragmatic for an international convention where no supranational court exists to moderate its application. In rare cases, this seemingly straightforward solution – the obligation on which the judgment ruled – may not be as straightforward as it appears. The guidance from *Barry v Bradshaw*[880] is that the 'obligation in question' in the context of Article 7(1)(a) of Brussels Ia will be determined by the pleadings or claims of the plaintiff. This is the common law approach, as the pleadings of the plaintiff determine the jurisdiction of the court. Under the Judgments Convention, the court in the State addressed will have to determine what was the place of performance of the obligation that the court in the State of origin gave its judgment on. It might do this based on the specific obligation in question as it had been pleaded by the claimant in the court addressed; it might, look at the judgment and – on seeing that the court established a principal obligation in question and ruled on all the obligations in dispute because it was the court of the place of performance of the principal obligation – agree with that court's assessment; or it might determine that if it were deciding the case based on the indirect ground of jurisdiction in the Convention, that ground would be established because the place of performance of the obligation ruled on the judgment (or, if more than one obligation is ruled on, the principal obligation ruled on in the judgment) is in the State of origin.

Concerns were raised over the 'obligation in question' approach by some members of the EU during the revision of the Brussels Convention. Notably, they expressed concern at the splitting of jurisdiction and the fact that where the obligation in question is one for the payment of money, it may confer jurisdiction over a court with a minor factual connection.[881] For the Hague Convention, this may not be a serious problem because the Convention does not seek to regulate direct jurisdiction and certainly has no interest in dealing with conflicts of jurisdiction. The often-cited criticism against the 'obligation in question' approach is when jurisdiction is exercised based on payments. In many cases, payments will often be due at the seller's location. This may correspond to the place of the characteristic obligation, for instance where a seller is to deliver goods at his premises. This means that the rule will likely work well in the majority of cases. Parties can opt out of this scheme through their contracts by simply specifying their preferred place of payment, bearing in mind the consequence that follows, or as Beaumont advises, to go for a choice of court agreement.[882] Consumer and employment contracts have already been excluded from this head of jurisdiction.

The next task is to examine the concept of 'the place of performance'. Unlike the CML which gives no clue on the determination of the place of performance,

---

[880] *Barry v Bradshaw* [2000] ILPr 706.
[881] Paul Reid Beaumont, 'The Brussels Convention Becomes a Regulation: Implications for Legal Basis, External Competence and Contract Jurisdiction' in James Fawcett (ed), *Reform and Development of Private International Law: Essays in Honour of Sir Peter North* (OUP 2002) 18.
[882] Ibid, 21.

the Convention partially follows the approach of Brussels Ia by giving prominence to party autonomy. In this approach, the first source of determination of
the place of performance is where the parties have chosen under the contract.[883]
While 'unless otherwise agreed', as provided under Brussels Ia, has created some
controversies,[884] the text of this Convention puts it in a clearer perspective and
beyond any doubt. For reasons best known to them, parties may specify a particular location, which may not really be the place where actual delivery took place. In
line with the general trends, the support for party autonomy in this head of jurisdiction for contracts in a global framework is welcomed. What should be added is
that it is required that the contract should have an *express* provision on the place
of performance. While the Convention does not place any restriction on party
autonomy, many national courts often require that parties' choice should be real
and have some factual connection with parties' locations.[885] It is suggested that
such restriction should not apply to the Convention, since the clear intention of
the drafters is to give full effect to party autonomy.[886]

The divergence starts from the determination of the place of performance in
the absence of an express choice. Brussels Ia has an autonomous definition of what
the place of performance is for goods and services where Article 7(1)(b) applies,
ie where the place of delivery of the goods or provision of the services is in an EU
Member State. This is fixed at the place of the delivery of goods or services according to the contract. Article 5(1)(g)(ii) of the Convention says it shall be determined
by the law applicable to the contract. One wonders why the drafters opted for
the applicable law route. The solution proposed by the Convention means that
parties have to first figure out the law applicable to the contract which governs the
obligation(s), and then that law determines the place where the obligation is to be
performed.[887] This is something that may be riddled with uncertainties in many
cases, considering how the law applicable to the contract has been determined in
the Commonwealth States.[888] Having noted the first uncertainty parties will face,
then another layer of uncertainty is added: determining the place of performance

---

[883] Art 7(1)(b), Brussels Ia.

[884] Beaumont, 'The Brussels Convention Becomes a Regulation: Implications for Legal Basis, External Competence and Contract Jurisdiction' (n 881) 20.

[885] See Yuko Nishitani, 'Party Autonomy in Contemporary Private International Law-The Hague Principles on Choice of Law and East Asia' (2016) 59 *Japanese Yearbook of International Law* 300. The following cases also support this position: *MSG v Gravières Rhénanes* [1997] ECR I-911; Case C-440/97 *GIE Groupe Concorde and Others v The Master of the vessel 'Suhadiwarno Panjan' and Others*, ECLI:E U:C:1999:456.

[886] See also a similar suggestion by Beaumont, Danov, Trimmings and Yuksel (ch 1, fn 40) 520 in their criticism of the CJEU's *obiter dictum* which tends to limit party autonomy.

[887] This is often referred to as the *Tessili* test in the ECJ jurisprudence. The test was laid down in Case 12/76 *Industrie Tessili Italiana Como v Dunlop AG*, ECLI:EU:C:1976:133.

[888] Generally, common law courts will consider the law that is most closely connected to the contract. They often examine a number of factors including the nature and subject matter of the contract, the place of performance, and the domicile of parties, amongst others. See *Lilydale Cooperative Limited v Meyn Canada Inc*, 2015 ONCA 281.

under the law applicable to the contract. This takes us to the question whether it is the substantive law or the private international law rules of the proper law that determine the place of performance. Neither the Convention nor the Explanatory Report gives any guidance on this issue.[889] This solution depreciates the objectives of legal certainty and predictability which the Convention seeks to pursue. In the absence of an express term, parties cannot predict the place of performance ex ante, since that decision can only be made after an inquiry on the proper law.

Pushing the determination of the place of performance to the doorsteps of national courts without more will not aid uniform interpretation. The choice of law system for some civil law jurisdictions prescribes rules for determining the applicable law. For instance, the Rome I Regulation identifies and prescribes such rules for about eight types of contracts: sale of goods, provision of services, rights *in rem* and tenancies, franchise, distribution, and sale of goods by auction. For some other contracts, it prescribes the habitual residence of the characteristic performer. It goes on to list connecting factors for other special contracts like carriage, consumer, insurance and employment contracts. In all cases, there is an escape clause from the rule to a law that has a manifestly closer connection to the contract.[890] The Chinese Foreign Economic Contract Law followed a similar approach by listing about 17 types of contracts, with choice of law rules focusing on who is performing the main (characteristic) obligation or the location where performance is factually required.[891] In the Anglo-American jurisdictions, there is no such codification. The basic formula remains the law that is most closely connected to the contract.[892] However, the practical application of that basic rule is not straight forward, as that depends on what factors the judge decides to emphasise in each case.

The approach adopted by this Convention is similar to that of the Brussels Convention,[893] and the uncertainties which trailed the latter led to the reform of that approach. The Brussels I Regulation and now Brussels Ia have rules that in many cases prescribe the place of performance for contracts for the sale of goods and services. From Beaumont's account, it is learnt that the solution emerged only on the very last day of the Brussels and Lugano Revision Working Party.[894] That proposal has led to some interpretative difficulties in practice, especially for

---

[889] See Garcimartín and Saumier (n 791) paras 192–194. Although Lord Diplock rules out renvoi in English choice of law rules in contract in *Amin Rasheed Shipping Corporation v Kuwait Insurance Co* [1984] AC 50, [1983] 3 WLR 241, it cannot be stated with certainty that other common law jurisdictions will follow the same approach.

[890] Articles 4–8, Regulation (EC) No 593/2008 of the European Parliament and of the Council of 17 June 2008 on the law applicable to contractual obligations (Rome I).

[891] Guangjian Tu and Muchi Xu, 'Contractual Conflicts in the People's Republic of China: The Applicable Law in the Absence of Choice' (2011) 7 *Journal of Private International Law* 179, 182–84.

[892] *Amin Rasheed Shipping Corporation v Kuwait Insurance Co* (n 889).

[893] *Tessili v Dunlop AG* (n 887).

[894] Beaumont, 'The Brussels Convention Becomes a Regulation: Implications for Legal Basis, External Competence and Contract Jurisdiction' (n 881) 19.

contracts which have multiple places of performance, amongst others.[895] On this note, some legal commentators such as Catherine Kessedjian are of the view that the adoption of the old Brussels' approach is unfortunate.[896]

The problem for the 2019 Convention is that if the indirect jurisdictional ground is not straightforward, a judgment debtor may often have justification to raise it as a defence at the recognition and enforcement stage and that will work against the overall objectives of the Convention. However, it has to be acknowledged that coming up with a simple and acceptable indirect contract jurisdiction that is always straightforward to apply may be an impossible dream.

Irrespective of which system of law the choice of law inquiry points to, one point that should still be emphasised is that the Convention settles for the obligation in question and not the characteristic obligation. This reminder is important because the choice of law process for some States focuses on the characteristic obligation and not the obligation in question while in other States the focus is on the contract as a whole. For instance, A Ltd, an English company, contracted to deliver goods to B Ltd, a German company, at its location in Germany. B Ltd defaulted in the payment for the goods. If the Rome I Regulation applies (Q1), the law governing the contract would likely be English law: the habitual residence of the seller.[897] The second stage of the inquiry (Q2) is to determine where the obligation in question – payment – is to be performed. English law says a debtor seeks its creditor, meaning that payment is due in England. Thus, England is the place of performance. If the English court were to apply the common law (focusing on the law of closest connection to the contract) and not Rome I, it might lead to a different result. On the first inquiry (Q1), the German law will most likely be the applicable law of the contract because that is where the goods are delivered.[898] However, under German law (Q2), the obligation in question – payment – is payable in the country of residence of the debtor. In this scenario, Germany becomes the place of performance.

One more issue with this head of jurisdiction is how the 'obligation in question' and the proper law requirements align with 'purposeful availment' and substantial connection. The draft Explanatory Report mentions that deference to the proper law of the contract can lead to places that have little or no connection to the contract.[899] This was of great concern to the United States whose law requires that a foreign court should be closely connected with the defendant and/or its activities in the State of origin. To meet this requirement, the Convention adds a proviso that the State

[895] Beaumont, Danov, Trimmings and Yuksel (ch 1, fn 40) 513–23.
[896] Catherine Kessedjian, 'Is the Hague Convention of 2 July 2019 a Useful Tool for Companies Who Are Conducting International Activities?' [2020] 1 *Nederlands Internationaal Privatrecht* 19, 29.
[897] See Art 4(1)(a). Although, by Art 4(3), where a contract is manifestly more connected to another State, the law of that State applies.
[898] It is assumed that the court favours the place of performance. Otherwise, the common law does not always regard the place of performance as the law of the closest connection.
[899] Garcimartín and Saumier (n 791) paras 195–96.

of origin will have international jurisdiction unless the activities of the defendant in relation to the transaction *clearly did not* constitute a purposeful and substantial connection to that State. Hence, a defendant will only escape civil jurisdiction under the Convention if his activities concerning the contract as a whole did not constitute a purposeful and substantial connection to the State of origin. A question arises here. Will the applicable law inquiry be dismissed if, for instance, it confers jurisdiction on the place of payment, which has little or no connection with the contract?[900] Also, will non-US courts be ready to embark on the analysis of a concept that is not effectively settled where it was coined? If the US joined the Convention, will its courts apply this head of jurisdiction differently from other courts, for instance where the obligation in question involves payment of money? Nevertheless, for most contracts, the US courts should arrive at the same result as other courts, since the State where a judgment debtor contracted to perform an obligation will presumably be closely connected and pass the purposeful availment analysis as it is crafted in the restrictive wording of the Convention. The overall objective of the 'purposeful connection' test is to ensure that a defendant is not hauled into a jurisdiction based on random or attenuated contacts of the defendant.[901]

G. Tenancies and Immovable Property

Article 6 reads:

> Notwithstanding Article 5, a judgment that ruled on rights in rem in immovable property shall be recognised and enforced if and only if the property is situated in the State of origin.

Article 5(1) reads:

> (h) the judgment ruled on a lease of immovable property (tenancy) and it was given by a court of the State in which the property is situated;
> (i) the judgment ruled against the defendant on a contractual obligation secured by a right in rem in immovable property located in the State of origin, if the contractual claim was brought together with a claim against the same defendant relating to that right in rem;

Article 5(3) reads:

> Paragraph 1 does not apply to a judgment that ruled on a residential lease of immovable property (tenancy) or ruled on the registration of immovable property. Such a

---

[900] The US courts have held that failure to pay a debt at the creditor's residence without more will fail the purposeful availment test. See *Milligan Electricity Co v Hudson Construction Co*, 886 F. Supp. 845 (N.D. Fla. 1995) noting that 'standing alone, mere nonpayment of a debt in Florida is not sufficient to subject a non-resident defendant to personal jurisdiction'. See also *CW Downer & Co v Bioriginal Food & Science Corp*, Civil Action No 13-11788-DJC (D. Mass. March 3, 2014).

[901] See *Burger King v Rudzewicz*, 471 US 462, 475 (1985); Brand and Mariottini (n 800); Garcimartín and Saumier (n 791) paras 195–96.

judgment is eligible for recognition and enforcement only if it was given by a court of the State where the property is situated.

These various heads of jurisdiction are brought together because of the similarities of the subject matter and the rules. The first one is Article 6, which concerns jurisdiction over immovable property. It adopts the *lex situs* rule which is one of the most settled rules of private international law. It deals with 'rights *in rem* in immovable property', ie, those rights over land or immovable property that are enforceable against the whole world. As stated in the draft Explanatory Report, these often include a determination of title to land and other interests ancillary to ownership of land such as mortgages, easements and usufructuary interests, but the key question is whether under the *lex situs* the particular right established in the judgment relating to immovable property has *erga omnes* effects (ie, the right is valid against everyone). The rationale for this rule has been offered in Chapter five above. There are public policy reasons why only the court of the State where land is situated should exercise jurisdiction over matters concerning ownership rights. These include the fact that enforcement of such decisions requires coercive powers of the court of the *situs*; the court of the *situs* has expertise in its land tenure system, and the decision may require rectification of the land register.[902] In line with these policy reasons, the Convention vests exclusive jurisdiction in the State where the immovable property is situated.[903] Judgments from other courts concerning *erga omnes* rights concerning that immovable property will neither circulate under the Convention nor be enforceable under the national laws of Member States. If the judgment ruled on the registration of immovable property and it did not have *erga omnes* effects in the State of origin, it can only circulate under the Convention if it was given by a court of the State where the property is situated (Article 5(3)). A judgment of this type from any other court could only circulate under Article 15 of the Convention where it is permitted under the national law of the State addressed.

One improvement made by the Convention is to add a contractual obligation secured by a right *in rem* (eg mortgage) for a property situated in the State of origin if the claim was brought against the defendant together with an action concerning a right *in rem*.[904] The example given in the draft Explanatory Report is apt. Assuming a defendant was sued for defaulting on a mortgage contract and the State of origin where the property is situated determined the mortgage and also ruled that the defendant is liable to indemnify the judgment creditor for any outstanding balance arising from the disposal of the property, such judgment will circulate under the Convention.[905] It should, however, be noted that this head of jurisdiction does not cover equitable claims arising from land or other contractual, trust or tort disputes concerning foreign lands.

---

[902] *Sterling v Rand & Another* [2019] EWHC 2560 (Ch).
[903] Art 6, Judgments Convention.
[904] This idea is borrowed from Art 8(4) of Brussels Ia.
[905] Garcimartín and Saumier (n 791) para 266.

The second aspect of this jurisdiction deals with leases/tenancies of immovable property. This ground has some similarities to Article 24(1) of Brussels Ia,[906] but it is not available in the judgments enforcement laws of the vast majority of the Commonwealth States. It is a major addition to a global judgments framework considering the burgeoning business of leases and holiday lettings. The text is different from the 2017 and 2018 drafts wherein the scope of the rule was limited to a tenancy for six months or more (long tenancies). This limitation was dropped at the Diplomatic Conference.

Two heads of jurisdiction are provided for disputes concerning tenancies. For residential leases Article 5(3) confers an exclusive indirect rule of jurisdiction under the Convention on the State where the leased property is situated. Judgments from other States on residential leases will not circulate under the Convention but can circulate under national law as a result of Article 15 of the Convention. Catherine Kessedjian, while commenting on this head of jurisdiction, wondered why the drafters separated Article 5(3) and Article 6 when the policy behind both provisions is the same. She also concluded that it might be because judgments that did not comply with Article 5(3) could still be enforced under national law.[907] On the other hand, Article 5(1)(h) confers a non-exclusive indirect ground of jurisdiction on the State of origin concerning non-residential leases situated in that State. This implies that judgments concerning non-residential leases that meet other jurisdictional requirements of Article 5 (eg choice of court agreements, and submission) will circulate under the Convention. Also, if Article 5(1)(h) is read in conjunction with Article 15, judgments on non-residential leases that do not come from the place of the immovable property may also be enforced under national laws. This is a significant addition that was secured at the Diplomatic Conference. It allows for wider circulation of judgments regarding non-residential tenancies which may be treated by some jurisdictions as *in personam* contracts. Therefore, if a non-residential leasing contract contains a non-exclusive jurisdiction clause, for instance, the judgment from the chosen court may be enforced under the 2019 Convention or national laws.

H. Non-contractual Obligations

Article 5(1)(j) reads:

> the judgment ruled on a non-contractual obligation arising from death, physical injury, damage to or loss of tangible property, and the act or omission directly causing such harm occurred in the State of origin, irrespective of where that harm occurred;

---

[906] The Brussels variant has a proviso which also vests jurisdiction in the domicile of the defendant for tenancies below six months. The additional conditions are that the defendant is a natural person and both the tenant and landlord are domiciled in the same State.
[907] Kessedjian (n 896), 28.

Non-contractual obligations can be described as obligations, which the law imposed on parties, as compared to those which they freely undertake. They are otherwise referred to as torts in common law, Brussels Ia and other bilateral treaties. The Convention limits the scope of non-contractual obligations to those arising from 'death, physical injury, damage to or loss of tangible property'. The draft Explanatory Report gives no reason for this restriction. Such restriction is not found in the CML, Brussels Ia or the national laws of most Member States. The reason may not be unconnected to the complexities surrounding some types of tort such as economic and cyber torts, especially in the context of locating the place where damage has occurred and the extent of damages recoverable.[908] Also, because some of those torts, such as negligent misstatement, are often connected to contractual obligations, litigants may plead them as a decoy to enable commencement of proceedings in a more favourable forum, other than the venue where the suit would have been brought based on the contract between the parties.[909]

Aside from limiting the scope of tort-related judgments, the Convention further adopts a restrictive jurisdictional ground by choosing the State which has the strongest connection to the tort – the place of the act or omission causing the harm. This text is very similar to the CML. No such ground exists for international jurisdiction under the common law and extant statutory frameworks of most Commonwealth States. The Convention emphasises 'the act or omission *directly causing such harm* (emphasis added)' thereby reducing the potential controversy surrounding whether damage is part of causation. Brussels Ia says 'the courts for the place where the harmful event occurred'. 'The harmful event' is ambiguous and could be broadly interpreted to include the event causing the harm, the initial damage, and any other harm that may flow from it. The CJEU in several cases, starting from *Bier v Mines de Potasse d'Alsace*,[910] interpreted the 'harmful event' to include the place of the event which gave rise to the harm and the place where the harm is suffered. This has been limited by subsequent cases such as *Marinari v Lloyds Bank*[911] to the place where the direct (initial) damage is suffered. So, the victim is not at liberty to sue in his home country, or other preferred places, where only subsequent harm took place. The English courts seem to retain the broader approach, especially for non-Brussels cases. In *Four Seasons Holdings Incorporated v Brownlie*,[912] the UK Supreme Court was of the view that in

---

[908] See Trevor C Hartley, 'Jurisdiction in Tort Claims for Non-Physical Harm under Brussels 2012, Article 7(2)' (2018) 67 *International & Comparative Law Quarterly* 987.

[909] For instance, see *In re The Alexandros T* [2013] UKSC 70 (where a shipping company sued in Greece, framing the dispute as a tort in order to avoid a jurisdiction agreement nominating an English court for the settlement of an insurance claim); Case C-220/88 *Dumez France SA and Tracoba SARL v Hessische Landesbank* ECLI:EU:C:1990:8 (where a French parent company sued in tort in France concerning loan cancellations between a German bank and its German subsidiaries).

[910] Case 21/76 *Handelskwekerij GJ Bier BV v Mines de Potasse d'Alsace SA*, ECLI:EU:C:1976:166.

[911] Case C-364/93 *Antonio Marinari v Lloyds Bank plc*, ECLI:EU:C:1995:289.

[912] *Four Seasons Holdings Incorporated v Brownlie* [2017] UKSC 80. See also *Cooley v Ramsey* [2008] EWHC 129 (QB) where the court sided with Prof Briggs' view that there is no compelling reason to apply Brussels Ia to non-Convention cases.

death and personal injury cases – which are more relevant to this Convention – the damage was sustained in England from an accident that occurred in Egypt because financial consequences of the physical damage were experienced in England: the loss suffered by the claimant as a dependant of Sir Ian Brownlie (the deceased) and other pecuniary loss for her own injury. The Court cited other cases from Canada and New South Wales with approval.[913] The Convention has attempted to minimise this ambiguity as much as possible by specifically stating in Article 5(1)(j) 'the act or omission directly causing such harm'. This emphasises the act causing the harm and not the harm itself or the effects of the harm. Thus, if the text of the Convention is to be properly construed, the UK court would not have international jurisdiction using the *Four Seasons Holdings Incorporated* as a case study.

To ensure a uniform interpretation, national courts need to stick to the objective of the Convention. This objective is to provide the closest connection between the court and the defendant's tortious conduct so that only the courts of the State where the event that led to the death or physical injury took place has international jurisdiction. For the majority of these torts, the place of the event giving rise to the harm should be easily ascertainable.[914] One type of case which may be problematic involves accidents arising from defective products, ie product liability cases. For those cases, the place of the event which caused the harm may be different from the State where the damage occurred.[915] The act or omission directly causing the harm may, depending on the facts of the case, be the place where the car was manufactured, designed or where it was purchased (eg, failure to warn about the way the specific car needed to be used safely).

It may be argued that the restrictive approach may deny tort victims the ability to sue at the place where an injury is suffered (usually their home State) or may compel parties to litigate at an inconvenient forum, perhaps where an accident or any fortuitous event occurs in a distant place.[916] While this is plausible, the objective of the Convention is to provide legal certainty and predictability. This is the general trend and it also informs why tortious claims are restricted to physical torts. Where plaintiffs have the choice of suing at home or other places where damage is suffered, it leads to the possibility of dragging tortfeasors (defendants) to jurisdictions which might not be reasonably foreseeable. The restrictive approach meets the jurisdictional requirements of most Hague Conference Member States including the United States whose apex court recently emphasised in *Bristol-Myers*

---

[913] These cases include *Skyrotors Ltd v Carrière Technical Industries* (1979) 102 DLR (3d) 323 and *Vile v Von Wendt* (1979) 103 DLR (3d) 356; *Challenor v Douglas* [1983] 2 NSWLR 405 and *Flaherty v Girgis* [1984] 1 NSWLR 56.

[914] Although, in some rare cases, the event giving rise to the wrongful death or personal injury may occur on the high seas or in space.

[915] For instance, in *World-Wide Volkswagen Corp v Woodson*, 444 US 286 (1980), an automobile was sold in New York to the residents of that state. While the owner was driving the car to his new home in Arizona, he had an accident while passing through Oklahoma.

[916] Patrick J Borchers, 'The Problem with General Jurisdiction' [2001] *University of Chicago Legal Forum* 119, 130–32.

Squibb Co v Superior Court of California[917] that for a special jurisdiction to be founded in tort cases, the action must have arisen out of the defendant's contact with the forum State, ie, the State of origin. The broader approach from EU/UK courts may fail the US due process tests, especially in cases where a foreign defendant is dragged before the courts of the place where the victim suffered the injury where it was not reasonably foreseeable to the foreign defendant that his act or omission would cause harm in that State.[918]

I. Trusts

Article 5(1)(k) reads:

> the judgment concerns the validity, construction, effects, administration or variation of a trust created voluntarily and evidenced in writing, and –
>
> (i) at the time the proceedings were instituted, the State of origin was designated in the trust instrument as a State in the courts of which disputes about such matters are to be determined; or
>
> (ii) at the time the proceedings were instituted, the State of origin was expressly or impliedly designated in the trust instrument as the State in which the principal place of administration of the trust is situated.
>
> This sub-paragraph only applies to judgments regarding internal aspects of a trust between persons who are or were within the trust relationship;

Trust is essentially a common law concept and it is well known in the common law jurisdictions. Its usage has, however, transcended the common law. Although many civil law jurisdictions do not have the concept of trust in their domestic laws, Brussels Ia provides for jurisdiction and enforcement of trusts judgments.[919] The use of trusts has continued to grow internationally especially in major international financial hubs and offshore jurisdictions.[920] Due to the economic benefits accruing from international trusts in modern times, there is a growing awareness from States on the need to draw trust assets to their jurisdictions, and various policies and legislation are being made to protect trust assets. Trust jurisdictions are also coming up with rules to protect settlors' autonomy,[921] with the hope that such protections are respected abroad, especially in non-trust States where trust assets

---

[917] *Bristol-Myers Squibb Co v Superior Court of California*, 137 S Ct 1773 (2017). See also *World-Wide Volkswagen Corp v Woodson* (n 915).

[918] Brand, 'Due Process, Jurisdiction and a Hague Judgments Convention' (ch 6, n 651) 694–95.

[919] Art 7(6), Brussels Ia. See also Jonathan Harris, 'The Trust in Private International Law' in James Fawcett (ed), *Reform and Development of Private International Law : Essays in Honour of Sir Peter North* (OUP 2002).

[920] See David Brownbill, 'The Role of Offshore Jurisdictions in the Development of the International Trust' (1999) 32 *Vanderbilt Journal of Transnational Law* 953; Rebecca Lee, 'The Evolution of the Modern International Trust: Developments and Challenges' (2018) 103 *Iowa Law Review* 2069.

[921] Jonathan Harris (n 919) 188.

may eventually be located. On the other hand, there is emerging 'firewall' legislation in other jurisdictions which seeks to shield local trust assets from foreign adjudication. These developments have led to a corresponding increase in trust litigation and requests for the recognition of foreign judgments concerning trust assets.[922] What all these developments suggest is that there is a need for a harmonisation of the divergent policies concerning trust assets litigation and judgments enforcement.

A trust can be created expressly or impliedly by a settlor. The implied trusts are known in common law jurisdictions as constructive or resulting trusts. They can also be created by law, ie statutes. Trust has been defined by the Hague Trusts Convention 1985 as 'the legal relationships created – *inter vivos* or on death – by a person, the settlor, when assets have been placed under the control of a trustee for the benefit of a beneficiary or for a specified purpose'. The scope of the Judgments Convention is also limited to trusts created 'voluntarily and evidenced in writing'. Thus, it is only judgments regarding express trusts that are enforceable under this Convention because, by default, constructive and resulting trusts are implied or imposed by law.[923] Restricting the scope to expressly created trusts will create a common understanding between the common and civil law traditions. Such common ground is desirable for uniform interpretation.

The last point leads to the examination of the nature of trusts and the rationale for the jurisdictional rules stated under subparagraph (k). Trusts affect both movable and immovable property. For trusts, the competing connections are the domicile of the trust, the location of trust assets, the domicile of the parties to the trust, party autonomy, and the system of law under which the trust was formed. In line with the general theme of the Convention, party autonomy is preserved. Since the scope of the trust has been limited to express trust, it is pragmatic that the settlor's choice of court should be respected. In furtherance of this, it is also suggested there should be no further inquiry as to whether the choice is real or not, thereby giving party autonomy its maximum effect. The choice of court covers only disputes expressly or impliedly mentioned in the trust instrument. Thus, if the instrument excludes matters relating to the validity of the trust, for instance, this ground of jurisdiction will not apply to such disputes.

The other jurisdictional basis is to find another close connection between a State of origin and the trust. The approved connection is the State which was expressly or impliedly named under the trust instrument as the principal place of administration of the trust. There is no dispute concerning an express designation of the principal place of administration of the trust by the instrument. However, it

---

[922] J Harris, 'Jurisdiction and Judgments in International Trusts Litigation – Surveying the Landscape' (2011) 17 *Trusts & Trustees* 236; Daniel Hochberg, 'Enforcement of Foreign Judgments and Firewall Legislation' (2015) 21 *Trusts & Trustees* 1006. See also *Schroder Cayman Bank Trust Co Ltd v Schroder Trust AG* [2015] JRC 125; *X Trust Co Ltd v RW* [2006] 4 WLUK 363; *FM v ASL Trustee Co Ltd* [2006] 2 WLUK 114; *Compass Trustees Ltd v McBarnett* [2002] 5 WLUK 421.

[923] See Garcimartín and Saumier (n 791) para 208.

is not clear how the principal place of administration can be implied, since differ-ent considerations apply under national laws. Would this be the State where the trust assets are located? The State under whose law it is formed? The State where physical administration takes place? It seems the drafters intend to confer jurisdic-tion only on the State where de facto administration takes place. In many cases, this may be the State where the trust assets are located or under whose law the trust instrument was established.

The conditions stipulated for courts of the State of the principal place of admin-istration are that the matters should relate to the internal aspects of a trust and between those in a trust relationship. Unlike Brussels Ia which specifies those in such a relationship – settlor, trustee or beneficiary – the Convention does not have such particularisation. The draft Explanatory Report suggests that only these three parties are intended under the Hague Judgments Convention.[924] Therefore, unless the final Explanatory Report is different, 'holders of trust powers, protectors, and enforcers',[925] as once envisioned by Professor Jonathan Harris, may not be covered under the Convention.

J. Non-exclusive Choice of Court

Article 5(1)(m) reads:

> the judgment was given by a court designated in an agreement concluded or docu-mented in writing or by any other means of communication which renders information accessible so as to be usable for subsequent reference, other than an exclusive choice of court agreement
>
> For the purposes of this sub-paragraph, an 'exclusive choice of court agreement' means an agreement concluded by two or more parties that designates, for the purpose of deciding disputes which have arisen or may arise in connection with a particular legal relationship, the courts of one State or one or more specific courts of one State to the exclusion of the jurisdiction of any other courts.

In Chapter six above, the HCCA was examined in some detail. One of the conclusions reached in that chapter is that those non-exclusive jurisdiction agree-ments which are outside the scope of the HCCA are covered by the Judgments Convention. By the Hague system of two Conventions, 'non-exclusive jurisdic-tion agreements' are agreements nominating the courts of two or more States and those nominating the court of a State but clearly indicating that the choice is not exclusive. Non-exclusive choice of court agreements are often mutual, giving both parties the option of suing in the agreed venues. There are, however, other variants. Some clauses may nominate State A for party X and State B for party Y (*Meeth v Glacetal* clause). In other cases, as prominently used in international finance, the

---

[924] Ibid, para 221.
[925] Harris (n 919) 238.

agreement may nominate State A for party X, and State A, B or others for party Y (*Rothschild* clause).[926]

The Convention deems a State nominated by parties as substantially connected to the dispute and thus the judgment from that State will circulate under this head of jurisdiction. It provides that the judgment should be from 'a court designated in an agreement'. What does this mean against the background of certain asymmetric jurisdictional clauses mentioned above? For a *Meeth v Glacetal* clause,[927] any of the nominated courts is 'a designated court'. However, because a choice of court agreement is synonymous with submission, the State of origin will only be closely connected if it was its court that the relevant party consented to be sued in. Of particular interest is *Me X v Société Banque Privé Edmond de Rothschild*[928] (*Rothschild* clause). Typically, this clause gives a party, usually a financial institution, the option of suing in a nominated court or *any other court* of its choice – eg where the borrower's assets are found. If we were to go by the ordinary meaning of 'designated', can those other courts which the financial institution may unilaterally choose be described as 'designated', bearing in mind that those courts are not specifically mentioned in the agreement? There are two approaches to this question under national laws. The English courts approve this type of asymmetric clause since it is freely negotiated by the parties.[929] Although the French courts had initially ruled that it was null and void for being asymmetric,[930] this position appears to have changed recently.[931] It is submitted that the English courts' approach is preferable. The borrower has impliedly submitted by contract to any court chosen by the bank that falls within the limits, if any, specified in the contract, and that court should be regarded as impliedly designated under the contract. Unfortunately, the draft Explanatory Report is silent on this point.

K. Consumer Contracts

Article 5(2) reads:

> If recognition or enforcement is sought against a natural person acting primarily for personal, family or household purposes (a consumer) in matters relating to a consumer

---

[926] Mary Keyes and Brooke Adele Marshall, 'Jurisdiction Agreements: Exclusive, Optional and Asymmetrical' (2015) 11 *Journal of Private International Law* 345, 366–77.

[927] *Meeth v Glacetal* [1979] CMLR 520.

[928] *Me X v Société Banque Privé Edmond de Rothschild* (Case No. 11-26022) Cour de Cassation, 26 September 2012.

[929] *Commerzbank Aktiengesellschaft v Liquimar Tankers Management Inc* [2017] EWHC 161 (Comm). See also Keyes and Marshall (ch 2, fn 127) 366–77.

[930] *Rothschild* (n 928); *Credit Suisse v Danne Holding Patrimoniale* (Appeal No 13-27264).

[931] *MJA société v Apple Sales International* [2016] ILPr 13, Cour de Cassation (noting that the agreement can be enforced where the venue at which the stronger party can sue may be objectively verified). See also the AG's Opinion in Case C-595/17 *Apple Sales International v MJA*, acting as liquidator of eBizcuss.com (eBizcuss).

contract, or against an employee in matters relating to the employee's contract of employment –

(a)   paragraph 1(e) applies only if the consent was addressed to the court, orally or in writing;

(b)   paragraph 1(f), (g) and (m) do not apply.

The Convention does not expressly provide international jurisdiction for consumer and employment contracts. It does, however, limit the application of some jurisdictional grounds where enforcement is sought against a consumer or an employee. A consumer is defined as a natural person who has contracted for personal, family or household items. This definition should be regarded as autonomous. National courts may not be able to vary it beyond the specific scope outlined by the Convention. At the Special Commission, some States such as Brazil pushed for a broader scope in the definition of consumers, to include non-natural persons and natural persons acting for professional purposes. However, this proposal did not see the light of the day.[932] Unlike consumers, employees are not defined. It seems that the ground will cover anyone employed under a contract of service/employment irrespective of his cadre. This does not, however, extend to independent contractors.

The protection of weaker parties is a growing concept in many legal systems including those of the Commonwealth. Professor Nadia de Araujo and Marcelo De Nardi note that international consumer transactions have recorded tremendous growth due to the development of tourism and e-commerce. Many of these transactions have smaller value, and most consumers (including employees) do not often have the resources to prosecute their cases in distant locations, thereby potentially leading to access to justice problems. Professor Briggs also suggests that those contracts rarely result from free and equal negotiation.[933] Thus, there is a vulnerable class of litigants that need special protection. The unwritten goal of the Convention is to restrict international jurisdiction for actions against employees and consumers to their habitual residence as much as practicable. Thus, it excludes alternative jurisdictional grounds that may be founded on contractual obligations and choice of court agreements altogether, since these are the grounds that are connected to their contracts. In addition, it excludes submission by arguing on the merits.

V.   Refusal of Recognition

Due to the diversity of laws, policies and the standards of justice across the globe, there is a need to protect judgment debtors against judgments that have been improperly procured or those that do not emanate from proceedings where due

---

[932] HCCH, 'Background to Working Document No 4 of 1 June 2016 on the Need of "Consumer" Definition', *Information Document No 3 of June 2016 for the attention of the Special Commission of June 2016 on the Recognition and Enforcement of Foreign Judgments* (2016) <https://assets.hcch.net/docs/eec804e8-b974-470e-92bc-dd593b96c12c.pdf> accessed 31 May 2020.

[933] Briggs, *The Conflict of Laws* (ch 1, fn 44) 66.

process was observed. This explains why some limited reviews may be necessary at the enforcement stage. There is equally a need to strike a balance between protecting judgment debtors from improperly procured judgments and placing too much burden on judgment creditors through an unnecessary waste of time and resources re-litigating issues that have been decided upon by foreign tribunals. A judgment creditor deserves a simple and cost-effective procedure to realise his judgment. The pragmatic way to set this balance is to provide clear indirect jurisdictional rules which direct parties to substantially connected court(s). Once parties have litigated the claims in one of those courts and due process was observed, the responsibility of the court addressed is to verify the checklist provided under Articles 5 and 6. If the foreign court had jurisdiction, the judgment should circulate under the Convention without much ado. The judgment debtor should only be able to challenge enforcement on very limited grounds of natural justice and public policy. That is the essence of Articles 4 and 7 of the Convention. Both articles provide that there should be no review of the merits of foreign judgments except for those reviews that are necessary to verify that the conditions imposed by the Convention are met. Where these conditions are met, Article 4 mandates recognition and enforcement. Recognition may only be refused where the judgment is caught by any of the refusal grounds under Article 7. The refusal grounds are discussed below.

A. Service of Writs/Originating Summons

Article 7(1) reads:

> Recognition or enforcement may be refused if –
>
> (a) the document which instituted the proceedings or an equivalent document, including a statement of the essential elements of the claim –
>
> > (i)   was not notified to the defendant in sufficient time and in such a way as to enable them to arrange for their defence, unless the defendant entered an appearance and presented their case without contesting notification in the court of origin, provided that the law of the State of origin permitted notification to be contested; or
> >
> > (ii) was notified to the defendant in the requested State in a manner that is incompatible with fundamental principles of the requested State concerning service of documents

Service of originating processes is a threshold matter in every jurisdiction. A defendant who did not receive the summons cannot be said to have participated in the proceedings. Non-service of processes is a violation of one of the cardinal principles of natural justice and the resulting judgment is not entitled to recognition as demonstrated in cases such as *Laserpoint Ltd v Prime Minister of Malta*.[934]

---

[934] *Laserpoint Ltd v Prime Minister of Malta* [2016] EWHC 1820 (QB).

The controversies in this area of law revolve around the manner of service and the adequacy of the time required for non-resident defendants to respond to a summons. In some jurisdictions, service can be effected by private process servers while other jurisdictions consider that as a breach of their sovereignty.[935] In *Louis Dreyfus Commodities Suisse, SA v Financial Software Systems, Inc*,[936] a judgment debtor opposed the enforcement of an English default judgment in the US because the summons had been served in Pennsylvania for the UK proceedings by a private process server, while Pennsylvania law requires that service be done by a sheriff. Although the court rejected that judgment debtor's argument in that case because the latter had had actual knowledge of the suit, such objection has been upheld in other enforcement cases especially in jurisdictions like China[937] and Malaysia[938] where service is regarded as a fundamental issue that affects State security and sovereignty.

The Convention expectedly adopts the position that will work in harmony with the laws of those States that consider service a public policy issue. It has provided the much-needed legal certainty because litigants can now make informed decisions concerning the issue of service, the law that governs it and when to raise objections. Judgment creditors should, therefore, be wary of the procedure for service of summons in the State where the defendant has his assets, as that can become a stumbling block at the enforcement stage. The restriction placed by Article 7(1)(a)(ii) must be emphasised. The ground can only be raised when the defendant was served in the State where enforcement is sought, and the manner of service violated the law of that State. This restriction is very pragmatic since the State's sovereignty is not affected by processes served elsewhere.

The Convention neither defines adequacy of time for arranging a defence nor the law that determines it. The law of the receiving State always governs grounds of refusal unless otherwise stated. While commenting on Article 7(1)(a), Niklaus Meier noted that the CJEU favours an autonomous interpretation of timeliness and appropriateness of service. He recommended a factual approach with the following guidelines as understood from CJEU cases and legal literature. These guidelines are: the method of service must be known in the State of origin, the defendant must be able to understand the nature of the notified documents, and there must be at least several weeks for the defendant to take necessary steps.[939]

---

[935] Hartley and Dogauchi also report this concerning the negotiation of the HCCA. This formed the basis of the 'service' ground which is *in pari materia* with the 2019 Judgments Convention. See Trevor Hartley and Masato Dogauchi (ch 5, fn 442) 829.

[936] *Louis Dreyfus Commodities Suisse, SA v Financial Software Systems, Inc*, 99 A.3d 79 (Pa. Super. Ct. 2014).

[937] Wenliang Zhang (ch 2, fn 158) 163.

[938] See Azmi Sharom, 'Private International Law in the Malaysia Courts' (2005) 9 *Singapore Year Book of International Law* 253 (citing *United Overseas Bank Ltd v Wong Hai Ong* [1999] 1 *Malayan Law Journal* (MLJ) 474; *Commerzbank (South East Asia Ltd) v Tow Kong Lian* [2002] 2 MLJ 353; *Ng An Chin v Panin International Credit (S) Pte Ltd* [2003] 3 MLJ 279).

[939] Niklaus Meier, 'Notification as a Ground for Refusal' (2020) 67 *Netherlands International Law Review* 81.

The only qualification to this suggested factual approach is that under the Convention the manner of service must comply with the law of the State addressed where the defendant was served in that State. However, a defendant is deemed to have waived this right if he defended an action on the merits without challenging the sufficiency of the time to make a defence, except where the law of the State of origin does not allow such objection to be raised.[940] In other words, a judgment debtor cannot contest the sufficiency of time at the enforcement proceedings unless he had raised it (unsuccessfully or otherwise) in the foreign court. This is a good case management strategy that will ensure that judgment debtors do not raise the defence at will.

One area that subparagraph (a) does not clarify is the non-service of amended claims or a scenario where a suit was withdrawn and later refiled but without a fresh service of the second claim. The first scenario came up in the 9/11 judgment enforcement proceedings cited earlier in section III. In that case, the court refused recognition because the main claim was substantially amended, and the amendment was never served on the respondents. The second scenario came up in *Giant Light Metal Technology (Kunshan) Co Ltd v Aksa Far East Pte Ltd*,[941] and the Singapore High Court granted recognition because submission to the initial action subsisted. The position of the Luxembourgish court is preferred because an amendment to the claim alters the claim, and a defendant ought to be given the benefit of deciding whether to pursue the new amendment or not. The same goes for a suit that is re-filed.

B. Fraud

Article 7(1)(b) reads:

> the judgment was obtained by fraud;

There seems to be a consensus in most legal systems that a foreign judgment which is tainted by fraud should not be recognised, as that violates both natural justice and fundamental morals and policy of every civilised State. The Convention agrees with that view that such judgments should not be recognised. It provides a simple rule, which is similar to that of the CML. In some other frameworks like Brussels Ia, fraud is subsumed under public policy.

Consensus does not go beyond the basic notion that fraud should lead to non-recognition. The questions to ask are what kind of fraud should lead to non-recognition, and can the defence be raised at any time? There is a divergence of thoughts on these two issues. The traditional common law rule[942] posits that

---

[940] Art 7 (a)(1)(i).
[941] *Giant Light Metal Technology (Kunshan) Co Ltd v Aksa Far East Pte Ltd* [2014] SGHC 16.
[942] *Abouloff v Oppenheimer* (1882) 10 QBD 295, reaffirmed by the House of Lords in *Owens Bank Ltd v Bracco* [1992] 2 AC 443.

fraud unravels everything. Any allegation of fraud, be it procedural or substantive, merits an examination by the court addressed. While there has been a modification to this rule in Singapore[943] and Canada,[944] it remains potent in the wider Commonwealth because it remains part of English law.[945] The *Abouloff* rule is not followed in the United States because the judicial practice leans towards 'extrinsic' fraud, which is closely related to the modified *Abouloff* rule.[946] It appears any allegation of fraud will also lead to a review in most civil law jurisdictions. The Convention favours a broad interpretation of 'fraud'. This view is reinforced by the rejection of the restrictive version of the HCCA where the fraud defence is limited to procedural fraud. Considering both drafts, one can hardly fail to conclude that the Judgment Convention applies to both procedural and substantive fraud. The draft Explanatory Report also confirms that this represents the consensus of the negotiators on this point.[947]

One cannot feign ignorance of the fact that some foreign judgments can be procured fraudulently through procedural and substantive fraud, as demonstrated by the *Donziger* scandal[948] and other cases where foreign judgments have been implicated by fraud.[949] This makes the argument for accommodating both substantive and procedural fraud appealing, especially in a global judgments framework. However, it will be unpragmatic to construe the fraud defence in a way that can resuscitate the already dying *Abouloff* rule and its obvious drawbacks. The House of Lords also agreed that the rule has outlived its usefulness. Therefore, the fraud defence should be restrictively interpreted to accommodate only those frauds that could not have been reasonably discovered by a diligent judgment debtor at the time of the foreign proceedings. In line with the general trend of the Convention, the fraud should be available only in three instances. First, it should be available in cases of default judgments because the judgment debtor did not have the opportunity of presenting his case. Second, it should be available for any fraud which only came to the knowledge of the judgment debtor after judgment had been issued. Third, it should apply where the fraud allegation was unsuccessfully challenged in the court of origin since the allegations may affect the judges. In all these cases, the fraud allegation should be specific, material and capable of altering the substance of the judgment. As depicted by the empirical research reported in Chapter five, these requirements will likely filter out unmeritorious applications from judgment debtors.

---

[943] *Hong Pian Tee v Les Placements Germain Gauthier Inc* [2002] SGCA 17.

[944] *Beals v Saldanha* (n 788).

[945] Briggs, 'Crossing the River by Feeling the Stones: Rethinking the Law on Foreign Judgments' (ch 3, fn 306) 19–21.

[946] Beaumont and Walker (ch 1, fn 59) 55.

[947] Garcimartín and Saumier (n 791) para 286.

[948] *Chevron Corp v Donziger*, No 14-826(L), 2016 WL 4173988 (2d Cir. August 8, 2016).

[949] *HJ Heinz Co Ltd v EFL Inc* [2010] EWHC 1203 (Comm); *Habib Bank Ltd v Ahmed* [2001] EWCA Civ 1270.

C. Public Policy

Article 7(1)(c) reads:

> recognition or enforcement would be manifestly incompatible with the public policy
> of the requested State, including situations where the specific proceedings leading to
> the judgment were incompatible with fundamental principles of procedural fairness of
> that State and situations involving infringements of security or sovereignty of that State;

The public policy defence is available in all legal systems. It seeks to prevent foreign judgments that violate the fundamental legal order of the receiving State. It has also been used to deny recognition to foreign judgments that violate the territorial integrity and sovereignty of the receiving State or its overriding mandatory laws. Public policy in its broader sense encompasses other key grounds like fraud and natural justice. But to restrict its usage, the Convention separates other grounds from public policy so that a court addressed does not hide under the public policy defence to unnecessarily review or reject foreign judgments.

The approach of the Convention is to restate 'manifest incompatibility' which has already been explained in Chapter five. The analysis in that chapter applies here as well, since the first part of Article 7(1)(c) fairly represents what is obtainable under Hague conventions and other regional/bilateral treaties. As mentioned in the draft Explanatory Report, it is to be interpreted restrictively and is only available in rare cases where a foreign judgment will lead to an 'intolerable result'[950] in the receiving State.[951]

Unlike other Hague Conventions, Brussels Ia, the CML and national laws, the Convention places procedural fairness and infringement of security or sovereignty under the public policy exception. Infringement of security or sovereignty is usually linked with the service of originating summons as shown by some of the cases cited in Chapter five, section V.A. Junhyok Jang states that the proposal to specially mention State sovereignty and security was spearheaded by Israel at the Special Commission. However, the preponderance of opinion was that this inclusion was not meant to expand the scope of public policy defence.[952]

A more serious provision is procedural fairness as a subset of the public policy defence. As stated earlier, this used to be a self-standing ground. Procedural fairness is not defined by the Convention. It will broadly be interpreted by national courts through the lenses of natural justice and the right to a fair trial, as these are analogous concepts. The Strasbourg jurisprudence has integrated the right to a fair

---

[950] Garcimartín and Saumier (n 791) paras 289–90.

[951] The research shows that most of the cases where public policy was successfully raised concern non-service of originating processes. See *Tavoulareas v Tsavliris & Others*; *Reeve & Others v Plummer*; *Laserpoint Ltd v Prime Minister of Malta & Others* (n 934); and *Maronier v Larmer* as discussed in Chapter 5, section V.A.

[952] Junhyok Jang, 'The Public Policy Exception Under the New 2019 HCCH Judgments Convention' (2020) 67 *Netherlands International Law Review* 97, 104–5.

trial, as enshrined in Article 6 of the ECHR, in the public policy of Member States and a court addressed is obliged to deny recognition where a foreign judgment breached Article 6. This represents the decision in *Pellegrini v Italy*.[953] However, the specifics of the right to a fair trial and what degree of violation will require denial were not discussed by the ECtHR. The implication is that procedural fairness, or right to a fair trial as some courts will construe it, is ambiguous. The guidance from *Pellegrini* may contrast with the English court's analysis of natural justice – a more restrictive concept – as the empirical research in Chapter five reveals. The result indicates that judgment debtors have sought to set aside recognition of judgments via the natural justice ground based on the allegation of partiality of judges,[954] incapacity to present their defence,[955] excessive delay of trial,[956] damages awarded on points not addressed at trial,[957] and deficiency in the judicial reasoning of foreign courts,[958] amongst others. While most of the cases failed, will the same result be achieved if courts elsewhere considered those objections under the right to a fair trial? Having placed procedural fairness under public policy, it is doubtful whether the defence can be realistically restricted to exceptional cases.

Having noted the possibilities of frequent usage of the public policy defence since it now encompasses 'procedural fairness', it is desirable that national courts keep the defence in line with the objectives of the Convention. It should be limited to a 'flagrant denial of justice' in cases which may not fit under Article 7(1)(a). Examples of such cases include *Krombach v Bamberski*,[959] where a foreign court's procedure prevented a debtor from presenting his case, without any fault on his part[960] and *Maronier v Larmer*,[961] where a debtor filed a defence, but was not notified of the reactivation of the case after a 12-year stay of proceedings. The courts should resist an invitation to set aside foreign judgments because of differences in procedural laws and standards under the guise of public policy. Procedural standards vary from one State to another. The US case of *Midbrook Flowerbulbs Holland BV v Holland America Bulb Farms, Inc*[962] is very illustrative on this point. In that case, the judgment debtor argued that a Dutch judgment should not be recognised because it violated the US standard of due process of law. The basis for the objection was that the Dutch court did not allow the judgment debtor's second application to have access to the 'majority of Midbrook's cost records and therefore

---

[953] *Pellegrini v Italy* [2001] ECHR 476.

[954] *Smith v Huertas* [2015] EWHC 3745 (Comm).

[955] *Ajay Kanoria and Others v Tony Francis Guinness* (ch 5, fn 566).

[956] *Smith v Huertas* [2015] EWHC 3745 (Comm); *Laserpoint Ltd v Prime Minister of Malta* (n 934).

[957] *Malicorp Ltd v Egypt* (ch 5, fn 568)

[958] *Superior Composite Structures LLC v Parrish* [2015] EWHC 3688 (QB).

[959] Case C-7/98 *Krombach v Bamberski*, ECLI:EU:C:2000:164. See also *Agbara & Others v The Shell Petroleum Development Company of Nigeria Ltd & Others* [2019] EWHC 3340 (QB).

[960] For instance, Case C-394/07 *Gambazzi v Daimler Chrysler Canada Inc & Another*, where the debtor had the opportunity to defend by obeying a court order but chose not to.

[961] *Maronier v Larmer* [2002] EWCA Civ 774.

[962] *Midbrook Flowerbulbs Holland BV v Holland America Bulb Farms, Inc*, 874 F.3d 604 (9th Cir. 2017).

deprived it of the opportunity to provide any defense' and that the Amsterdam Court of Appeal 'arbitrarily and without basis overturned the Alkmaar District Court's credibility rulings regarding whether the parties had reached a settlement'. The Ninth Circuit Court of Appeal notes that:

> Our conclusion that section 4(c)(8) requires only 'fundamental fairness' is buttressed by the prefatory note to the UFCMJRA, which states that the act's purpose is to 'make it more likely that money judgments rendered in that state would be recognized in other countries.' Certainly, it would undermine this purpose to enforce only those foreign judgments which resulted from proceedings that conformed to our own notions of constitutional due process. *See Ashenden,* 233 F.3d at 476 (rejecting the argument that foreign courts should have to follow 'the latest twist and turn of our courts regarding, for example, the circumstances under which due process requires an opportunity for a hearing in advance of the deprivation of a substantive right rather than afterwards'). Such a high bar would encourage foreign powers to condition the enforcement of *our* judgments on the satisfaction of *their* procedural requirements, which could be just as onerous as our own.[963]

The Court concludes that to succeed, a judgment debtor needs to establish more than mere differences in the procedural standards of the State of origin and the court addressed. He must establish specific deprivation of basic procedural fairness, like evidence of corruption or that the judgment was awarded for political reasons.[964] In the same vein, the German courts have also maintained a similar attitude. In several enforcement actions, they have rejected an invitation by judgment debtors to deny recognition to US judgments on the basis that US discovery rules violate German public policy simply because the US method is wider than what is available in Germany, or because the US method of allocation of litigation cost varies from that of German civil procedure.[965] This approach accords with the results of the empirical research in Chapter five. It is recommended as the appropriate attitude of courts towards procedural fairness and the public policy defence in general. The same conclusion was reached by the English High Court in *Lenkor Energy Trading DMCC v Puri,*[966] where the judgment debtor attempted to argue that a DIFC judgment should not be enforced on public policy grounds because the interest rate awarded by the Dubai court is higher than what obtains under English law and that the underlying transaction was illegal. The English court held that the mere fact that the Dubai law imposes personal liability on a cheque drawn on a company's account (corporate veil was pierced) does not offend English public policy and the interest rate is just 1 per cent higher than the English judgment debt rate.

---

[963] Ibid, 616–17.
[964] Ibid.
[965] Wolfgang Wurmnest, 'Recognition and Enforcement of U.S. Money Judgments in Germany' (2005) 23 *Berkeley Journal of International Law* 175, 197–98.
[966] *Lenkor Energy Trading DMCC v Puri* [2020] EWHC 75 (QB).

D. Breach of a Choice of Court Agreement or Designation in a Trust Instrument

Article 7(1)(d) reads:

> the proceedings in the court of origin were contrary to an agreement, or a designation in a trust instrument, under which the dispute in question was to be determined in a court of a State other than the State of origin;

This refusal ground underscores the importance of party autonomy and its dominance in modern private international law jurisprudence. Since the HCCA prioritises exclusive choice of court agreements which impose obligations on parties to litigate in a particular chosen forum, its effectiveness can only be guaranteed by disincentivising any attempt to litigate elsewhere. This Convention protects such exclusive choice of court agreements. Also, where a judgment was given by a court not designated in a trust or by any court which was specifically excluded under a choice of court agreement, the judgment from that court may be refused recognition under this ground.[967] It accords with a growing international policy of denying recognition to judgments obtained in breach of jurisdiction/arbitration agreements generally.[968] Thus, it is pragmatic that the same treatment is given to judgments in breach of a choice of a court agreement and those in breach of the designation of a court in a trust instrument. Although this ground is not available in most national and regional judgments frameworks, there should be no difficulty in its application.

E. Inconsistent Judgments

Article 7(1) continues:

> (e) the judgment is inconsistent with a judgment given by a court of the requested State in a dispute between the same parties; or
>
> (f) the judgment is inconsistent with an earlier judgment given by a court of another State between the same parties on the same subject matter, provided that the earlier judgment fulfils the conditions necessary for its recognition in the requested State.

The two grounds deal with inconsistent judgments given in a dispute between the parties either in the receiving State or a third State. They are similar to those of the HCCA and are also available in national and regional judgments frameworks. In a global simple convention, which does not regulate direct jurisdictional grounds,

---

[967] Garcimartín and Saumier (n 791) 297–99.

[968] Section 7(4)(b) Foreign Judgments Act 1991 (Australia); Article V, s 2(b), Canada-United Kingdom Civil and Commercial Judgments Convention; s 32(1) Civil Jurisdiction and Judgments Act 1982 (United Kingdom); s 3 Foreign Judgments (Restriction on Recognition and Enforcement) Ordinance (Hong Kong); *Philip Alexander Securities and Futures Ltd v Bamberger* [1997] ILPr 72.

there is a high degree of probability that litigation may be pursued by parties in different Member States, resulting in conflicting judgments. It becomes practically impossible to enforce such judgments where court A rules that Mr X is liable, and another competent court B says otherwise. A practical example is *Thai-Lao Lignite (Thailand) Co v Gov't of the Lao People's Democratic Republic*[969] where a US court was faced with an English court's judgment enforcing an arbitral award and a Malaysia court's judgment nullifying the same award.

The conditions for the applicability of the two grounds are very clear. First, the earlier judgment must be enforceable under the Convention. In other words, it must pass the Article 5 and 6 tests and must not be vitiated by any of the refusal grounds in Article 7. For instance, Mr A, a Greek national established a trust concerning some property in France. He appointed German Trust Ltd as the trustee. The trust agreement nominated an English court for the settlement of all disputes arising from the administration of the trust. A dispute arose between the company and the beneficiaries. The company sued in Germany where it has its principal place of business while the beneficiaries who were then resident in England also commenced an action in England. The German proceedings were concluded first with a judgment in favour of the trustees. The English proceedings came to a different conclusion and gave judgment for the beneficiaries. The beneficiaries sought to enforce the judgment in France. In this instance, subparagraph (f) does not apply because the earlier judgment was not enforceable under the Convention since it violated Article 5(1)(k).

The second condition is that the earlier judgment should affect the same parties and decide the same subject matter. Otherwise, where the parties are not the same or the issue decided by both judgments is not the same, then subparagraphs (e) and (f) will not apply. There is a subtle difference between subparagraphs (e) and (f). Subparagraph (e) does not include 'the same subject matter'. The Explanatory Report states that it is meant to be wider than subparagraph (f) and will cover situations where findings of fact or conclusions of law in separate disputes between the same parties are irreconcilable. While this may not be a regular occurrence, it is not impossible.[970] In this situation, the other conflicting judgments will always give way for the judgments rendered by the receiving State.

One other qualification that should be noted in subparagraph (f) is that, as for judgments of other Member States, priority is given to the judgment which is earlier in time while the later one is expected to be denied recognition. This explanation is necessary as it is very much possible that it is the first judgment that is the subject of enforcement proceedings. The implication is that the judgment debtor cannot challenge the proceedings because of a later inconsistent judgment. This was the scenario in *Thai-Lao Lignite (Thailand) Co v Government of the Lao*

---

[969] *Thai-Lao Lignite (Thailand) Co v Government of the Lao People's Democratic Republic* 864 F.3d 172 (2d Cir. 2017).
[970] See Case 145/86 *Hoffmann v Krieg*, ECLI:EU:C:1988:61.

People's Democratic Republic.[971] In this case, a US court was asked to recognise and enforce an English judgment which confirmed an arbitral award. The action was opposed because there was another Malaysian judgment, which set aside the award. The US court denied recognition to the English judgment because of the inconsistent Malaysian judgment that was later in time. The reason for that decision was that Malaysia was the seat of the arbitration and its court was more closely connected to the dispute. Assuming Malaysia, the United Kingdom and the United States were parties to the 2019 Judgments Convention, the US court would be obligated to recognise the English judgment which was first in time, provided it meets the conditions for recognition. On the other hand, if it were the Malaysian judgment that was the subject of the enforcement proceedings, recognition would be denied because of the earlier inconsistent judgment, assuming the English judgment meets the conditions for recognition. The first-in-time principle applies in most jurisdictions[972] based on the doctrine of *res judicata*. This has been dealt with in more detail in Chapter five (Section V.D). The first judgment validly issued has determined the issue(s) thereby rendering any subsequent determination ineffective. This principle has been applied in several English cases like *Showlag v Mansour*,[973] *Vervaeke v Smith*,[974] and *People's Insurance Co of China (Hebei Branch) v Vysanthi Shipping Co Ltd 'The Joanna V'*.[975]

VI. Other Sundry Matters

A. Non-Money Judgments

Article 3 defines judgment to include any decision on the merits. This entails that money and non-money judgments are enforceable under the Convention. Two basic points that are stressed by Article 3 are that the decision must be on the merits and interim measures are not judgments. A decision on the merits includes a judgment in default of appearance or pleadings. The draft Explanatory Report

---

[971] *Thai-Lao Lignite (Thailand) Co v Government of the Lao People's Democratic Republic* (n 969).

[972] This is the result of the comparative inquiry carried out by Kevin Clermont on conflicting foreign judgments under common law, civil law, and EU law amongst others. See Kevin M Clermont, 'Limiting the Last-in-Time Rule for Judgments' (2017) 36 *Review of Litigation* 1, 31–39. The practice in the United States favours the last-in-time principle for inter-state judgments. The authorities are not decisive and consistent on conflicting foreign judgments. However, Kevin Clermont and Ruth B Ginsburg suggest that first-in-time rule might apply to conflicting non-American judgments. This position is supported by the Uniform Act as well. See Kevin M Clermont, ibid, 44–53; Ruth B Ginsburg, 'Judgments in Search of Full Faith and Credit: The Last-in-Time Rule for Conflicting Judgments' (1969) 82 *Harvard Law Review* 798, 804.

[973] *Showlag v Mansour* (ch 5, fn 637).

[974] *Vervaeke v Smith* (ch 5, fn 632).

[975] *People's Insurance Co of China (Hebei Branch) v Vysanthi Shipping Co Ltd 'The Joanna V'* [2003] EWHC 1655 (holding that an arbitral award, which was first in time had *res judicata* effect over a later conflicting Ningbo Maritime Court judgment).

indicates that the judgment must be a final judgment.[976] This takes interlocutory or procedural rulings outside the scope of enforceable judgments. Therefore, all final judgments which compel the judgment debtor to perform an act or prohibiting him from acting in a particular way are enforceable. Examples of such judgments include injunctions and an order for specific performance issued after the final determination of a case.

Some issues may arise from the enforcement of non-money judgments. The orders may be couched in a manner that is not entirely clear or the relief may not be available in the receiving State. In some cases, it may be unduly burdensome for the receiving State to supervise the enforcement of the judgment as earlier explained in Chapter four. The Convention is silent on these important issues. It is entirely up to the receiving State to determine how best non-money judgments can be enforced. It will run contrary to the objective of the Convention to simply reject a non-money judgment based on some of the factors that have been mentioned above. It is suggested that national courts may borrow a leaf from the CML's approach. This entails an amendment of the judgment to suit local circumstances or granting of whatever variant of the foreign relief may be available under the law of the receiving State.

B. Punitive Damages

Article 10 governs the enforcement of punitive damages. There is a substantial divergence of approaches under national law on this point. Punitive damages are well known in US law and have been criticised both within and outside the United States.[977] They are, however, not limited to the United States, as they are occasionally granted in other legal systems as well. They are considered contrary to the public policy of many States and as such not enforceable. In recent times, there is a growing positive attitude towards punitive damages. The approach in some Commonwealth States, such as Australia, and as recently adopted under the CML, is to allow for the severability of the non-compensatory part of the judgment. Some European States have followed suit.[978]

The Convention adopts the severance approach. Article 10(1) permits a court addressed to refuse the enforcement of a foreign judgment that awards damages that do not compensate for actual loss or harm suffered. Where the court addressed can determine the compensatory and the punitive part, then the compensatory part should be severed and enforced while the punitive part may be rejected. This approach is pragmatic and produces better results than cases where the whole judgment is deemed unenforceable.

---

[976] Garcimartín and Saumier (n 791) para 80.

[977] Ronald A Brand, 'Punitive Damages Revisited: Taking the Rationale for Non-Recognition of Foreign Judgments Too Far' (2005) 24 *Journal of Law and Commerce* 181.

[978] See Stefania Bariatti, Luigi Fumagalli and Zeno Crespi Reghizzi (eds), *Punitive Damages and Private International Law : State of the Art and Future Developments* (CEDAM 2019).

Article 10(2) governs costs and other expenses relating to the foreign proceedings. The same approach is maintained concerning costs. A court addressed is permitted to consider the extent to which the costs compensate for litigation expenses. Where the costs order is meant to punish the judgment debtor, then enforcement may be refused. Costs are often awarded to compensate parties for litigation expenses. The procedure for the award of costs differs from one legal system to the other. As such, a costs order is not punitive simply because a lower amount would have been ordered if the case were to be conducted in the court addressed.[979]

C. Forum Shopping, *Forum Non Conveniens* and *Lis Pendens*

The analysis of this Convention will not be complete without some comments on forum shopping, *forum non conveniens* and *lis pendens*. The earlier attempts at negotiating a mixed convention failed partly because of the difficulty in obtaining consensus on rules that will govern parallel litigation. This Convention does not, therefore, address conflicts of jurisdiction. The fact that it provides several alternative venues for the plaintiff implies that it is highly probable that litigation may proceed in different jurisdictions.

Pending such time as harmonisation will be feasible, litigants will have to make do with the solutions offered by national laws. The Convention confers jurisdiction mostly on courts that are closely linked to parties and disputes. These close connections suggest that in one way, the Convention has set some limit to parties' choice. Hopefully, national courts may give additional support to the Convention's modest solution by staying proceedings in favour of courts that are more connected to a dispute, even though such obligation is not required by the Convention. Having set guidelines for appropriate jurisdictional connections, the Convention then gives priority to a judgment that is first in time. Recognition and enforcement cannot be challenged except through the limited grounds specified under Article 7. Thus, *forum non conveniens* and *lis pendens* are not relevant at the recognition and enforcement stage.[980]

D. Relationship with Other International Instruments

Treaty conflicts are not unusual considering the multiplicity of international legal instruments available on specific subject matters. Some of these international instruments may conflict because some Member States may wish to extend or

---

[979] A recent decision of the Greek Supreme Court made this fine distinction. See Apostolos Anthimos, Mutual Trust v Public Policy: 1-0, *Conflict of Laws.net*, 6 November 2019, <http://conflictoflaws. net/2019/mutual-trust-v-public-policy-1-0/> accessed 12 November 2019.
[980] See Art 13(2) of the Convention.

limit the scope of application of existing treaties on the subject matter amongst themselves.[981] There are extant bilateral and multilateral treaties on foreign judgments. Recently, several court-to-court agreements have also been concluded. These international instruments can create incompatible obligations for the Contracting States of the Judgments Convention.

The basic international framework for resolving treaty conflicts is the 1969 Vienna Convention on the Law of Treaties (VCLT). Article 30 of that Convention provides that when a treaty specifies that it is subject to, or not to be incompatible with an earlier or later treaty, the provision of the other treaty prevails.[982] Also, when all parties to an earlier treaty are also parties to a later treaty and the earlier treaty is not terminated or suspended, the earlier treaty applies to the extent of its compatibility with the later treaty.[983]

The management of existing treaty arrangements on foreign judgments requires a more detailed approach. For instance, the EU is a party to some Hague conventions as an REIO. It has different mechanisms for jurisdiction and judgments amongst its Member States (eg Brussels Ia, and IIa). It also has a parallel convention with some members of the European Free Trade Association (ie the Lugano Convention). There are bound to be conflicts between the obligations imposed by the Hague conventions and those created under the intra-EU or Lugano schemes. There may also be potential conflicts when the litigants are resident in EU and non-EU States respectively.

The approach of the Convention is to forestall the occurrence of conflicts as much as practicable. The Convention uses four basic conflict management approaches: interpretation, subordination, disconnection and adaptation.[984] Article 23(1) requires that the statute should be interpreted in such a way as to make it compatible with other treaties in force between the Contracting States. This applies to treaties which came into force before or after the Judgments Convention. Just like Article 30 of the VCLT, Article 23(2) subjects the Judgment Convention to an earlier treaty in force between the Contracting States.

Article 23(3) and (4) govern situations where one or more Contracting States conclude a treaty after the Judgments Convention came into force. Contracting States are allowed to apply the later convention on issues concerning recognition and enforcement provided both parties are also Contracting States of the later convention. For instance, this clause will take care of conflicts that may emerge

---

[981] Surabhi Ranganathan, 'Responding to Deliberately Created Treaty Conflicts' in Christian J Tams, Antonios Tzanakopoulos and Andreas Zimmermann (eds), *Research Handbook on the Law of Treaties* (Edward Elgar 2014) 448–53.

[982] Art 30(2),

[983] Art 30(3).

[984] For a more extensive analysis on the four approaches, see European Parliament, 'The Hague Conference on Private International Law "Judgments Convention": Study' (April 2018), pp 19–21. The text is available at: https://www.europarl.europa.eu/RegData/etudes/STUD/2018/604954/IPOL_STU(2018)604954_EN.pdf (Accessed 10 February 2021).

from future intra-EU treaties. For the avoidance of doubt, the later EU treaty will apply provided the judgment in question is from another EU State. The same applies to bilateral or multilateral treaties among Contracting States. The only exception is if the judgment touches on Article 6 of the Judgments Convention (rights *in rem* in immovable property) and the other Contracting State is not a party to the later treaty.

The conflict management rules of the Convention are similar to those of the HCCA and other PIL conventions recently concluded by the Hague Conference.[985] No serious difficulty has been experienced so far from the application of extant conflict management rules. This can be attributed to the adopted approach, which seeks not to disturb existing treaty relations/obligations freely assumed by Contracting States. This approach does not strictly require other treaties entered into by Contracting States to promote or be consistent with the objectives of the Judgments Convention.[986] By way of illustration, the operation of Brussels Ia (and future recast) cannot be impeded by the EU's ratification of the HCCA and the Judgments Convention, provided the State of origin and the State addressed are both EU members. This is, of course, subject to the overriding provision of Article 6 of the Judgments Convention. This position is correctly stated by the English Court of Appeal in *Etihad Airways PJSC v Professor Dr Lucas Flother*[987] when considering the relationship between Brussels Ia and the HCCA whose provisions are similar to those of the Judgments Convention as follows:

> The effect of the [conflict management] provision, as I understand it and as Mr Joseph submitted, is that priority is afforded to the rules of Brussels Recast in any case where both parties are resident in Member States of the EU, but not where only one of the parties is so resident.[988]

The same applies to treaty obligations between the EU and third States (eg Lugano Convention) or bilateral and multilateral treaties concluded by Contracting States.

E. Procedural Matters

The position of the Convention is that procedural matters for recognition and enforcement of foreign judgments are to be governed by national laws.[989] This implies that litigants and their lawyers may still need to familiarise themselves with the recognition and enforcement procedures of their targeted State.

---

[985] See Art 26 of HCCA; Art 51 of the 2007 Convention on the International Recovery of Child Support and other Forms of Family Maintenance (Maintenance Convention); Art 39 of the 1993 Convention on Protection of Children and Co-Operation in respect of Intercountry Adoption.
[986] For instance see Art 51(2) of Maintenance Convention.
[987] *Etihad Airways PJSC v Professor Dr Lucas Flother* [2020] EWCA Civ 1707.
[988] Para 42.
[989] See Art 13.

In many civil law countries, foreign judgments must undergo a special procure for declaration of enforceability (*exequatur* proceeding) before foreign judgments can be enforced. In some legal systems, recognition and enforcement are automatic. The drafters of the Convention missed a great opportunity of harmonising enforcement rules or introducing a simple efficient mechanism that can be adopted by States. A good example is the use of Central Authorities to facilitate the issuance and transmissions of required documents for enforcement of foreign judgments. Besides, this arrangement may also be used for the enforcement of small claims or uncontested judgments. This will improve access to justice as it saves this category of litigants the cost of hiring lawyers for enforcement of judgments.

While the law of the State addressed governs recognition and enforcement procedures, the Convention (Article 12) recommends that the following documents must be produced by the judgment creditor:

a.   a complete and certified copy of the judgment;
b.   a document establishing that the originating processes were served on the judgments debtor (for default judgments);
c.   any document establishing that the judgment is enforceable in the State of origin;
d.   for judicial settlements, a certificate issued by the State of origin indicating that the judicial settlement is enforceable in the State of origin.

The Convention also recommends that an application for enforcement may be accompanied by a prescribed form to be published by the Hague Conference on Private International Law.

National laws will always require the judgment creditor to present the judgment or its certified true copy. So, the first document stated under Article 12 of the Convention should not be a problem. Items (c) and (d) are also not unusual. The problematic area may be the item (b), which requires judgment creditors to also exhibit a document indicating that the judgment debtor was served if the judgment was given in default of appearance or pleadings. For default judgments, the court of origin may not make specific reference to how the judgment debtor was served and, certainly from practical experience, it is doubtful whether any separate document or certificate on service of the judgment debtor will be issued. This underscores the need for some degree of harmonisation of the procedure for enforcement and the nature of documents to present. A practical illustration of this point is the Singaporean case of *Ermgassen & Co Limited v Sixcap Financials Pte Limited*,[990] which has already been discussed in Chapter six above.

As suggested in the Hartley and Dogauchi Report,[991] national courts should avoid excessive formalism in matters of procedure. This was the attitude adopted by the Singaporean court in the above-mentioned case where the judgment creditor

[990] [2018] SGHCR 8.
[991] Hartley and Dogauchi (ch 5, fn 442) 61.

failed to attach all the documents listed under Article 13 of the HCCA. Where a judgment creditor has placed sufficient documents from which the court addressed can verify the authenticity of the judgment and the requirements of Article 5 of the Convention (jurisdictional filters), the judgment should be enforced.

The last point of interest to litigants and practitioners on procedural matters is that security for costs or other deposits shall not be required from judgment creditors.[992] The statutory frameworks in most Commonwealth States empower a court addressed to require security for costs, even though this is rarely exercised. What is common is a situation where defendants ask for security for costs where the claimant is resident abroad and there is a likelihood that the defendant will not be able to enforce any judgment or costs awarded in that case against the claimant abroad.[993] Be that as it may, the Convention has altered the rule requiring a judgment creditor to pay the costs of his application. States are, however, permitted to declare that their courts shall not apply this provision.[994]

VII. Has the Convention Met the Practical Needs of Litigants?

The preceding sections examine the key provisions of the 2019 Judgments Convention, its pragmatism, and the extent to which the analysed provisions meet the pragmatic goals suggested in Chapter three of this book. Most commentators who have written on the Convention agree that it is a modest framework that will meet the practical needs of cross-border litigants to a large extent.[995] However, some scholars have also raised several issues concerning the effectiveness of the Convention. The criticisms are largely based on the limited scope and some provisions that could endanger uniform interpretation.[996]

The expectation of many is that the Convention should provide a simple framework like the 1958 New York Convention on the Recognition and Enforcement of Foreign Arbitral Awards with bright-line rules on indirect jurisdictional rules, recognition and enforcement. Admittedly, the ultimate goal of a global judgments enforcement framework is to provide simple, clear and predictable rules which cross-border litigants who are the end-users of the Convention can easily consult to make strategic decisions on venues that will guarantee a wider circulation of judgments. The reality of negotiating a global judgments convention indicates that

---

[992] Art 14(1).
[993] See *Pisante v Logothetis* [2020] EWHC 3332 (Comm); *Bestfort Developments LLP v Ras Al Khaimah Investment Authority* [2016] EWCA Civ 1099.
[994] Art 14(3).
[995] Kessedjian (n 896); Michael Wilderspin and Lenka Vysoka, 'The 2019 Hague Judgments Convention through European Lenses' [2020] 1 *Nederlands Internationaal Privaatrecht* 34.
[996] For instance, see Saumier (n 872) 65.

cross-border litigants may not get a simple framework that mirrors the New York Convention, due to the deep divergence in laws, States' interests and policies on judgments.

Admittedly, one area that may depreciate the effectiveness of the Convention is the lack of clarity in the way some of the jurisdictional filters are drafted; mechanisms such as declarations, and reservations which allow States to further limit or exclude the application of some provisions; and the permissibility of enforcement under national law in cases that may not meet the standards set by Article 5 (jurisdictional filters). While the policy behind that permissibility is to give maximum circulation to foreign judgments just as the same was allowed under the New York Convention, and to allow as many States as possible to join the Convention, the drawback is that it reduces the predictability which the Convention intends to offer cross-border litigants. As Saumier puts it, Article 15 and other mechanisms like reservations and declarations are 'necessary compromises inherent in the negotiation of international instruments.'[997]

VIII. Conclusion

The Hague Judgments Project has been one of the most arduous tasks embarked upon by the HCPIL. It has taken 27 years thus far, with two conventions successfully negotiated. The first fruit of the project, the HCCA, was finalised in 2005 and it became effective in 2015. The second fruit, the 2019 Judgments Convention was finalised in July 2019 and it secured its first signature on the same day. The HCPIL is currently promoting the Convention, intending to get States' ratification as soon as practicable. It organised the first global conference on the Judgments Convention in September 2019 in Hong Kong. An Experts' Group met in February 2020 to consider the feasibility of a convention on direct jurisdiction and conflicts of jurisdiction.[998]

The 2019 Judgments Convention was received with much enthusiasm from the delegates at the Conference, academics and practitioners as well. The cheers should not be surprising considering the accruable benefits to litigants and lawyers when the Convention becomes effective. Together with the HCCA, the two instruments will further enhance access to justice, legal certainty and predictability in international litigation. This is very essential because judgments enforcement law in many States is old-fashioned and inefficient.

The Convention is a modest framework, which is expected to solve many prevailing problems bedevilling international litigation. It meets the basic principles of a pragmatic global judgments enforcement framework. It prioritises party

---

[997] Saumier (n 872) 65.
[998] HCCH 'Third meeting of the Experts' Group on Jurisdiction' <https://www.hcch.net/en/news-archive/details/?varevent=720> accessed 15 May 2020.

autonomy, efficiency and justice. These formed the core philosophy of identifying sufficient connections between foreign courts and disputes. Where parties nominate a court, that court's judgment will freely circulate under either the HCCA or the Judgments Convention. The restriction placed on connections for consumer and employment contracts is essentially justice driven. On the other side of the spectrum, efficiency principles dictate the connections for other subject matters like contracts, torts, property, trust and so on. The cumulative effect is that the Convention should meet the practical needs of international litigants who have longed for such a simple, clear and predictable global framework to support their contracts and other civil engagements. It is also expected that the Convention should enjoy the support of States and wide ratification in the nearest future because it is flexible enough to accommodate States' interests and policies. This accounts for why there is a long list of exclusions from scope, restrictive international jurisdictional grounds and seemingly broadly drafted refusal grounds.

One of the perceived disadvantages of the Convention is that it appears to be largely pro-judgment creditors. It only guarantees the circulation of judgments which meet the conditions outlined under the Convention. It is reasonable to argue that judgment debtors can also benefit from the legal certainty provided by the jurisdictional grounds in Articles 5 and 6. However, there is more to that. A judgments debtor's Achilles' heel may lie in Article 15, which allows a judgment to be enforced if it meets the requirements under the national law of the receiving State, unless it is contrary to Article 6. While this is aimed at giving maximum circulation to judgments, it may be disadvantageous to judgment debtors who may not make an informed decision on how the national laws may affect them. However, this should not be exaggerated, as the Convention contains enough safeguards that ensure that improperly procured judgments are denied recognition.

8

Summary of Findings and Conclusion

I. Summary

Private international law has been transforming since the beginning of the twentieth century. This change has largely been felt only in the EU, US and Canada. The Westphalian system, which led to the emergence of modern European States, the codification of private law, and burgeoning cross-border trading activities, amongst other things, gave the impetus for the developments in Europe. The American conflict of laws revolution has also been attributed to the nature of the United States' federalism, the size of its population, the strength of its economy and the diversity of its legal policies. These factors challenged American scholars to articulate home-grown solutions to the peculiar American conflict of laws problems.

The responses from scholars and judges were fixated on the adoption of certain doctrinal bases to deal with the varieties of cross-border issues that came before the courts. Reciprocity was the famous approach adopted in most European States. This reflects the highly revered doctrines of territorial sovereignty and independence of States. The harsh realities observed from the application of reciprocity to the recognition and enforcement of foreign judgments consequently forced treaty relations among trading partners in the late nineteenth and early twentieth centuries. From this perspective, reciprocity has some utilitarian value. However, treaty relations are often established by only a few States. This will not help the case for the global judgments liberalisation agenda as no State is insignificant in modern times. Some of the developing countries which might have been considered unimportant in the nineteenth century are global players in cross-border trade and investments today. Also, the supposedly small offshore States are now international hubs for trust assets and tax havens for corporate and financial institutions. Judgments enforcement has, however, greatly improved at least for intra-EU judgments, since the establishment of the EU single market.

Comity was popularised by Huber, a Continental scholar, as an alternative doctrinal basis for cross-border legal cooperation. While this theory was developed in Europe, it was imported into the common law majorly by Lord Mansfield and Justice Joseph Story.[999] It became the most useful mechanism ever developed

---

[999] Paul (ch 2, fn 101) 17, 19–20.

and applied to entire branches of private international law. It has greatly mitigated the harshness of territoriality and assisted greatly in judgments recognition and enforcement in the Commonwealth and the United States.

While these doctrinal bases and others discussed in Chapter two have their merits and drawbacks, the major problem that has been observed over the years is that national courts have held on to one theory or the other as the basis for the recognition of foreign judgments. While these theories might have seemed to work fine in the past centuries, they are not well equipped to deal with the numerous challenges which are being experienced by cross-border litigants today. The inability to adapt these theories to new challenges, or the upholding of a theory regardless of whether it is solving practical problems, necessitated the need for a paradigm shift; shopping for alternative approaches to the enforcement of foreign judgments.

This book considers the practical problems faced by both judgment creditors and debtors in the course of enforcing or challenging foreign judgments. These challenges are rife in all legal systems, from the supposedly liberal regimes to the more restrictive ones where foreign judgments are hardly enforced. It is argued that these myriad problems cannot be solved by various unilateral, and in some cases parochial, approaches. The solution does not exclusively lie in any single theoretical basis. Rather, what is needed is a functional approach which investigates practical problems and develops solutions that are tailored towards solving those problems.

Legal pragmatism fits into the functional approach that has been described above. Pragmatism has its roots in philosophy and has been applied to other branches of knowledge, including law in different shades. In the field of private international law, it is conspicuously absent in most legal English texts except for *Anton's Private International Law*,[1000] at least in the Commonwealth, which has considered it as a theoretical tool for private international law discourse. The first major task in this research was to consider the concept of pragmatism not only in philosophy but also in the legal field, particularly, private international law.

Legal pragmatism can be described as a concept that seeks to solve live legal problems with solutions that produce maximum valuable results. The next stage of the inquiry was geared towards identifying the pragmatic tools that can be used to investigate practical problems and measurement of results. Having an idea of the real problems gives the policy-makers a clear picture of the substantive goals to be pursued and the most efficient methods that can deliver those goals. The substantive goals keep the policy-makers on track in their search for solutions. This is imperative so that pragmatism does not become an 'anyhow' method of solving problems.

[1000] Paul Beaumont and Peter McEleavy (eds), *Anton's Private International Law* (3rd edn, W Green 2011).

The analysis of case law from different jurisdictions reveals that litigants are unable to make informed choices at the litigation or pre-litigation stages due to the divergent approaches of States to foreign judgments; both litigants and States waste scarce resources in re-litigating matters already decided in another forum and judgment creditors are unable to enforce judgments at all in some cases. Thus, it is suggested that the substantive goals of a typical judgments enforcement framework include justice, efficiency, parties' reasonable expectations, legal certainty and predictability. These broadly represent the parameters that can be used to evaluate the utility of the proposed framework. The pragmatic theory rejects a one-size-fits-all approach to solving legal problems. Thus, in designing a judgments scheme, policy-makers should mix and match ideas and concepts that have a bearing on the suggested goals to form unique solutions that are valuable and practical in nature.

This book demonstrates how the concept of pragmatism can be applied by judges, and national and international legislators, respectively. For these categories of actors, different considerations apply. Multilateralism is the best method of dealing with global problems like the diversity of laws and policies in cross-border litigation and enforcement of foreign judgments. This was used to advance support for the work of the Hague Conference as the best platform to deliver on the harmonisation of the divergent judgments enforcement laws. The 2019 Judgments Convention was analysed to see the extent to which it delivers on the pragmatic goals that have been earlier mentioned. The CML was used to illustrate what a pragmatic judgments framework should entail for a very significant group of countries, using the same parameters earlier highlighted. Lastly, the book also demonstrates how judicial pragmatism may be actualised within the limited scope permitted by law.

II. Conclusion

Pragmatism has a role to play at any level of rule or decision-making. The hallmark of the theory remains that law is a tool for social engineering and, as such, there is the need to constantly examine the law to ensure that it addresses live problems. Generally, the task is best suited for the legislators, who have adequate resources and time to carry out a critical examination of the challenges at hand and come up with solutions that best fit the problems. Pending such time as these legislative interventions come on board, the judges should be able to tweak the law as and when necessary to respond to societal needs.

In the absence of a robust legislative framework, judicial pragmatism is welcomed provided it is aimed at meeting the ends of justice, parties' reasonable expectations, efficiency, and judicial economy. The common law courts have been widely acknowledged to be pragmatic in their approach to legal issues in general. When most legal systems were unreceptive to foreign judgments, they formulated an action on a judgment debt as a functional way of bypassing the harsh effects of the concept of territoriality and reciprocity. They developed several equitable reliefs to support cross-border litigation. *Mareva* injunctions, *Chabra* injunctions,[1001] anti-suit injunctions and remedies for the breach of choice of court agreements are examples of pragmatic tools that give the common law courts an edge over their counterparts in the civil law systems. Perhaps many developments were not seen in the area of foreign judgments partly because of the codification that visited this area of law and the Europeanisation of English private international law in general. It is not surprising why some other Commonwealth States, such as Canada, have parted ways significantly from the traditional common law of judgments recognition and enforcement.

The Canadian experience informs the need for a cautious approach to the use of judicial pragmatism because it may become a threat to legal certainty and predictability. Thus, the book recommends that a robust statutory framework should be a top priority. National legislators need to step in through law reforms. They should endeavour to intervene at the right time in order not to create a void, which has been the exact experience with the Commonwealth extant statutory schemes. They can get direct feedback from various stakeholders like litigants, lawyers, and judges on the practicality of the extant laws, and then propose amendments as and when necessary. Judicial pragmatism should be restricted to statutory interpretation and the formulation of efficient procedural rules which advance the substantive rights entrenched in statutory frameworks. In this limited role, they should be guided by judicial empiricism and comparative inquiry. These two tools will enable them to evaluate the functionality of their rules and those being developed elsewhere, and they can interpret national, and more importantly, multinational frameworks to create an international harmony of judgments enforcement rules.

The 2017 Commonwealth Model Law represents a modest attempt at modernising the outdated judgments enforcement laws in the Commonwealth. It is cheering to see that the Member States are gradually embracing legal pragmatism. This has been demonstrated through the methodology adopted by the drafters and the content of the law. As analysed in Chapter four of this book, the law is a significant improvement when compared with the extant statutory schemes that apply in most Commonwealth States. The adoption of several jurisdictional bases which hitherto were not available will greatly address the problem of international jurisdiction, which has been a major stumbling block to the recognition of foreign judgments. The move to remove reciprocity by extending the simple registration process to all foreign judgments will also boost the global judgments liberalisation agenda.

While the modest framework is highly commendable and good enough to ensure access to practical justice, the drafters could have done more in the area

---

[1001] *TSB Private Bank International SA v Chabra* [1992] 1 WLR 231. A *Chabra* injunction is an injunction affecting a third party who holds assets beneficially for a defendant.

of legal certainty and predictability, which are major goals of every judgments recognition framework. Most grounds for international jurisdiction are drafted in a simple and broad form which may make them be applied too flexibly. This may be a legitimate concern considering the orientation of a typical common law judge. A nuanced approach, with explanations of certain concepts, can produce a better result than the current draft. Perhaps the courts can fill this gap through comparative law inquiry. While the English courts and their decisions will have greater impacts in the Commonwealth, the courts should be open to the solutions developed elsewhere, within and outside the Commonwealth, and in particular, the Hague instruments. Litigants will gain more when the national laws are interpreted in such a way that they work in harmony with the global Judgments Convention, at least in areas where the provisions have the same substance.

The next task for the Commonwealth is the implementation of the model law. Pragmatism does not end with the enactment of fine laws; the goal is to get them to become effective so that they become usable by litigants to solve the myriad problems facing international litigation and judgments enforcement. The Commonwealth has several platforms for continuous engagement with legal developments within the bloc. The Law Ministers now meet bi-annually to examine the latest developments in different legal fields within and beyond the Commonwealth. Having adopted the model law in 2017, one would expect that it should have formed part of the agenda for the 2019 meeting and reports should have been laid concerning how Members intend to implement this important piece of legislation. Unfortunately, the Commonwealth Senior Officials of Law Ministries meeting, which was held in October 2018 to prepare the agenda for the 2019 Law Ministers' meeting, failed to include the model law on the agenda.[1002] In effect, nothing may be heard of the model law anytime soon. In a related development, Singapore amended its judgments enforcement statute in October 2019 without considering the model law.[1003] Although this statute made some improvements, mainly in the area of the enforcement of non-money judgments, none of the new jurisdictional grounds introduced in the model law were considered in the amended Act. Also, the reciprocity requirement which the Member States agreed to remove was retained.[1004] One can safely conclude that the model law was not considered. The Commonwealth Secretariat needs to adopt the approach of the Hague Conference by promoting the new law amongst its Members. It should make it a major agenda item in subsequent Law Ministers' Meetings and carry out some soft diplomacy to stimulate the political will needed to implement the law. Without these conscious efforts, Commonwealth States may pay little or no attention to the law. The extant schemes were successfully implemented throughout

---

[1002] 'Senior Officials Report "Good Progress" Ahead of 2019 Law Ministers' Meeting' (*The Commonweath*, 5 October 2018) <https://thecommonwealth.org/media/news/senior-officials-report-"good-progress"-ahead-2019-law-ministers'-meeting> accessed 29 October 2019.
[1003] See Reciprocal Enforcement of Foreign Judgments (Amendment) Act 2019.
[1004] Reciprocal Enforcement of Foreign Judgments Act (chapter 265) (Revised Edition 2001), s 3.

the Commonwealth due to Britain's influence in her colonies or as direct legislation. Unfortunately, that influence rarely exists today. It may well be that after Brexit, the United Kingdom will provide more leadership in the Commonwealth and in giving effect to the model law.

Beyond the national schemes, the 2019 Judgments Convention and the HCCA are two key international instruments that can potentially deliver global judgments liberalisation. They provide a harmonised and simple scheme, which largely agrees with the law and policy of most legal systems. The Hague Conference Permanent Bureau is commended for a good job in promoting the Conventions, as it recently jointly organised a global conference on the 2019 Judgments Convention in Hong Kong.[1005]

This book focuses on the Commonwealth and the Hague Conference because of the influence of the latter on the former and the potential impact that the former can have on the latter. The Commonwealth has been following the activities of the Hague Conference, and reports are often presented at its Law Ministers' meetings. The successive negotiations at The Hague inspired the Commonwealth framework. This explains why the model law is very similar to the Judgments Convention both in structure and content, except that some of the grounds in the model law, such as submission and counterclaims, are broader than those of the Convention.

The Commonwealth is a global player considering its status, size and geographical spread. At present, it has 54 Member States. The Association needs to deepen its relationship with the Hague Conference by urging its members to join the Conference and its conventions. The success of the HCCA and the Judgments Convention lies in their widest possible ratification. These conventions will certainly grow faster if the Commonwealth shows more attention to The Hague's works. Of the 54 Member States, only 13 are members of the Hague Conference.[1006] Also, the HCCA is ratified by only four Commonwealth States: United Kingdom, Cyprus, Malta, and Singapore. There is undoubtedly a need for deeper and more meaningful cooperation between the two bodies to yield better results for the Hague conventions on time.

The HCCA and the Judgments Convention will have a greater impact in the Commonwealth. The conventions cover jurisdictional grounds for exclusive choice of court agreements, non-money judgments, private anti-trust claims, tenancies, consumer contracts, general contracts and torts all of which are not available under the 1922 and 1933 schemes. While many of these grounds are available under the new model law, joining the Hague conventions will, nevertheless, allow Commonwealth judgments to freely circulate in major civil law

---

[1005] See 'Inaugural Global Conference on the 2019 HCCH Convention on the Recognition and Enforcement of Foreign Judgments in Civil or Commercial Matters', 9 September 2019. The conference was Jointly organised by the HCCH and the Department of Justice of the Government of the Hong Kong, Special Administrative Region of the People's Republic of China.

[1006] They are Australia, Canada, Cyprus, India, Malaysia, Mauritius, Malta, New Zealand, Sri Lanka, South Africa, Singapore, United Kingdom and Zambia.

jurisdictions, notably the EU Member States, which will hopefully ratify the Judgments Convention in no distant time. In addition, having removed reciprocity from its new model law, joining the Hague Judgments Convention is the only guarantee for favourable treatment of Commonwealth judgments abroad. This is a smart move that will reward the proposed extension of the statutory scheme to all foreign judgments.

The Commonwealth Trade Ministers met in October 2019 to discuss ways of boosting intra-Commonwealth trade.[1007] The meeting resolved to continue its push for global free trade, and the removal of protectionist policies amongst other things. One way the Commonwealth can demonstrate its commitment to global free trade and removal of trade barriers is to push for the ratification of the two Hague conventions by all its Member States. First, these conventions are essential for the development of free trade. This book has demonstrated in previous chapters the role of private international law in the promotion of global trade. Restrictive and inefficient judgments enforcement schemes and general uncertainties surrounding dispute resolution increase transaction risks which have negative effects on the cost of doing business. Therefore, the teeming SMEs and multinational businesses in the Commonwealth have a lot to gain from the two Hague conventions. Second, not joining the conventions is counterproductive for the Commonwealth States as the bloc will be left behind in the global scheme of things. Litigators will be attracted to fora whose judgments have a global reach. It will affect the development of their judiciaries because complex and high-value cases will be moved elsewhere. The effect will cascade down to the availability of business for the local bar, and other sectors supporting international commercial litigation.

The above-highlighted gains apply to other States as well. Beyond the Commonwealth, the majority of States are civil law jurisdictions or those whose legal systems have been significantly influenced by civil law. The leading economies amongst these States, like China, Russia, Japan, have witnessed increasing requests for the enforcement of judgments from their courts abroad and vice versa. Several other States have recently relaxed their reciprocity requirements or abolished them completely. For instance, China recently adopted a presumptive reciprocity understanding in the Nanning Statement of June 2017. With the growing global liberalisation, the net gain to be made by States is that their judgments will be favourably treated in all Contracting States. There is little or no cost that the ratification of or accession to the Hague conventions attracts since they are minimum harmonisation instruments and do not inhibit the development of national laws.

Regional Economic Integration Organisations (REIOs) such as the EU, likewise, have much to gain from ratifying the Judgments Convention. The EU has the

---

[1007] UK Department for International Trade, 'Commonwealth Trade Ministers: Reform WTO and Resist Protectionism' (*Press release*, 2019) <https://www.gov.uk/government/news/commonwealth-trade-ministers-reform-wto-and-resist-protectionism> accessed 29 October 2019.

competence to join the Convention on behalf of its Member States. As a union of 27 Member States, the EU is a major player at the Hague Conference and a major destination for both international litigation and enforcement of foreign judgments. The HCCA did not come into force until it was ratified by the EU. Therefore, the EU's decision on ratifying the Judgments Convention might likely determine how soon the Convention will become effective. An EU Parliament commissioned study on the Judgments Convention expressed a pessimistic view on the desirability of the EU's ratification.[1008] The learned authors are of the considered view that the Convention's scope is limited and that it will add another layer of complexity to the EU judgments framework.[1009] We respectfully disagree with them. The EU negotiators had taken care of possible negative impacts the Convention might have in the EU. Largely, the text of the Convention is inspired by Brussels Ia and, overall, the Convention is closer to Brussels Ia than any other national law or bilateral treaty. The Convention can fill the current vacuum which exists in Brussels Ia concerning judgments from non-EU States. Thus, it will provide legal certainty and predictability for both EU and non-EU litigants, and will enhance the circulation of EU judgments abroad. It has a good conflict management provision which ensures that the operation of the Convention does not disturb any bilateral or regional judgments treaties already existing or to be agreed upon in the future by the Contracting Parties subject to the mandatory observance of Article 6 of the Judgments Convention.[1010] With this approach, it is less likely that there will be any clash between the Convention and Brussels Ia.

III.   Contributions to Knowledge and Avenues for Further Research

This book has made three key contributions to knowledge. First, it has significantly expanded the understanding of the theory of pragmatism in private international law and how it applies to recognition and enforcement of foreign judgments. It has developed a pragmatic model that can be adopted in modernising national, bilateral and multilateral judgments frameworks. Second, since the CML was finalised in 2017, no critical evaluation has been carried out on the law. This book is the first systemic analysis of the model law from a pragmatic perspective. Third, the book is also one of the first systemic analyses of the 2019 Judgments Convention, highlighting the pragmatism in the making of the Convention, the utilities of the text, and the extent of its convergence and divergence from the Commonwealth and Brussels frameworks.

[1008] See European Parliament (ch 7, fn 984).
[1009] Ibid, 38.
[1010] Art 23, 2019 Judgments Convention.

The Hague Judgments Project is still a work in progress. Two conventions have been delivered while the Council has given the nod for the meeting of an Experts' Group in February 2020 to consider the desirability or otherwise for a convention on direct jurisdiction and conflicts of jurisdiction. The Judgments Convention also excludes some important subject matters, especially intellectual property judgments. The Hague Conference has not given up on intellectual property judgments. It recently published 'When Private International Law meets Intellectual Property Law – A Guide for Judges'[1011] in conjunction with the World Intellectual Property Organization on the intersection between private international law and intellectual property. The growing importance of the subject matter will continue to stimulate academic debates. Thus, there is a need to monitor the developments in these areas under national laws and the activities of the Hague Conference. It will be worthwhile to examine how the pragmatic theory of international law can help in these undertakings, especially the future works on direct jurisdiction of courts.

The Judgments Convention and the HCCA are the first multilateral instruments to be delivered by the Hague Judgments Project. Concerns have been raised on how uniform interpretations can be achieved since that is the only way that the Conventions can deliver maximum benefits to both litigants and their advisers. There is a need to continuously monitor national courts' engagements with the Conventions and to observe the extent to which they meet or deviate from the consensus reached at the Diplomatic Conference and the views expressed in the Explanatory Reports. This and other ongoing works of the Hague Conference are areas that are to be further researched.

Lastly, this book emphasises the place of empiricism in the development of private international law. Having highlighted the broad goals and objectives of the two Conventions and the Commonwealth model law, there is a need for more studies on how these latest frameworks impact cross-border trades and international commercial litigation. These studies will determine whether the new frameworks are meeting practical needs and the key indicators to measure their success or otherwise. Empiricism has a greater role to play in the discoveries.

[1011] Annabelle Bennett and Sam Granata, *When Private International Law Meets Intellectual Property Law: A Guide for Judges* (The Hague: Hague Conference on Private International Law; World Intellectual Property Organization 2019).

BIBLIOGRAPHY

Andrews J and Allin C, 'Developments in Freezing Foreign Assets' (2015) 2 *Journal of International Banking and Financial Law* 111

Ahmed M and Beaumont P, 'Exclusive Choice of Court Agreements: Some Issues on the Hague Convention on Choice of Court Agreements and Its Relationship with the Brussels I Recast Especially Anti-Suit Injunctions, Concurrent Proceedings and the Implications of BREXIT' (2017) 13 *Journal of Private International Law*

Alexander JG and Phillimore GG, 'Preface' (1873) 1 *International Law Association Reports of Conferences* iii

Allsop, Justice James, 'Comity and Commerce' (FCA) [2015] *Federal Judicial Scholarship* 27 <http://www.austlii.edu.au/au/journals/FedJSchol/2015/27.html> accessed 4 July 2017

Almeder R, 'A Definition of Pragmatism' (1986) 3 *History of Philosophy Quarterly* 79

ALRUD Law Firm, 'Enforcement of Foreign Court Judgments in Russia: A Wind of Change' (2017) <http://www.alrud.com/upload/iblock/dc5/Newsletter_recognition and enforcement.pdf> accessed 29 November 2017

American Bar Association, 'Hague Choice of Court Agreement: Recommendation' (2006) <https://www.americanbar.org/content/dam/aba/migrated/intlaw/policy/investment/hcca0806.pdf> accessed 24 June 2019

Amram PW, 'Uniform Legislation as an Effective Alternative to the Treaty Technique' (1960) 54 *Proceedings of the American Society of International Law at its Annual Meeting* (1921–1969), 62

——, 'Report on the Eleventh Session of the Hague Conference on Private International Law' (1969) 63 *The American Journal of International Law* 521

Anderson K and Davis J, 'Annual Survey of Recent Developments in Australian Private International Law 2000–2003' (2005) 24 *Australian Year Book of International Law* 443

Anthimos A, 'Mutual Trust v Public Policy: 1-0', *Conflict of Laws.net*, 6 November 2019, <http://conflictoflaws.net/2019/mutual-trust-v-public-policy-1-0/>

Antonov M, 'Foreign Court Decisions, Arbitral Awards and Sovereignty in Russia' (2013) 38 *Review of Central and European Law* 317

Arzandeh A, 'The English Court's Service-Out Jurisdiction in International Tortious Disputes' (2017) 133 *Law Quarterly Review* 144

Asensio PADM, 'Recognition and Enforcement of Judgments in Intellectual Property Litigation: The CLIP Principles' in J Basedow, T Kono and A Metzger (eds), *Intellectual Property in the Global Arena-Jurisdiction, Applicable Law and The Recognitions of Judgements in Europa, Japan and the US* (Mohr Siebeck 2010)

Aslett P, 'Cross-Border Asset Protection: An Offshore Perspective' (2003) 10 *Journal of Financial Crime* 229

Association for Reform & Codification of the Law of Nations, 'Seventh Annual Conference' (1879) 7 *Association for Reform & Codification of the Law of Nations Reports of Conferences* 1

Association for Reform & Codification of the Law of Nations, 'Foreign Judgment' (1880) 8 *Association for Reform & Codification of the Law of Nations Reports of Conferences* 175

Atiyah PS, *Pragmatism and Theory in English Law* (Stevens & Sons 1987)

Baldwin SE, 'The Comparative Results, in the Advancement of Private International Law, of the Montevideo Congress of 1888–9 and the Hague Conferences of 1893, 1894, 1900, and 1904' (1905) 2 *Proceedings of the American Political Science Association* 73

Banerji A, 'The Commonwealth of Nations: A Force for Democracy in the 21st Century?' (2009) 97 *The Round Table* 813

Bariatti S, Fumagalli L and Crespi Reghizzi Z (eds), *Punitive Damages and Private International Law: State of the Art and Future Developments* (CEDAM 2019)

Barnett PR, *Res Judicata, Estoppel, and Foreign Judgments: The Preclusive Effects of Foreign Judgments in Private International Law* (Oxford University Press 2001)

Basedow J, 'Methods of Private International Law' in J Basedow and others (eds), *Encyclopedia of Private International Law* (Edward Elgar Publishing 2017)

Baudenbacher C, 'Judicial Globalization: New Development or Old Wine in New Bottles?' (2003) 38 *Texas International Law Journal* 505

Baumgartner SP, 'How Well Do U.S. Judgments Fare in Europe ?' (2007) 40 *George Washington International Law Review* 173

——, *The Proposed Hague Convention on Jurisdiction and Foreign Judgments: Trans-Atlantic Law Making for Transnational Litigation* (Mohr Siebeck 2003)

——, 'Understanding the Obstacles to the Recognition and Enforcement of U.S. Judgments Abroad' (2013) 44 *New York University Journal of International Law and Politics* 965

Beaumont P, 'Hague Choice of Court Agreements Convention 2005: Background, Negotiations, Analysis and Current Status' (2009) 5 *Journal of Private International Law* 125

——, 'The Revived Judgments Project in The Hague' (2014) 4 *Nederlands Internationaal Privaatrecht* 532

—— (eds), *Cross-Border Litigation in Europe* (Hart Publishing 2017)

——, 'A United Kingdom Perspective On the Proposed Hague Judgments Convention' (1998) 24 *Brooklyn Journal of International Law* 75

——, 'The Brussels Convention Becomes a Regulation: Implications for Legal Basis, External Competence and Contract Jurisdiction' in James Fawcett (ed), *Reform and Development of Private International Law: Essays in Honour of Sir Peter North* (OUP 2002)

——, 'Reflections on the Relevance of Public International Law to Private International Law Treaty Making', *Collected Courses of The Hague Academy of International Law – Recueil des cours* (M Nijhoff 2010)

——, 'Judgments Convention: Application to Governments' (2020) 67 *Netherlands International Law Review* 121

Beaumont P and McEleavy P, *Anton's Private International Law* (3rd edn, W Green/Thomson Reuters 2011)

Beaumont P and Walker L, 'Recognition and Enforcement of Judgments in Civil and Commercial Matters in the Brussels I Recast and Some Lessons from It and the Recent Hague Conventions for the Hague Judgments Project' (2015) 11 *Journal of Private International Law* 31

Beaumont P and Danov M, 'Introduction: Research Aims and Methodology' in P Beaumont, M Danov, K Trimmings and B Yuksel (eds), *Cross-Border Litigation in Europe* (Hart Publishing 2017)

Beaumont P and Yuksel B, 'Cross-Border Civil and Commercial Disputes Before the Court of Justice of the European Union' in P Beaumont and others (eds), *Cross-Border Litigation in Europe* (Hart Publishing 2017)

Beck U, *The Cosmopolitan*, vol 24 (OUP 2015)

Beckers P, 'German Court Takes First Step on Road to Mutual Recognition with China' (*International Law Office Newsletter*, 2007)

Bennett D, 'The Hague Convention on Recognition and Enforcement of Foreign Judgments – A Failure of Characterisation' in T Einhorn and K Siehr (eds), *Intercontinental Cooperation Through Private International Law: Essays in Memory of Peter E. Nygh* (TMC Asser Press 2004)

Bennett A and Granata S, *When Private International Law Meets Intellectual Property Law: A Guide for Judges* (Hague Conference on Private International Law; World Intellectual Property Organization 2019)

Bentham J, *Introduction to the Principles of Morals and Legislation (Collected Works of Jeremy Bentham)*, JH Burns and HLA Hart (eds) (Oxford University Press 2000)

Berman PS, 'The Globalization of Jurisdiction' (2002) 151 *University of Pennsylvania Law Review* 311

Bernhardt R, *Encyclopedia of Public International Law: History of International Law, Foundations and Principles of International Law, Sources of International Law, Law of Treaties* (1984)

Black V, 'Enforcement of Foreign Non-Money Judgments: *Pro Swing v. ELTA*' (2005) 42 *Canadian Business Law Journal* 81

Bleimaier JK, 'The Doctrine of Comity in Private International Law' (1978) 24 *Catholic Lawyer* 327

Borchers PJ, 'A Few Little Issues for the Hague Judgments Negotiations' (1998) 24 *Brooklyn Journal of International Law* 157

——, 'The Problem with General Jurisdiction' [2001] *University of Chicago Legal Forum* 119

Bradford A and Ben-Shahar O, 'Efficient Enforcement in International Law' (2012) 12 *Chicago Journal of International Law* 375

Brand RA, 'Transaction Planning Using Rules on Jurisdiction and the Recognition and Enforcement of Judgments' (2014) 62 *Netherlands International Law Review* 485

——, 'Recognition of Foreign Judgments as a Trade Law Issue: The Economics of Private International Law' in JS Bhandari et al (eds), *Economic Dimensions in International Law* (Cambridge University Press 1997)

——, 'Due Process, Jurisdiction and a Hague Judgments Convention' (1999) 60 *University of Pittsburgh Law Review* 661

——, 'Community Competence for Matters of Judicial Cooperation at the Hague Conference on Private International Law: A View from the United States' (2002) 21 *Journal of Law and Commerce* 191

——, 'Punitive Damages Revisited: Taking the Rationale for Non-Recognition of Foreigh Judgments Too Far' (2005) 24 *Journal of Law and Commerce* 181

——, 'Withdrawn: Federal Judicial Center International Litigation Guide: Recognition and Enforcement of Foreign Judgments' (2014) 74 *University of Pittsburgh Law Review*

——, 'New Challenges in the Recognition and Enforcement of Judgments' (2018) *University of Pittsburgh Legal Studies Research Paper No 2018–29*

——, 'The Circulation of Judgments Under the Draft Hague Judgments Convention' (2019) *Working Paper No 2019-02*

Brand RA and Herrup P, *The 2005 Hague Convention on Choice of Court Agreements: Commentary and Documents* (Cambridge University Press 2008)

Brand RA and Jablonski SR, *Forum Non Conveniens: History, Global Practice, and Future under the Hague Convention on Choice of Court Agreements* (Oxford University Press 2007)

Briggs A, 'Crossing the River by Feeling the Stones: Rethinking the Law on Foreign Judgments' (2004) 8 *Singapore Year Book of International Law* 1

——, 'Distinctive Aspects of the Conflict of Laws in Common Law System: Autonomy and Agreement in the Conflict of Laws' (2005) 57 *The Doshisha Law Review* 21

——, 'Recogntion of Foreign Judgments: A Matter of Obligation' (2013) 129 *Law Quarterly Review* 87

——, *The Conflict of Laws* (Oxford University Press 2013)

——, 'The Principle of Comity in Private International Law', *Hague Academy of International Law: Recueil des cours* vol 354 (Martinus Nijhoff 2011)

Brownbill D, 'The Role of Offshore Jurisdictions in the Development of the International Trust' (1999) 32 *Vanderbilt Journal of Transnational Law* 953

Brownlie I, *Principles of Public International Law* (7th edn, Oxford University Press 2008)

——, *Foreign Relations Law* (Cambridge University Press 2014)

Carmody C, 'Obligations versus Rights: Substantive Difference between WTO and International Investment Law' (2017) 12 *Asian Journal of WTO and International Health Law and Policy* 75

Castel J-G, 'Canada and the Hague Conference on Private International Law: 1893–1967' (1967) 1 *Canadian Bar Review* 1

——, 'Recognition and Enforcement of Foreign Judgments in Personam and in Rem in the Common Law Provinces of Canada' (1971) 17 *McGill Law Journal* 11

——, 'The Uncertainty Factor in Canadian Private International Law' (2007) 52 *McGill Law Journal* 555

Cavers D, *The Choice-of-Law Process* (University of Michigan Press 1965)

Cebula RJ, 'A Critique of the Evidence' (1979) 47 *Harvard Law Review* 173

Chao CC and Neuhoff CS, 'Enforcement and Recognition of Foreign Judgments in United States Courts: A Practical Perspective' (2002) 29 *Pepperdine Law Review* 147

Childress III DE, 'Comity As Conflict: Resituating International Comity As Conflict of Laws' (2010) 44 *UC Davis Law Review* 11

Chong S, 'Cross-Border Dispute Resolution: Innovations From Singapore', *2nd China-ASEAN Justice Forum* (8 June 2017)

——, 'Singapore International Commercial Court: A New Opening in a Forked Path' (Speech delivered by Justice Steven Chong at the British Maritime Law Association Lecture and Dinner in London, 15 October 2015)

Clermont KM, 'Limiting the Last-in-Time Rule for Judgments' (2017) 36 *Review of Litigation* 1

——, 'Res Judicata as Requisite for Justice' (2016) 68 *Rutgers University Law Review* 1067

Coffey DK, 'The Right to Shoot Himself': Secession in the British Commonwealth of Nations' (2018) 39 *The Journal of Legal History* 117

Cohen MR and Cohen FS, *Readings in Jurisprudence and Legal Philosophy* (Beard Books 1951)

Collins L, *Essays in International Litigation and the Conflict of Laws* (OUP 1996)

——, 'Professor Lowenfeld and the Enforcement of Foreign Public Law' (2009) 42 *International Law and Politics* 125

——, 'The Territorial Reach of Mareva Injunctions' (1989) 105 *Law Quarterly Review* 262

——, 'Comity in Modern Private International Law' in J Fawcett (ed), *Reform and Development of Private International Law: Essays in Honour of Sir Peter North* (Oxford University Press 2002)

Collins S, 'The Last Frontier: Enforcing Foreign Judgments against Offshore Trusts after Pattni v Ali' (2009) 15 *Trusts & Trustees* 18

Commonwealth Secretariat, 'Charter of the Commonwealth' <http://thecommonwealth.org/sites/default/files/page/documents/CharteroftheCommonwealth.pdf> accessed 10 October 2018

——, 'Singapore Declaration of Commonwealth Principles 1971' <http://thecommonwealth.org/sites/default/files/history-items/documents/Singapore Declaration.pdf> accessed 26 February 2019

——, *Recognition and Enforcement of Judgments and Orders and the Service of Process within the Commonwealth: A Report of a Working Meeting Held at Apia, Western Samoa, 18–23 April 1979* (Commonwealth Secretariat 1979)

——, 'Recognition and Enforcement of Judgments and Orders and the Service of Process within the Commonwealth – Multiple Damages Judgments: LMM(80)24', *1980 Meeting of Commonwealth Law Ministers: Barbados, 28 April–2 May 1980: Memoranda* (Commonwealth Secretariat 1980)

——, *2005 Meeting of Commonwealth Law Ministers and Senior Officials Accra, Ghana, 17–20 October 2005* (Commonwealth Secretariat 2006)

——, 'Commonwealth Practice in the Recognition of Foreign Judgments' (2009) 35 *Commonwealth Law Bulletin* 345

——, 'Meeting of Commonwealth Law Ministers and Senior Officials' (5–8 May 2014, Gaborone, Botswana) <http://thecommonwealth.org/sites/default/files/inline/Commonwealth_Law_Ministers_Meeting_2014_Communique.pdf> accessed 6 December 2018

——, 'Small States and the Commonwealth: Strengthening Resilience for Sustainable Development' (2014) <http://thecommonwealth.org/sites/default/files/events/documents/P743_commonwealth_smallstates_150814_FINAL_CE_ammend.pdf> accessed 22 February 2019

——, *Commonwealth Secretariat Strategic Plan: 2017/18–2020/21* (Commonwealth Secretariat 2017)

——, 'Improving the Recognition of Foreign Judgments: Model Law on the Recognition and Enforcement of Foreign Judgments' (2017) 43 *Commonwealth Law Bulletin* 545

——, 'Meeting of Commonwealth Law Ministers and Senior Officials: Outcome Statement' (2017) <http://thecommonwealth.org/sites/default/files/inline/CLMM2017OutcomeStatement.pdf> accessed 3 November 2018

——, 'Praise for Commonwealth's New "momentous" Justice Reform Office' (*News*, 2017) <http://thecommonwealth.org/media/news/praise-commonwealths-new-momentous-justice-reform-office> accessed 8 November 2018

——, 'Declaration on the Commonwealth Connectivity Agenda for Trade and Investment' (2018) <http://thecommonwealth.org/sites/default/files/inline/DeclarationontheCommonwealth ConnectivityAgendaforTradeandInvestment_0.pdf> accessed 10 October 2018

——, 'Model Law on the Recognition and Enforcement of Foreign Judgments' (2018) <http://thecommonwealth.org/sites/default/files/key_reform_pdfs/D16227_1_GPD_ROL_Model_Law_Rec_Enf_Foreign_Judgements.pdf> accessed 7 November 2018

——, 'Senior Officials Report "Good Progress" Ahead of 2019 Law Ministers' Meeting |' (2018) <https://thecommonwealth.org/media/news/senior-officials-report-"good-progress"-ahead-2019-law-ministers'-meeting> accessed 29 October 2019

——, 'Meeting of Commonwealth Law Ministers, Edinburgh, 7–10 July 2008: Communiqué To' (2009) 35 *Commonwealth Law Bulletin* 85

——, *Commonwealth Trade Review 2018: Strengthening the Commonwealth Advantage* (The Commonwealth Secretariat 2018)

——, 'Maldives Becomes 54th Member of Commonwealth Family'

Constable C, 'International Marriage Brokers, Cross-Border Marriages and the US Anti-Trafficking Campaign' (2012) 38 *Journal of Ethnic and Migration Studies* 1137

Cowen Z, 'The Contemporary Commonwealth: A General View' (1959) 13 *International Organization* 204

Cox PN, 'An Interpretation and (Partial) Defense of Legal Formalism' (2003) 36 *Indiana Law Review* 57

Coyle JF, 'Rethinking Judgements Reciprocity' (2014) 92 *North Carolina Law Review* 1109

——, 'The SPEECH Act and the Enforcement of Foreign Libel Judgments in the United States' (2017) 18 *Yearbook of Private International Law* 245

Cuniberti G, *Conflict of Laws: A Comparative Approach: Text and Cases* (Edward Elgar Publishing 2017)

Curzon LB, *Dictionary of Law* (6th edn, Pearson Education Ltd 1998)

Dale W, 'Is the Commonwealth an International Organisation?' (1982) 31 *International and Comparative Law Quarterly* 451

Dammann J and Hansmann H, 'Globalizing Commercial Litigation' (2008) 94 *Cornell Law Review* 1

De Araujo N and De Nardi M, 'Consumer Protection Under the HCCH 2019 Judgments Convention' (2020) 67 *Netherlands International Law Review* 67

De Jong J, 'The Dutch Golden Age and Globalization: History and Heritage, Legacies and Contestations' (2011) 27 *Macalester International* 46

De Miguel Asensio PA and others, 'The Hague Conference on Private International Law "Judgments Convention"' (April 2018) <http://www.europarl.europa.eu/thinktank/en/document.html?reference=IPOL_STU(2018)604954>

Del Mar K, 'The Effects of Framing International Legal Norms as Rules or Exceptions: State Immunity from Civil Jurisdiction' (2013) 15 *International Community Law Review* 143

Dicey AV, *A Digest of the Law of England with Reference to the Conflict of Laws* (2nd edn, Stevenson & Sons Ltd 1922)

Dickinson A, 'Keeping up Appearances: The Development of Adjudicatory Jurisdiction in the English Courts' (2017) 86 *British Yearbook of International Law* 6

Dodge WS, 'International Comity in American Law' (2015) 115 *Columbia Law Review* 2071

Dogauchi M, 'The Hague Draft Convention Convention from the Perspective of Japan', *Seminar on the Draft Convention on Jurisdiction and Foreign Judgments in Civil and Commercial Matters Organised by Union International des Avocats* (20–21 April 2001, Edinburgh)

Droz A and Dyer A, 'The Hague Conference and the Main Issues of Private International Law for the Eighties' (1981) 3 *Northwestern Journal of International Law & Business* 155

Driscoll M QC, 'Common Law Recognition of Foreign Judgments by English and Commonwealth Courts: What Are You Implying?' (2016) 7 *Journal of International Banking and Financial Law* 396

Dworkin R, *Law's Empire* (Belknap Press 1986)

Elbalti B, 'Spontaneous Harmonization and the Liberalization of the Recognition and Enforcement of Foreign Judgments' (2014) 26 *Japanese Yearbook of Private International Law* 1

——, 'Reciprocity and the Recognition and Enforcement of Foreign Judgments: A Lot of Bark but Not Much Bite' (2017) 13 *Journal of Private International Law* 184

El Chazli K, 'Recognition and Enforcement of Foreign Decisions in Egypt' (2013) XV *Yearbook of Private International Law* 387

Elias O, 'Globalisation and Private International Law: Reviewing Contemporary Local Law' [2001] 36 *Amicus Curiae* 5

——, *Judicial Remedies in the Conflict of Laws* (Hart Publishing 2001)

Elliott R, 'The Hague Convention on Choice of Court Agreements – Will It Be a Game Changer for International Litigation?', *European Law Firm* (19 April 2016)

Elms D and Sriganesh B, 'Trump's Trade Policy: Discerning between Rhetoric and Reality' (2017) 12 *Asian Journal of WTO and International Health Law and Policy* 247

Endicott T, 'Comity among Legal Authorities' (2015) 68 *Current Legal Problems* 1

Epstein DZ, 'Rationality, Legitimacy, & the Law' (2014) 7 *Washington University Jurisprudence Review* 1

Erin O'Hara (ed), *Economics of Conflict of Laws* (Edward Elgar 2007)

'EU/US Disagreements Highlighted as USPTO Rejects Inclusion of Intellectual Property in Hague Convention' (*World Trademark Review*) <https://www.worldtrademarkreview.com/governmentpolicy/euus-disagreements-highlighted-uspto-rejects-inclusion-intellectual-property> accessed 8 November 2019

Eyffinger A, *Dreaming the Ideal, Living the Attainable: T.M.C. Asser [1838–1913] Founder of The Hague Tradition* (TMC Asser Press 2011)

Fentiman R, *International Commercial Litigation* (OUP 2015)

Fitt VA, 'The Tragedy of Comity: Questioning the American Treatment of Inadequate Foreign Courts' (2010) 50 *Virginia Journal of International Law* 1022 <http://www.vjil.org.> accessed 6 July 2017

Foreign Affairs Committee, 'The Role and Future of the Commonwealth' (2012) <https://publications.parliament.uk/pa/cm201012/cmselect/cmfaff/writev/commonwealth/com23.htm> accessed 10 October 2018

Forsyth C, 'The Eclipse of Private International Law Principle? The Judicial Process, Interpretation and the Dominance of Legislation in the Modern Era' (2005) 1 *Journal of Private International Law* 93

Fuller LL, 'American Legal Realism' (1934) 82 *University of Pennsylvania Law Review* 428

Gan Y, 'Jurisdiction Agreements in Chinese Conflict of Laws: Searching for Ways to Implement the Hague Convention on Choice of Court Agreements in China' (2018) 14 *Journal of Private International Law* 295

Garcimartín F and Saumier G, 'Judgments Convention: Revised Draft Explanatory Report' (*Preliminary Doc No 1 of December 2018*)

Garnett R, 'The Hague Choice of Court Convention: Magnum Opus or Much Ado About Nothing?' (2009) 5 *Journal of Private International Law* 161

Gerber DJ, 'Sculpting the Agenda of Comparative Law: Ernst Rabel and the Facade of Language' in A Riles (ed), *Rethinking the Masters of Comparative Law* (Hart Publishing 2001)

Ginsburg RB, 'Judgments in Search of Full Faith and Credit: The Last-in-Time Rule for Conflicting Judgments' (1969) 82 *Harvard Law Review* 798

Glenn HP, 'Foreign Judgments, the Common Law and the Constitution: De Savoye v. Morguard Investments Ltd' (1992) 37 *McGill Law Journal* 537

Goddard D, 'The Judgments Convention – The Current State of Play' (2019) 29 *Duke Journal of Comparative & International Law* 473

Goldberg JCP, 'Pragmatism and Private Law' (2012) 125 *Harvard Law Review* 1640

Golomb A, 'Recognition of Foreign Money Judgments: A Goal-Oriented Approach' (1969) 43 *St John's Law Review* 604

Gómez MA, 'The Global Chase: Seeking the Recognition and Enforcement of the Lago Agrio Judgment Outside of Ecuador' (2013) 1 *Stanford Journal of Complex Litigation* 429

Govare JP, 'Convention Internationale Pour l'Execution Des Jugements Etrangers' (1924) 33 *International Law Association Reports of Conferences* 169

Graupner R, 'Some Recent Aspects of the Recognition and Enforcement of Foreign Judgments in Western Europe' (1963) 12 *International and Comparative Law Quarterly* 367

Graveson RH, 'The Ninth Hague Conference of Private International Law' (1961) 10 *International and Comparative Law Quarterly* 18

Graziano TK, 'Is It Legitimate and Beneficial for Judges to Use Comparative Law' in M Andenas and D Fairgrieve (eds), *European Review of Private Law*, vol 21 (Oxford University Press 2013)

Greenwood G, 'Australia's Triangular Foreign Policy' (1957) 35 *Foreign Affairs* 689

Grey TC, 'Holmes and Legal Pragmatism' (1988) 1 *Stanford Law Review* 787

——, *Formalism and Pragmatism in American Law* (Brill 2014)

Grishchenkova A, 'Recognition and Enforcement of Foreign Judgments in Russia: Recent Trends' (2013) 15 *Yearbook of Private International Law* 439

Haack S, 'On Legal Pragmatism: Where Does "The Path of the Law" Lead Us?' (2005) 50 *The American Journal of Jurisprudence* 71

——, 'The Pluralistic Universe of Law: Towards a Neo-Classical Legal Pragmatism' (2008) 21 Ssrn 453

Halkerston G, 'Enforcement of Foreign Non-Money Judgments at Common Law in Offshore Jurisdictions: Back to Basics?' (2015) 21 *Trusts & Trustees* 969

Halperin-Walega ES and others, *Adverse Effect of a Sucrose-Based Semipurified Diet on Development and Postnatal Growth of Fischer Rats*, vol 80 (Harvard University Press 1985)

Harder S, 'Recent Judicial Aberrations in Australian Private Law' (2012) 19 *Australian International Law Journal* 161

Harris J, 'Jurisdiction and Judgments in International Trusts Litigation – Surveying the Landscape' (2011) 17 *Trusts & Trustees* 236

——, 'The Trust in Private International Law' in James Fawcett (ed), *Reform and Development of Private International Law: Essays in Honour of Sir Peter North* (OUP 2002)

——, 'Jurisdiction and Judgments in International Trusts Litigation – Surveying the Landscape' (2011) 17 *Trusts & Trustees* 236

Harrison R, 'Why Have Two Types of Civil Court?' (1999) 149 *New Law Journal* 65

Harten G Van, 'The Transformation of International Law' (2007) 460 *Investment Treaty Arbitration and Public Law* 95

Hartley TC, *International Commercial Litigation: Text, Cases, and Materials on Private International Law* (Cambridge University Press 2009)

——, *International Commercial Litigation: Text, Cases, and Materials on Private International Law* (Cambridge University Press 2009)

——, *Choice-of-Court Agreements under the European and International Instruments: The Revised Brussels I Regulation, the Lugano Convention, and the Hague Convention* (OUP 2013)

——, 'Jurisdiction in Tort Claims for Non-Physical Harm under Brussels 2012, Article 7(2)' (2018) 67 *International & Comparative Law Quarterly* 987

Hartley TC and Dogauchi M, 'Explanatory Report: Convention of 30 June 2005 on Choice of Court Agreements' (2005)

Hazelhorst M, *Free Movement of Civil Judgments in the European Union and the Right to a Fair Trial* (TMC Asser Press 2017)

HCCH, 'Conventions, Protocols and Principles' <https://www.hcch.net/en/instruments/conventions> accessed 13 June 2019

——, 'Ongoing Work in the Area of Judgments', *Preliminary Doc No 7B of January 2016*

——, 'Status Table: Convention of 1 February 1971 on the Recognition and Enforcement of Foreign Judgments in Civil and Commercial Matters' <https://www.hcch.net/en/instruments/conventions/status-table/?cid=78> accessed 18 June 2019

——, 'Status Table' (*Statute of the Hague Conference on Private International Law*) <https://www.hcch.net/en/instruments/conventions/status-table/?cid=29> accessed 13 June 2019

——, 'Conclusions of the Special Commission of June 1992 on General Affairs and Policy of the Conference', *Preliminary Doc No 18 of August 1992 in Proceedings of the Seventeenth Session* (1993)

——, 'Conclusions of the Working Group Meeting on Enforcement of Judgments', *Preliminary Doc No 19 of November 1992 in Proceedings of the Seventeenth Session* (1993)

——, 'Some Reflections of the Permanent Bureau on a General Convention on Enforcement of Judgments', *Preliminary Doc No 17 of May 1992 in Proceedings of the Seventeenth Session* (1993)

——, 'International Jurisdiction and Foreign Judgments in Civil and Commercial Matters: Report Drawn up by Catherine Kessedjian', *Preliminary Doc No 7 of April 1997 for the attention of the Special Commission of June 1997 on the question of jurisdiction, and recognition and enforcement of foreign judgments in civil and commercial matters* (1997)

——, 'Report on the First Meeting of the Informal Working Group on the Judgments Project of October 2002', *Preliminary Doc No 20 of November 2002* (2002)

——, 'Some Reflections on the Present State of Negotiations on the Judgments Project in the Context of the Future Work Programme of the Conference', *Preliminary Doc No 16 of February 2002* (2002)

——, 'Council on General Affairs and Policy of the Conference (7–9 April 2010): Conclusions and Recommendations Adopted by the Council' (2010)

——, 'Background to Working Document No 4 of 1 June 2016 on the Need of "Consumer" Definition', *Information Document No 3 of June 2016 for the attention of the Special Commission of June 2016 on the Recognition and Enforcement of Foreign Judgments* (2016) <https://assets.hcch.net/docs/eec804e8-b974-470e-92bc-dd593b96c12c.pdf> accessed 31 May 2020

——, 'Explanatory Note Providing Background on the Proposed Draft Text and Identifying Outstanding Issues: *Preliminary Doc No 2 of April 2016 for the Attention of the Special Commission of June 2016 on the Recognition and Enforcement of Foreign Judgments*' (2016) <https://assets.hcch.net/docs/e402cc72-19ed-4095-b004-ac47742dbc41.pdf> accessed 1 October 2019

——, 'Note on Article 1(1) of the 2016 Preliminary Draft Convention and the Term "Civil or Commercial Matters"', *Preliminary Doc No 4 of December 2016 for the attention of the Special Commission of February 2017 on the Recognition and Enforcement of Foreign Judgments* (HCCH 2016) <https://assets.hcch.net/docs/9be83162-a32b-457c-8232-16748c841789.pdf> accessed 29 May 2020

——, 'Annual Report 2018' (2019)

——, 'Council on General Affairs and Policy Meeting of 5–8 March 2019: Conclusions & Recommendations' (2019) <https://assets.hcch.net/docs/c4af61a8-d8bf-400e-9deb-afcd87ab4a56.pdf> accessed 29 October 2019

Henshaw A, 'Reciprocity after Brexit' (2017) 2 *Journal of International Banking and Financial Law* 69

Hess B, 'Not a Simple Footnote: 9/11 Litigation in the Civil Courts of Luxembourg' (2019) 5 *Praxis des Internationalen Privat- und Verfahrensrechts*

Hess B and Martinez Cristian O, 'Civil and Commercial Matters' in J Basedow and others (eds), *Encyclopedia of Private International Law* (Edward Elgar Publishing 2017)

Hess B, Pfeiffer T and Schlosser P, 'Report on the Application of Regulation Brussels I in the Member States' (CF Müller 2007)

Hesselink MW, *The New European Private Law: Essays on the Future of Private Law in Europe* (Kluwer Law International 2002)

Hill J, 'Jurisdiction in Matters Relating to a Contract under the Brussels Convention' (1995) 44 *International and Comparative Law Quarterly* 591

Hill J and Chong A, *International Commercial Disputes: Commercial Conflict of Laws in English Courts* (Hart Publishing 2010)

HM Courts and Tribunals Service, 'Civil and Family Court Fees From 6 April 2015' (2015) <http://hmctsformfinder.justice.gov.uk/courtfinder/forms/ex050-eng.pdf> accessed 30 August 2018

HM Government, 'Review of the Balance of Competences between the United Kingdom and the European Union Civil Judicial Cooperation' (2014) <https://assets.publishing.service.gov.uk/government/uploads/system/uploads/attachment_data/file/279228/civil-judicial-cooperation-report-review-of-balance-of-competences.pdf> accessed 3 November 2018

Ho HL, 'Policies Underlying the Enforcement of Foreign Commercial Judgments' (1997) 46 *International and Comparative Law Quarterly* 443

Hochberg D, 'Enforcement of Foreign Judgments and Firewall Legislation' (2015) 21 *Trusts & Trustees* 1006

Hoeflich MH, 'Law & Geometry: Legal Science from Leibniz to Langdell' (1986) 30 *The American Journal of Legal History* 95

Holmes, Oliver Wendell J, *The Common Law* (William S Hein & Compan 1881)

House of Commons Library, 'The Privy Council' (*Briefing Paper: Number CBP7460*, 8 February 2016)

House of Commons Foreign Affairs Committee, *The Role and Future of the Commonwealth: Fourth Report of Session 2012–13* (The Stationery Office Limited 2012)

Hsu J, 'Judgment Unenforceability in China.' (2013) 19 *Fordham Journal of Corporate & Financial Law* 201

Institut de Droit International, 'Exécution Des Jugements' (1878) <http://www.idi-iil.org/app/uploads/2017/06/1878_paris_01_fr.pdf> accessed 18 July 2019

——, 'Autorité et Exécution Des Jugements Étrangers' (1924) <http://www.idi-iil.org/app/uploads/2017/06/1924_vien_03_fr.pdf> accessed 18 July 2019

International Bar Association, 'Report of the International Bar Association (IBA) on the 2016 Preliminary Draft Convention', *Information Document No 8 of February 2017 for the attention of the Special Commission of February 2017 on the Recognition and Enforcement of Foreign Judgments* (HCCH 2017) <https://assets.hcch.net/docs/03311845-08cd-4048-953b-285914e44e25.pdf> accessed 30 May 2020

International Institute for the Unification of Private Law, *UNIDROIT Principles of International Commercial Contracts 2016* (UNIDROIT 2016)

International Law Association, 'Foreign Judgments', *Report of the Twentieth Annual Conference* (Williams Clowes and Sons Ltd 1901)

——, 'Enforcement of Foreign Judgments' (1960) 49 *Reports of the Forty-Ninth Conference* 290

——, 'Enforcement of Foreign Judgments' (1962) 50 *International Law Association Reports of Conferences* 491

Jackson LJ, 'Speech by Lord Justice Jackson: Fixed Costs – The Time Has Come', *IPA Annual lecture* (2016) <https://www.judiciary.uk/wp-content/uploads/2016/01/fixedcostslecture-1.pdf>

Jang J, 'The Public Policy Exception Under the New 2019 HCCH Judgments Convention' (2020) 67 *Netherlands International Law Review* 97

Janis MW, *America and the Law of Nations 1776–1939* (Oxford University Press 2010)

Juenger FK, *Choice of Law and Multistate Justice* (Martinus Nijhoff Publishers 1993)

——, 'The Lex Mercatoria and Private International Law' (2000) 60 *Louisiana Law Review* 1134

Kalensky P, *Trends of Private International Law* (Springer Netherlands 1971)

Kegel G, 'Paternal Home and Dream Home: Traditional Conflict of Laws and the American Reformers' (1979) 27 *The American Journal of Comparative Law* 615

——, 'Fundamental Approaches' in Kurt Lipstein (ed), *International Encyclopedia of Comparative Law: Private International Law* (JCB Mohr 1986)

Kellogg FR, 'American Pragmatism and European Social Theory' (2012) IV *European Journal of Pragmatism and American Philosophy* 107

Kessedjian C, 'Is the Hague Convention of 2 July 2019 a Useful Tool for Companies Who Are Conducting International Activities?' [2020] 1 *Nederlands Internationaal Privaatrecht* 19

Keyes M, *Jurisdiction in International Litigation* (Federation Press 2005)

Keyes M and Marshall BA, 'Jurisdiction Agreements: Exclusive, Optional and Asymmetrical' (2015) 11 *Journal of Private International Law* 345

Koch C, 'The Advantages of the Civil Law Judicial Design as the Model for Emerging Legal Systems' (2003) 11 Ssrn 139

Koskennjemi M, 'Gustave Rolin-Jaequemyns and the Establishment of the Institut de Droit International (1873)' (2004) 37 *Revue Belge de Droit International / Belgian Review of International Law*

Krishnan S, 'Nobody's Commonwealth? The Commonwealth in Britain's Post-Imperial Adjustment' (2006) 44 *Commonwealth & Comparative Politics* 257

Kruger T, 'The Quest for Legal Certainty in International Civil Cases', *Recueil Des Cours* vol 380 (Martinus Nijhoff 2016)

Kupelyants H, 'Recognition and Enforcement of Foreign Judgments in the Absence of the Debtor and His Assets within the Jurisdiction: Reversing the Burden of Proof' (2018) 14 *Journal of Private International Law* 455

Lee R, 'The Evolution of the Modern International Trust: Developments and Challenges' (2018) 103 *Iowa Law Review* 2069

Lee S, 'Title to Foreign Real Property in Transnational Money Claims' (1995) 32 *Columbia Journal of Transnational Law* 607

Lee SH, 'Foreign Judgment Recognition and Enforcement System of Korea' (2006) 6 *Journal of Korean Law* 110

Lenhoff A, 'Reciprocity in Function: A Problem of Conflict of Laws, Constitutional Law, and International Law' (1953) 15 *University of Pittsburgh Law Review* 44

——, 'Reciprocity and the Law of Foreign Judgments: A Historical-Critical Analysis' (1955) 16 *Louisiana Law Review* 466

Leonard TM (ed), *Encyclopedia of the Developing World* (Routledge 2006)

Lind D, 'The Mismeasurement of Legal Pragmatism' (2012) 4 *Washington University Jurisprudence Review* 213

Llamzon AP, 'Jurisdiction and Compliance in Recent Decisions of the International Court of Justice' (2007) 18 *European Journal of International Law* 815

Loon H Van, 'The Hague Conference on Private International Law: Asser's Vision and an Evolving Mission' (2007) 2 *Hague Justice Journal* 3

——, 'The Global Horizon of Private International Law', *Recueil des Cours* (Brill Nijhoff 2016)

Lord Collins of Mapesbury and others (eds), *Dicey, Morris and Collins on the Conflict of Laws* (15th edn, Sweet & Maxwell Ltd 2012)

Lord Reed, 'Comparative Law in the Supreme Court of the United Kingdom' (Centre for Private Law, University of Edinburgh, 2017) <https://www.supremecourt.uk/docs/speech-171013.pdf> accessed 22 August 2018

Lorenzen EG, 'Huber's De Conflictu Legum' (1919) 13 *Illinois Law Review* 375

Luban D, 'What's Pragmatic About Legal Pragmatism?' (1996) 18 *Cardozo Law Review* 43

Lundstedt L, 'The Newly Adopted Hague Judgments Convention: A Missed Opportunity for Intellectual Property' (2019) 50 *IIC – International Review of Intellectual Property and Competition Law* 933

Lussier L, 'A Canadian Perspective' (1998) 24 *Brooklyn Journal of International Law* 31

Maier HG, 'Extraterritorial Jurisdiction at a Crossroads: An Intersection between Public and Private International Law' (1982) 76 *American Journal of International Law* 280

Mance, Lord, 'The Future of Private International Law' (2005) 1 *Journal of Private International Law* 185

Mann FA, *Foreign Affairs in English Courts* (Oxford University Press 1986) <http://www.oxford scholarship.com/view/10.1093/acprof:oso/9780198255642.001.0001/acprof-9780198255642> accessed 23 September 2017

Marshall B, 'The 2005 Hague Convention: A Panacea for Non-Exclusive Asymmetric Jurisdiction Agreements Too?' in V Bath and others (eds), *Commercial Issues in Private International Law: A Common Law Perspective* (Hart Publishing 2019)

Mattei U and Pes LG, 'Civil Law and Common Law: Toward Convergence?' in GA Caldeira, RD Kelemen and KE Whittington (eds), *The Oxford Handbook of Law and Politics* (OUP 2008)

McClean JD, 'The Contribution of the Hague Conference to the Development of Private International Law in Common Law Countries', *Collected Courses of The Hague Academy of International Law – Recueil des Cours* (Nijhoff 1992)

McClean JD and Patchett KW, *The Recognition and Enforcement of Judgments and Orders and the Service of Process within the Commonwealth* (Commonwealth Secretariat 1977)

McDougal LL, 'Toward Application of the Best Rule of Law in Choice of Law Cases' (1983) 35 *Mercer Law Review* 483

McIntyre WD, *A Guide to the Contemporary Commonwealth* (Palgrave 2001)

McLachlan C, 'The Jurisdictional Limits of Disclosure Orders in Transnational Fraud Litigation' (1998) 47 *International & Comparative Law Quarterly* 3

Meier A, Burrer S and Fufurina A, 'Hamburg Higher Regional Court: (Still) No Recognition and Enforcement of Russian Court Judgments in Germany Due to Reciprocity Not Being Warranted' (*Newsletter*, 2016) <https://www.noerr.com/en/newsroom/News/no-recognition-and-enforcement-of-russian-court-judgments-in-germany.aspx> accessed 15 July 2017

Meier N, 'Notification as a Ground for Refusal' (2020) 67 *Netherlands International Law Review* 81

Menand L, *The Metaphysical Club*, vol 20 (Flamingo 2009)

Menon S, 'International Commercial Courts: Towards a Transnational System of Dispute Resolution' in P Sooksripaisarnkit and SR Garimella (eds), *Opening Lecture for the DIFC Courts Lecture Series 2015* (2015)

Michaels R, 'The Functional Method of Comparative Law' in M Reimann and R Zimmermann (eds), *The Oxford Handbook of Comparative Law* (OUP 2006)

——, 'Comparative Law and Private International Law' in J Basedow and others (eds), *Encyclopedia of Private International Law* (Edward Elgar Publishing 2017)

——, 'Globalizing Savigny? The State in Savigny's Private International Law and the Challenge from Europeanization and Globalization' in M Stolleis and W Streeck (eds), *Aktuelle Fragen zu politischer und rechtlicher Steuerung im Kontext der Globalisierung* (Nomos 2007)

——, 'Recognition and Enforcement of Foreign Judgments' in R Wolfrum (ed), *Max Planck Encyclopedia of Public International Law* (Oxford University Press 2009)

Mills A, 'The Private History of International Law' (2006) 55 *International and Comparative Law Quarterly* 1

——, 'Rethinking Jurisdiction In International Law' (2014) 84 *The British Yearbook of International Law* 187

——, 'Variable Geometry, Peer Governance, and the Public International Perspective on Private International Law' in H Muir Watt and DP Fernández Arroyo (eds), *Private International Law and Global Governance* (OUP 2014)

Monestier TJ, 'Foreign Judgments at Common Law: Rethinking the Enforcement Rules' (2005) 28 *The Dalhousie Law Journal* 163

——, '(Still) A "Real and Substantial" Mess: The Law of Jurisdiction in Canada' (2013) 36 *Fordham International Law Journal* 396

Morse CGJ, 'Making English Private International Law' in JJ Fawcett (ed), *Reform and Development of Private International Law: Essays in Honour of Sir Peter North* (Oxford University Press 2002)

Mousourakis G, *Comparative Law and Legal Traditions: Historical and Contemporary Perspectives* (Springer 2019)

Mussa M, 'Factors Driving Global Economic Integration' (IMF 2000) <https://www.imf.org/en/News/Articles/2015/09/28/04/53/sp082500> accessed 27 May 2020

Nadelmann KH, 'The Common Market Judgments Convention and a Hague Conference Recommendation: What Steps Next ?' (1969) 82 *Harvard Law Review* 1282

Nadelmann KH and Droz GAL, 'The Hague Conference on Private International Law Ninth Session' (1960) 9 *American Journal of Comparative Law* 583

Nadelmann KH and von Mehren AT, 'The Extraordinary Session of the Hague Conference on Private International Law' (1966) 60 *American Journal of International Law* 803

Nadelmann KH and Reese WLM, 'The American Proposal at the Hague Conference on Private International Law to Use the Method of Uniform Laws' (1958) 7 *The American Journal of Comparative Law* 239

——, 'The Tenth Session of the Hague Conference on Private International Law' (1964) 13 *American Journal of Comparative Law* 612

Newman LW (ed), *Enforcement of Money Judgments* (Juris Publishing LLC 2000)

Nishitani Y, 'Party Autonomy in Contemporary Private International Law – The Hague Principles on Choice of Law and East Asia' (2016) 59 *Japanese Yearbook of International Law* 300

Noodt Taquela MB, 'Applying the Most Favourable Treaty or Domestic Rules to Facilitate Private International Law Co-Operation', *Hague Academy of International Law Recueil des Cours* vol 377 (Brill Nijhoff 2015)

Noodt Taquela MB and Abou-Nigm VR, 'The Draft Judgments Convention and Its Relationship with Other International Instruments' (2018) 19 *Yearbook of Private International Law* 449

Nwabueze BO, *A Constitutional History of Nigeria* (C Hurst 1982)

O'Brian WE, 'The Hague Convention on Jurisdiction and Judgments: The Way Forward' (2003) 66 The Modern Law Review 491

O'Neill M, 'Top London Lawyers Charge £1,000 an Hour, Study Finds', *Financial Times* (2 May 2016) <https://www.ft.com/content/29151078-ca73-11e5-a8ef-ea66e967dd44> accessed 23 August 2018

OECD, *Free Movement of Workers and Labour Market Adjustment* (OECD Publishing 2012) <http://www.oecd-ilibrary.org/social-issues-migration-health/free-movement-of-workers-and-labour-market-adjustment_9789264177185-en> accessed 5 July 2017

——, 'Better Civil Justice Systems Can Boost Investment, Competition, Innovation and Growth' (2013) <http://www.oecd.org/economy/betterciviljusticesystemscanboostinvestmentcompetition innovationandgrowththeoecdsays.htm> accessed 27 February 2019

Oestreicher Y, 'The Rise and Fall of the "Mixed" and "Double" Convention Models Regarding Recognition and Enforcement of Foreign Judgments' (2007) 6 *Washington University Global Studies Law Review* 339

——, '"We're on a Road to Nowhere" – Reasons for the Continuing Failure to Regulate Recognition and Enforcement of Foreign Judgments' (2008) 42 *The International Lawyer* 59

Olawoyin AA, 'Enforcement of Foreign Judgments in Nigeria: Statutory Dualism and Disharmony of Laws' (2014) 10 *Journal of Private International Law* 129

Oppong RF, 'Recognition and Enforcement of Foreign Judgments in Ghana: A Second Look at a Colonial Inheritance' (2005) 31 *Commonwealth Law Bulletin* 19

——, *Private International Law in Commonwealth Africa* (Cambridge University Press 2013)

——, 'Enforcing Foreign Non-Money Judgments: An Examination of Some Recent Developments in Canada and Beyond' (2006) 39 *University of British Columbia Law Review* 257

Øren JS, 'International Jurisdiction Over Consumer Contracts in E-Europe' (2003) 52 *International and Comparative Law Quarterly* 665

Palmer VV (ed), *Mixed Jurisdictions Worldwide: The Third Legal Family* (2nd edn, Cambridge University Press 2012)

Palumbo G and others, 'Judicial Performance and Its Determinants: A Cross-Country Perspective' [2013] *OECD Economic Policy Papers*

'Papers Relating to the Foreign Relations of the United States Transmitted to Congress with the Annual Message of the President', *Foreign Relations of the United States (FRUS)* (1874)

Paul JR, 'Comity in International Law' (1991) 32 *Harvard International Law Journal* 1

Permanent Bureau of, the Hague Conference on Private International and Law, *Practical Handbook on the Operation of the Hague Convention of 15 November 1965 on the Service Abroad of Judicial and Extrajudicial Documents in Civil or Commercial Matters* (Wilson & Lafleur 2006)

Pertegás M, 'The Brussels I Regulation and the Hague Convention on Choice of Court Agreements' (2010) 11 *ERA Forum* 19

Peterson CH, 'Res Judicata and Foreign Country Judgments' (1963) 24 *Ohio State Law Journal* 291

Pier LP, Monti G and Botta M (eds), *Private Enforcement of EU Competition Law: The Impact of the Damages Directive* (Edward Elgar Publishing 2018)

Pitel SGA, 'Enforcement of Foreign Non-Monetary Judgments in Canada (and Beyond)' (2007) 3 *Journal of Private International Law* 241

Plessis JD, 'Comparative Law and the Study of Mixed Legal Systems' in M Reimann and R Zimmermann (eds), *The Oxford Handbook of Comparative Law* (1st edn, OUP 2006)

Poon F, 'The Hague Choice of Court Convention and the Current Judgment Project', *UNCITRAL Judicial Summit* (2017) <http://uncitralrcap.org/wp-content/uploads/2018/03/10.13-Judicial-Conference-slides-Session-4.pdf> accessed 24 June 2019

Posner EA and Sykes A, 'Efficient Breach of International Law: Optimal Remedies, "Legalized Noncompliance," and Related Issues' (2011) 110 *Michigan Law Review* 243

Posner RA, *How Judges Think* (Havard University Press 2008)

——, 'What Has Pragmatism to Offer Law?' (1990) 63 *Southern California Law Review* 1653 <http://chicagounbound.uchicago.edu/journal_articles> accessed 23 July 2017

——, 'Pragmatic Adjudication' (1996) 18 *Cardozo Law Review* 1

——, 'Legal Pragmatism' (2004) 35 *Metaphilosophy* 147

——, *Law, Pragmatism, and Democracy* (Harvard University Press 2005)

——, 'Legal Pragmatism Defended' (2013) 71 *University of Chicago Law Review* 683

Pound R, 'Mechanical Jurisprudence' (1908) 8 *Columbia Law Review* 605

Prott LV, 'Judicial Reasoning in the Common Law and Code Law Systems' (1978) 64 *Archives for Philosophy of Law and Social Philosophy* 417

Queen Mary University of London, '2018 International Arbitration Survey: The Evolution of International Arbitration' (2018)

Quevedo SM, 'Formalist and Instrumentalist Legal Reasoning and Legal Theory' (1985) 73 *California Law Review* 119

Rabel E, 'A Draft of an International Law of Sales' (1935) 5 *University of Chicago Law Review* 543

——, 'Interim Account on Comparative Conflicts Law' (1948) 46 *Michigan Law Review* 625

Raffai K, 'The New Hungarian Private International Law Act – a Wind of Change' (2017) 6 *Acta Universitatis Sapientiae: Legal Studies* 119

Ramsey MD, 'Comity' (1998) 1 *Iowa Law Review* 893

Ranganathan S, 'Responding to Deliberately Created Treaty Conflicts' in CJ Tams, A Tzanakopoulos and A Zimmermann (eds), *Research Handbook on the Law of Treaties* (Edward Elgar 2014)

Reese WL, 'The Status in This Country of Judgments Rendered Abroad' (1950) 50 *Columbia Law Review* 783

Reyes A (ed), *Recognition and Enforcement of Judgments in Civil and Commercial Matters* (Hart Publishing 2019)

Reynolds TH, *Foreign Law Guide* (Brill 2000)

Rheinstein M, 'Comparative Law and Conflict of Laws in Germany' (1935) 2 *University of Chicago Law Review* 232

Rogerson P, 'Habitual Residence: The New Domicile?' (2000) 49 *International & Comparative Law Quarterly* 86

Roodt C, 'Venue in Transnational Litigation: Party Autonomy Adds New Impetus to the "Judgment Project"' (2006) 16 *South African Mercantile Law Journal* 13

Rossouw M, *The Harmonisation of Rules on the Recognition and Enforcement of Foreign Judgments in the Southern African Customs Union* (Pretoria University Law Press 2016)

Rühl G, 'The Problem of International Transactions: Conflict of Laws Revisited' (2010) 6 *Journal of Private International Law* 59

——, 'Foundations of Private International Law' in J Basedow and others (eds), *Elgar Encyclopedia of Comparative Law* (2nd edn, Edward Elgar Publishing 2017)

Ruiz Abou-Nigm V, 'Ancillary Jurisdiction for Interim Measures of Protection in Support of Cross-Border Litigation' (2005) 10 *Uniform Law Review*

Salacuse JW, *An Introduction to Law in French-Speaking Africa*, vol 1 (Michie Company 1969)

Saumier G, 'Has the CJPTA Readied Canada for the Hague Choice of Court Convention?' (2018) 55 *Osgoode Hall Law Journal* 141

——, 'Submission as a Jurisdictional Basis and the HCCH 2019 Judgments Convention' (2020) 67 *Netherlands International Law Review* 49

Saunders ML, 'The Hague Conference on Private International Law' (1966) 2 *Australian Yearbook of International Law* 115

Schlosser P, 'Jurisdiction and International Judicial and Administrative Co-Operation', *Recueil des Cours*, vol 284 (Martinus Nijhoff 2001)

Schreiber A, 'Granting of Reciprocity within the German-Russian Recognition Practice' (2017) 4 *Praxis des Internationalen Privat- und Verfahrensrechts (IPRax)* 139

Schultz T and Mitchenson J, 'Navigating Sovereignty and Transnational Commercial Law: The Use of Comity by Australian Courts' (2016) 12 *Journal of Private International Law* 344

Schultz T and Ridi N, 'Comity and International Courts and Tribunals' (2017) 50 *Cornell International Law Journal* 576

Seinfeld G, 'Reflections on Comity in the Law of American Federalism' (2015) 90 *Notre Dame Law Review* 1309

Shackleton SR, 'Annual Review of English Judicial Decisions on Arbitration – 2000' [2001] *International Arbitration Law Review* 178

Shapiro S, *Legality* (Harvard University Press 2011)

Sharom A, 'Private International Law in the Malaysia Courts' (2005) 9 *Singapore Year Book of International Law* 253

Silberman L, 'Can the Hague Judgments Project Be Saved?: A Perspective from the United States' in JJ Barceló and KM Clermont (eds), *A Global Law of Jurisdiction and Judgments: Lessons from the Hague* (Kluwer Law 2002)

——, 'Comparative Jurisdiction in the International Context: Will the Proposed Hague Judgements Convention Be Stalled?' (2002) 52 *DePaul Law Review* 319

Siltala R, *Law, Truth, and Reason*, vol 97 (Springer Netherlands 2011)

Sinclair M, 'What Is the "R" in "Irac"' (2002) 46 *New York Law School Law Review* 457

Singal V, 'Preserving Power Without Sacrificing Justice' (2007) 59 *Hastings Law Journal* 943

Singapore Academy of Law, 'Report of the Law Reform Committee on Enforcement of Foreign Judgments' (2005)

Slapper G and Kelly D, *The English Legal System* (14th edn, Routledge 2004)

Slaughter and May, 'Private Enforcement of Competition Law in the UK' (2017) <https://www.slaughterandmay.com/media/2534704/private-enforcement-of-competition-law-in-the-uk.pdf> accessed 10 August 2019

Slinn P, 'The Commonwealth and the Law' in J Mayall (ed), *The Contemporary Commonwealth: An Assessment 1965–2009* (Routledge 2010)

Smaghi LB, 'Legal System and Financial Markets', *Legal issues related to the financial markets* (26 October 2007) <https://www.ecb.europa.eu/press/key/date/2007/html/sp071026.en.html> accessed 27 February 2019

South African Law Reform Commission, 'Report: Consolidated Legislation Pertaining to International Judicial Co-Operation in Civil Matters' (2006) <www.doj.gov.za/salrc/index.htm> accessed 27 February 2019

Stein T, 'International Law Association (ILA)', *Max Planck Encyclopedia of Public International Law* (OUP 2015)

Steiner E, *French Law: A Comparative Approach* (2nd edn, OUP 2010)

Stephan PB, 'Courts on Courts: Contracting for Engagement and Indifference in International Judicial Encounters' (2013) 100 Ssrn 17

——, 'Foreign Court Judgments and the United States Legal System' in PB Stephan (ed), *Foreign Court Judgments and the United States Legal System* (Brill 2014)

Stevens SL, 'Commanding International Judicial Respect: Reciprocity and the Recognition and Enforcement of Foreign Judgments' (2002) 26 *Hastings International & Comparative Law Review* 115

Stewart DP, 'The Hague Conference Adopts a New Convention on the Recognition and Enforcement of Foreign Judgments in Civil or Commercial Matters' (2019) 113 *The American Journal of International Law* 772

Strong S, 'Recognition and Enforcement of Foreign Judgments in U.S. Courts: Problems and Possibilities' (2014) 33 *Review of Litigation* 45

Sullivan M, 'Pragmatism and Precedent: A Response to Dworkin' (1990) 26 *Transactions of the Charles S. Peirce Society* 225

Sullivan MN and Solove DJ, 'Can Pragmatism Be Radical? Richard Posner and Legal Pragmatism' (2003) 113 *Yale Law Journal* 687

Summers RS, 'Pragmatic Instrumentalism in Twentieth Century American Legal Thought – A Synthesis and Critique of Our Dominant General Theory about Law and Its Use' (1980) 60 *Cornell Law Review* 861

Symeonides SC, *The American Choice-of-Law Revolution: Past, Present and Future* (M Nijhoff 2006)

——, *American Private International Law* (Kluwer Law International 2008)

——, 'Choice of Law in Cross-Border Torts: Why Plaintiffs Win and Should' (2009) 61 *Hastings Law Journal*

——, 'Result-Selectivism in Conflicts Law' (2009) 46 *Willamette Law Review* 1

——, *Private International Law : Idealism, Pragmatism, Eclecticism: General Course on Private International Law* (M Nijhoff 2016)

Tamanaha BZ, *Realistic Socio-Legal Theory: Pragmatism and a Social Theory of Law* (Clarendon Press 1997)

Tang ZS, '"The Belt and Road" and Cross-Border Judicial Cooperation' (2019) 49 *Hong Kong Law Journal* 121

Tang ZS, Xiao Y and Huo Z, *Conflict of Laws in the People's Republic of China* (Edward Elgar Publishing 2016)

Tanja Domej, 'Recognition and Enforcement of Judgments (Civil Law)' in J Basedow and others (eds), *Encyclopedia of Private International Law* (Edward Elgar 2017)

Teitz LE, 'The Hague Choice of Court Convention: Validating Party Autonomy and Providing an Alternative to Arbitration' (2005) 53 *American Journal of Comparative Law* 543

Terradas BA, 'Restrictions on Jurisdiction Clauses in Consumer Contracts within the European Union' (2003) *Oxford University Comparative Law Forum* 1

Thiede T, 'Fine to Follow-on? Private Anti-Trust Actions in European Law' (2017) 5 *China-EU Law Journal* 233

Tomkins FJ, 'Execution of Foreign Judgments', *Association for the Reform and Codification of Law of Nations: Report of the Thirteenth Conference* (1887)

Torremans P and others (eds), *Cheshire, North & Fawcett: Private International Law* (15th edn, OUP 2017)

Tsang KF, 'Chinese Bilateral Judgment Enforcement Treaties' (2017) 40 *Loyola LA International & Comparative Law Review* 1

Tu G and Xu M, 'Contractual Conflicts in the People's Republic of China: The Applicable Law in the Absence of Choice' (2011) 7 *Journal of Private International Law* 179

UK Department for International Trade, 'Commonwealth Trade Ministers: Reform WTO and Resist Protectionism' (*Press release*, 2019) <https://www.gov.uk/government/news/commonwealth-trade-ministers-reform-wto-and-resist-protectionism> accessed 29 October 2019

Umstetter LJ, 'Enforcing Foreign Judgments: In Search of a Treaty to Locate Assets Abroad' (2007) 3 *South Carolina Journal of International Law and Business* 85

Uzelac A, 'Goals of Civil Justice and Civil Procedure in Contemporary Judicial Systems' in A Uzelac (ed), *Goals of Civil Justice and Civil Procedure in Contemporary Judicial Systems* (Springer International Publishing 2014)

Vanham P, 'A Brief History of Globalization' (2019)

Vanleenhove C, 'The Enforcement of American Punitive Damages in the European Union', *Punitive Damages in Private International Law* (Intersentia 2016)

Von Mehren AT, 'Recognition and Enforcement of Foreign Judgments : A New Approach for the Hague Conference ?' (1994) 1993 *Law and Contemporary Problems* 271

——, 'Drafting a Convention on International Jurisdiction and the Effects of Foreign Judgments Acceptable World-Wide: Can the Hague Conference Project Succeed?' (2001) 49 *American Journal of Comparative Law* 191

——, 'Recognition and Enforcement of Foreign Judgments – General Theory and the Role of Jurisdictional Requirements', *Recueil Des Cours* (Martinus Nijhoff Publishers 2002)

Von Mehren AT and Trautman DT, 'Recognition of Foreign Adjudications: A Survey and a Suggested Approach' (1968) 81 *Harvard Law Review* 1601

Walker A, *The Commonwealth: A New Look* (Pergamon Press 1978)

Walker J, 'Canada's Position on a Multilateral Judgments Convention' in C Carmody, Y Iwasawa and S Rhodes (eds), *Trilateral Perspectives on International Legal Issues: Conflict and Coherence* (3rd edn, American Society of International Law 2003)

Walker L, *Maintenance and Child Support in Private International Law* (Hart Publishing 2015)

Walker L and Beaumont P, 'Empirical Study on the Early Operation of the EU Maintenance Regulation' in P Beaumont and others (eds), *The Recovery of Maintenance in the EU and Worldwide* (Hart Publishing 2014)

Wass J, 'The Court's *In Personam* Jurisdiction in Cases Involving Foreign Land' (2014) 63 *International and Comparative Law Quarterly* 103

Watt A, *The Evolution of Australian Foreign Policy: 1938–1965* (Cambridge University Press 1968)

Watt HM, 'Globalization and Private International Law' in J Basedow and others (eds), *Encyclopedia of Private International Law* (Edward Elgar Publishing 2017)

Wheare KC, 'Is the British Commonwealth Withering Away?' (1950) 44 *The American Political Science Review* 545

Whincop MJ, 'The Recognition Scene: Game Theoretical Issues in the Recognition of Foreign Judgments' (1999) 23 *Melbourne University Law Review* 416

——, 'Three Positive Theories of International Jurisdiction' (2000) 24 *Melbourne University Law Review* 379

Whincop MJ, Mary Keyes and Richard A. Posner, *Policy and Pragmatism in the Conflict of Laws* (1st edn, Routledge 2017)

Whytock CA, 'Conflict of Laws, Global Governance, and Transnational Legal Order' (2016) 1 *UC Irvine Journal of International, Transnational, and Comparative Law* 117

——, 'Enforcement of Foreign Judgments: Governance, Rights, and the Market for Dispute Resolution Services' in H-W Micklitz and A Wechsler (eds), *The Transformation of Enforcement: European Economic Law in a Global Perspective* (Hart Publishing 2016)

Wilderspin M and Vysoka L, 'The 2019 Hague Judgments Convention through European Lenses' [2020] 1 *Nederlands Internationaal Privaatrecht* 34

Witz C, 'The Place of Performance of the Obligation to Pay the Price: Art. 57 CISG' (2005) 25 *Journal of Law and Commerce* 325

World Bank Group, 'Enforcing Contracts' <http://www.doingbusiness.org/en/data/exploretopics/enforcing-contracts/why-matters> accessed 27 February 2019

Wurmnest W, 'Recognition and Enforcement of U.S. Money Judgments in Germany' (2005) 23 *Berkeley Journal of International Law* 175

Xianwei P, 'Choice of Court Agreement and the Practical Connection Principle: A Comment on Chinese Supreme Court's Civil Ruling Regarding the "Hero" Online Game Jurisdiction Dispute Case' (2013) (3) *Journal of Business Law* 317

Yakushko O and Rajan I, 'Global Love for Sale: Divergence and Convergence of Human Trafficking with "Mail Order Brides" and International Arranged Marriage Phenomena' (2017) 40 *Women and Therapy* 190

Yekini A, 'Foreign Judgments in Nigerian Courts in the Last Decade: A Dawn of Liberalization' (2017) 2 *Nederlands Internationaal Privaatrecht* 205

Yeo TM, 'The Choice of Court Agreement: Perils of the Midnight Clause', *12th Yong Pung How Professorship of Law Lecture* (22 May 2019, Singapore Management University) <https://cebcla.smu.edu.sg/sites/cebcla.smu.edu.sg/files/Paper2019.pdf> accessed 4 July 2019

——, 'Jurisdiction Issues in International Tort Litigation: A Singapore View' (1994) 7 *Singapore Academy of Law Journal* 1

——, 'Hague Convention on Choice of Court Agreements 2005 : A Singapore Perspective' (2015) 114 *Journal of International Law and Diplomacy* 50

Zeynalova Y, 'The Law on Recognition and Enforcement of Foreign Judgments: Is It Broken and How Do We Fix It ?' (2013) 31 *Berkeley Journal of International Law* 150

Zhang W, 'Recognition and Enforcement of Foreign Judgments in China: A Call for Special Attention to Both the Due Service Requirement and the Principle of Reciprocity' (2013) 12 Chinese Journal of International Law 143

——, 'Sino-Foreign Recognition and Enforcement of Judgments: A Promising "Follow-Suit" Model?' (2017) 16 Chinese Journal of International Law 515

Zweigert K and Kötz H, *Introduction to Comparative Law* (3rd edn, OUP 1998)

Zweigert K and Siehr K, 'Jhering' s Influence on the Development of Comparative Legal Method' (1971) 19 The American Journal of Comparative Law 215

INDEX

Lightning Source UK Ltd.
Milton Keynes UK
UKHW021908180821
389039UK00002B/187